MAPLE LEAF
MOMENTS

A Thirty Year Reflection

Howard Berger

Warwick Publishing Inc.

Toronto   Los Angeles

Second Printing: December 1994

Published by the Warwick Publishing Group
Warwick Publishing, Inc., 24 Mercer Street, Toronto, Ontario M5V 1H3
Warwick Publishing Inc. 1300 N. Alexandria, Los Angeles, California 90027

Front cover photographs: Harold Barkley, Dan Hamilton
Cover Design: Dave Hader/Studio Conceptions
Text Design & Editing: Nick Pitt

ISBN 1-895629-38-1

Distributed in Canada by:
Firefly Books Ltd.
250 Sparks Avenue
Willowdale, Ontario
M2H 2S4

Printed and bound in Canada

To my parents, Sandee and Irv, who allowed a young,
impressionable hockey fan to stay up late
on Saturday nights in the 1960s.

And to the memory of Pierre Dorion,
whose love for the game was simply infectious.

TABLE OF CONTENTS

ACKNOWLEDGEMENTS

Writing a book is an enormous undertaking, requiring the thoughtfulness and cooperation of many people. This project was no exception and I'd like to sincerely thank the following:

Carl Hadfield, whose brother Vic forms the basis of Chapter 10, was invaluable to me and really gave the book a kick-start. His good-natured assistance in the face of my constant badgering helped me track down many of the subjects for chapters THE SIMMONS SAGA and SAWCHUK'S LAST HURRAH. This book would not have materialized without him.

Jim Gregory, the former Maple Leaf general manager, bridged the gap between me and several difficult-to-reach players. Few executives in the history of the game were as underrated as this man.

Bobby Orr and Bernie Parent, a couple of hockey legends and Hall of Famers who were kind enough to return phonecalls.

Joe Bowen, voice of the Maple Leafs since 1982 and my colleague at The Fan-1430, provided a flattering endorsement of this project in the FOREWORD. Only Foster Hewitt has called more Leaf games than Joe and *nobody* has done it better.

Bruce Bennett, hockey's very best photographer and a good friend, took a few moments out of his hectic schedule at the '94 NHL draft in Hartford to snap the photo that appears on the back cover.

Don Pagnutti, Paul Williams, Allan Davis, Bob Mackowycz and Nelson Millman — the "Lords" of Telemedia and The Fan-1430, for their support and encouragement in this non-radio enterprise.

Scott Metcalfe, news and sports director at The Fan-1430, for his patience and leniency in the face of numerous disruptions while his senior reporter scrambled to complete this project.

And last, but not least, Nick Pitt and Jim Williamson of Warwick Publishing for believing in the idea.

A tip of my hat to you all.

FOREWORD

The history of the Toronto Maple Leafs is full of moments that we, as hockey fans, vividly remember. In his book *MAPLE LEAF MOMENTS, A 30-YEAR REFLECTION*, Howard Berger captures many of them.

From Don Simmons' 11-0 loss to the woeful Boston Bruins in 1964 to Pat Burns' triumphant return to the Montreal Forum three decades later, the book is full of anecdotes as told to the author by those involved.

I've known Howard for many years while broadcasting Leaf games on the *Telemedia* Sports Network and *Global* TV. During that time, Howard has written and talked about the team — discovering behind-the-scene stories that have contributed to its success or failure. Having grown up in Toronto, he's had to juggle his emotions from being a fan and a journalist.

MAPLE LEAF MOMENTS contains so many unforgettable highlights — from Pat Quinn's thunderous hit on superstar Bobby Orr, to the Leafs' major upset of the New York Islanders (thank-you Lanny McDonald) in the 1978 playoffs.

But the storied Leaf franchise has had other moments.

Who can forget the catastrophic fall from grace during the 1980s, culminating in the 48-point season of 1984-85. Or the humorous exploits of Vic Hadfield, who dampened Maple Leaf spirits by simply throwing the goalie-mask of Bernie Parent into the throng at Madison Square Garden during a playoff game in 1971.

MAPLE LEAF MOMENTS will re-introduce the characters of the past 30 years... Jim Dorey, Jim McKenny, Mike Palmateer, Dave (Tiger) Williams, Darryl Sittler, and many more. If you're a Leaf fan, you are in for a treat. If you're merely a hockey fan, stay tuned for an enjoyable read.

After spending almost a decade-and-a-half behind the microphone, I can tell you without equivocation that the Toronto Maple Leafs are one of the most remarkable pro sports franchises in the world. Good, bad, or indifferent, the support this club has garnered is the envy of all leagues and sports.

Howard Berger's efforts in the following pages will give you yet another reason why this is so.

Joe Bowen
"Voice of the Maple Leafs"

VISIONS OF BLUE AND WHITE

I never saw Bob Baun score that goal.

The one on the broken ankle. In 1964.

But there's precious little about the game that night at Detroit's Olympia that I *can't* tell you about. Baun's overtime winner in Game 6 of the Stanley Cup final saved the Leafs. It is folklore... legendary in the annals of hockey, and a darned good piece of Canadiana. A moment that will stand on its own for as long as the game is played.

Too bad I was in bed.

But, what do you want from a five-year old?

I sure as hell wasn't sleeping when Lanny McDonald scored that overtime goal against the Islanders in 1978. Cripes, an unruly group of friends and I almost tore my old bedroom apart that night. Broke a real nice lamp, in fact. And never told Mom and Dad.

By the time Nikolai Borschevsky *next* won a playoff series for the Maple Leafs in overtime of Game 7 — just more than 15 years later — I had graduated to the status of media mogul. That was in Detroit, too. At Joe Louis Arena. And I covered the game. Even got my photo in the next issue of *Sports Illustrated*. Interviewing Nicki. He and I were smiling. Couldn't speak a word between us, but we were smiling. It was the thing to do that night.

The anthology of Maple Leaf moments you are about to read spans without question the most inglorious epoch in Toronto's National

Hockey League history. Imagine, if you will, a fat-man lying face-down on a hammock. You'd have quite an under-belly. That's roughly the graphical pattern of the Maple Leafs between 1964 and 1994.

It begins at a high point with a Stanley Cup victory — the third in succession, dips way down low with a 48-point season in 1984-85, and gradually curves upward again to meet the start of the Pat Burns era. In between, there are enough sagas and yarns, *we* think, to fill a book.

In the 30 hockey seasons between 1964-65 and 1993-94, the Maple Leafs captured one Stanley Cup and lost four semifinals. That's it. On nine other occasions, the club failed to qualify for the post-season tournament. Early playoff exits dominated the years in which it *did* qualify. Harold Ballard had his ruinous stamp on much of the era. At least he provided some sophomoric entertainment along the way.

But, there *were* moments of relative glory. Relative in the sense that a fan of the Montreal Canadiens the past 30 years would look over and yawn. Still, they served celebratory purposes in Toronto. And we remember many of them with compassion beyond their realm.

As a not-so impartial observer of the Maple Leafs for much of the past three decades, I feel qualified to compose a not-so impartial list of the top ten Maple Leaf moments.

1) THE 1967 STANLEY CUP VICTORY: This is an easy one. Kind of hard to recall, but obviously the high point. Terry Sawchuk's goaltending... the Pulford-Pappin-Stemkowski line... George Armstrong's empty net goal to clinch the final championship of the Original Six era. May 2, 1967. Beat the Canadiens *that* time. Haven't done much with them since.

2) DARRYL SITTLER'S TEN-POINT GAME: This one came right out of left field, but it's still in the record book. Most points in one game. The Maple Leaf captain should have bought a lottery ticket on February 7, 1976. Might've won a few more bucks than Harold was paying him back then. Sittler scored six goals and set up four others that incredible night at the Gardens as a very average Maple Leaf team — in the throes of a horrendous slump — lambasted a very good Boston club, 11-4. If you don't believe us, just ask "Grapes". He saw it all. From ice level. Without question the most magical evening of the past 30 years. And the record seems not to be in jeopardy. After all, Wayne and Mario have had plenty of cracks at it.

3) LANNY'S GOAL: That's all you have to say to most Leaf fans of the past 30 years, and they'll know exactly what you're referring to. April 29, 1978. A Saturday night at the Nassau Coliseum. Game 7 with the Islanders and nobody gave Leafs a chance. But they hung in there. Kept the score even at 1-1 after three periods then almost died early in overtime. Billy Harris had a breakaway. But Mike Palmateer stopped him. Then, suddenly — too quick for the TV camera to catch it all — the puck caromed to Lanny McDonald at the Islander blueline. He strode forward and planted a snapshot behind Chico Resch. There was momentary disbelief. For a second or two, time stood still. "Is it *really* in? No whistle?" Then came unfettered euphoria. Lasted all night. Thousands met the team at the airport in the wee small hours. It was just a quarterfinal victory, but a rare night for Maple Leaf fans to cherish.

4) NICKI'S DEFLECTION: A radio reporter's nightmare! The Leafs beat Detroit in overtime of the deciding game and the player who scores the winning goal knows one english word... *"Brutal!"* It was Nikolai Borschevsky's pat-response during his rookie season. He'd pump three past Eddie Belfour and we'd ask him, "How d'ya feel, Nicki?"

"Brutal!"

Oh well... *my* problem, not your's. Never mattered much that night at Joe Louis. May 1, 1993. A night to wear blue and white. But, who'da thunk it? Like they did against the Islanders in '78, the Leafs clawed back from a 2-0 series deficit to create hockey's ultimate hour: Game Seven. It looked bad there for awhile. Detroit led 3-2. Late. But then Doug Gilmour spun his usual magic and Peter Zezel almost won it in regulation. Overtime lasted only 2:35. Nicki tipped in Bob Rouse's lazy shot from the right-wing circle. The Red Wings were Dead Things.

5) THE RECORD-BREAKER IN TAMPA: This one got buried. Trampled. Annihilated. What timing, huh? The Leafs beat Tampa Bay to fashion the longest win streak from the start of a season... and Joe Carter hits a three-run homer to win the World Series. Happened within 60 minutes of one another. October 23, 1993. Hockey season it wasn't. Not just yet. But, what an achievement. Nine games played, nine victories. Better than the '34-35 Leafs and the '75-76 Sabres. Better than anyone... ever. Turned into Mark Osborne's night. He scored twice. Leafs won, 2-0. Felix blanked 'em at the other end. The ThunderDome was silent.

6) SITTLER'S FIVE AGAINST PHILLY: Another one of those shake-your-head nights in the mid-70s at Maple Leaf Gardens. Almost surreal. April 22, 1976. Just two-and-a-half months after his ten-point outburst against Boston, Darryl Sittler massacred hockey's premier goaltender. He buried a playoff record-tying five goals behind Bernie Parent of the Flyers: defending Stanley Cup champions. Try scoring five on Patrick Roy today. By yourself. Good luck. The captain's hot night kept the playoff quarterfinal alive. Sent it back to Philly for a Game 7. Jack Valiquette scored early, but the Leafs lost big. Sittler wound up tying Maurice Richard's modern-day record. The Rocket had scored five 32 years earlier. Incredibly (ironically, too), Reggie Leach of Philadelphia matched the record only 14 days after Sittler. And Mario Lemieux did it again in 1989.

7) TURNBULL'S FIVE AGAINST DETROIT: Almost a year to the day of Sittler's ten-pointer and the Gardens rocked again. February 2, 1977. The Maple Leafs beat Detroit, 9-1, and Ian Turnbull put his name in the record book. Five goals: most ever by a defenceman in one NHL game. Like Sittler's 10 points, the mark has survived. Paul Coffey, Denis Potvin, Raymond Bourque and Bobby Orr are the top four goalscorers among defencemen in hockey history. Coffey had four one night against Calgary. But only one man has five. Turnbull's victims? Ed Giacomin and Jim Rutherford. He broke the record on a breakaway. The place went nuts. Again.

8) GILMOUR'S SPINERAMA: An outlandish goal ended the Maple Leafs' second-longest playoff game of the past 30 years. Against St. Louis. May 3, 1993... only 48 hours after Nicki's deflection in MoTown. The opener of a Norris Division final. More than four periods of pulsating drama ended on a play from behind the net. Doug Gilmour got the puck, but he seemed dreadfully unsure of what to do with it. Nicki was covered. Andreychuk was covered. Dougie faked coming out to his left... spun around and faked to his right... then again to his left, like someone trapped between two walls closing fast. Finally, he emerged to the right of bewildered Curtis Joseph and stuffed the puck into the net on his backhand. At 3:16 of the second overtime. CuJo slumped. Who could blame him. He had stopped 62 shots.

9) SALMING'S BIRTHDAY BREAKAWAY: Ooooh, was this sweet revenge! For millions of Maple Leaf fans and, especially, for Borje Salming. In the same playoff quarterfinal in which Darryl Sittler would later score his five goals, Salming almost tore the roof off the Gardens. It was Game 4. A Saturday night. April 17, 1976. Borje Salming's 25th birthday. Two nights earlier, the Swedish defenceman had been flogged by the Broad Street Bullies. In one of hockey's premier acts of cowardice, Philadelphia rookie Mel Bridgman chose Borje as his dancing partner. Bludgeoned him half to death. Right in the Gardens. Beside the goal in the north end. It wasn't pretty. Black and blue from head to toe — but stubbornly undaunted — Salming re-emerged for Game 4 and stuck it right down Bridgman's throat (or *up* his you-know-what). He carried the puck to his own blueline and passed to Sittler along the boards in front of the penalty box. He then broke straight up the middle of the ice and let out one of his patented whistles. Darryl re-planted the puck on his tape and B.J. was in alone. He whipped a snapshot past Bernie Parent, generating what remains the loudest and most unabashed moment of celebration in my years of watching hockey at the Gardens. Leafs won that night, 4-3.

10) "MOTOR CITY'S" MAGIC: This was easily the most exciting single moment of the 1980s for the Maple Leafs. And there weren't more than a handful to chose from. April 16, 1987. At the Gardens. For the second consecutive spring, it seemed as if the Leafs were going to bely their typically abysmal regular season with a surprising playoff effort. They had a better St. Louis team on the ropes: down 3-2 in the Norris Division semifinal with Game 6 on home ice. Leafs hadn't won a playoff series since 1979, against Atlanta. The crowd was pumped. An awkward but lovably rugged forward named Brad Smith had endeared himself to fans at the Gardens. They knew him as "Motor City Smitty" for his Windsor roots and his earlier NHL days in Detroit. He scored goals like Bill Berg... rarely, and without flair. But all of a sudden, there he was, early in Game 6 and on a breakaway. The crowd rose so quickly that *Hockey Night In Canada* had to switch to its high-angle camera. Smitty deked and scored on Greg Millen. The Gardens erupted. Leafs went on to win, 4-0. Series over.

While this may not be a Letterman-like Top Ten, it does represent the rare peaks in 30 years of innumerable Maple Leaf valleys. Other, less-heralded moments deserve honourable mention.

Like Bruce Gamble's incredible ascent to Maple Leaf stardom late in the 1965-66 season. Summoned from Tulsa to replace Johnny Bower and Terry Sawchuk — both of whom were injured — Gamble played in eight consecutive games and recorded four shutouts. On a memorable Saturday night at the Gardens, he prevented Chicago's Bobby Hull from becoming the first player to score more than 50 goals in one season. Hull came at the Leafs in waves, pressing for No. 51, but Gamble stoned him.

There was Blaine Stoughton's overtime winner against the Kings in 1975 that sent the Maple Leafs back to Los Angeles to clinch their first playoff series since the 1967 Stanley Cup.

Or how about winning the first two games of the 1977 playoffs... right in Philadelphia!

Who can forget the three-goal outburst in 23 seconds against the Flames in the 1979 playoffs? At the Gardens. North end. First period. Sittler, Sittler, then Ellis. Still a post-season record for the fastest three by one team.

Fast-forwarding to the current era, we'll always remember the joy and relief on the face of Pat Burns the night he triumphantly returned to the Montreal Forum in January, 1993. His new team beat his old team, 5-4. Todd Gill scored a Bobby Orr-like goal.

*   *   *   *   *   *

Hockey is a game for kids. Adults watch it, too. Write about it. Broadcast it. And play it. But nothing in *my* life has ever compared to those impressionable years of the mid and late-1960s, when hockey and the Maple Leafs seemed bigger than life itself. Everything about the game intrigued me.

Dad would buy issues of *Hockey Illustrated* Magazine and I'd immerse myself in trying to understand the articles. I would then spend countless hours cutting out the photos and pasting them into my scrapbook. I'd struggle to stay awake and listen to Maple Leaf games that began at 11 p.m. from Los Angeles and Oakland. An innocence and naivety prevailed that none of us could possibly maintain.

Everything in life was simpler.

The details are fuzzy, but I do remember my first-ever trip to the Gardens. It was sometime early in the 1965-66 season and Dad bought a pair of tickets for a Sunday afternoon Junior 'A' game. The Toronto Marlboros were playing the Peterborough Petes. Mom dressed me in a shirt and tie and I recall laying on my parents' bed, nauseous with anticipation, in the moments before we left the house.

While driving to the Gardens, I somehow remember The Beatles' song "*Michelle Ma Belle*" playing on the car radio. And to this day, whenever I hear Paul McCartney sing that melody, I get some pangs of deja vu.

Several visions remain from that wonderfully exciting afternoon. Dad and I sat in the red seats (now golds), between the blueline and the goal the Marlies defended for two periods. The Marlies wore their white home uniforms — replicas of the Maple Leaf road duds. The Petes were in their predominantly maroon outfits, with the white trim.

To be in the same place where the Maple Leafs played *their* home games was a ghostly feeling.

Gazing curiously around the cavernous building, I recall that the mezzanine blues weren't yet in place. The sections that today comprise the north and south reds were the only end-zone seats in 1965. Without the balconies, there was plenty of wall space at each end of the arena.

Up to my right was a huge portrait of Queen Elizabeth. At the far end, to my left, I remember sunlight shining through four cathedral-like windows, underneath which were electronic clocks for out-of-town scores. There were only six NHL teams back then, each starting with a different letter. On a night the Leafs were at home and, say, Chicago was at Montreal and Boston at Detroit, the simple, but effective out-of-town scoreboard would appear like so:

C 2   B 1
M 4   D 3

I somehow recall only four players from that first visit to the Gardens. Al Smith was in goal for the Marlies and Fern Rivard for Peterborough. Smith later played briefly for the Maple Leafs while Rivard had a cup of tea with Minnesota in 1968-69. Brent Imlach, Punch's son, was in the Marlie line-up that afternoon. And I remember how big Wayne Carleton dominated the game offensively. The Petes couldn't deal with. his size and strength.

Within a few weeks, I was back at the Gardens for a Friday night encounter between the Marlies and St. Catharines Blackhawks. The game must have been on television somewhere as I recall the splendour of the bright TV lights which, to this day, remain suspended high above the arena floor along the west side of the building. With the lights on, the ice took on a pure and brilliant whiteness.

I remember how excited I was to see the Hamilton Red Wings for the first time. Another Friday night game at the Gardens. The Wings were more familiar to me than the Marlies because Hamilton's Thursday night home games were televised each week by CHCH-TV (Channel 11). Live from the Hamilton Forum. Norm Marshall and Sandy Hoyt called the action with Joe Watkins of the Hamilton *Spectator* providing intermission anlysis. If you missed the game, it was replayed in its entirety the following Sunday morning at 9:30. Brought to you by *Wilkinson Sword*.

The Hamilton players were household names. Jim Rutherford, Eddie Hatoum, Ron Climie, Lee Cunningham, Rene LeClair, Danny Lawson, Bart Crashley, Sandy Snow. And they wore Detroit's home red uniforms. What a treat *that* was!

Experimenting with mischief, I almost got myself kicked out of the Gardens that night. Not even seven years of age and already in trouble. We had rail (front-row) seats in the corner. The programs at the Marlie games back then were three-page cardboard fold-ins, with the line-ups and a 5"-by-7" black-and-white photo of a Toronto player in the middle.

Earlier in the game, I noticed that a teenaged fan sitting behind me had heaved his program onto the ice during a stoppage in play. For no apparent reason. The referee blew his whistle, allowing the linesman to skate over and pick it up. I thought that was kind of neat. One guy up in the blues was able to interrupt the whole game. So, a few minutes later, during another halt in play, I casually slipped *my* program through the small space between the glass and the top of the boards.

This wasn't quite as dramatic a scene, as one of the linesmen was hunched over with his butt practically in my face, awaiting the drop of the puck. He merely had to bend to his right and retrieve the program.

Still, I was damned proud.

Within a few seconds, however, I felt a tap on my right shoulder. Turning around, I noticed a Gardens' usher and a Metro policeman, both of whom summoned me away from my seat. I almost crapped myself walking to a small room in a corridor where the Maple Leaf Gardens Board of Directors' Lounge is still located. The two men gave me a stern lecture about the heinous crime I'd committed, then generously returned me to my location for the rest of the game.

At that time, Maple Leaf games were events that I listened to on radio and watched on television. We had two black-and-white TVs in the house — a console in the livingroom, and a smaller portable model that sat atop the dresser in my parents' bedroom. On Saturday nights, the ritual was always the same.

I'd have a bath after dinner, then lay in my bed and listen to Foster Hewitt describe the first half-hour of the hockey game on CKFH Radio, where I now work. I would pay extra-special attention to Foster's description of a scoring play — knowing that I'd ultimately see a replay of all the goals during the first intermission, with Ward Cornell, on *Hockey Night In Canada*.

The telecast started at 8:30 p.m. and I'd be planted at the foot of my parents' bed in plenty of time to see the opening. Bill Hewitt, Foster's son, called the TV action with Brian McFarlane doing the colour. I remember asking Mom why the Maple Leafs wore dark uniforms and the opposition white ones. In a peculiar stab at comedy, she told me the Leaf players smeared mud on their sweaters. And I believed her.

My favourite TV moments were Cornell's player interviews. To see the faces and hear the voices of these divine creatures was perpetually inspiring and it sent me on the path towards my current-day pursuits. I remember Ward standing one night beside Detroit goalie Roger Crozier, who was sweating profusely from the heat of the studio lights. Having played the first period, Crozier patiently diagrammed a Maple Leaf scoring play on a blackboard between he and Cornell.

At the time, the thought of actually attending a Maple Leaf game never even crossed my mind until Dad unwittingly showed me a pair of tickets he'd brought home.

I don't think he took *Mom* to a game for the next ten years!

The seats were east-side blues, and I still have the program from that momentous evening: Detroit at Toronto — Saturday, December 4, 1965. My first Leaf game. Walking into the seating area, I was again astounded by the brightness of the TV lights but this time, everything was larger than life. Especially the players I had known only by their black-and-white TV images.

I stood practically in a daze during the warmup. There was Dave Keon, Frank Mahovlich, Johnny Bower, Tim Horton... AND GORDIE HOWE! My gawd. While the Maple Leafs were perfectly colour-coordinated in their navy blue uniforms (dispelling Mom's mud-smearing doctrine), I remember thinking how strange the Detroit players looked wearing beige-coloured gloves with their white and red outfits.

Then there was the booming sound of Paul Morris over the Gardens' P.A. system. Again, louder and bigger than I ever imagined.

"Ladies and gentlemen, these are the officials for tonight's game. The referee, Vern Buffey. The linesmen, Neil Armstrong and John D'Amico. The official scorer, Bill Graham. Timekeeper, Joe Lamantia. Penalty timekeeper, Red Hewitt. Goaljudges, at the north end, Eddie Mepham. At the south end, Grant Easson."

Then, after a pregnant pause: *"In goal for Detroit and wearing number one, Roger Crozier."* Another pause. *"In goal for Toronto and wearing number one, Johnny Bower."* Almost 30 years have passed since that announcement but Paul is still doing it the same way. Only the names have changed. Morris hasn't missed his P.A. assignment at a Leaf regular-season or playoff game since 1962.

Looking back on the summary from my first-ever Maple Leaf game, I suppose there must have been mild disappointment as Detroit skated off with a 5-3 win. A lot of great names were in the line-up that night:

DETROIT: Goal- Roger Crozier, Hank Bassen. Defence- Bert Marshall, Warren Godfrey, Doug Barkley, Bryan Watson, Gary Bergman. Forwards- Norm Ullman, Gordie Howe, Alex Delvecchio, Andy Bathgate, Floyd Smith, Paul Henderson, Ab McDonald, Val Fonteyne, Ron Murphy, Billy Harris, Bruce MacGregor, Don McKenney.

TORONTO: Goal- Johnny Bower, Terry Sawchuk. Defence- Tim Horton, Allan Stanley, Marcel Pronovost, Bob Baun, Kent Douglas. Forwards- Red Kelly, Ron Ellis, George Armstrong, Brit Selby, Peter Stemkowski, Dave Keon, Bob Pulford, Frank Mahovlich, Eddie Shack, Larry Jeffrey, Orland Kurtenbach.

Bruce MacGregor and former Leaf Andy Bathgate gave Detroit a 2-0 lead after the first period, but Ron Ellis and Eddie Shack tied it up with goals late in the second. The third period was all Detroit. The Red Wings outshot the Maple Leafs 21-6. Gordie Howe (at 11:14) and Bathgate (at 12:39) put the Wings ahead, 4-2. Bob Pulford scored with 1:59 left to make it interesting but future Maple Leaf Paul Henderson clinched the win with an empty net goal at 19:58. I was zero-for-one. But, who cared? I had actually seen my first Maple Leaf game.

I'll never forget the morning of my seventh birthday: February 3, 1966. Mom and Dad rushed into my bedroom and awakened me with immense excitement around 5:30. I remember feeling cranky at being so rudely disturbed, but my grouchiness subsided upon entering my parents' room. On the floor at the foot of their bed was a full Maple Leaf uniform. Blue and white sweater, blue pants, gloves and socks.

I though I'd died and gone to heavan.

I hurriedly pulled the sweater on over top my pyjamas. It was made of the same woollen material the players wore in those days. Mom and Dad helped me on with the rest of the outfit and took some black and white photos that are still laying around the house somewhere. It was a moment I'll carry with me forever.

My first hockey hero was Leaf goalie Terry Sawchuk. I knew nothing about his glory days with the Red Wings more than a decade earlier, but it didn't matter. I loved his mask. It absolutely fascinated me how he could wear that thing over his face and still see the game. Initially, someone (probably Mom) told me it was made of thick leather, but I soon discovered it was fibreglass.

Having seen Sawchuk only during hockey games, and with the mask in place, I never knew what he looked like. Then one night, I was watching on TV when a Chicago player crashed into the Maple Leaf goal, toppling it backward off its moorings. A couple of maintenance men had to come out and reset the pins and while they were working, Sawchuk tilted the mask up onto his head. Seconds later, a television close-up finally revealed my hero's features. And I was mortified.

Sawchuk looked 60 years old.

He had wrinkles and scars.

And a brush-cut. A *brush-cut*. Damn, I was already listening to Beatle albums and my idol looked like a porcupine. Oh well, it was only a momentary let-down. He soon re-fastened the mask and I loved him all over again.

In March, 1966, Dad took me to see the Montreal Canadiens for the first time (still have *that* program, too). And a pair of visions from that game have stayed with me. First, I remember how Orland Kurtenbach beat the shit out of Montreal defenceman Terry Harper. We had great seats, in the reds, several rows up and to the left of the Toronto bench. And the fight happened just to the right of us. Poor Harper bled like a stuck pig.

Later in the game, I could have sworn that Sawchuk waved at me. Sitting so close to the ice, I frantically tried to get his attention every time he appeared to look my way. Finally, he waved back. Or so I thought. I'm sure *now* that he was merely adjusting his catching glove. But his arm came up and rotated several times. And for that moment, he and I were the only two people in Maple Leaf Gardens.

I think I saw all of the other five Original Six teams play the Leafs in the two years before expansion. When I was eight years old, the NHL doubled in size, adding six new clubs for the 1967-68 season. Dad took me one night to pick up Chinese food at the *Sea Hi* restaurant on Bathurst Street. A radio report talked about the soon-to-be expanded NHL and he explained that teams would be added in Oakland, Los Angeles, Minnesota, St. Louis, Philadelphia and Pittsburgh.

Where the hell *were* these places?

Expansion came at a time when I was starting to memorize all the elements of the six-team league: the cities, the uniforms, the players, the arenas. It was difficult enough for a grade-schooler to know, for example, that Bob Nevin was captain of the New York Rangers, who played their games at Madison Square Garden, wore blue uniforms with red and white trim at home; white uniforms with blue and red trim on the road.

Absorbing all the facts about six new clubs seemed overwhelming and I remember not enjoying my Chinese dinner that night.

When I first saw the Maple Leafs *play* one of the expansion teams, it threw me for a loop. Dad took me to a game on October 28, 1967 and for some reason, I didn't bother to inquire about the opposition. When we got to our seats, the action was underway and the Maple Leafs were playing a team wearing green pants. It made no sense to me at all until Dad explained that these were the California Seals, one of the six new expansion teams.

Dad then pointed to someone he felt I would recognize, and he was correct. Wearing number 21 in the white and green uniform was Bob Baun. I remembered him wearing the same number for the Maple Leafs just the year before. When I asked why he was now playing for California, Dad mumbled something about an expansion draft. Another brain-drain.

I quickly grew to enjoy the concept of expansion. The new colour schemes were great. California and Minnesota wore green. Philadelphia wore orange. And Los Angeles wore *purple!* I went out and bought a set of coloured pencils and had a joyous time sketching the new uniforms.

The entire process of going to a Maple Leaf game in the late-1960s remains vivid. After watching the *Bugs Bunny/Roadrunner* Hour from 5 to 6 on Saturday afternoon, I'd have dinner with my family. Around 6:45, we'd leave our house in North York and Dad would take Yonge St. most of the way downtown. I'll always remember the big **"PROCTER AND GAMBLE"** sign atop the office tower at Yonge and St. Clair.

Dad would make his way over to Church St. and we'd drive past *Julie's* Steakhouse (now *The Keg* Mansion). Back then, people attending the hockey game could park their car at *Julie's*, have dinner, then be driven to the Gardens on a double-decker bus like the ones you see in England.

Heading further down Church, we'd pass *Harry's* Steakhouse on the right. It no longer exists but it used to be a popular hangout for the Toronto sporting set. Once past *Harry's*, the Gardens would come into view. Lights shining through the windows on the upper part of the arena produced a blue-grey colour and I knew we were close. Dad would turn right on Carlton St. and park in the massive lot across the road from the Gardens. The large business/apartment complex that now sits on the south side of Carlton St. was not built until the late-70s.

Upon entering the Gardens, the first thing you noticed was the smell of popcorn. Every corridor had the same hot-buttered aroma. Dad's accounting firm had tickets in the west-side blues, Section 46, Row M, Seats 11 and 12: almost directly between the blueline and the south goal.

At the top of the stairwell in the second-floor lobby, you could see directly through the ramp-like openings to the seats on the other side of the arena. That was always an enthralling moment.

When I first attended Maple Leaf games, *God Save The Queen* was still played as the national anthem. And it was quite a ceremony.

The arena lights would all be extinguished, except for a cluster beneath the sportstimer at center-ice, and a singular beam that illuminated Queen Elizabeth's portrait on the south wall. The *Union-Jack*, and the soon-to-be adopted flag of Canada hung from an extension of the sportstimer, flapping rhythmically with the aid of large fans.

The game would start just after 8, and during the first period, I'd often keep my eye on one of the clocks at the end of the arena. At 8:30, I would think about the TV viewers just tuning in on *Hockey Night In Canada*. And I'd feel privileged to have witnessed the portion of the game they had missed.

I'd often spend the intermissions watching one of the TVs in the lobby. Ward Cornell would interview a player and when the teams skated out for the start of the next period, I'd look at that player and think how amazing it was that he had just been on television. I had no idea at the time that the dressing rooms were mere feet from the studio. The entire process of appearing on TV seemed complex and intriguing.

When the game ended, and the arena emptied, it came time for the parking-lot vigil. As they still do on game nights, parking attendants crammed cars into their lots like sardines. Forget about laneways. Unless you flew a helicopter to the game, you had to sit and wait for the vehicles surrounding you to clear out. If the people who owned the cars on your front and rear fenders decided to go for a late dinner, you were screwed.

Fortunately, Dad and I never had to camp out for the night. We'd usually start moving towards the exit within 20 minutes of arriving at the car. To pass time, Dad would turn the heat up nice and toasty and read me the articles in the program. On the way home, we'd occasionally stop for a hamburger. They were nice times.

Not so nice was the day the Maple Leafs traded Frank Mahovlich to Detroit (March 3, 1968). Hockey fans in the city erupted with anger and protested outside the Gardens. I was too young to consider activism but I do recall feeling somewhat mournful that day. In spite of the taunts that occasionally greeted him at the Gardens, Mahovlich was an icon in Toronto and it wasn't easy for an eight-year old to comprehend why he would no longer be playing here.

Looking back at newspaper accounts of reaction to the trade, it's apparent that Torontonians of all ages had the same problem.

Therefore, one of the strangest sights for any Maple Leaf fan in the 1960s was Mahovlich skating onto the Gardens' ice just six days later in a white Detroit uniform. Dad took me to that game on March 9, 1968. All eyes were on the Big 'M' during the warmup and I'll always remember the look of contentment on his face, as he had finally escaped the incessant chiding of Punch Imlach. Like always, his jet-black hair was impeccably combed and parted.

Still wearing his familiar No. 27, Mahovlich scored a breakaway goal on Bruce Gamble in the first period. Detroit built an early 3-0 lead, but the Maple Leafs came back to win a thriller, 7-5. Mike Walton beat Roger Crozier on a penalty shot.

The first hockey personality I recall meeting was Bill Hewitt: the voice of the Maple Leafs on television in the 1960s and 70s.

And I think I over-reacted.

It was sometime during the 1968-69 NHL season. My Grade 4 class at Wilimington Avenue Public School took a day trip to the old CKFH Radio offices on Grenville Street, near the Gardens. The station (FH standing for Foster Hewitt) had broadcast Maple Leaf games from the days of the Mutual Street Arena and was owned and operated by the Hewitt family.

An underling escorted us on a brief tour of the place and we later gathered in the reception area. We were told that Foster was signing a stack of autographs for us in his office. Just then, Bill walked out and introduced himself. *Bill Hewitt...* whose nasal twang had become so familiar on Wednesday and Saturday nights in the winter-time. And there he was, standing no more than three feet away.

I was truly in awe of this man but I felt obliged to up-hold my reputation as class clown. So I walked over to Bill and pretended to faint. Dropped like a rock right at his feet. It drew the desired response from my class-mates, who were howling with laughter, but I'll never forget the mortified look on my teacher's face. She was dying of embarrassment and upon offering Bill a sheepish apology, she took me onto the stairwell for a tongue-lashing. I vowed my repentance and was allowed to go back in and meet Foster.

A more thrilling and unexpected encounter took place a year later at Maple Leaf Gardens. The husband of one of my grade-school teachers, Elizabeth Dees, had season-tickets along the glass in the west rails — right next to the visitor's penalty box. Mr. Dees was a dental patient of my uncle, Ralph Blatt, and he occasionally offered him the tickets.

During games, whenever an opposing player skated to the box, the television angle would incorporate the people sitting in those rail seats. One night, a puck deflected off Maple Leaf captain George Armstrong, fluttered over the glass, and landed right in Elizabeth's lap. Watching it all on TV, I desperately hoped she would bring the puck to school the following day.

Well, not only did she *bring* it... she actually GAVE the puck to me! Just like that. I almost passed out.

And I remember marvelling with envy the few times I saw my uncle on TV in those front-row seats. To sit there was beyond my imagination.

As a result, I don't think I'll ever forget the night of Saturday, January 3, 1970. Watching TV earlier in the day, I got a telephone-call from Uncle Ralph, who said he was taking me to the game that night. *And he had the rails.* Wow!! Adding to my excitement was the fact that Bobby Hull and the Chicago Blackhawks were in town to play the Maple Leafs. And it was Hull's 31st birthday.

Uncle Ralph picked me up and drove us to the Gardens in plenty of time to watch the pre-game warmup. The glass along the side-boards was low enough in those days that even a scrawny 11-year old could stand up and see over top. Chicago warmed up at that end of the ice and as Hull came past me at one point, I stood on my toes and wished him a happy birthday. He skated down the left-wing boards and looked back over his left shoulder to see where the greeting had come from.

Thinking nothing more of it, I sat down and proceeded to thumb through the program-magazine. Seconds later, Uncle Ralph nudged me with his right elbow. I looked up, and standing directly in front of me, was hockey's Golden Jet. I was staring right into that Indian-head logo on the front of his white Blackhawk uniform.

Hull removed his right glove and reached over the glass to shake my hand. He thanked me for the birthday wish and offered to sign my program. I was wobbly. I wanted to speak but the words got caught between my brain and my tonsils. I sat back down feeling like the most special human being in the world.

In the first period of that game, the Leafs scored a goal that Chicago's rookie netminder Tony Esposito contested rather vehemently. He stormed out of his net towards the late Vern Buffey, who refereed the game, and I can still hear Esposito shouting over and over again through his mask, *"Bullshit! Bullshit!"* Such were the advantages of sitting in front-row seats.

At the time, I was absolutely astonished that a professional athlete could use that sort of language and get away with it. How could Buffey ignore Esposito's outburst the way he did? If I said "Bullshit" back then, I'd get a slap.

It bothered me and I decided to do something about it.

The officials went on and off the ice about six inches away from me, through the gate of the visitor's penalty bench. So when Buffey emerged for the start of the second period, I called him over to the glass. Surprisingly, he consented to hear my beef.

Upon advising him that I felt Esposito should have received a 10-minute misconduct for his diatribe, Buffey smiled and calmly explained that hockey was an emotional game, and that the referee had to allow players to blow off a little steam now and then. It opened my eyes to an aspect of the game I had not previously understood. I figured that any four-letter word was punishable by the rulebook. But Uncle Ralph carefully explained that a referee's ancestry would have to be brought into question before issuing a misconduct.

Of course, all I wanted at the time was a Chicago player to take a penalty, so he could sit down next to me. Secretly, I was hoping for a bench-emptying brawl. You know, the kind in which eight players from each team overflow the penalty benches. It would've been great!

Instead, all I got was a single, solitary visit.

Keith Magnuson, the obnoxious rookie defenceman, contributed a minor to his eventual league-leading total of 213 penalty minutes. He *also* cursed Buffey on the way to the box and I wondered if he was in any mood for a greeting. But I said hello and he was very pleasant. He reached over with his left glove, tapped me on the knee, and asked, "How ya doin' young fella?" I thought to myself, "Gee, this guy isn't the ogre he seems to be on the ice." Yet another eye-opener.

Earlier in the evening, I had walked behind the penalty bench and noticed the pail of frozen pucks by the timekeeper's table. I thought, boy, would I love to get my hands on one of those. During the second intermission, the pail was sitting right there, seemingly unattended. I looked around, shifty-eyed, and briefly considered larceny. But my developing conscience prevailed and I resisted the temptation.

When the timekeeper, "Banana" Joe Lamantia, returned to his position for the third period, I summoned enough valour to go over and *ask* him for a puck. He looked at me, growled something imperceptible, and told me to get back to my seat. The wretch.

Bummed out, I saw the rest of the game and stayed behind for the announcement of the three stars. As Uncle Ralph and I were walking out through the corridor to the lobby, a man approached us from behind and tapped me on the shoulder.

It was "Banana" Joe.

And he had a puck.

*   *   *   *   *   *

Maple Leaf memories are a subjective lot.

I've presented you with a mere sampling, based on the experiences of a youngster born in 1959. Those of you older than me will revel in the nostalgia of the late-1940s, when Kennedy, Apps, Broda and Co. won four Stanley Cups in five seasons for Conn Smythe.

Others will point to the Punch Imlach era, encompassing the very beginning of this book, and bringing with it another four Stanley Cup triumphs between 1962 and 1967.

Whatever your preference, I'm hoping these pages will re-kindle some latent recollections. Perhaps enlighten you to some stories you're not familiar with. Or enhance your perception of more recent Maple Leaf moments.

This trip down memory lane has sure been fun.

Enjoy the ride *with* me.

Howard Berger,
Toronto,
September, 1994.

SAWCHUK'S LAST HURRAH

Chicago Stadium
April 15, 1967

As the National Hockey League enters the final quarter of its first century, any singular mention of the game's greatest players is neither justified, nor complete, without the name Terry Sawchuk.

Considered by many to be the finest goaltender who ever lived — and having died in his youth a full generation ago — Sawchuk's preeminence as a hockey legend seems to grow with the passage of time. The NHL's career leader with 103 regular-season shutouts, he is immortalized for his astounding playoff efforts on behalf of the 1950s Detroit Red Wings: four-time Stanley Cup champions. In fact, many still consider his brilliance in the spring of 1952 to be one of hockey's most spectacular individual achievements.

But, long-time fans of the Toronto Maple Leafs are more likely to recall Sawchuk for a Saturday afternoon in the late-1960s, when a bruised and battered veteran of 38 turned back the clock en route to the most implausible of NHL triumphs.

Having won the Stanley Cup on three previous occasions that decade, the 1966-67 Maple Leafs appeared to be an over-the-hill collection of players rapidly approaching retirement. In the years since they were last champions, notable warriors like Sawchuk, Tim Horton, Johnny Bower, George Armstrong, Allan Stanley and Marcel Pronovost had gracefully aged to the point where genuine pride was all that kept them competitive.

Presumably, other variables more consistent with youth, like speed and endurance, had passed them by. And when they embarked on a semifinal playoff against a young and explosive Chicago club — 19 points superior during the regular season — they were chosen to succumb with minimal resistance.

That the Leafs ultimately prevailed in that series, and went on to win another Stanley Cup, is a lasting tribute to Sawchuk's goaltending savvy. The singular highlight of the playoff round will forever be his spectacular performance in relief of a faltering Bower, during the pivotal fifth game, at Chicago.

*   *   *   *

Sawchuk became a Maple Leaf, almost by accident, on June 10, 1964, at the age of 35. He was plucked off Detroit's roster by Punch Imlach in round three of the NHL's intra-league waiver draft.

For the better part of 15 years, he had been a stalwart in goal for the Red Wings, having also played briefly with Boston in the mid-1950s. He backstopped Detroit to three Stanley Cup triumphs in a four-year span, beginning in 1952 — *that* spring featuring the most emphatic playoff statement in hockey history.

While blitzing Toronto and Montreal in the minimum eight games, the Red Wings yielded only five scores. Sawchuk wasn't beaten for a single goal on home ice — wracking up four shutouts — and an infinitesimal 0.63 goals-against average. Only the 1959-60 Montreal Canadiens were able to match Detroit's eight-game Stanley Cup sweep.

Sawchuk was virtually unbeatable again in the 1954 playoffs, when he permitted only 20 goals in 12 playoff games for a 1.60 average. From that point forward, the native of Winnipeg had a standing reservation in hockey's Hall of Fame.

Sawchuk became the NHL's all-time shutout king on the night of January 18, 1964 — midway through his 15th season. He achieved that milestone, ironically, on the same night his *future* team — the Maple Leafs — were being hammered 11-0 by Boston. Detroit blanked Montreal 2-0 at the Forum: Sawchuk recording his 95th career shutout, breaking the mark held by George Hainsworth, who had played for Montreal and Toronto between 1926 and 1937.

By the *end* of his 15th season, however, the years of toil had seemingly caught up to Sawchuk. His right arm had been terribly damaged while playing rugby at a young age and was two inches shorter than the left. Combining that with the emotional upheaval all goalies faced in the six-team era — while playing every minute of every game — Sawchuk often wore the look of a much older man.

Upon losing the '64 Stanley Cup final to the Maple Leafs, Red Wing management no longer perceived Sawchuk to be a worthy number-one netminder. General manager and coach Sid Abel, formerly a star centerman with the club, had lofty expectations for an acrobatic young- ster named Roger Crozier, whom the Wings had acquired from the Chicago organization a year earlier. Abel believed Crozier could handle the bulk of Detroit's goaltending chores, with occasional relief from a similarly young, but less-heralded partner.

At the June NHL meetings in Montreal, Abel followed through with his plan. In round three of the intra-league waiver draft, he selected goalie George Gardiner — a former Niagara Falls junior — from the Boston organization. Having then to drop a goalie from his existing NHL roster, Abel chose to spare Sawchuk the indignity of expulsion to the minors, and he made the storied veteran available for selection by any of the other five NHL clubs.

The Maple Leafs were next in line and were planning to draft veteran Lorne (Gump) Worsley from the Canadiens' roster. Montreal had Charlie Hodge, and wanted to make room for promising youngster Ernie Wakely — the Central League's leading goalie with Omaha in 1963-64. Worsley had been demoted to the minors by Montreal for all but eight games of that season, and had battled a hamstring injury as well. So, the Gumper was available at draft time and Imlach was all set to try and resuscitate his career in Toronto.

But when Abel made *his* unexpected move, the Maple Leaf general manager changed his mind and grabbed Sawchuk for the $20,000 waiver fee. Suddenly, the three-time defending Stanley Cup champions had an unparalleled netminding tandem. Bower was the incumbent starter, while Sawchuk instantly up-graded the Leafs' goaltending depth. His arrival created a rung of demotion for both Don Simmons and Gerry Cheevers — neither of whom would play another game in a Maple Leaf uniform. The shocking turn of events thoroughly con- founded rival NHL executives, several of whom spoke out.

"If the Red Wings wanted to go with Crozier, why didn't they try to trade Sawchuk?" wondered Chicago coach Billy Reay. "They surely would have gotten something better than 20,000 dollars."

Added another rival coach: "Imlach is the luckiest bastard in the world. If he and I fell overboard and there was only one life preserver, you know who'd get to it first, don't you?"

Meanwhile, Sawchuk had mixed emotions about the whole thing.

He was deeply hurt that Detroit would merely release him after his many years of loyalty and service to the club. On the other hand, he realized his chances of winning another Stanley Cup were much greater in Toronto.

"I was knocked for a loop when I heard the news... too stunned to think properly," Sawchuk told Red Burnett in the Toronto *Star*. "I had a good year last season and never believed Detroit would leave me unprotected. But after a couple of hours, I decided it was a hell of a break. Toronto has a lot more talent than Detroit.

"It means moving up one notch right away and I think it will be the way to first place because I believe Leafs are that good. But don't forget, I have to beat out Don Simmons and Gerry Cheevers to prove I should share the job with Johnny Bower. It's no secret I have no intention of going to the minors.

"I wouldn't object, however, to rotating with another goalie," Sawchuk continued. "I don't think that either Bower or myself can be at our best for 70 games anymore."

Like everyone else, Bower was taken aback by the acquisition of Sawchuk and he remembers there being a myriad of thoughts swirling through his mind that day. Five months away from his 40th birthday, Bower showed no discernable signs of regression. He had completed his fifth full season in a Maple Leaf uniform with a stellar 2.12 goals-against average in 50 appearances. That level of performance then carried over through 14 playoff matches, as Bower backstopped the Leafs to their third consecutive Stanley Cup.

"I remember feeling sort of confused on the day we acquired Sawchuk," Bower says. "At first, I was worried about my own job, because I was the oldest of any goalie the Leafs had. And I began to wonder why Punch would bring in a goalie of Terry's calibre to compete with me. Did he feel I was at the end of the line? Those were the negative kind of thoughts that I initially had.

"But, I got along pretty well with Punch and I knew my record with the Leafs was strong. As the hours passed, I began to realize that with me *and* Terry in goal, we might win another Stanley Cup. And with the number of games we had played through the years, it turned out to be the best thing for both of us. Punch usually knew what he was doing back then... he was pretty shrewd."

Indeed, Imlach obtained the goaltending results he sought in 1964-65, although his hockey club had an otherwise ordinary season. The Maple Leafs finished in fourth place with only 74 points, their lowest total in any of Imlach's ten full years behind the bench. But the ageless tandem of Bower and Sawchuk sparkled between the pipes, winning the Vezina Trophy for allowing the fewest number of goals during the 70-game schedule (173). Their individual records for the season appeared like so:

	GP	GA	SO	AVE.
BOWER	34	81	3	2.38
SAWCHUK	36	92	1	2.56

Unfortunately for the Maple Leafs, they were eliminated by the Canadiens in a six-game semifinal playoff — Claude Provost scoring the series winner in overtime at the Gardens — officially ending Toronto's three-year Stanley Cup reign. Montreal then went on to beat Chicago for the '65 championship. But the Bower-Sawchuk duo proved it still had lots to contribute.

*   *   *   *

Despite his brilliance on the ice, Sawchuk — or "Ukey", as he was known — is universally remembered as a sad, almost pathetic human being. He had a terribly grim disposition and he rarely mixed well with people, in or out of hockey.

A difficult and tragic up-bringing in Winnipeg may have been the catalyst for his personality. His older brother, Mike, with whom he was very close, died of complications from a heart murmur when Terry was 10 years old — a traumatic experience from which the young Sawchuk never completely recovered. A second brother, Roger, died of pneumonia a few years later. Misfortune of that nature undoubtedly hardened Sawchuk and he became morose and introspective during his hockey playing days.

"Terry was a loner," recalls Bower. "He just wanted to go his own way and be by himself. After a game, the guys would go to a restaurant and have a beer, and Terry would be off on his own at a separate table. On a train ride to another city, he'd usually sit by himself and read a book, not saying much to anybody. That's the way he was most of the time and we just let him be. We didn't want to upset him because few people could play goal the way he could."

On several occasions during their netminding partnership, Bower tried to befriend Sawchuk, but the response was minimal.

"We were two very different people," Bower says. "I used to enjoy the camaraderie and shenanigans with the rest of the guys, but Terry wanted no part of that. Every once in awhile, I'd try to sit down and have a chat with him, but our conversations rarely went beyond hockey. He was a goalie I'd admired for a long time and I tried to get to know him away from the arena. But, it was very difficult."

The dissimilarity between Bower and Sawchuk extended to the ice. "I used to hate having a goal scored on me at any time, in a practice or a game," Bower recalls. "But Terry didn't give a shit about practice. He'd just stand there in the net like a statue, with his glove-hand extended, and the guys would usually lob their shots at him. Meanwhile, I'd be getting all the *real* action at the other end.

"Punch used to get mad at Terry for not trying and he'd call him into his office. But, Terry would say, `I do all my work in games, not practices.' During a stretch one year, he was playing so well that I couldn't get into a game. I was sitting out night after night and it was frustrating. So as a joke, I told Eddie Shack to really fire one at Terry during practice — thinking that maybe he'd get shaken up and I'd be able to play again.

"Of course, I was only fooling around, but Shackie took it seriously. Terry was standing there like a statue and Eddie fired a bullet at him and broke his finger! I couldn't believe it but Shackie skated by and said, `Well, I got you back in the net, pal.' I think I played the next 10 games."

During the three years in which they were teammates, Bower remembers Sawchuk letting loose only once.

"It was just after we won the Vezina Trophy together. The team threw a big party at a hotel Charlie Conacher used to own and, oh boy, what a different guy Terry was. The season was over, the pressure was off, and he was just like one of the boys — he had a hell of a time with us that night. But, that was the *only* time I remember seeing him have any fun. He was usually very withdrawn."

Apart from Sawchuk's family, the individual who knew him best was Hall of Fame defenceman Marcel Pronovost — his long-time teammate and roommate in both Detroit and Toronto. Pronovost was somehow able to recognize the complexities of Sawchuk's nature and he became one of the few people the goalie trusted as a friend.

"Terry's moodiness was his way of protecting himself from the outside," Pronovost explains. "Fame and fortune never sat well with him and he had a tough time accepting criticism or accolades. He cherished his privacy and looked upon all the public focus as an intrusion. Being rude and abrupt was his defence mechanism... it was not the *real* Terry Sawchuk. He was actually a wonderful man."

Unlike the majority of players in the NHL, Pronovost endured and accepted his illustrious teammate — warts and all.

"I could turn Terry like a pretzel because I understood his ways," Pronovost says. "I knew when to allow him his space and when to give him hell. I *learned* that only by living with him on the road for so many years. If he woke up the morning of a game and didn't say a word, then I didn't say a word. It would be breakfast in 20 minutes and see you there. On the other hand, if he brushed by a group of admirers, I could tell him to ease up and sign a few autographs.

"Most of the other players never really tried to understand Terry. He'd be rude or abrupt with them and he'd freeze them out. That seemed to be the way he wanted it most of the time."

Pronovost recalls Sawchuk as a highly competitive person, both on and off the ice.

"I remember one year in Detroit, some loud-mouth in the Olympia was giving Terry a hard time. He'd yell down at him after a goal, `Hey *Sawbuck*, you should be able to make that save.' The guy always called him `Sawbuck'. Well, one night, before a faceoff in our zone, Terry called me over and said, `The next time that cocksucker yells at me, try to look up there and find out who it is.'

"A few games later, I finally spotted the guy and told Terry where he was sitting. He wasn't playing because of an injury and during that game, he walked right up to the guy, tapped him on the shoulder, and said, `Hey pal, my name is Sawchuk, not Sawbuck.' He wasn't one to shy away from confrontation."

Another man who knew Sawchuk better than most was Hall of Famer Leonard (Red) Kelly. The two were teammates and Stanley Cup champions in Detroit and Toronto, and Kelly was Sawchuk's coach with the Los Angeles Kings in 1967-68, the year the NHL expanded to 12 teams. To this day, Kelly's nature precludes him from denigrating his fellow man, but he does acknowledge that Sawchuk could be an unpleasant associate.

"I enjoyed playing with Terry because he may have been the best goalkeeper of all time," Kelly says. "But, I saw the same weaknesses that others did. Most of his problems occurred when he had a bit too much to drink. He could become antagonistic in those situations, and it may have been a circumstance like that which ultimately caused his death. *[More on that later]*

"He just wasn't a good drinker," Kelly continues. "Some guys could drink a lot and it wouldn't really bother them. But Terry wasn't like that. He didn't react well to alcohol."

Often moody and unpredictable, Sawchuk was no more congenial in his rapport with members of the press. Milt Dunnell, the former sports editor and columnist at the Toronto *Star*, covered many of Sawchuk's greatest moments, including his miraculous performance for Detroit in the '52 playoffs, and the Maple Leafs' run to the '67 Stanley Cup.

"If you caught him at the right time, he could be quite the conversationalist, but those times were rare," Dunnell recalls. "I often found him to be rather surly and I remember thinking how much Dave Stieb, the former Toronto Blue Jay pitcher, resembled Sawchuk in personality. They were both very unpleasant to deal with."

Familiarity with Sawchuk meant nothing if he was in one of his snits. He would spurn even his closest acquaintance. Dunnell remembers an incident in the Maple Leaf dressing room involving Sawchuk and the late Bob Pennington — then a columnist with the *Telegram*.

"Pennington was a very refined individual, who rarely swore," Dunnell says. "One night, after a game, he approached Sawchuk to ask him a question and Sawchuk looked up and said, `Fuck off.' To which Pennington, in his refined manner, calmly replied, `Very well, Terry, if that's how you feel, I shall.'

"Well, Sawchuk couldn't believe what he'd just heard, and he yelled at Pennington, `Hey, okay, come back.'"

The incident was classic Terry Sawchuk, according to Pronovost. "That's exactly the way he was. If you went back at him with kindness, he'd feel bad and apologize. It was the Jekyl and Hyde in him. Most of the time, he didn't even realize the rude things he said."

Sawchuk also had a quick and volatile temper, as former *Globe & Mail* hockey writer Lou Cauz discovered late in the '66-67 season. The Maple Leafs were in Montreal to play the Canadiens (March 29), and on the afternoon of the game, Cauz was chatting with several of the players in the lobby of the Mount Royal Hotel.

"That was a pretty common scene back then," remembers Cauz, who covered the Leafs from 1966-69. "The players would sit in the lobby and it was a good opportunity for the writers to shoot the breeze with them and maybe get a story. Well, on this particular day, we were gathered around, and Sawchuk happened to say he wouldn't be returning to the Maple Leafs the following season.

"He elaborated quite extensively on the comment — saying the only place he'd consider playing was back in Detroit, where he had his home — and I wrote a story around it for the next day's paper."

Among the quotes Cauz attributed to Sawchuk were:

* *"Three more games, then the playoffs, and that's it. Twenty years is a long time; I want to start spending more time with my family. You know, our seventh (child) is on the way this summer."*

* *"I've thought very hard about it and right now, I'm ninety percent sure I'll retire. It's getting pretty rough."*

* *" I'm beat. I've lost a lot of weight; I don't know what I weigh, all I know is I'm under 170 pounds. (The Maple Leafs) aren't going to protect an old guy like me with a bad back (for the 1967 expansion draft). It'll be John Bower or one of the younger guys."*

The Maple Leafs lost 5-3 in Montreal that Wednesday night and returned to Toronto following the game. They practised at the Gardens the next morning and afterwards, during a media scrum with Imlach, Cauz unexpectedly drew the full wrath of Sawchuk's fury.

"Punch was pedalling away on an exercise bike in his office and several of us (the writers) were talking with him," Cauz remembers. "All of a sudden, Sawchuk came storming into the office in full equipment — with his mask still on — screaming at *me* for misquoting him in the retirement story. He was waving his big goal-stick around like a meat cleaver, while denying everything he had said during that chat in the Montreal hotel.

"And Imlach was making the whole situation worse by saying, `Yeah, you tell him, Ukey!' I was doing all I could to prevent from getting clubbed by Sawchuk's goal-stick, while screaming back at him, `You *did* say those things to me, for Chrissake. I've got them all here in my notes.' It was quite a scene."

Milt Dunnell believes the root of Sawchuk's acrimony may have been his unpleasant two-year stint with Boston (1955-57). Sawchuk went to the Bruins as part of a nine-player transaction in June, 1955, and he never got comfortable in Beantown.

"It was a disaster for him," Dunnell says. "He didn't play well in his first year there and it wasn't long before he was snapping back and forth with the media. In his second year, he contracted mononucleosis and wound up missing a good part of the season. He wanted out of Boston and at the same time, Detroit decided to trade Glenn Hall to Chicago. So the Red Wings re-aquired Sawchuk (for Johnny Bucyk in

July, 1957) and he quickly reverted to his all-star form. He was just a man fit for certain places and certain atmospheres."

Pronovost agrees that Sawchuk's bout with mononucleosis changed him forever. "Terry was a strapping, wide-shouldered man of 215 pounds when he started his NHL career," Pronovost says. "But the mono took a lot out of him. He lost almost 40 pounds and never again made it past 180. It left him with a different personality because he couldn't accept the way his body had changed."

While his gruff exterior was no illusion, Sawchuk *did* possess qualities of sensitivity and playfulness. He rarely displayed them in public, but Kelly will always remember sharing an emotional moment with his long-time friend and teammate.

"It was after our year together in Los Angeles," Kelly recalls. "We traded Terry to Detroit (for Jimmy Peters) at the start of the 1968-69 season and when I told him the news, he broke down and cried. In almost 20 years together, I'd never seen that side of him. It was quite a surprise."

Pronovost also remembers how Sawchuk never blamed a teammate for a goal being scored. On the afternoon of March 6, 1994, Pronovost took part in a pre-game ceremony at Detroit's Joe Louis Arena, during which Sawchuk's Red Wing uniform was retired and hoisted to the rafters. In a brief tribute to his late buddy, Pronovost told the audience a story, on which he later elaborated.

"We were playing in Toronto one night and leading the Maple Leafs 1-0 after the first period," he recalled. "Terry was having a fabulous game, stopping shots left, right and center. Well, in the third period, I ended up losing the game all by myself. One puck went past Terry off my skate; one went in off my leg, and I accidentally tipped another one under the crossbar. I think we ended up losing 5-1 or something.

"In the dressing room afterwards, I turned to him and said, `Sorry Uke, I had a horseshit night putting those three goals past you.' And he said, `Yeah, but you beat me cleanly on all three.' Then he started to laugh. That was his way of shifting the blame. He *always* did that.

"Anytime I either screened him on a goal or had a puck deflect in off of me, I'd go over and apologize and he'd say, `Aw shit, I got a piece of the damned thing and should've stopped it.' He was a very good teammate in those situations."

The demure, untroubled aspect of Sawchuk's personality wasn't easily uncovered, under any circumstance. However, former Leaf Peter Stemkowski remembers getting along quite nicely with the grizzled veteran. Despite an age differential of 14 years, the two players had a couple of things in common — being from Winnipeg, and of Ukranian descent.

Stemkowski was single at the time and Sawchuk's family (his wife, Pat, and seven children) lived in the Detroit area, year-round. So, at one point, the two Maple Leafs shared an apartment on Jarvis Street in downtown Toronto, and Sawchuk took the young forward under his wing. When Sawchuk had a day or two to visit his family, he'd often come back with a pot of cabbage rolls Pat had cooked up. He and Stemkowski would enjoy them over dinner.

"Terry seemed to like me for some reason," Stemkowski remembers. "I knew he was moody and preferred being by himself but there was a fun side to him as well. He had a very dry sense of humour and he enjoyed a joke. Every now and then, he'd walk into the dressing room in one of his terrible moods and someone would throw a good line at him. He'd usually lighten up and laugh.

"After practice now and then, I'd be sitting around and he'd come up and say, 'Hey kid, let's go for lunch.' Those were nice times for me and I can tell you that for all his moodiness, Terry wasn't a bad guy at all... once you got to know him."

Stemkowski would often get a rise out of Sawchuk when he mimicked the ailing goaltender.

"He was a physical wreck most of the time and he used to shuffle along, hunched over and limping," Stemkowski says. "One of his elbows was twice the size of the other because of floating bone-chips... he just looked like someone ready to fall apart. Every so often, I'd move up beside him and imitate the way he was walking. After a few seconds, he'd look over at me — a smile would come across his face — and he'd toss a few obscenities in my direction.

"The veteran players never really tried to humour Terry. They knew what he was like most of the time and left him alone. But, I was young and brash, and Terry seemed to enjoy it when I clowned with him."

Larry Hillman was a veteran defenceman with the 1966-67 Maple Leafs whose association with Sawchuk dated back to his rookie season, 12 years earlier, when the two played in Detroit. Hillman remembers Sawchuk's dour temperament, but doesn't feel he was much different than many of his colleagues.

"Just about all the goaltenders of that era had the stigma of being loners, and the majority of them were," Hillman says. "So, Terry really wasn't all that unusual. I actually got along quite well with him and don't remember him being as miserable as other people do."

Hillman occasionally saw the easygoing side of Sawchuk, and he remembers a moment of levity involving the veteran goalie and Maple Leaf defenceman Tim Horton.

"Tim was a big, playful guy, but he was as strong as an ox," Hillman says. "Back in the early '60s, he was sort of famous within the hockey world for lifting hotel-room doors off their hinges. He'd have a couple of beer, go back to the hotel, and enter his room *without using the key*.

"Well, when Terry came to our club in '64, he'd heard about this habit of Tim's but he didn't believe it. He had to be shown. So, one night after a game in Boston, Terry, Tim, Allan Stanley, Bob Baun, Johnny Bower and myself went out for a couple of drinks. We came back to the hotel a few hours later and got on the elevator to the third floor. When we got off, Terry began to egg Tim on, saying, `I've heard you can break down these doors but I think it's a lot of bullshit.'

"Tim was all loosened up from the beer and he walked over to a door, put his shoulder up against it, and lifted the damned thing right off its supports. Terry's eyes almost bulged out of his head and he just walked away laughing.

"The next morning, when we were going for breakfast, we passed by that room and saw a maintenance man painting the trim around the door. Tim said, `Geez, I wonder what could've happened *here* last night?!' It was quite hilarious."

*   *   *   *   *   *

The Chicago Blackhawks breezed to the NHL regular-season title in 1966-67 with a team-record 94 points. By finishing atop the standings for the first time in club history, the 'Hawks removed the so-called "Muldoon Curse" — placed on them by Chicago's first-ever coach, Pete Muldoon. Upon being fired after the Blackhawks' inaugural season of 1926-27, Muldoon suggested the club would never finish in first place during the regular season. His proclamation held true for 40 years, and was finally eradicated by the '66-67 team.

The Blackhawks scored 264 goals that season, the highest total in the 18 years the NHL operated with a 70-game schedule. And they permitted a league-low 170 tallies — netminders Glenn Hall and Denis Dejordy sharing the Vezina Trophy.

The club placed five players in the top nine of league scoring: Stan Mikita and Bobby Hull finishing one-two, with Ken Wharram, Phil Esposito and Doug Mohns close behind. A solid, mobile defence corps featured veteran captain Pierre Pilote, and youngster Pat Stapleton. No previous Chicago side — including the 1960-61 Stanley Cup-championship team — was considered to be so deeply talented.

For the second consecutive season, the Maple Leafs finished in third place with 75 points, only two behind second-place Montreal, but a whopping 19 points in back of Chicago. As was his custom back then, Punch Imlach managed to extract the optimal performance level from a veteran-laden team. But, the Maple Leafs of that season were *so* collectively antiquated that few observers believed they'd have enough resilience to withstand another playoff grind.

Consider the ages of the following Leaf players: Johnny Bower, 42... Allan Stanley, 41... Red Kelly, 39... Tim Horton, 37... Terry Sawchuk, 37... George Armstrong, 36... Marcel Pronovost, 36. By the end of the 1966-67 season, those seven players had a combined 120 years of NHL experience — with the wrinkles and scars to prove it.

Comedian John Wayne (of Wayne and Shuster) said of the 1966-67 Maple Leafs: "It won't be wonky knees or sore ankles that does this team in... it'll be prostate surgery."

The aging Leafs had been clearly inferior during 14 regular-season meetings with Chicago, compiling a 4-8-2 record. As well, Toronto's erratic and unpredictable efforts against the league, in general, were borne out remarkably between mid-January and early March. A calamitous 10-game losing streak (Jan. 15 - Feb. 8) was followed, promptly, by a six-game win streak (Feb. 15 - 26).

In the midst of that turmoil, Imlach entered hospital on the verge of a nervous breakdown, suffering from full-blown exhaustion. While he refuelled, King Clancy took over behind the bench and proved to be the perfect antidote. Frazzled by Imlach's oppressive style, the Leafs responded immediately to Clancy's more cavalier approach and got themselves back on the beam. In mid-March, after a month of repose, Imlach returned to his customary role.

"That really set the table for our success the remainder of the season," recalls Stemkowski, by then a full-time centerman with the Maple Leafs. "Punch was a tough man and his philosophy was to get the players so mad at him that they'd take it out on the other team. Sometimes it worked, sometimes it didn't.

"During that bad stretch we had in '67, most of us were absolutely sick of him. He had no idea when or how to let up, and we were going through torture during practice. I remember coming home by train after a terrible loss in Montreal (7-1, February 1). We had travelled all night and I didn't get a wink of sleep. I was pissed off to begin with and, being a young player, I had an upper-berth on the train.

"You rattled around pretty good up there and it was very tough to nod off. We got back to Toronto early in the morning, around 8 o'clock, and Punch said to us, `Okay guys, on the ice at nine!' Which meant we had to drag our weary bodies straight to the Gardens.

"That approach just wore on us. It was the only time I recall Punch actually losing the guys. No one wanted to see him get sick but if he hadn't entered hospital at that point — and Clancy hadn't come in to settle things down — I don't believe we would have won the Stanley Cup that season."

During his stint behind the bench, Clancy made the most fortuitous coaching decision of the season. Midway through a practice at the Tam-O-Shanter ice rink, he placed veteran Bob Pulford on a forward unit with youngsters Stemkowski and Jim Pappin. Clancy's brainwave would contribute mightily to a surprise Stanley Cup championship.

"It was really a fluke," remembers Pappin. "Stemmer and I were the extra players that season and during the practice, Clancy told Pulford to do his line rushes with us — basically to keep us company. Well, the next night, we were playing Montreal and losing 2-0, so Clancy sent the three of us onto the ice and we ended up scoring twice. We came back to tie the Canadiens 3-3 and we stayed together as a line for the remainder of the season."

The playoff format back then had the top four teams in the NHL qualifying, with first-place versus third, and second-place versus fourth. In 1967, that meant Chicago against Toronto, and Montreal against New York: the Rangers making it to post-season play for the first time since 1963. The 'Hawks and Habs were heavily favoured to meet in the Stanley Cup final, as they had two years earlier.

Pre-series forecasts appeared to be well on their way to fruition when the Blackhawks stomped the Maple Leafs 5-2 in the semifinal opener, at Chicago. Mikita and Hull scored second-period goals to break a 1-1 tie and Sawchuk was less-than spectacular in the Maple Leaf net.

But, "Ukey" would own the next two games of the series: both 3-1 Toronto victories.

Dave Keon and Stemkowski put the Leafs ahead 2-0 in the first period of Game 2, and that's all Sawchuk needed.

Back in Toronto for Game 3, Ron Ellis scored in the first period, with Frank Mahovlich and Pappin adding goals in the middle frame, for an insurmountable 3-0 Leaf lead. Hull beat Sawchuk in the third period, but the Leafs had a 2-1 edge in the series.

The Blackhawks fought back to win Game 4 on Gardens ice, 4-3, sparked by Ken Wharram's goal only nine seconds after the opening faceoff. Sawchuk had faced Mikita, Hull and company four times in a one-week span and was suffering from innumerable aches and pains. Most worrisome was a severely bruised right shoulder and the veteran goalie seemed physically spent as the series shifted back to Chicago for the pivotal fifth game — an matinee affair — Saturday, April 15.

In his 1969 autobiography, *HOCKEY IS A BATTLE,* Imlach recalled Sawchuk's condition. "Terry had played the first four games and was so battered and bruised that he asked to be allowed to sit that one out," the coach remembered of the scene prior to Game 5.

Brian Conacher, a right-winger on the '67 Maple Leafs, is *still* amazed that Sawchuk even showed up at the rink that afternoon in Chicago. "The poor guy looked like a reject from a concentration camp," Conacher says. "I still have a picture that someone took of us in the dressing room during that series and Terry looks like a refugee. He had a bad shoulder, a bad arm, one of his elbows could hardly move back and forth, and he was bruised from head to toe. God only knows how he sucked up the strength and courage to play as well as he did."

Maple Leaf trainer Bobby Haggert also recalls the extent to which Sawchuk was ailing. "You have to remember that Terry wasn't a youngster at that stage of his career," Haggert explains. "He had played in more than a thousand games by the playoffs of 1967 and the years of pressure had taken quite a toll on him. He had thinned out considerably late in his career. Every game had more and more of an effect."

Imlach realized Sawchuk needed a rest and he named Bower as his starting netminder for the all-important fifth game. It couldn't have been an overly taxing decision, as Bower had performed wondrously in the playoffs throughout his career as a Maple Leaf. But this particular afternoon in Chicago would prove to be an exception.

The game started at 1 p.m. Chicago time and was televised by CBS in the United States, and *Hockey Night In Canada* north of the border. It was unseasonably warm in the Windy City and with almost 20,000 fans jammed into every nook and cranny of the Stadium, the temperature inside was close to 90 degrees. As a result, the ice surface was dotted with numerous slush-puddles.

Unfazed by the adverse conditions, the Leafs started quickly, as rookie Mike Walton scored on Toronto's first shot of the game. Neatly set up by Pappin, Walton found the far corner on Blackhawk goalie Denis Dejordy from the high slot. In a situation similar to the Maple Leafs, Dejordy was subbing for a battered and fatigued Glenn Hall.

But, Chicago answered soon-after, scoring a pair of goals in a 90-

second span with the teams skating five aside. Maple Leafs' Stemkowski and Blackhawk defenceman Ed Van Impe were in the penalty box for a high-sticking altercation when center Lou Angotti tied the score at the 9:31 mark. Bower was unusually clumsy on the play.

Attempting to clear the puck up the left-side boards, his feeble pass was intercepted by Pierre Pilote, who immediately sent it back towards the Toronto goal. The shot hit Angotti in the leg and deflected into the net off Bower's stick. That mistake seemed to unsettle the veteran goalie and, moments later, he flubbed a weak shot from the point by Chicago defenceman Doug Jarrett. Fortunately for Bower, the puck sailed wide of the net, but it was quickly retrieved by Blackhawk forward Bill (Red) Hay.

Hay found Bobby Hull in the slot and Hull scored on a quick wrist shot at the 11:01 mark — Bower lunging awkwardly at the puck as it found the upper portion of the net. Mahovlich knotted the count three minutes later, but Bower continued to fight the puck on almost every Chicago rush.

With four minutes remaining in the period, Imlach called Bower over to the bench to try and determine why the goalie appeared so jittery. In *HOCKEY IS A BATTLE*, Imlach rehashed that conversation:

"...(Bower) admitted he was shaky, but said he wanted to finish the period anyway. I let him. We talked again in the dressing room after the period. I could see he wasn't himself and he knew it too. He agreed with me that he should come out and we'd put Terry Sawchuk in.

"...(Sawchuk) was on the bench, of course, I'd asked him in the first, when Bower looked shaky, if he felt well enough to go in. But Terry said he'd rather wait until the start of the second if he had to go in at all, so that made it unanimous."

Bower remembers how disappointed he was at that moment, knowing all the while it was the proper decision. "Punch told me he couldn't depend on me anymore that day because I didn't look sharp," Bower says. "I wanted to play. I knew millions of people were watching the game on TV, so who wouldn't want to play? But, I hadn't seen much action in recent games and I was scared I would continue to make costly mistakes. So, I couldn't argue the decision to put Terry in.

"He was a guy who could sit on the bench for a period or two, then come into the game and play great, regardless of how he was feeling."

Milt Dunnell was in Chicago that day. In his *Toronto Star* column, he wrote: "When Terry waddled out to replace Bower, there was a buzz of speculation in the packed and perspiring Stadium. The partisans didn't like Sawchuk's arrival. He'd been poison in the third game at Toronto."

That premonition turned out to be frighteningly accurate for the Chicago rooters, but not before Sawchuk nearly had his upper body decimated by one of Bobby Hull's cannons. The second period wasn't two minutes old when Hull scooped up the puck at a steep angle to the right of Sawchuk. The Maple Leaf goalie had never been fond of high shots, and would frequently storm off the ice in practice whenever a teammate sent one up around his ears. Undoubtedly aware of that obsession, Hull wired a rising missile at Sawchuk from the corner.

Had Sawchuk ducked, the shot would almost certainly have cleared the top of the net and rattled around the protective glass. In a reflex move, however, the goalie leapt several inches off the ice, trying to take the puck in his chest padding. Instead, Hull's bomb caught him flush on his bruised right shoulder and Sawchuk dropped like a rock.

"Everyone thought he was dead," recalls Stemkowski, who was on the ice at the time. "For a moment there, I had the feeling it was all over — that we may as well fold up our tent. As Bobby Haggert rushed onto the ice, I remember looking at our bench and everyone's head was down. I knew what they were thinking, because I was thinking the same thing... Bower hadn't been at all sharp and didn't seem ready to play. If he had to go back in, it would give Chicago a major boost."

In spite of his objectives, Hull cringed when he saw his howitzer flatten Sawchuk. "I was scared I'd hit him in the neck or the throat," said the Golden Jet. Covering the game for the *Globe & Mail*, the late Dick Beddoes recounted the scene around the Maple Leaf net:

"...The puck struck Sawchuk's left shoulder and knocked him down, another crack on the same shoulder with blue-green bruises from two shots in recent practices. Other players skated around the Toronto net, watching — the Leafs in some chagrin, the 'Hawks curious.

"Pierre Pilote, the Chicago captain, crafty, conny, got out his barbs. 'How'd you feel, Terry? You should have let it go, Terry. Might've been a goal.'"

Haggert scurried onto the ice, unaware if the Maple Leaf goalie was conscious. When he arrived, he asked Sawchuk, "Are you alright?"

"I stopped the puck, didn't I?" was the goalie's reply.

At that point, Haggert knew the veteran would stay in the game. "That was typical Terry Sawchuk," recalls the former Leaf trainer. "He really got clobbered by that shot, right under the collarbone. There's not a lot of padding there and I remember his arm went a little numb. Between periods, we had him checked over by a doctor just to make sure the collarbone wasn't broken: he had a welt the size of a grapefruit.

"But, nothing surprised me when it came to Terry's courage. He was always such a gamer. Even though he asked Punch Imlach not to use him that afternoon in Chicago, once he went in (to replace Bower), nothing was going to get him out of there."

All things considered, what followed the scary incident may still rank as the most heroic goaltending performance in Stanley Cup history. Sawchuk picked himself up off the ice and performed flawlessly the remainder of the day, amid a relentless Chicago attack. Hull, Mikita, Wharram, Mohns, Stapleton — they fired incessant bullets from varied angles and ranges: 37 in total over the two-period duration. Not one got past the gritty netminder.

The second period was scoreless, with the Blackhawks outshooting the Maple Leafs 15-9. But it was Sawchuk's third-period splendour that many Leaf fans recall to this day. The banged-up goalie dove, sprawled and smothered like never before — blocking a 22-shot barrage — as the Maple Leafs counted twice for a spellbinding 4-2 victory.

Stemkowski scored the winning goal at the 2:11 mark. The hastily arranged line of Stemkowski, Pulford and Pappin would be Toronto's most effective throughout the '67 playoffs and it struck for the biggest goal of the Chicago series. Stemkowski looked awkward in mis-directing a perfect feed from Pappin in among the spectators behind the Chicago goal. But seconds later, Pappin had two whacks at the puck from close range before it scooted over to Stemkowski, who whipped it past Dejordy for the only tally Sawchuk would require.

His exhausted body performing on instinct, Sawchuk repeatedly spun magic to protect the one-goal cushion. In his *Globe & Mail* game story, Lou Cauz penned an example of the netminder's heroics:

> "...(Doug) Mohns and Sawchuk held a private meeting with the score 3-2 in Leafs' favour late in the game. They met eyeball to eyeball. Mohns jiggled his shoulders, waggled his stick as he moved across the face of the goal. Sawchuk met every deke masterfully and finally smothered the drive."

But Sawchuk's most memorable save of the afternoon occurred a few seconds after he out-guessed Mohns. Once again it was Hull winding up from close range. But this time, his booming drive was smartly deflected by Mikita. The puck changed directions and seemed labelled for the upper corner until Sawchuk miraculously got his arm in the way of it. The unflappable Hull continued to fire his hardest and most accurate drives at Sawchuk... but to no avail. Pappin iced the win for Toronto with 2:46 remaining on the clock.

"I saw him make those saves, but I still can't believe it," Hull would lament after the game. "That was the most frustrating experience of my career."

In the happy Maple Leaf dressing room, Sawchuk barely had enough strength to peel off his soaked equipment. When asked if he saw Hull's shot that almost annihilated him, he answered, "Are you kidding? All you do is hope that it hits you. There's no skill in that."

Dick Beddoes visited the dressing quarters of both teams after the game and described the atmosphere in his *Globe & Mail* column:

> "...Bobby Hull dressed slowly and said little. What he did say had disbelief in it. 'Never! Sawchuk never gave us that much trouble before.' A reporter said, 'He simply pitched a no-hitter at you.' Hull, slipping a ring on one thick finger — 'Yes.'
>
> "The Toronto dressing room was cheerful, but not ecstatically so; there was some jubilance in the hangers-on, but the players seemed aware there is another game tomorrow. And that somewhere, in the Laurentian hills, the Montreal Canadiens are waiting.
>
> "Sawchuk sat in his socks and underwear a long time, head down, hands cupped around a can of Coke, absorbing what he had done.
>
> "Finally, he looked up, wan, spent. 'I feel 57, not 37.'"

The superlatives for Sawchuk flowed freely in both rooms. Red Burnett recorded several of them in the Toronto *Star*.

"Sawchuk was that good. He gave us nothing, not a rebound," said Pierre Pilote. "That, my friend, is perfect goaltending."

Added an exasperated Mikita: "Everything broke right for Sawchuk and wrong for us, and mostly it was because he made the right moves. Maybe we'll start getting them in bunches on Tuesday. Certainly we're overdue to break loose."

And Blackhawk coach Billy Reay said, "That was the greatest game of hockey (Sawchuk) has played in the Stadium in the four years I've been coach. It was a terrific hockey show and he dwarfed the rest of the players with his work."

The Maple Leafs finished off the Blackhawks two nights later in Game 6 of the semifinal series at Maple Leaf Gardens. Typical of their 1967 playoff run, they received goal-scoring savvy from an unexpected source — rookie Brian Conacher connecting twice in a 3-1 victory. Once again, Sawchuk was absolutely brilliant.

When reflecting on the series more than a quarter-century later, the participants are split in their views of just how monumental an upset it was.

"I don't think we were as well-prepared for the playoffs," admits Pilote. "We were an entertaining, offensive-oriented team, not really capable of changing our style. The Leafs weren't as explosive, but they could shut you down effectively. Combine that with the goaltending of Sawchuk, and there's no way we were going to beat them that year."

Stan Mikita isn't necessarily on the same page as his former teammate and captain.

"I don't know how anybody could say we were a one-dimensional team," Mikita bristles. "Sure, we scored a lot of goals but we also ended up winning the Vezina Trophy that season. You don't do that by accident. Even though Toronto beat us, the scores weren't exactly one-sided. Sawchuk stood tall for them, but if we had gotten one or two past him at certain times, *we* would have come out on top."

Defenceman Pat Stapleton, a second-team All-Star with Chicago the year before, believes the series turned irrevocably in Toronto's favour the moment Sawchuk recovered from Bobby Hull's wicked blast in Game 5.

"That was the turning point, no question," he insists. "Bobby could really wire them in those days and he used his shot as a device for intimidation. When Sawchuk went down, very few of us in the Stadium thought he would get up. But, he did... and he performed as well as any goalie I'd ever seen. It was awfully frustrating."

Stapleton agrees with Mikita that there wasn't much to choose from between the two teams. "A shot here or a shot there would have made the difference," he says. "When I look back on it, we may have peaked a bit too early that season. I remember how thrilling it was to finish atop the standings and maybe it all came together for us at the wrong time. But, give the Leafs credit. They had loads of experience on that team and they played us perfectly."

The Maple Leaf front-liners like Frank Mahovlich, Dave Keon and a young Ron Ellis were expected to generate scoring opportunities against Chicago, but it quickly became a series that showcased Toronto's deep supporting cast.

"Sawchuk was great, no doubt about it, but Pulford, Stemkowski and Pappin were the guys who stood out for Toronto," says former Blackhawk winger Chico Maki. "The Maple Leafs' young players really made the difference in that series because they weren't expected to carry such a big load. I don't think we had the same depth on our club."

Hall of Fame defenceman Allan Stanley, who played such a dominant physical game against the Blackhawks, doesn't remember anything too complicated about the Maple Leafs' strategy in that series.

"Chicago had Hull and Mikita," he says. "There were many other good players on that team, but Bobby and Stan were the mainstays — if you could slow them down, you could beat the Blackhawks. I remember the team meeting we had just before the series. Davey Keon got up and said that if we didn't keep a close watch on Hull and Mikita, Chicago would kill us. That was a bit strange, because it wasn't often a forward got up in one of those meetings and talked about defence.

"But, Davey was absolutely right and we decided, generally, that the closest man to Hull or Mikita on the ice would go over and stand beside them. We didn't want them to carry the puck or work themselves into good shooting positions. Our approach was to stick close and make them pass it off. And, basically, it worked."

Buoyed by their upset of Chicago, the Maple Leafs went on to win their fourth Stanley Cup of the 1960s. They beat the Montreal Canadiens in six games — utilizing the same elements of success: depth in goal, and in the forward ranks.

Sawchuk started the series opener at the Forum but had a difficult night and was yanked by Punch Imlach after the second period of a 6-2 Montreal romp. Bower took over and proceeded to duplicate Sawchuk's accomplishments of the Chicago series.

He was extraordinary during a 3-0 Maple Leaf victory in Game 2, and equally brilliant in the most memorable game of the series — two nights later — at Maple Leaf Gardens. That was the evening Bower and rookie Montreal goalkeeper Rogatien Vachon took turns performing magic through almost four-and-a-half periods of thrilling hockey.

Dubbed inaccurately by Imlach as a "Junior `B' goalie", Vachon handled 62 shots in the Montreal net, while Bower had 54 directed his way. The line of Pulford, Stemkowski and Pappin did all the scoring damage for Toronto: Pulford ricocheting the puck into the Canadiens' net off defenceman Terry Harper's skate at 8:26 of the second overtime.

Montreal tied the series in Game 4 — a replay, in many respects, of the opener. Bower pulled a groin muscle in the pre-game warmup and Sawchuk got blitzed *again* by the Canadiens, 6-2. Not expecting to play, a story alleges — and persists — that Sawchuk had been drowning his sorrows in a local watering hole the night before, and was still half-in-the-bag when he replaced Bower. True or false, it appeared as if the veteran goalie had lost all of his recuperative powers.

But then he bounced back. Like magic. And he turned the series in Toronto's direction — exactly as he had done against the Blackhawks. A brilliant performance backstopped the Leafs to a 4-1 win in the all-important fifth match at Montreal, a game in which the Canadiens (like Chicago in the previous series) had been decided favourites.

Back home for Game 6, Sawchuk again stood out as the Maple Leafs won the Stanley Cup with a 3-1 victory. The image of captain George Armstrong loping towards center ice and firing the puck into a vacated Montreal net for the series clincher, remains among the most vivid in a decade replete with Maple Leaf memories.

*   *   *   *

For Terry Sawchuk, life was never the same after that Maple Leaf triumph. The NHL doubled in size for the 1967-68 season, adding teams in Philadelphia, Pittsburgh, St. Louis, Minnesota, Los Angeles and Oakland. The six established clubs were each allowed to protect only one goaltender for the expansion draft, and Imlach chose to keep Bower.

Left unprotected, Sawchuk was claimed early by Los Angeles and he performed adequately for the first-year Kings. Sharing the netminding chores with Barrie native Wayne Rutledge, he compiled a 3.07 average in 36 appearances. But the wheels fell off for good in the playoffs that spring. Los Angeles and Minnesota went the distance in a West Division quarterfinal and Sawchuk foundered in Game 7.

A crowd of 11,214 at the L.A. Forum looked on dejectedly as the North Stars poured five goals past Sawchuk in a 7:31 span of the second period. Losing 8-2, he was replaced by Rutledge after the middle frame and Minnesota coasted to a 9-4 series-clinching victory.

Sawchuk returned to the Red Wings for the 1968-69 season but he played in only 13 games. He then went to New York for 1969-70, and spelled Ed Giacomin on eight occasions. Little did anyone realize that his life would come to a sudden and tragic ending only weeks after the Rangers were eliminated by Boston in the 1970 playoffs.

Sawchuk died in a New York hospital on May 31 of that year. He was 40. The circumstances surrounding his demise are still shrouded by mystery and intrigue almost a generation later. What is known, albeit vicariously, is that Sawchuk and Ranger teammate Ron Stewart became embroiled in some kind of a drunken confrontation on the night of April 29, 1970. During that scuffle, Sawchuk took a swing at Stewart and lost his balance. He fell awkwardly over the side of a barbecue pit and Stewart apparently came down on top of him, knee-first.

Sawchuk's liver — enlarged from his years of alcohol abuse, and protruding below his ribcage — took the brunt of the trauma and he began to haemorrhage. Suffering from a split liver, he was rushed to Long Beach Memorial Hospital, where doctors packed his injured organ and stopped the bleeding.

Sawchuk should have been moved to a better-equipped facility at that point but, craving his privacy, he apparently refused a transfer. The decision cost him his life. Several days later, Sawchuk's liver began to haemorrhage once again, at which point he *was* rushed to the New York University Hospital. But it was too late. Unable to withstand the shock, his body shut down and the great former goalie passed away.

What remains unknown about the entire episode is whether there was any intent on Stewart's part to injure Sawchuk. The two veteran players were great friends, but they were both known to lose their tempers when under the influence of alcohol.

An article in the November, 1970 edition of *Hockey Illustrated* magazine, seems to absolve Stewart of any blame. Shirley Fischler, the wife of hockey author and columnist Stan Fischler, visited Sawchuk in Long Beach Memorial and is the last reporter to interview the goalie. During her visit, Fischler asked Sawchuk about the scuffle with Stewart and Sawchuk replied, "It was just a fluke, a complete fluke-accident." He then made it clear to Fischler that he no longer wanted to discuss the controversial incident.

When asked if he would ever again play hockey, Sawchuk told Fischler, "I'm retired, man. Look at me. I can never come back from this." Upon Sawchuk's death four days later, involuntary manslaughter charges against Stewart were considered, but never filed. Which sheds sufficient light on why Stewart has always refused to discuss the incident publicly.

"Terry died on my wife's birthday," recalls Marcel Pronovost. "We were celebrating at a friend's house in Toronto — sitting around the pool — when I heard about it on the radio. And I'm not ashamed to tell you that I broke down and cried. Terry was so insistent on his privacy that I didn't even know he was ill."

The last man to see Terry Sawchuk was Emile Francis, the Rangers' general manager and coach in that era. In broadcaster Dick Irvin's acclaimed book, *BEHIND THE BENCH*, Francis recounted the eerie spectre of identifying Sawchuk's body.

> "...I had to go to the morgue on Second Avenue. ...There were about 30 bodies lying there, and the first thing that hit me was that they were in bags just like the bags we use to carry hockey sticks in.
>
> "And there he was, his head out of one end of the bag with a tag around his neck. They had 'Terry Sawchuk' written on the tag."

And so ended the life and the career of one of hockey's most enigmatic stars. The saga of Terry Sawchuk lingers almost 30 years after that storied afternoon of April 15, 1967, when a legend in his own time singlehandedly reversed the playoff fortunes of two teams.

Terry Sawchuk's last hurrah.

WHERE ARE THEY NOW? ...

JOHNNY BOWER, 70, blossomed at a late age and did not make it to the NHL till he was 29. He played parts of three seasons in New York and was drafted by the Maple Leafs in June, 1958. Known as the "China Wall", Bower was the Leafs' number-one netminder through their glory days in the 1960s. He played an integral role on all four Stanley Cup teams and remained with the Leaf organization as a scout for more than 20 years after his retirement in 1970. He currently spends his summers in Mississauga, Ont. and his winters in Fort Myers Beach, Fla.

MARCEL PRONOVOST, 64, was a stalwart defenceman for Detroit in the Red Wings' Stanley Cup dynasty of the 1950s. Traded to the Maple Leafs as part of a seven-player deal in May, 1965, he finished his career in Toronto and retired after the 1969-70 season. He coached the Buffalo Sabres in 1977-78 and was elected to the Hockey Hall of Fame that same year. Living in Windsor, he is now a scout for the New Jersey Devils.

LARRY HILLMAN, 57, was an unheralded but steady defenceman in the NHL and WHA from 1954 to 1976. He played with the Maple Leafs from 1960 to 1968 and was a member of all four Stanley Cup teams under Punch Imlach. He remains among the most travelled hockey players in history: his NHL log including Detroit, Boston, Toronto, Minnesota, Montreal, Philadelphia, Los Angeles and Buffalo. He played for Cleveland and Winnipeg in the WHA. He currently operates an outdoor tourist camp in Charlton, Ont., 33 miles south of his native Kirkland Lake.

JIM PAPPIN, 55, was one of the true heroes of the Maple Leafs' unexpected Stanley Cup team in 1967. Playing on a line with Peter Stemkowski and Bob Pulford, he scored seven goals in the 12 playoff games that spring, and notched the eventual Cup winner in Game 6 against Montreal. Traded to Chicago for Pierre Pilote in May, 1968, Pappin enjoyed his finest NHL seasons in a Blackhawk uniform, playing on the famed "M-P-H" line with Pit Martin and Dennis Hull. He scored more than 30 goals four times and finished his playing career with the NHL's Cleveland Barons in 1977-78. He and Pulford are still together in the Chicago organization: Pulford as Senior V-P and general manager, and Pappin as the Blackhawks' pro scout.

BRIAN CONACHER, 53, joined the Maple Leafs in the mid-1960s after several years as a member of Canada's national hockey team. He played for Canada in the 1964 Winter Olympics at Innsbruck, Austria and became a full-time Maple Leaf in 1966-67. Among Punch Imlach's least-favourite players, Conacher didn't last very long in Toronto. He briefly played with Detroit in 1971-72, then with Ottawa of the WHA the following year. The son of Lionel Conacher, Canada's athlete of the half-century, Brian lives in Toronto and is currently vice-president of building operations at Maple Leaf Gardens.

PIERRE PILOTE, 63, was the NHL's premier defenceman in the era preceding Bobby Orr. Captain of the Chicago Blackhawks, he combined sound defensive work with an ability to move the puck, and he won the Norris Trophy three years running (1962-63/ 1963-64/ 1964-65). Pilote played 13 years in Chicago and was traded to the Maple Leafs for Jim Pappin in May, 1968. He retired after the '68-69 season and was elected to the Hockey Hall of Fame in 1975. Nowadays, he raises cattle (Black Aberdeen Angus) on a farm near Milton, Ont.

STAN MIKITA, 54, is one of hockey's all-time great players. A brilliant center-iceman, he skated 22 years for the Blackhawks (1958 - 1980) and won the Art Ross Trophy as the NHL's leading scorer four out of five seasons between 1963 and 1968. He also won consecutive Hart Trophies as League MVP in 1966-67 and 1967-68. He was elected to the Hall of Fame in 1983. Still living in Chicago, Mikita is a partner in a Plastics company, *Mikita-Skov*, with former NHLer Glen Skov.

PAT STAPLETON, 54, was an excellent, mobile defenceman with the Blackhawks between 1965 and 1973. But he never really made his mark until the 1972 Canada-Soviet summit series, during which he played so effectively for Team Canada. In the early 70s, at Chicago, he teamed with Bill White to form one of the NHL's top defensive duos. Stapleton played with Chiacgo, Cincinnati and Indianapolis of the WHA before retiring in 1978. He currently does some farming in Strathroy, Ont. and gives inspirational talks to young hockey players and their families.

RONALD (CHICO) MAKI, 55, is best remembered for being the right winger on Bobby Hull's line throughout the 1960s. Maki and Hull played with various center-icemen, most notably Phil Esposito and Lou Angotti. Maki's brother, Wayne, played with St. Louis and Vancouver in the NHL before dying of brain cancer in 1971. Chico retired after the 1975-76 season. He now lives in Port Dover, Ont. and is service manager for *L-P International* of Brantford, a company that manufactures electrical equipment to move household appliances.

ALLAN STANLEY, 68, had his NHL career resurrected by Punch Imlach in October, 1958, when he was traded from Boston to the Maple Leafs for fellow defenceman Jim Morrison. Starting out with the Rangers in 1948-49, Stanley fell into disfavour with the hockey fans of New York and was practically booed out of Madison Square Garden in 1954. He played briefly with Chicago and the Bruins before joining Toronto. During the 1960s, Stanley teamed with Tim Horton to provide one of the League's strongest defence combinations. He was a standout on all four Stanley Cup teams and he finished his career with the Philadelphia Flyers in 1968-69. In later years, Stanley operated a golf resort and hockey camp near Fenlon, Falls, Ont. He sold the resort in 1988 and now spends the winter in Venice, Fla. He lives in Bobcaygeon, Ont. in the summertime.

LEONARD (RED) KELLY, 67, is one of the NHL's all-time great defencemen, having played 20 years with Detroit and Toronto (1947-67). He was a member of four Stanley Cup teams with the Red Wings. Acquired by the Maple Leafs in February, 1960, he was converted to a center-iceman by Punch Imlach and he won four more Stanley Cups in Toronto. Kelly was the first winner of the James Norris Memorial Trophy as the NHL's top defenceman (in 1954), and was a four-time winner of the Lady Byng Trophy. He retired following the Leafs' last Stanley Cup victory in 1967 and became the original coach of the Los Angeles Kings. He later coached Pittsburgh for two years and was coach of the Maple Leafs from 1973-77. He was inducted into the Hockey Hall of Fame in 1969. A former Member of Parliament, Kelly still lives in Toronto and is president of *C.A.M.P Systems of Canada*, an aircraft-maintenance company.

PETER STEMKOWSKI, 51, was part of Punch Imlach's blockbuster trade that sent Frank Mahovlich to Detroit in March, 1968. He went to New York in 1970 and had his most productive NHL seasons with the Rangers. Stemkowski scored 206 goals and finished his career with Los Angeles in 1977-78. He currently lives in San Jose, Calif. and does TV colour commentary for the Sharks.

... Leafs in Spring ...

Intro:

Have you ever wondered what it's like to travel with and cover the Maple Leafs during the Stanley Cup playoffs?

Dirty work, huh?

Well, someone has to do it.

As part of my job at The Fan-1430 in Toronto, Canada's first all-sports radio station, I had the opportunity to follow the Leafs during their post-season revivals of 1993 and '94. Untold years of springtime mediocrity became a distant memory as the Maple Leafs flourished under the crafty stewardship of general manager Cliff Fletcher and coach Pat Burns. They advanced to the Stanley Cup semifinals and played 39 games: equalling their post-season total for the entire decade of the 1980s.

My itinerary included three trips to Detroit, two to Chicago, and one each to Los Angeles, San Jose and Vancouver. While recovering from surgery, I missed the '93 Norris Division final against St. Louis, but I had twice been to the Gateway City when the Maple Leafs last made the playoffs: in 1990.

That was the year grandstanding owner Harold Ballard upstaged even his own team... by dying. As the Buds were jetting to Missouri for Game 5 with the Blues — facing elimination — Ballard succumbed to an array of circulatory problems at Toronto's Wellesley Hospital. As if to honour the legacy of their late general, the Maple Leafs then expired the following night and weren't heard from again at flower-blooming time for three years.

Even the pilfering of Doug Gilmour from Calgary took awhile to bare tangible results. Acquired in that record ten-player blockbuster on Jan. 2, 1992, Gilmour couldn't salvage a lost season.

Grouped with an equally inept Minnesota team in the old Norris Division, Leafs remained in contention for a playoff spot through the very late stages of 1991-92. But their waterloo occurred — for all intents and purposes — on a sunny March afternoon in San Francisco.

I was at the Cow Palace that day as the expansion San Jose Sharks beat the Leafs 4-1. It was practically comical to watch the offensively impaired Toronto club toss a season's worth of scoring opportunities at goalie Jeff Hackett, and come so close to drawing a blank.

The Maple Leaf players could have been standing on the Golden Gate Bridge with a pail of pucks, and not one of their shots would have made it into San Francisco Bay.

When Pat Burns, Nikolai Borschevsky, Felix Potvin and Dave Andreychuk were added to the mix the following season, the Maple Leaf karma did an about-face. Riding an emotional tidal-wave — and playing what it repeatedly called "in-your-face" hockey — the team came within four agonizing minutes of making it all the way to the 1993 Stanley Cup final. It took some guy named Gretzky to mess things up.

All indications pointed rather emphatically to another serious run at the championship during the early stages of the 1993-94 campaign. In hindsight, the timing couldn't have been more regrettable for an NHL-record ten-game win streak to start the season. The accolades deserving of such a feat were smothered by the Toronto Blue Jays' simultaneous march to a second World Series triumph.

Unfortunately for hockey fans in Toronto, the climactic moments of the baseball season jibed with the pinnacle of the Maple Leaf campaign. While staggering through a inordinate sequence of injuries, the Leafs were barely a .500 team after their blazing start, and were downright ordinary during the stretch run. Nobody was quite sure what to expect on the eve of the Stanley Cup tournament.

Despite hanging in there for three rounds once again, the novelty and passion of '93 never quite materialized. An opening-game victory over Vancouver in the Western Conference final proved to be Toronto's swan-song. Leafs were vanquished in five by the Canucks — falling two games short of matching their post-season fling of the previous year.

While reflecting on the two playoff rides with the Maple Leafs, a number of images come to mind. At the suggestion of my editor, they appear at the conclusion of each chapter.

"CAPTAIN VIDEO" COMES TO TOWN

The Maple Leafs of 1977-78

Red Kelly had to know his days as Maple Leaf coach were numbered when Toronto blew a grand opportunity to upset Philadelphia in the 1977 Stanley Cup quarterfinals. Leafs won the first two games of the series at the Spectrum and should have swept the Flyers back at the Gardens.

But, Rick MacLeish knocked down Borje Salming's futile clearing attempt in the dying seconds of Game 3 and beat Mike Palmateer to send the match into overtime. MacLeish then won it for Philadelphia at 2:55 of the extra period.

Even more gut-wrenching was the loss in Game 4, two nights later, as Lanny McDonald's four goals had the Leafs in front, 5-2, with less than six minutes remaining in the third period. The roof then caved in with Mel Bridgman, Tom Bladon and Bobby Clarke blitzing Palmateer in a 4:16 span — Clark tying the game with 1:33 left in regulation. Reggie Leach scored at 19:10 of overtime and Philadelphia went on to eliminate the demoralized Maple Leafs in six.

Harold Ballard pinned the loss on Kelly and dumped him, hiring the young and innovative Roger Neilson to coach the team. Having spent many successful years behind the bench of the Junior 'A' Peterborough Petes, Neilson coached the Maple Leafs' top farm team in

Dallas in 1976-77 and Ballard tracked him down in late-June, while Neilson was on a safari in Johannseburg, South Africa.

An impressive nucleus of players that included Palmateer in goal, Darryl Sittler, McDonald, Errol Thompson and Tiger Williams up front, with Salming and Ian Turnbull on defence, had the Maple Leafs within a hair of busting out in the playoffs. Twice, they upset Pittsburgh in the preliminaries and extended the powerful Flyers beyond expectations. Ballard felt the one missing ingredient was a sophisticated coaching blueprint that seemed beyond Kelly's grasp.

For that, he turned to the 43-year-old Neilson, labelling his new man a "hockey genius." As part of Neilson's sketch in the 1977-78 Maple Leaf fact book, publicity director Stan Obodiac quoted Ballard. "I'm making a drastic change in the operation of the hockey club," said the owner. "We are going into the second 50 years of the Leafs and this is the launching of a new era. I have selected a youth-oriented coach to deal with the modern-life problems of the current hockey player.

"All the reports I have seen on Neilson seem to fit this image. I hope Roger can turn the Leafs around into a Stanley Cup seeking team."

Naturally, there was no mention in that passage of general manager Jim Gregory, whose right it should have been to hire his *own* coach. In fact, Ballard's entire sermon was a lot of malarkey. Rarely, if ever, did he take a bright, contemporary approach to running the hockey club. Saving money was his usual mandate and Neilson — as a rookie coach — would not have drained his resources by any sizeable amount.

Having said that, hiring Neilson turned out to be one of Ballard's truly wise decisions... perhaps his *lone* example of genuine prudence in the years he was free of the law and fully in control of the Maple Leaf organization. Neilson brought with him a teacher's philosophy that offset the brash, unhewn deportment of the young Toronto nucleus.

His constant use of audio-visual equipment to break down games and opponents' tendencies earned him the derisive nickname "Captain Video", after the factitious TV character of the 1950s. But Neilson put form to the Maple Leaf mold and the team enjoyed the most prosperous season in Ballard's ownership tenure.

Neilson's first remarks upon accepting Ballard's appointment set the tone for his entire coaching career in the NHL.

"We must improve defensively because this team can score plenty of goals," he said, emphasizing his close-checking philosophy. "We simply cannot be a contender until we lower our goals-against average below 3.00 per game. That means giving up 46 goals fewer than last season, when the opposition scored 285.

"We can ice a five-man unit which is as good as anyone the league. But, the Montreal Canadiens are champions because their foot-soldiers, the workers who fill out their roster, are so strong. That's an area where the Leafs must improve."

To that end, Neilson and Gregory would make several alterations to the roster that began the regular season, Oct. 13, in Detroit. On that night at the Olympia, only five of the 19 Maple Leaf skaters were new to the team. Gord McRae returned as back-up to Palmateer, replacing the departed Wayne Thomas. Rookies Trevor Johansen and Randy Carlyle earned defence positions, while Jimmy Jones, a penalty-killing specialist who had played for Neilson in Peterborough, made the club at center.

The most prominent addition was veteran Ron Ellis, who re-joined the Leafs after a two-year retirement. A 276-goal scorer during his 12-year career, Ellis had toiled for the Canadian entry at the 1977 World Hockey Championships in Vienna. He fared so well in the tournament that he decided to come back and play in the NHL.

"I think I played some of the best hockey in Austria that I have in my entire career," he said. "It was a pleasant surprise for me."

The season began on a bit of a downer, as the Maple Leafs blew a two-goal lead against Detroit in the third period. Pat Boutette scored his second goal of the night to give the Leafs a 3-1 advantage early in the final frame. But Rick Bowness and Dan Maloney spoiled the night — Maloney tying the match with only 1:36 left on the clock.

The Maple Leafs walked into a lion's den that night, as the Red Wings, who had been pushovers for so many years, adopted the slogan: "Aggressive Hockey Is Back In Town." The new general manager was former Detroit winger Ted Lindsay — one of the most callous and unrelenting players during his wondrous career in the 1940s and '50s. The new coach was Bobby Kromm, who had broken his teeth with the explosive WHA teams in Winnipeg that featured Bobby Hull, Ulf Nilsson and Anders Hedberg. Together, they promised to instill some flash and dash to a stale Red Wing franchise that had missed the playoffs seven years in a row.

With the fierce promotional campaign, more than 12,000 fans showed up at the Olympia expecting some form of bloodshed. But a minor high-sticking incident between Boutette and Detroit veteran Terry Harper in the second period was the only emotional flare-up.

Two nights later, on a Saturday, the Maple Leafs began their 40-game home schedule and were badly outclassed by Buffalo. A dazzling goal by Gilbert Perreault in the second period broke a 1-1 tie and sent the Sabres on to a lop-sided 5-2 victory. With George Ferguson serving a penalty for Toronto, Perreault put a nifty fake on Borje Salming at the Maple Leaf blueline and broke in alone on Palmateer. He then deked the Leaf goalie and scored on his backhand.

Darryl Sittler tied it up for Toronto midway through the period, but Richard Martin's goal, 14 seconds later, proved to be the winner. Don Luce and Craig Ramsay added some insurance in the third period. Leafs out-shot the Sabres 41-38, forcing Don Edwards to play well in the Buffalo net. But the shot total did not impress Neilson.

"Buffalo just checked better than we did, no matter how the shots might indicate we played," he said. "We didn't play defensively and we didn't take the man very well, either."

Neilson's first NHL coaching victory occurred the following Wednesday, at the Gardens, as the Maple Leafs edged the pesky Colorado Rockies 5-4. Ian Turnbull's powerplay goal at 15:38 of the third period proved to be the difference in a game that saw Colorado battle back to tie the score on four separate occasions. Four of Toronto's five goals were counted with the man advantage.

The final blow came as a result of a questionable holding call on Colorado's rookie defenceman Barry Beck. Referee Andy Van Hellemond sent Beck off with 4:28 left in the game, even though Salming appeared to enhance the foul with an exaggerated pratfall.

"If Salming had made that dive in the Olympics, he would have received a few scores in the nines," chaffed Rockies' coach Pat Kelly. "Beck barely touched him, but Salming turned it into a penalty." To which the slick Swede responded: "What is he talking about? If that guy hadn't grabbed me and pulled me down, I would have been around him."

Neilson had worked diligently on the powerplay during practice sessions that week. But, his top checking forward — Jack Valiquette — did most of the offensive damage with a goal and two assists.

"That's the way it is in this game... things don't go quite the way you plan them," said Neilson. "The Valiquette line has been our best unit in the three games so far. I'm happy to get my first win and I wasn't too concerned about how we did it. Colorado worked well and they kept coming back. But we kept bouncing back as well."

The victory over the Rockies began the Leafs' first hot streak of the year and it preceded one of the most satisfying weekends in many a season for Toronto hockey fans. A home-and-home sweep of Philadelphia proved that the 1977-78 Maple Leafs were going to be just a little bit different. And it made a loud statement to many of the veteran Flyers, who had come out on top in two playoff battles against Toronto.

Sittler's hattrick paved the way to a 6-1 Maple Leaf trouncing on Saturday night at the Gardens. The Flyers had romped to a 4-0-0 early season record, outscoring their opposition 31-3, and were coming off an 11-0 destruction of Pittsburgh just two nights earlier at the Spectrum. But the Leafs jumped out to a 2-0 first-period lead, made it 4-0 after two, and actually bettered the Flyers in the physical department.

Neilson set the tone and had the crowd buzzing when he started a mucking forward unit of Tiger Williams, Kurt Walker and Bob Neely.

"We know Philadelphia's whole game-plan is dominating the corners and we wanted to take that away from them," said the very happy coach. "The guys truly felt they could beat Philadelphia and that surprised me a bit. I told them about the 31 goals Philly had scored, but it didn't seem to bother them a bit."

The Flyers stepped up the physical tempo on home ice the following night but again were no match for the Leafs in a 6-3 Toronto victory. A wild first period that saw fights break out every few minutes was completely dominated by the Maple Leafs, who built a 4-1 lead. In so doing, they reversed the upsetting trend of so many prior visits to the Spectrum, when the Flyers would flex their collective muscle and send the passive Torontonians scurrying for cover.

As per usual, Tiger Williams was front-and-center, picking up fighting majors with Paul Holmgren and Andre Dupont. Kurt Walker and Mel Bridgman fought late in the period. Two more battles broke out in the third: Sittler taking on Dupont, and Williams battling Bridgman.
"This Leaf team is different," said Philadelphia captain Bobby Clarke after the game. "That roster has been falling into place slowly over the past couple of seasons. They have some of the best players in the game — Sittler, McDonald, Salming, Turnbull — and the guys they have added are strong, grinder-type workers.

"Now they have a good coach to improve the team technically and give it a system. They're tough physically and they're playing with confidence. When a good team gets rolling and has momentum, it can be very tough to stop.

"And I have a feeling that a lot of NHL teams are going to have a problem with the Leafs this season."

The Leafs passed another early season test, but barely, when they played the Stanley Cup-champion Canadiens to a 2-2 tie at the Gardens, Oct. 26. Although Larry Robinson and Steve Shutt gave Montreal a 2-0 first-period lead, the Habs would have been home and cooled out had it not been for the brilliance of Palmateer. Montreal outshot the Maple Leafs 19-5, and held a 30-15 edge after 40 minutes.

An exciting late rally earned Toronto the tie. Jimmy Jones scored his first NHL goal at 12:38 of the third period, taking a pass from Don Ashby and beating Ken Dryden with a quick shot to the glove side. And Ian Turnbull knotted the score with only 1:24 left on the clock when his point drive bounced into the Montreal net off Robinson.

"I saw it was going low so I lifted my stick to avoid deflecting it," explained the Habs' defenceman. "But it hit my stick and changed direction. It was just like what would happen in a barn-yard using old-style pucks. But then, the ice surface here was a bit like a barnyard."

Turnbull's goal sparked an avalanche of Maple Leafs, who poured over the boards to mob the night's hero. In 1977-78, there had yet to be a rule implementation that prevented such delays.

"I was kind of worried after the first," Palmateer said while assessing his strong performance. "I had a good period but I gave up two goals. I said to myself, three times two is six — I was in for a six-goal game. But we came out stronger in the second period. We just never gave up, kept plugging away, and eventually it paid off.

"We always seem to get up for Montreal. I've been with the team for five games against Montreal and we've lost just one. It's hard to explain. As good as they are, they bring out the best in us."

It was the third game in four nights for the Canadiens, which may have contributed to their late slide. "Actually, I'm satisfied with the tie," said Montreal coach Scotty Bowman. "We're coming off five road games in 10 days and we were dragging in the third period. Also, with Guy Lapointe out, I had to use Robinson and (Serge) Savard for extra penalty killing duty and they got tired."

The Leafs extended their winning streak to four games with a 7-4 victory over Detroit, but Neilson was unhappy with the club's defensive work. As a result, three days later, he put his first real stamp on the team. On Nov. 1, Jim Gregory traded veteran Inge Hammarstrom to the St. Louis Blues for right-winger Jerry Butler. It was strictly an exchange of scoring potential for checking proficiency, as Butler possessed few of Hammarstrom's polished skills. But it tailored to the Neilson system of defence first, and Gregory was simply providing his coach with the style of player he required.

"We had to give up a guy who had played well for us and who was well-respected," said Gregory, admitting it was a difficult move. "Inge was always a gentleman and a heck of a favourite with the fans."

Not an aggressive player, Hammarstrom had been hurt three years earlier by the inane ranting of Ballard, who uttered his now-famous line: "If that Swede went into the corner with six eggs, he wouldn't break any of them." But, he rose above the owner's criticism to score 85 goals in a Toronto uniform.

Hammarstrom and fellow-Swede Salming had joined the Maple Leafs four years earlier after being scouted by Gerry McNamara. "I don't feel too great, but it could be worse," said Hammarstrom. "It's kind of hard to believe. I've never been in this situation before. I made so many friends in this city and I really enjoyed the Toronto organization. It's difficult... very difficult."

Both players debuted for their new teams the following night. In Richfield, Ohio, Hammarstrom scored two goals, helping St. Louis to a 4-4 tie with the Cleveland Barons. Hockey writer Rick Fraser, then of the Toronto *Sun*, covered the game and found out that Hammarstrom had considered quitting hockey after Gregory informed him of the trade.

"Jim said there was a team really interested in having me," Inge told Fraser. "He said it was St. Louis and he wanted to make the trade. I was shocked. I went back to my apartment and thought about it for a few hours. I probably wasn't thinking straight, but I honestly thought about leaving pro hockey.

"But then I figured if the Leafs didn't want me, it was nice to know that another team in the NHL did. So I got back to Jim on Tuesday morning and told him I was prepared to go."

St. Louis coach Leo Boivin used Hammarstrom on a forward unit with Bob MacMillan and Claude Larose. The former Leaf winger took 16 shifts and later said, "I haven't had that much ice time since I played with Darryl Sittler and Lanny McDonald last year. I was very nervous at the beginning but after a couple of shifts, I got my act together."

On that same Wednesday evening, Butler joined the Maple Leafs in Vancouver for the start of a six-game road trip — the first three out west. "I hope I'll fit in," said the 26-year-old native of Sarnia. "I understand Inge was popular but if I go out and do my job, I think the people of Toronto are good enough fans to appreciate it."

Butler admitted the trade from St. Louis came as no big surprise. "I knew something was up when the Blues picked up Bill Fairbairn (from Minnesota) on waivers last week," he said. "He plays the same style as I do. I told my wife to expect something, and I was right."

Butler played a typically aggressive game in his Toronto debut as the Maple Leafs began their road trip with an easy 5-1 victory over the Canucks. It raised the club's record to 5-1-2 after eight games — the best

Leaf start to a season in 27 years. Once again, the Leafs came out blazing, as Errol Thompson, Pat Boutette and Lanny McDonald beat goalie Cesare Maniago in the first 5:20 of play. Borje Salming made it 4-0 at the 10:21 mark of the opening period.

Don Ashby scored in the second while Ron Sedlbauer of the Canucks ruined Gord McRae's shutout bid with 6:57 left in the game.

McRae made his first start of the season, as Palmateer battled an ear infection and cold. "The boys played well," he said. "It's nice to know they're willing to come up with a big game for me. The point is we blitzed them early. Cesare didn't have a chance on the goals."

Maple Leaf road games were carried on TV during the regular season that year for the first time. Hamilton independent CHCH-TV (Channel 11) assumed the midweek package from Toronto's CFTO (Channel 9) and decided to telecast every Wednesday night game the Leafs played. Viewers had to stay up late, as the match from Vancouver began at 11 p.m. And many of them were disappointed when CHCH lost the TV picture at the end of the first period. A C.N. Communications microwave station near Milton, Ont. malfunctioned, causing the loss of signal. But viewers were still able to hear the play-by-play call of announcer Bill Hewitt.

The six-game Leaf unbeaten streak came to an end two nights later in Los Angeles — the Kings prevailing 4-2. But Toronto made it close, as Sittler and Turnbull scored third-period goals to cut into L.A.'s 3-0 lead. Mike Palmateer was pulled for an extra attacker with 59 seconds left on the clock and the Leafs buzzed around the Kings' net. But, Mike Murphy clinched the win with an empty net goal at the 19:45 mark. Lanny McDonald pulled a rib-muscle early in the first period and had to sit out the remainder of the game.

Toronto completed its western swing with a 5-2 triumph in Denver over the Colorado Rockies — Sittler scoring twice — then moved on to Atlanta to continue the road trip.

Veteran newspaper columnist Trent Frayne reminded Maple Leaf fans of their early season fortune in the Toronto *Sun*:

> "The Leafs are off to their briskest start in 27 years, and if you want to know what that means, it means the year Hap Day was elevated from coach to general manager and Gentleman Joe Primeau became coach.
>
> "...There've been three very rugged additions to the line-up (this season) — the mysterious Jimmy Jones (anybody named Jimmy Jones is mysterious)... Trevor Johansen, a solid kid built like Tim Horton on

defence, and Jerry Butler, a guy who when he goes into the corner with six eggs in his pocket will break six eggs.

"Johansen, a native of Thunder Bay and a 20-year-old grad of the Junior Marlies, is young enough to require a sitter. Indeed, Randy Carlyle, who is all of 21 himself, referees to him as 'the kid.'

"Anyway, they're all part of the new marauding Leafs, quickest out of the gate in 27 years. They may even be for real."

Ron Ellis scored for the first time since returning to the Maple Leafs, as Toronto blanked Atlanta 4-0 at the Omni. He then added a pair in a 3-1 victory at Washington two nights later. "The legs are feeling fine and I'm starting to feel comfortable out there," he said. "Mind you, playing with (Tiger) Williams and Darryl Sittler doesn't hurt."

By the end of November, the Maple Leafs had a 12-5-3 record and stood sixth overall in the NHL standings (a spot in which they'd remain for most of the season). On Dec. 5, defenceman Jim McKenny's career in Toronto effectively came to an end as Roger Neilson demoted him to the club's Central League farm team in Dallas, along with Don Ashby. Young forwards Bruce Boudreau and John Anderson were promoted.

The 31-year-old McKenny possessed none of the defensive acumen Neilson was preaching. "I won't be back," he declared.

Another one of Harold Ballard's infamous stunts took place on the night of Dec. 7, while the Maple Leafs were beating Minnesota 6-3 at the Gardens. In a World Hockey Association game at Birmingham, Gordie Howe of the New England Whalers scored the 1,000th goal of his pro hockey career, beating goaltender John Garrett of the Bulls. Howe had netted 786 goals with the Detroit Red Wings between 1946 and 1971 and scored the remaining 214 in four-plus WHA seasons. Ballard, however, showed his contempt for the WHA by refusing to acknowledge Howe's achievement on the electronic message-board at the Gardens.

"Why should I show it... a blind man can score in that league," chided the Leaf owner. "A thousand goals in *this* league would mean something, but not there. It's like playing street hockey. Last year, they had playoff scores like 11-2 and 10-1. Can you imagine that?"

Of course, Ballard hated the WHA only because he had so blatantly misjudged its resolve five years earlier. Figuring the league owners were bluffing with their extensions of wealth, Ballard refused to match salary demands and wound up losing the core of his young hockey club.

The Leafs made another short western trip the second week of

December and came home with a pair of victories. Sittler's goal with 2:22 remaining gave Toronto a 3-2 victory at Colorado, before a Friday night crowd of 15,376 at the McNichols Arena — largest in the Rockies' two-year history. Mike Palmateer stopped 27 shots the following night in Los Angeles, and the Maple Leafs beat the Kings 4-0. Veteran Kings' goalie Rogie Vachon was so impressed with Palmateer, he delivered one of his patented cigars to the Leaf dressing room after the game.

One of the season's best games occurred the following Wednesday at the Gardens, as the Maple Leafs edged the New York Islanders 3-2. Borje Salming put on an absolute clinic that night, and scored a breath-taking goal at 3:50 of the third period to give Toronto the victory. Speeding towards the net from an angle, Salming took Bruce Boudreau's pass and flicked a rising shot over the shoulder of Chico Resch. He then went flying over top the Islander goalie.

Sittler also had a great game, setting up first-period goals by McDonald and Williams, and he drew praise from one of his most esteemed counterparts in the NHL — Islander sparkplug Bryan Trottier.

"If Sittler isn't the No. 1 center in the league, then he's in the top two," Trottier said. "I figured we had as many chances to score as their line, but they just popped in one more than we did."

Back-to-back romps against Minnesota and Chicago lifted Toronto's record to 13 games over .500. Salming set up five goals in an 8-5 whipping of the North Stars at Minnesota. Boudreau had a hattrick for the Leafs. Sittler then popped two goals and three assists the next night at the Gardens in a 7-1 Maple Leaf bombing of the Blackhawks. A sign at one end of the Gardens accurately read: **THE NIGHT CHICAGO DIED.**

"The guys are up and ready now," said Roger Neilson, commenting on the superb play of his team. "We're still trying for first place in our division and while it's tough the way Boston and Buffalo are winning, I think it's making us play better."

After games of Dec. 18, the Adams Division race appeared like so:

	GP	W	L	T	PTS
BUFFALO	31	20	7	4	44
BOSTON	31	19	7	5	43
TORONTO	28	19	6	3	41

Inge Hammarstrom made his return to the Gardens with St. Louis on Dec. 19. The Leafs came back from a 3-0 second-period deficit to tie the Blues 4-4 and Salming flattened his good friend with a clean, hard bodycheck in the neutral zone. A number of signs dotted the building — welcoming back the popular ex-Leaf.

"All my friends called," said Hammarstrom. "You know, even though it's not my home, it feels like I'm coming home. It's the same feeling Borje and I had when we played for Sweden against Team Canada in the Canada Cup (at the Gardens) last year."

Salming got kicked out of a game against Montreal (Dec. 21) and the Canadiens beat the Leafs 3-2 with a last-minute goal. Defenceman Larry Robinson scored at 19:12 of the third period. Goals by Boudreau (at 11:26) and Sittler (at 13:35) had brought the Leafs back from a 2-0 deficit and sent a surge of electricity through the Gardens' crowd. But with 4:40 left on the clock, Salming was tripped by Doug Risebrough of the Canadiens, and referee Bob Myers declined to call what appeared to be a certain penalty.

Salming got up, made an obscene gesture at Myers, and the referee handed him a 10-minute misconduct. The Toronto fans pelted the ice with debris. Minus their kingpin defenceman, the Maple Leafs were ripe for Montreal's last-minute rally.

"What's the use... they won't let me play the game," muttered an exasperated Salming in the Leaf dressing room.

Neilson felt there should have been a penalty call on the play, but would not condone Salming's tantrum. "We looked at the video and it certainly looked like a trip," said the Leaf coach. "However, Borje has to learn to control his feelings or he's going to cost us games. The last four minutes of a game against Montreal is when we need him on the ice and he may have cost us this one tonight."

Just five days later, the Leafs lost another heartbreaker at the Gardens: 5-4 to Pittsburgh. A Boxing Day crowd saw Toronto blow a 3-0 first-period lead, but then cheered wildly as Lanny McDonald appeared to give Leafs a tie by scoring on Denis Heron at 19:06 of the third period. However, Blair Chapman of the Penguins beat Palmateer on a breakaway 22 seconds later and Pittsburgh won the game.

Maple Leaf fans were put through a humiliating experience early in the New Year, during an exhibition game against the touring Kladno team of Czechoslovakia. Practically the entire Leaf club came down with sudden and mysterious ailments the morning of the game and Palmateer, McDonald, Salming and Turnbull sat out. The crowd, which paid regular prices as part of the season-ticket package, lustily booed the pre-game announcement of the no-shows. Kladno won, 8-5.

"How's Gord McRae supposed to feel after getting a reception like that?" asked Leaf scout (and former goalie) Johnny Bower. The Gardens' crowd had chanted "We want Mike!" when McRae's name was announced.

Of course, the Leafs used the game to rest their better players and the con-job took on disgraceful proportions two nights later, when all four skaters miraculously recovered for a game against the Colorado Rockies. Tiger Williams added to the miserable display by pitch-forking Frantisek Kaberle of Kladno late in the third period, and was handed a well-deserved spearing major by referee Wally Harris.

The entire debacle smelled suspiciously like a Harold Ballard production and Trent Frayne made some very good (albeit futile) points in a Toronto *Sun* column entitled: **LEAF FANS ENDURE ANOTHER FAILURE.**

"...After Monday's exhibition game, during which fans repeatedly showed their displeasure, the majority stockholder of the team and the rink, Harold Ballard, spelled out the management's philosophy. 'We're not going to bust our butts trying to kick theirs,' he said. 'These games are utterly stupid, a very foolish way to do business.'

"So why did he book one of the games into his rink? It would be by no means a precedent if he had refused. Two years ago, when two Soviet clubs toured NHL cities, Ballard kept them out of his rink.

"...As the principal owner of the only rink in town, doesn't he have an obligation to let the fans make a choice? And in this case, having booked the Czechoslovaks, doesn't he have an obligation to give the fans the best possible production?

"...Has Ballard no real pride in the hockey club?"

Sadly, the answer to the last question was painfully obvious.

A bizarre and scary incident *off* the ice occurred after a 2-1 loss in Detroit, Jan. 5. Shots rang out in the parking lot of the Olympia as the Maple Leafs were boarding their team-bus. A man was killed by the hail of bullets and Detroit police returned the fire at a speeding car before abandoning their chase.

"A car came flying through with somebody shooting," said Lanny McDonald. "The car hit a pick-up truck and then pulled out of the lot with the cops shooting. There must have been 15 shots. I guess in Detroit, they shoot first and ask questions later."

Recalled Ballard: "There was a murder in this same parking lot last year. In fact, the Wings' team doctor was attacked in this lot and left in a pool of blood."

The Maple Leafs' season-long consistency waned during the month of January. The club went 7-9-7 in a 24-game span between Dec. 19 and Feb. 5 to effectively bow out of the race for top spot in its division. A 3-3 tie in Boston, Feb. 5, left the first-place Bruins 11 points ahead of Toronto, and second-place Buffalo was nine points up.

Typical of the Leaf misfortune was a game against Buffalo at the Gardens, Feb. 1. With Toronto ahead 2-1 early in the second period, Sittler poked a loose puck out of a scramble and into the Sabres' net. But referee Bryan Lewis waved off the goal, claiming he had blown the play dead. Maple Leafs argued it was a quick whistle and it ultimately came back to haunt them, as Craig Ramsay scored the game-tying goal at 19:50 of the third period.

"It was bad and he wasn't in a position to call it properly," said Sittler about the disallowed goal. "He probably called it right from where he was standing...which is too bad. He was out near the blueline, wasn't he?"

There was more heartache in Boston four nights later during a game the Leafs absolutely had to win to stay within radar distance of the Bruins. Toronto was leading 3-2 with 24 seconds left on the clock when referee Bruce Hood penalized Tiger Williams for tripping Gregg Sheppard in the Maple Leaf zone. Sheppard then rammed the tying goal past Mike Palmateer on the powerplay with only two seconds remaining.

"That's probably the only time Hood will call a penalty in the last minute this season, but the way our luck has been going lately, it figured that we'd get it," lamented Neilson. "There had been several guys in a scramble for the puck along the boards. Tiger just swiped his stick out and knocked somebody down. He was on his knees."

Bruins' coach Don Cherry took delight in gloating over the turn of events. "How sweet is it, this has rounded out a perfect day," he said. "We deserved the tie. In fact, we deserved more. It seemed like we had a powerplay out there for 60 minutes the way we controlled things. This puts us 11 points ahead of the Leafs. It will take quite an effort on their part to cut that margin."

In his assessment of the NHL's top teams heading into the stretch run of the season, Toronto *Star* hockey writer Frank Orr penned a column entitled: **LEAFS STILL SHORT OF JOINING NHL'S BIG FIVE**. He wrote:

> "New coach Roger Neilson has inspired an overall improvement in the team, but a change in emphasis from offence to defence is not

accomplished overnight. Leafs sometimes appear a trifle confused about which approach to take. They can ice a starting line-up which matches any in the league but they still lack size and belligerence on the wings. Lately, there's been too large a gap between the number of scoring chances and the number of goals. Leafs lack snipers."

The club finally did some late-game damage of its own against St. Louis, at the Gardens, Feb. 8. Pat Boutette and Errol Thompson scored third-period goals to give Toronto a 5-4 victory over the Blues. The winning marker came with just 2:43 left on the clock: Thompson beating Phil Myre with a backhand shot on a clear breakaway. The win over St. Louis came as part of a seven-game unbeaten streak that had the Leafs again thinking about a higher standing in the Adams Division.

Lanny McDonald ripped a pair of shots past Don Edwards in Buffalo on a Monday-night game televised nationally in the U.S. Leafs beat the Sabres 4-2 and moved to within seven points of both Boston and Buffalo. A home-ice encounter against the Bruins was next on the agenda.

"The Bruins are a different team than the one we beat tonight," said Neilson after the game. "They're not a *better* team than Buffalo, but they're tougher. We need to be ready to be tough along the boards in order to catch them."

But the Maple Leafs' inability to handle Boston prevented them from joining the NHL's high-rent district that season. The Bruins won all the physical battles in a 4-2 victory over Toronto, Feb. 15. It was a typical slow-paced game between the two grinding clubs but as usual, Boston's grinding was a little more effective. Third-period goals by Al Simms and Peter McNab proved to be the difference.

"Nothing fancy, just play for the win," observed Bruin coach Cherry. "Our wingers — I call them the SS Squad — have been the difference all year. If we hold an advantage over other teams, it's our size on the wings. I would like to see any team in any sport give more than my guys do on a nightly basis."

Neilson was dejected after the game. "The Bruins just played a little better than we did tonight," he said. "I thought we had them going in the second period, but they just kept coming at us. We knew we had to outhit them, but they were stronger along the boards.

"It will be very difficult for us to catch them now. However, the Bruins haven't had a flat spot all season, so you never know."

Maple Leaf vice-president King Clancy turned 75 on Feb. 25 and the

Leafs were in town for a game against Washington. Ballard feted his pal with a luxurious pre-game ceremony that saw Clancy blow out candles on a 300-pound cake rolled to center-ice. The lights in the building were all extinguished, except for those shining on Clancy and the cake. Ian Turnbull scored the only goal the Leafs would need at 1:06 of the first period in a 4-0 whitewashing of the Capitals.

Ballard was front-and-center again the following night in Chicago. A 5-3 victory for the Leafs was overshadowed by one of the owner's all-time wacko stunts. The previous summer, NHL governors had instituted a bylaw stating that all players were to have their surnames sewn to the back of their sweaters for identification purposes. Everyone complied except Ballard, who claimed such a move would hinder program sales at the Gardens.

League president John Zeigler began to threaten Ballard with fines of up to $5,000 per game if he didn't fall in line. A compromise was struck whereby the Maple Leafs would only have to wear the names on the back of their road sweaters. So, for the Chicago game, Ballard followed through. Only he did it in typical Harold fashion.

He had trainer Guy Kinnear sew blue lettering on the blue jerseys, rendering the players' names undecipherable. Close-up photographs of the sweater-backs showed the three-inch blue letters but no one would have been able to notice them from any distance.

"I'll never make it as a colour-coordinator, will I," Ballard chortled after the game. "I've complied with the NHL bylaw. The names are stitched on, three inches high. It's a pity you can't see them.

"Zeigler is just going to have to keep his little nose out of my business. This move was done to make a compete mockery of the ruling."

Of course once Ballard got the attention he was seeking, the jersey lettering was never again an issue. Regulation white letters were sewn to the Maple Leaf uniforms for their road game against the New York Rangers one week later. And Leaf names appeared on the back of the home sweaters the following season.

March rolled in like a lion, as Toronto won a big game at the Gardens against Philadelphia. Sittler's slapshot from just inside the blueline at 10:40 of the third period dipped under the glove of rookie goalie Rick St. Croix and gave Leafs a 3-2 victory. McDonald had tied the game earlier in the period. With the winner, Sittler extended his torrid streak to 14 goals and 12 assists in his past 12 games.

The Ballard circus was at it again. Having purchased the Hamilton

Tiger-Cats of the Canadian Football League several days earlier, he had two Ti-Cat logos painted in the large center-ice circle — flanking the Maple Leaf symbol. He also instructed his Zamboni driver and ice staff to wear Tiger-Cat uniforms for the Maple Leafs' next home game, three nights later, against Vancouver.

And the Leafs won that match, 4-3, thanks in part to a goal and an assist from rookie left-winger Ron Wilson, who had been called up from Dallas the previous day. Wilson played on the big line with Sittler and McDonald. "Wow! I just can't believe it," he exclaimed afterwards. "All I wanted was to get on for a couple of shifts. A goal and an assist... it's unbelievable!"

That same Ron Wilson would one day become the first head coach of an expansion team called the Anaheim Mighty Ducks.

Ron Ellis also had a memorable night against Vancouver, scoring his 300th career goal in the second period. It was classic Ellis, as he beat Vancouver goalie Kurt Ridley with a slapshot from the right-wing circle. "Possibly a third of my goals have been scored from that area," he noted. "I remember the first one was against Boston with Ed Johnston in goal. Frank Mahovlich sent the pass to me and I scored from there."

On Mar. 7, the Maple Leafs and Tiger Williams agreed on a new multi-year contract, worth more than $100,000 per season. The 24-year-old left-winger was in the fourth (and option) year of his original pact with the team. "He's invaluable to this club," said Neilson. "We couldn't get along without him."

Darryl Sittler continued towards the best season of his career, breaking two of his own Maple Leaf team records in a 7-1 romp at Pittsburgh, Mar. 12. His two goals and three assists gave him 103 points on the season — three more than the total he achieved in 1975-76. And he scored his 42nd goal to establish a new single-season mark for Maple Leaf centermen (he had 41 in '75-76). But the Leaf captain insisted he wasn't concentrating on establishing new standards.

"If you go out and consciously play for records, you'll get into trouble," he said. "All I do is play as hard as I can to help the team finish as high in the standings as possible. That's the only approach I can take; the only one I know much about.

"I've seen guys going for records and changing their games to try and get them, instead of playing relaxed hockey in their usual style. It causes their game to fall apart. I don't want that to happen."

The Maple Leafs had little time to savour their lop-side victory over Pittsburgh. The following day — just prior to the trade deadline —

general manager Gregory made a blockbuster deal with Detroit. In a move aimed at toughening up the forward ranks, Gregory acquired veteran Dan Maloney from the Red Wings for winger Errol Thompson. He also gave Detroit two first-round draft choices and a second-rounder. Both he and Neilson had long coveted Maloney, but the outlay seemed exorbitant.

"LEAFS TRADE THEIR FUTURE FOR MUSCLE", said the sports headline in the Toronto *Star*. **"FOR DETROIT, IT'S GRAND LAR-CENY"**, screamed the *Sun*. But, Gregory wasn't concerned.

"We've made a nice trade by landing someone we've wanted for a long time," he said. "We tried to get Maloney back when John McLellan was coaching our team (in the early '70s). That's how much we think of Maloney. Sure, we didn't like to give up the first and second-round draft choices, but those picks have to make the team. This guy can step right in and play a very important role for us."

Maloney's size and abrasiveness were his endearing qualities and Neilson had little use for the offensive-minded Thompson, a player too one-dimensional for the coach. Thompson had scored 43 goals on a line with Sittler and McDonald in 1975-76, but he suffered a broken wrist early in the next season and never regained his touch around the net. Still, the deal left Sittler with some mixed emotions.

"I'm sorry to see Errol go because I enjoyed playing with him through the years," said the captain. "I hope he does well in Detroit. But I think Maloney has some of the ingredients we've been missing and he should help." Sittler and Maloney were former Junior teammates with London of the OHA.

Thompson realized that he and Neilson were simply not a match. "I tried to play his style and I thought I was doing a good job at it," said the ex-Leaf. "My best game has always been skating and scoring, but I worked hard at playing the way Roger wanted. He just didn't seem to appreciate it."

But Neilson preferred to look ahead. "A guy like Danny puts us a little closer to a Stanley Cup," he said. "Along with Tiger Williams and Pat Boutette, left-wing is now probably our toughest position physically. With Lanny McDonald, Ron Ellis and Jerry Butler on the right side, we have good experience on the wings in all six positions.

"Danny's a great team man... everyone has said that about him since he was a Junior. He's a strong two-way player who is respected by all the other players in the NHL. And, he's experienced."

Reaction to the trade was mixed, but there was a definite feeling that

Gregory had compromised the club's future. Columnist George Gross pulled no punches in the *Sun*.

> "Two years ago, Ontario attorney general Roy McMurtry's office initiated action against Detroit Red Wings' captain Dan Maloney for decking Maple Leafs' Brian Glennie in a game at the Gardens.
>
> "This time, McMurtry should issue a warrant for the arrest of Detroit general manager Ted Lindsay — for grand larceny.
>
> "What else can you call the `deal' in which he sent Maloney to the Leafs in exchange for — now get this — Errol Thompson and TWO first-round draft choices. I'm surprised Leafs didn't throw in the key to the Carlton Street cashbox as part of this `let's save the Detroit Red Wings arrangement.'"

Toronto *Star* columnist Jim Proudfoot was a bit more pragmatic.

> "Maloney's a splendid acquisition, there's no doubt about that. There was no place in Leafs' new system for the artistry of Thompson. He tried to adapt, but couldn't. He was out of step and, like Inge Hammarstrom, was disposable goods.
>
> "But it'll be years before the Leafs can properly calculate what Maloney cost, whether it was too much. If, by then, they've taken a Cup title and Maloney has helped, they won't care. But if they haven't, and he hasn't, they may decide that March 13, 1978 was unlucky. Even if it wasn't a Friday."

Maloney made his debut in a Maple Leaf uniform two nights later in Washington and set up McDonald for a third-period goal in a 5-2 Toronto victory over the Capitals. He played his usual aggressive game, but said the entire experience was a bit overwhelming.

"I had a pretty good case of butterflies," he admitted. "But, I suppose it's a natural reaction in your first game with a new team. You want to play well and make a good impression. My linemates, Darryl and Lanny, helped a great deal by talking to me a lot. The Leafs play a different system than we used in Detroit. Playing with two players of their calibre is a great break for anybody."

The Maple Leafs lapsed into their worst slump of the season during March, and finished the regular campaign with a 2-10-0 record in their final 12 games — losing their last four. Included (naturally) was two more losses to Boston, which wound up first in the Adams Division with 106 points: two ahead of Buffalo and a distant 25 more than the Leafs.

In Toronto's final regular-season home game, Apr. 8, the Bruins had some fun at the expense of Ballard. During the national anthem, two Boston equipment boys unveiled a 10-foot Toronto Argonauts banner and draped it over the boards in front of the Boston bench. It was, of course, a dig at Ballard for his purchase of the Hamilton Tiger-Cats.

Leafs finished with a 41-29-10 record for 92 points, the second-highest total in franchise history. The 1950-51 Stanley Cup champions — considered by many to be the best Maple Leaf team ever — enjoyed a 95-point season. Defensively, the club accomplished Neilson's aim by reducing its goals-against allowance by 48 from the previous year. The Leafs also *scored* 30 less goals.

Placing sixth in the overall standings created a preliminary round playoff match-up with the 10th-place Los Angeles Kings: a best-of-three rematch from 1975. The Kings had won three out of five regular-season meetings, including a 5-1 victory at the Gardens, Mar. 8, in arguably Toronto's worst home-ice performance of the entire campaign. But, the Leafs played a better physical brand of hockey than the Kings and were hoping to use it to their advantage.

"We have to play aggressively and use the body on them," pointed out Neilson. "We want to play as tough as we possibly can."

The series turned out to be a laugher.

In the opener at the Gardens, George Ferguson scored three goals as the Maple Leafs clobbered Los Angeles 7-3. Toronto had a 6-0 lead before the Kings scored their first goal, at 9:41 of the third period. Defensive center Jimmy Jones did a masterful job of blanketing L.A. star Marcel Dionne and Neilson counted a total of 45 Maple Leaf hits during the game. Just as he had prescribed.

Toronto eliminated Los Angeles two nights later at The Forum, blanking the Kings 4-0 for a two-game sweep. Ron Ellis scored the only goal Toronto would need at the 1:12 mark of the first period. McDonald and Jones made it 3-0 before the period was over and Sittler added another with 6:45 left in the game. Again, the Leafs smothered the Kings, limiting L.A. to only 21 shots at Mike Palmateer. In the dying moments, many of the 12,889 fans sang *"Goodbye Stewart"* to Kings' coach and former Leaf Stanley Cup warrior Ron Stewart.

"We played solid tonight, a very strong game," said Ellis. "The team was really high for this series. We were never concerned about what happened at the end of the season. We realized we had the people to get it done once the playoffs began."

The victory over Los Angeles set up a best-of-seven quarterfinal meeting with the New York Islanders, who had finished third in the NHL overall standings with 111 points. Gearing up for their championship reign of four years (1980 - 1983), the Islanders had assembled a cast of front-line players that included Bryan Trottier (second in scoring with 123 points), rookie Mike Bossy (second in the NHL with 53 goals), superstar defenceman Denis Potvin, menacing winger Clark Gillies, and clutch goaltenders Chico Resch and Billy Smith. Understandably, they were prohibitive favourites to beat the Maple Leafs.

But, Roger Neilson was defiant.

"We've worked hard in conditioning all year and we're in good shape," he said. "The longer the series goes, the more confidence our guys will gain. If we play as well against the Islanders as we did against Los Angeles, we'll win."

Added defenceman Brian Glennie: "There's no way the Islanders can outhit or out-muscle us and the goaltending is equal. So, if we take the man and concentrate on good positional play we can win. I think it will be a low-scoring and physical series."

The quarterfinal round opened at the Nassau Coliseum on Mon. Apr. 17 and the Islanders breezed to a 4-1 victory. New York coach Al Arbour threw a curve at the Leafs by removing Mike Bossy from the club's top scoring unit with Trottier and Gillies. He inserted Bob Nystrom on the right side and placed Bossy with Mike Kaszycki and Bob Bourne. Bossy and Kaszycki each had a goal and an assist, while Nystrom also scored.

"It was nothing very complicated," Arbour said. "A hockey team has to have players who are inter-changeable... who can play effectively in all sorts of combinations. Leafs were using their big line (Sittler, McDonald and Maloney) against the Trottier line and I wanted to shake things up a little."

It served to throw the Leafs off their game in the first period, and the Islanders had a 3-0 lead by the 16:39 mark. Sittler scored the only Toronto goal at 12:48 of the second, but Wayne Merrick restored New York's three-goal margin 1:18 later.

Neilson confessed to being surprised that Bossy was moved from the Islanders' top line. "We thought they couldn't break it up and if they did, it would be to our advantage," he said. "I'm sure if they keep it that way, it *will* be to our advantage. Arbour has the last change at home and he obviously wanted Nystrom, instead of Bossy, on Maloney. It worked well for them tonight."

The Islander coach re-united Bossy and Trottier in the second game of the series, two nights later, and again came up smelling like roses. Bossy scored a controversial goal at 2:50 of the first overtime to give New York a 3-2 victory over Toronto and a 2-0 lead in the best-of-seven affair. Bossy was on the seat of his pants when he swiped the puck past Mike Palmateer.

Television replays supported the Leafs' contention that Trottier had shovelled the puck to Bossy with his glove. Leafs felt that referee Andy Van Hellemond should have blown the play dead. Denis Potvin took the initial shot from the blueline and Palmateer stopped it. Trottier jammed the first rebound into Palmateer's pads before sliding the puck — with his hand — to Bossy, who swept it into the open net.

"I haven't seen the replay but someone said he (Trottier) used his hand," commented Leaf coach Roger Neilson. "It's too late now, anyway. Once again, we outhit the Islanders. If we keep doing that, we'll win the series. It was an even game and we feel we can play even tougher at home. I'm confident we'll come back here for Game 5 all tied up."

Ian Turnbull had opened the scoring for the Maple Leafs at 13:03 of the first period, but Clark Gillies tied it up a few minutes later. After a scoreless middle frame, Bob Bourne put the Islanders ahead 2-1 early in the third. George Ferguson's goal at the midway point of the period ultimately sent the game into overtime.

Neilson's prediction of physical dominance materialized in grand fashion for his Maple Leafs when the series shifted to the Gardens for Games 3 and 4. The Toronto players hit everything that moved in a blue and orange Islander uniform, and the Leafs wound up tying the series.

Goals by Ellis and Turnbull were more than enough in a thorough 2-0 victory in Game 3 — Fri. Apr. 21. The persistent Maple Leaf checking limited the Islanders to only 19 shots at Palmateer, who recorded his second playoff shutout. The game was every bit as one-sided as the Islanders' victory in the series opener.

"Anytime we finish off our checks as we did tonight, we will be there," said a satisfied Neilson. "It was a tough, physical game and we beat them at it. So far, we've been controlling the boards very well."

Ellis opened the scoring at 14:37 of the second period, pouncing on a loose puck in front of Chico Resch. Turnbull made it 2-0 at 5:37 of the third when he beat Resch with a shot from the blueline. Jerry Butler provided a screen on the play.

Canadian Prime Minister Pierre Elliott Trudeau attended the game and visited the Leaf dressing room afterwards. "Thanks for coming," Tiger Williams told the P-M. "You brought us some luck. Come back on

Sunday, we'll even pay your expenses."

With the Islanders in need of a physical response to the Maple Leafs, Game 4 turned ugly and is best remembered for a serious eye injury suffered by Borje Salming eight minutes into the second period. Toronto prevailed once again in a three-hour and 15-minute marathon, but everyone's post-game thoughts were on the Maple Leaf defenceman.

Ironically, one of the most reticent players on either club was responsible for the injury. Islander center Lorne Henning, who had all of 16 penalty minutes during the regular season, tried to check Salming as he carried the puck over the New York blueline on a powerplay. Both players fell, and Henning's stick came up and clipped Salming over the right eye. The Leaf rearguard dropped to his knees, clutching his face. Blood spurted from the wound and stained the ice, as an ominous silence enveloped the entire arena. Obviously worried about Salming, Henning immediately skated over to the fallen Leaf.

"I was trying to check Borje and when I couldn't, I tried to hook him," Henning explained. "We fell backward and my stick came around and cut him. It was an accident. I bent over and told him so but I guess he was in too much pain and didn't hear me.

"I skated to him because I was concerned. I knew it was either his eye or his nose. Or both. It's ironic that during a night of so many cheap shots, such a thing would happen in an innocent collision. There is no way anyone would want to see Salming get hurt like that. He's not the type of player you'd try to hurt."

Salming was helped off the ice and rushed to Wellesley Hospital with damage to his eye and nose. A few minutes later, Leaf enforcer Dan Maloney skated over to Henning and jumped him from behind: a move that seemed curious to even the most die-hard of Maple Leaf fans.

"He was sent out to get me and he suckered me from behind," said Henning, who absorbed a flury of punches. "He came straight out and told me he was getting me for hurting Salming. I guess that's his style — to attack from behind. He hit me in the face, then I covered up."

Salming's injury was the low point in a brutal evening of stick-work and intimidation. The Leafs won the game, 3-1. Salming and Stan Weir scored 16 seconds apart early in the second period to put Leafs ahead 2-0. Bob Nystrom then counted for the Islanders but Pat Boutette restored the two-goal Toronto cushion early in the third.

The teams clawed and gouged one another from the outset. Williams and Nystrom fought in the first period and Tiger emerged from the bout with teeth marks on his left cheek. While the players cooled off in the penalty box, Williams flipped a towel to Nystrom, "so he could wipe off the wounds he had over him."

Williams and Gary Howatt exchanged words at the 20-minute mark of the opening period and the players from both teams engaged in a lengthy waltz before heading to their dressing rooms. Williams fought Islander defenceman Dave Lewis in the second period, in the altercation sparked by Maloney jumping Henning. Even Mike Palmateer got involved, duelling Howatt in the third. Nystrom and Leaf defenceman Mike Pelyk rounded out the evening's wrestling card.

Jude Drouin of the Islanders was handed a five-minute major by referee Bob Myers for spearing Brian Glennie in the opening period. In all, Myers wound up assessing 111 penalty minutes.

A banner headline in bright red on the front page of Monday's Toronto *Star* said: **"SALMING HURT, McMURTRY WANTS LEAFS, ISLANDERS TO COOL IT."** The accompanying article contained warnings from Ontario Attorney General, Roy McMurtry, of possible assault charges should the series continue with its brutal pattern.

"We're not looking for excuses to lay charges but anything that amounts to criminal assault will bring a charge," McMurtry said. "There are policemen in the Gardens capable of dealing with the situation."

McMurtry's crusade against hockey violence dated back to November, 1975, when he charged Dan Maloney — then of Detroit — with assaulting Leaf defenceman Brian Glennie. Maloney lost his temper, grabbed Glennie by the back of his sweater, and repeatedly slammed him to the ice.

During the 1976 playoffs, McMurtry levied assault and weapons charges against three Philadelphia players for their part in a melee with the Leafs. Defenceman Joe Watson of the Flyers was charged with possession of an offensive weapon after he swung his stick over the glass near the penalty box and struck a policeman on the shoulder.

Tiger Williams then drew charges of assault causing bodily harm and possession of an offensive weapon when he pole-axed Pittsburgh defenceman Dennis Owchar in a game at the Gardens, Oct. 20, 1976. Owchar required 22 stitches in his head to close a gaping wound.

"We have seen worse when it comes to mindless viciousness," McMurtry told the *Star* after the Leaf-Islander game. "What we saw in the Toronto-Philadelphia series was much worse. But I am disappointed that professional hockey seems incapable of growing up."

Salming's injuries were diagnosed as a badly broken nose and a deep gash in his eyelid. He was admitted to hospital wearing patches over both eyes. A uniformed security officer guarded Salming's room on the ninth floor and doctors and nurses had to obtain special passes to enter the room. Salming was finished for at least the remainder of the quarterfinal series with the Islanders.

"Everyone must dig down deep now to make up for Borje not being there," said Pat Boutette. "We've been doing everything possible to win this series; now we'll have to do a little more."

Neilson remained stubbornly optimistic the Leafs could beat the Islanders without his top defenceman. "Anytime you lose a great player, it's bound to have a psychological effect," he said. "I just hope the guys come up big. Ian Turnbull and Brian Glennie will get all the ice time they can stand. They'll have to play their hearts out.

"We've said all along we were going to outhit the Islanders, which we have. They're too good a team not to fight back. In fact, I'm hoping they will because the tougher this series is, the better chance we have of winning."

That chance appeared bleak after another Islander overtime victory in Game 5, two nights later, at the Nassau Coliseum. Bob Nystrom deked Brian Glennie out of his athletic-supporter and beat Palmateer with a shot from the right faceoff circle at 8:02 of the first overtime. The goal came only seconds after Lanny McDonald had rung one off the post at the other end. It moved New York to within a victory of eliminating the Maple Leafs.

After the game, Tiger Williams uttered his latest in a series of unforgettable remarks. "We started the series having to win one game in here and we'll do it in the seventh game Saturday night," he promised Leaf fans. "They were life and death to beat us here, even though we didn't have Salming. And we came so bloody close to winning it that it was robbery when we didn't."

The last reference was to McDonald's clanging of the goalpost. "I was in pretty deep but I had about a foot of the net to shoot at," said Lanny. "It just hit the post, that's all. I might have tried pulling it to a better angle and shooting, but I didn't know if I had the time."

Again, the Maple Leafs opened the scoring as Turnbull deflected Sittler's pass into the net at 1:10 of the second period. The teams were skating five-aside at the time. Denis Potvin tied it for New York at 13:39 of the middle frame, beating Palmateer cleanly from the slot. Islanders held an edge in play during the third period, outshooting the Leafs 15-7, but Palmateer kept the score even.

Nystrom made a super move on Glennie to end it in overtime.

"He had stopped me several times when I faked inside and tried to go outside," explained the Islander hero. "This time, I faked outside and when he made a little lunge that way, I slipped the puck between his feet and went to the inside. Palmateer gave me a small hole on the short side and I was able to hit it."

The Leafs toned down their physical play in Game 5, but Neilson promised that, "In the next game in our rink, we'll be playing tough hockey once again."

How correct he was.

Two nights later at the Gardens, a punishing effort by just about every member of the Toronto team produced the most lop-sided game of the series. Leafs set the physical tone early and buried the Islanders in the opening period, building a 4-0 lead by the 12:53 mark, en route to a 5-2 victory. The game was marred by an incident late in the second period that had everyone in the Gardens concerned about the health of Islander freshman Mike Bossy.

Leaf winger Jerry Butler bumped into Bossy from behind in the New York end of the rink. It was by no means a violent collision, but Bossy jammed his neck on the boards and collapsed to the ice.

He laid motionless for several minutes, as doctors assessed the situation. He was then carefully removed on a stretcher and transported to Wellesley Hospital (where Salming was still recovering). The sight of the Islander winger in apparently grave condition had a dramatic effect on some people, as hockey writer Jim Kernaghan pointed out in the Toronto *Star*.

"When Bossy was carried away, one of New York's sportswriters leaned against a Zamboni machine and wept uncontrollably," he wrote.

Upon further examination at the hospital, everyone breathed a sigh of relief as Bossy was found to have merely a sprained neck. X-rays of the neck area proved negative and he was pronounced fit to play in the seventh and deciding game of the series, two nights later.

Still, the insults and accusations flew back and forth between the dressing rooms after Bossy returned to the Gardens.

"He got me after the whistle and it was a cheap-shot," said Bossy. "I was sort of relaxed on the play. I heard a little crack and I didn't want to take any chances, so I just lay there."

Butler, however, professed his innocence.

"I took him with the body in an effort to freeze the puck," he explained. "It's the kind of play that happens many times during a game. I just glided into him and he went low."

Meanwhile, in another corner of the Leaf dressing room, Tiger Williams was at it again. The previous year, prior to the deciding game of a playoff series in Pittsburgh, Williams had said, "Them Penguins is done like dinner." He was right. The Leafs beat them handily.

After the victory over the Islanders in Game 6, he was reminded of that comment and uttered, unquestionably, the most memorable line of his colourful career.

"Them Islanders is *worse* than done dinner... they're burnt toast!" Tiger exclaimed. He then turned to a group of New York writers and asked, "What are you guys going to do after Saturday? Cover baseball?"

Unorthodox as it may have been, Williams seemed to personify the entire Maple Leaf spirit with his bravado. The Leafs truly appeared to have the Islanders over a barrel with their unrelenting physical play and they didn't mind telling people about it.

The pressure was squarely on the Islanders to win the series in Game 7, as Dave Anderson pointed out in the Saturday New York *Times*.

> "In other years, the New York Islanders could rationalize their elimination from the Stanley Cup playoffs. Until now, they were always ousted by a team that was considered superior — Montreal in the semi-finals the last two years; Philadelphia in the semis three years ago.
>
> "...(But), if the Islanders lose to the Toronto Maple Leafs tonight in the deciding game of their Stanley Cup conflict at Nassau Coliseum, they will have only themselves to blame. No complaints. No alibies.
>
> "Tonight, the Islanders are EXPECTED to win."

Alas, the *unexpected* happened, and every Maple Leaf fan old enough to remember that Saturday night in April, 1978, will be indebted to Lanny McDonald for making an impossible dream come true.

A wire-mask dangling from his helmet to protect a broken nose, the Leaf winger scored on Chico Resch at 4:13 of the first overtime to win the series for Toronto. It gave the Leafs a 2-1 victory and sent them to the Stanley Cup semifinals for the first time in 11 years. Montreal would be their next opponent.

McDonald gobbled up a loose puck inside the Islander blueline and cruised in on Resch. He took careful aim and cleanly beat the New York goalie to the far side. He then flipped his gloves high in the air, touching off an explosion of joy from his teammates, as the Maple Leaf players poured off the bench to mob him.

"It's a play we've tried a few times in practice but we needed a little luck to make it work," McDonald explained of the series winner. "(Ian) Turnbull brought the puck up the ice and I cut into the middle to spread the defence. He flipped a high pass to me which hit an Islander (defenceman Stefan Persson), hit *me*, and dropped at my feet.

"All of a sudden, there was nobody between me and Resch and I needed an instant to realize I was in the clear. Chico came out to cut down the angle and I had to get the puck over his glove. I did."

Resch faulted himself for the goal.

"I thought McDonald was going to his backhand and I wasn't completely set for the shot," he said, confessing he had lost the puck when Turnbull flipped it high. "For a second, I just couldn't find the puck against McDonald's dark-blue sweater. I can't believe it."

Indeed, it *was* unbelievable — particularly when considering a glorious, almost can't-miss scoring opportunity that Bryan Trottier failed to convert early in the second period. An incredible photo of the play shows Trottier skating through the Maple Leaf goalcrease with the puck on his backhand and a wide-open net. Palmateer is to the left and slightly behind the goal, scrambling to get back. But somehow, the puck stayed out. Palmateer threw his body across the crease at the last possible millisecond — his big goal-stick fully extended — and made a miraculous stop.

Then there was a breakaway by Billy Harris of the Islanders in the overtime period, just moments before McDonald's goal. Again, if you're a Leaf fan who recalls watching that game, you may remember a momentary feeling of panic and resignation. This was it: the Islanders were going to win once again in overtime. You may have looked away; or turned off your television for a few seconds.

Harris intercepted an errant pass by Randy Carlyle intended for defence-mate Brian Glennie. But Palmateer again made the save.

"We had the better scoring chances and just didn't capitalize," said Islander coach Al Arbour. "I'm very disappointed."

Absolute bedlam ensued among the Maple Leafs and George Gross of the *Sun* witnessed much of it.

"McDonald couldn't calm down for some time," he wrote. "He was charging up and down the corridor like a young colt, shouting and waving his arms in ecstasy.

"'We did it, boy, we did it. Do ya hear, people? We did it, we won,' he shouted in jubilation.

"Tiger Williams...didn't try to hide his exuberance. He picked up the nearest fire-extinguisher, dragged it into the dressing room, and used it on whomever was in his way, screaming, 'Now where are those guys who've been saying we can't do it? Where the hell are they?'"

Roughly 1,500 euphoric fans gathered at Toronto International Airport and waited till 4:15 a.m. for the Maple Leafs to arrive. They hoisted Sittler on their shoulders and had an old-fashioned party.

The Toronto newspaper headlines reflected that joy.

"BRING ON MONTREAL! MAPLE LEAFS WIN 2-1" said the front page of the *Star*. **"HALLELUJAH!"** screamed the *Sun* in three-inch block letters.

When analyzing the Maple Leaf upset, two points were clear: The Leafs simply hammered the Islanders into submission with their bodies. They out-muscled a more talented club and proved their coach right when he said the longer the series went, the greater advantage Toronto would have. Secondly — but of equal importance — was the superb play of Ian Turnbull, who enjoyed his finest three-game stretch as a Maple Leaf.

Often a lazy performer whose attitude restricted what could have been a Hall of Fame career, Turnbull was magnificent in the absence of defence partner Borje Salming. He took complete charge of the Maple Leaf blueline and played with his full and abundant capabilities.

Ironically, in so doing, he proved how sinful a waste of talent he really was. His career, which began in 1973 at age 19, fizzled out 10 years later in Los Angeles. He had the athletic genius to play double that amount of time.

After expending so much energy in beating the Islanders, the Leafs were easy prey for a vastly superior Montreal team in the semifinals. The Canadiens cruised to a four-game sweep, then went on to defeat Boston for their third of four Stanley Cup victories in succession.

No one in Toronto seemed to mind.

Not after the great season of "Captain Video" and his boys.

... Leafs in Spring ...

APRIL 27, 1993
Joe Louis Arena, Detroit

The Maple Leafs looked like duck-soup in the first two games of their '93 Norris Division semifinal with Detroit. The Red Wings breezed to 6-3 and 6-2 wins at Joe Louis Arena and seemed capable of dismissing their long-time rivals in four straight.

But, "in-your-face" hockey then came into vogue.

Back on home ice, the Maple Leafs suddenly got that "feeling" — whatever it is that prompts underdog teams to overachieve — and they deadlocked the semifinal at two games apiece. After the victory in Game 4, Pat Burns was fielding questions from the media in the Gardens' press lounge when one of life's inherent dilemmas ruffled the proceedings.

During an ill-fated lull in the questioning, a loud and crackly fart emanated from the direction of a well-known Toronto sportswriter: puncturing the sudden quietness. Burns reacted like a Secret Service agent — quickly snapping his head in the direction of the blast. Media members discreetly shuffled to the other side of the room, fearing an aftershock, and the press conference resumed.

Several days later, the culprit and I were riding to Joe Louis Arena on the "People Mover": an outdoor monorail system that encircles downtown Detroit. And he enlighened me on the press-room gas attack.

"Geez, I tried to time it so there would be enough noise to drown out the sound," lamented the sportswriter. "But just as I reached the point of `no return', everyone suddenly stopped talking."

While contemplating the moment, a perverse curiosity overcame me. I began to wonder if Burns had indeed recognized the offender. But short of initiating a discussion about flatulence with the Maple Leaf coach, I had few ideas on how to broach the subject. Thankfully, the situation looked after itself.

Moments after arriving at Joe Louis Arena, the gaseous writer and I were slowly walking past the corridor outside the Maple Leaf dressing room. As the Toronto players warmed up for the pivotal fifth game with Detroit, Burns nervously paced back and forth: seemingly oblivious to his surroundings. We offered him a cursory wave and continued towards the pre-game buffet area, at which time we became fully aware that he wasn't in too deep a trance.

"No farting in the press box!" hollered the Leaf coach.

At least he knew.

3

THE SIMMONS
SAGA

Maple Leaf Gardens / Chicago Stadium
January 18-19, 1964

On the 1963-64 National Hockey League schedule, it looked like just another Saturday night home game for the Toronto Maple Leafs: one of 24 such engagements throughout the season. And none too big an attraction, either. Boston would provide the opposition, having already suffered the ignominy of missing the playoffs four years running, with a fifth likely to follow. No Jean Beliveau, Gordie Howe or Bobby Hull to fear on this night. Easy pickings.

Just past the halfway point of the season, the Leafs were poised, it seemed, to strongly challenge for their third Stanley Cup triumph in succession. They sat third in the old six-team league, but only three points in arrears of first-place Chicago. The Bruins, on the other hand, were again providing a black, gold and white doormat for the rest of the league: firmly entrenched in the NHL basement with only 26 points, 22 less than Toronto. Boston had left the Gardens with that familiar empty feeling on four prior occasions that season. Could the Bruins' fifth visit be anything more than a foregone conclusion?

Well, more than 30 years later, the answer to that question remains an ear-splitting *YES!* And any hockey fan old enough to recall turning on CBC television at 8:30 p.m. EST, January 18, 1964, will concur. "I remember seeing the graphic, which read 6-0 for Boston, and thinking it was someone's idea of a bad joke," says Joe Bowen, the current-day voice of the Maple Leafs. "Then I turned the volume up and, holy shit, it was true!"

A 13-year-old student at Lansdowne Public School in Sudbury, Bowen was far from alone in his disbelief. In fact, thousands of hockey fans all across Canada still remember gawking at their TV sets on that Saturday evening more than a generation ago.

Hockey Night In Canada went to air at 8:30 in those days, following local programming on CBC affiliates (including the game show *To Tell The Truth*). Invariably, the hockey game would be nearing the conclusion of the first period and the telecast would begin with a wide-angle shot from a camera mounted in the west-side Greens. For those who had listened to Foster Hewitt's *radio* description of the game to that point, the accompanying score graphic confirmed what they already knew. But for others, many of whom had just finished a relaxing dinner, the first TV images were their sole source of information. And for Maple Leaf fans of the early 1960s, the news was often pleasant... especially with the Bruins in town. But, not on this night.

An experience that Maple Leaf players and fans recall as the most humiliating of the 1960s Stanley Cup dynasty ended with Boston on the front end of an 11-0 massacre. The NHL's perennial also-ran came to town and rode roughshod over a Toronto team on its way to a Stanley Cup hattrick. No wonder they still talk about it today.

"An equivalent would be the bad Maple Leaf teams of the mid-1980s going into Edmonton and beating Gretzky, Messier and company something like 23-0!" says Bowen. "That's how much better the Leafs were than Boston in 1964 and how incredible an 11-goal outburst was back then. It just didn't happen, especially when the worst team in the league went on the road to play the best."

The principals involved in that game were no less astounded than the observers. Several of the players appeared in more than 1,300 games during their NHL careers, but they recall *that* night as if it were yesterday. Some, like Bruins' coach Milt Schmidt, were in such a state of bewilderment that they required a second look. "That's the only time in my entire career as a player or a coach that I had to watch a video replay of a game to make sure I wasn't dreaming," Schmidt recalls. "When we got home to Boston the next day, I watched the game all over again. It was unbelievable."

For Maple Leaf goalie Don Simmons, it would mark the beginning of a remarkably improbable weekend. A veteran of eight NHL seasons,

Simmons was generally regarded as the premier back-up netminder in hockey, at a time when the two-goalie system was starting to become the norm. A native of Port Colborne, Ont., Simmons did his minor-league apprenticeship in Springfield of the American Hockey League, amid the ravings of the cantankerous Eddie Shore. That pretty much prepared him for anything he'd encounter later on — including his rabble-rousing Maple Leaf boss, Punch Imlach.

Something of a nonconformist, Simmons bucked the trend of the early-60s by wearing an odd-looking goalie mask — one of those multi-stranded, fibreglass relics of that era. Full of gaps, the mask seemed to afford little protection, but Simmons swore by it.

"I really haven't heard a good, sound argument against masks," he said in a 1963 interview. "Terry Sawchuk and Jacques Plante are good advertisements for them. At first, I didn't think it gave me any extra confidence, but I now think it must provide a subconcious feeling of security. I forget I have it on most of the time."

After appearing in 167 games for Boston over five seasons, Simmons was traded to the Maple Leafs for fellow goalie Ed Chadwick in January, 1961. He quickly emerged as a dependable stand-in for the ageless, but fragile Johnny Bower and he gained instant renown for an heroic pinch-hitting display in the 1962 Stanley Cup final.

In Game 4 of that series, with the defending-champion Blackhawks attempting to tie the set at 2-2 in Chicago, Bower suffered a serious hamstring injury while making an acrobatic save on Bobby Hull. Simmons played the balance of the series in goal for the Leafs, who prevailed in six games to win their first Stanley Cup of the decade.

The following year (1962-63), Simmons subbed for Bower on 28 occasions in the regular season, but Bower played in all 10 playoff games as the Maple Leafs up-ended Montreal and Detroit to win their second championship in a row.

The Bower-Simmons combo returned for 1963-64 and Bower required time off in mid-January to rest a hand injury. The veteran goalie was also at odds with Imlach over an incident at the Gardens, in which he displayed genuine concern at the end of a period for injured Montreal rookie John Ferguson. Bower was a human being first, a hockey player second, but if ever there was a no-no in the 1960s NHL, it was showing that type of compassion for an opponent... on or off the ice.

So, it was Simmons who had the spotlight once again as the Maple Leafs continued their quest for first place, midway through the '63-64 schedule. His stand-in role began promisingly, with home-ice victories over Montreal and Boston. But he then lost twice (to the Bruins and Rangers) and the Leafs took that mini slump into a weekend of seemingly immense contrast, January 18-19. They would host the NHL's worst team (Boston) on Saturday night at the Gardens before railing it to Chicago for a Sunday night encounter with the league's best. A split seemed highly probable.

"I don't think it was any great disadvantage having me in goal back then," Simmons recalls. "John was obviously number-one, but I saw a fair amount of action in those days. It wasn't as if I played only once a month or something; I'd get into an average of one game every week or 10 days and I felt prepared to hold down the fort any time Punch called my name."

Simmons was also experienced enough to realize that no hockey game was a sure thing, regardless of the standings. The Leafs were indeed favoured to beat Boston any time they played back then, but the Bruins came to the Gardens with consecutive victories over New York and Detroit. Still, Simmons probably never imagined he'd live through an evening so bizarre that people would still be talking about it three decades later.

The same undoubtedly applies to Peter Stemkowski, a centerman who would play in more than 1,000 NHL games with Toronto, Detroit, the Rangers and Los Angeles. On January 18, 1964, the 20-year-old native of Winnipeg was midway through his final year of Junior 'A' hockey with the Toronto Marlboros and was playing very well. A 10-point explosion in three games had vaulted him to third in the Ontario Hockey Association scoring race, behind only Andre Boudrias and Yvan Cournoyer of the Montreal Junior Canadiens. As far as Stemkowski knew, his next task would be a home game the following afternoon against Bobby Orr and the Oshawa Generals.

"I was sitting at home watching TV on Saturday when the phone rang," recalls Stemkowski, who was boarding with a Polish family in Toronto. "It was King Clancy on the other end saying I was going to play for the Maple Leafs that night. Jim Pappin was sick with strep throat or something, and they were calling me up. It was hard to believe, mainly because I never gave that situation a thought. If the Leafs needed a replacement player in those days, they usually went to their (AHL) farm team in Rochester.

"But there I was — a kid from the West with white socks and penny loafers — getting ready to play his first NHL game with the Stanley Cup champions. It was a trip!"

The Bruins came to town not having made the playoffs since the

1959-60 season, and they wouldn't qualify again till 1967-68, when the NHL expanded to 12 teams. Of the 16 players who dressed for Boston, only two (winger Johnny Bucyk and goalie Ed Johnston) would still be with the team when it won a Stanley Cup six years later.

"We weren't a good club but we went into Toronto that night playing quite well," recalls former Bruin defenceman Leo Boivin, one of hockey's all-time great hip checkers. "There wasn't really a lot of pressure on us in those days because nobody ever expected us to win, so we probably went into Toronto feeling pretty loose. And every time somebody reminds me of what happened that night, it brings a big smile to my face. I still can't believe the score when I think of it 30 years later — how we were able to demolish such an excellent and proud team like the Leafs."

The officiating crew for the game consisted of referee Bill Friday, with linesmen Dave Smith and Matt Pavelich. Thanks to a quirk in his travel schedule, Friday remembers feeling somewhat edgy prior to the opening faceoff.

"I was scheduled to work the Montreal at Boston game the following night and the NHL had made arrangements for me to fly to Boston on a charter flight with the Bruins," he recalls. "I wasn't too thrilled with that idea but Carl Voss (NHL referee-in-chief) said it was the only way I could get there on time, so I had no other choice.

"Now going into a game knowing that you have to fly with one of the teams afterwards, is not an ideal situation for a referee and I remember feeling some pressure. I don't think I prepared differently but in the back of my mind, I was hoping I wouldn't be forced into doing something harsh against the Bruins. If I had to throw a player out of the game, or make a ruling on a disputed goal, it could cause some hard feelings and the flight wouldn't be very pleasant.

"But as it turned out, someone up there must've been looking out for me that night."

Indeed, there would be no reason at all for any member of the Bruin organization to pout, grumble or sneer. Rarely did the *great* Boston teams of the early 70s possess the artistry and magic of the hum-drum Bruin collection that night in '64.

The evening began quickly for Boston, and ominously for the Leafs, when rookie right-winger Gary Dornhoefer opened the scoring 53 seconds into the first period. It was only Dornhoefer's third of 214 goals he'd score in the NHL — the vast majority with the "Broad Street Bullies" in Philadelphia a decade later — but he still recalls taking Johnny Bucyk's pass and beating Simmons to open the floodgates.

"I sure didn't think there'd be 10 more goals after that one — not for us, anyway," he laughs. "It was my first-ever game at the Gardens and a big thrill for a 20-year-old kid who'd grown up in Kitchener always wanting to be a Maple Leaf. Then, to score a goal in the first minute of play... wow! My parents and some friends were in the stands that night and it was a great feeling."

Veterans Andy Hebenton, Murray Oliver and Dean Prentice added goals for Boston and it was 4-0 Bruins before the 10-minute mark. Hebenton and Prentice scored again late in the period for a 6-0 Boston lead heading into the first intermission.

"We were all wondering what the hell was going on and I'm sure the Leaf players were as well," says Dornhoefer. "I mean, we didn't have a whole lot of offensive firepower on that team. Most nights were an exercise in survival for us and we were usually intent on trying to keep the opposition from scoring.

"Then we go into Toronto and get six in the first period against the Stanley Cup champions. We were all kind of light-headed during the intermission."

Hebenton and Prentice were playing on a makeshift forward unit with rugged center Orland Kurtenbach. They had been teammates for a brief time during the 1960-61 season in New York, when Kurtenbach played 10 games for the Rangers, and were thrown together by Milt Schmidt just a few days before the Leaf massacre. For some reason, the line would soon be dismantled — "probably, because we began losing again," reasons Schmidt — but it was a trio of contrasting styles and terrific balance.

Hebenton was the NHL's ironman of that era, setting an all-time record by playing in 630 consecutive games with the Rangers and Bruins. He had nine complete 70-game seasons between 1955-56 and 1963-64 — a record that endured for almost 12 years, and was broken by Garry Unger of the St. Louis Blues in March, 1976. Doug Jarvis, Steve Larmer and Craig Ramsay have all since joined Unger in bettering the mark established by Hebenton. An excellent two-way winger, Hebenton combined a scoring touch (189 career goals in his nine seasons) with a disciplined checking game.

"From a coaching standpoint, Andy was an absolute delight to have as a player," Schmidt says. "You could use him in any given situation and he'd perform well, especially when you had to protect a one-goal lead late in the game."

Hebenton remembers the 11-0 Boston whipping of the Leafs as, "probably the second-most memorable night of my NHL career" —

second only to the semifinal playoff game in 1958, when he scored an overtime goal for the Rangers against Montreal at Madison Square Garden. "That's the moment which stands out for me, but scoring three goals against the Maple Leafs in that terribly one-sided game is pretty close," Hebenton says. "I just remember that everything we shot at poor Simmons seemed to go in and the harder the Leafs tried, the worse it got for them."

Prentice was Boston's most talented forward at the time and one of hockey's smoothest skaters. He would play 22 years in the NHL with the Rangers, Bruins, Detroit, Pittsburgh and Minnesota — totalling 391 career goals.

Kurtenbach was a lanky, hard-nosed center — devoid of any great offensive skills — but one of the most feared warriors of his time. If you dared fight Kurtenbach in those days, you'd lose badly, and have your features rearranged.

"Dean, Andy and I had occasionally been used as a checking line, but we sure clicked with the puck in Toronto that night," Kurtenbach recalls. "On one of the goals, I remember banking the puck perfectly off the corner boards to Dean, who was flying in on his wing. He one-timed it past Simmons. It was sure nice to see those goals go in because we weren't a very high-scoring team, and if we fell behind by two or three, we'd almost certainly lose. To have a 6-0 lead at the end of the first period was miraculous."

By comparison, the Bruins took it easy on the Maple Leafs in the middle frame, adding only one goal to their total, as Hebenton completed his hattrick on passes from Prentice and Bob Leiter. But the onslaught picked up again in the third, as Oliver and Prentice (with *his* third of the night) scored early to give Boston a 9-0 lead and officially convert Maple Leaf Gardens into a funny farm.

"Our fans had turned against us by that time and were chanting `We want 10!'" chuckles Billy Harris. "In fact, as the situation got more and more out of hand, we were trying hard not to giggle on the bench. It got to a point where our frustration was overcome by embarrassment and we began to see some humour in what was happening out there. Our feeling was `let's get this thing over with as soon as we can. No offsides or icings, let's just get the hell out of the building!' It was a humiliating experience."

In his 1989 book, *THE GLORY YEARS*, Harris wrote that at 9-0,

"...Imlach wanted me to play left wing with Keon and Armstrong and he muttered, not just to the three of us, but the entire team, `If you ever let them score their tenth, I will get even at practice on Monday.' When we finished our shift, the score was 10-0 and the fans were cheering, `We want eleven.'"

Johnny Bucyk had granted the Gardens' faithful their first wish at the 7:04 mark, taking passes from Oliver and Dornhoefer. "The fans wanted ten so I obliged," Bucyk laughs. "Actually, I shouldn't sound cocky. There were very few highlights playing for Boston in the early 60s — the Stanley Cup years were still more than a half-decade away — and that game was just a fluke. But it sure broke the monotony of losing, as we did so often back then."

Harris got another shift moments later, this time with the devilish Eddie Shack, who was never beyond having a little fun at the expense of his coach — regardless of the circumstance. "Punch didn't say much behind the bench that night but I could tell just by looking at him that he was in a rage," Shack recalls. "With the score 10-0, he sent me and Harris over the boards, so I turned to him and said, `What do you want us to do, *tie* it or *win* it?' I don't think he appreciated my humour."

Shack had been in ill-humour, himself, during a shift early in the second period when he was toppled heavily by Boston center Bob Leiter. Shack's skate came up and shattered a pane of glass along the west-side boards. He then righted himself and pummeled the much-smaller Leiter for the only decision the Leafs would win on this night (Shack and Leiter would briefly be teammates on the 1971-72 Pittsburgh Penguins).

The 14,011 spectators at the Gardens razzed Simmons unmercifully, and actually began to cheer *Boston's* advances in the third period. "Ah, that stuff didn't bother me, I never listened to the crowd," asserts Simmons, who faced 38 Bruin shots. "But, I'll say one thing: nobody ever gave me any credit for stickin' in out that night. Nowadays, the goalies run to the bench when they're having a bad game, but I just stood there and took all the abuse. I never even looked at Imlach."

The extent to which Simmons and his teammates were ridiculed by the fans appeared in Hal Walker's Toronto *Telegram* column on Monday morning:

"...In years of recording the heroics of the Leafs, I've never heard a Toronto crowd swing away from their team as the Saturday night audience did. They began a chant for the Bruins to hoist the score and the sturdy walls of the building must have shed some plaster in remorse."

Little-used forward Jean-Guy Gendron, who would play a leading role with the Philadelphia Flyers in their infant years, finished off the rout, scoring Boston's 11th goal with 4:13 remaining in the game. Winger Forbes Kennedy and defenceman Bob McCord drew assists on the play and referee Friday remembers another moment of levity. "I was back at center ice with the puck when Kennedy skated by and said, `Well, *that* should be the clincher.' It was typical Forbsie and I almost fell over laughing."

Veteran Eddie Johnston stopped all 26 Toronto shots to record an almost-forgotten shutout at the other end of the rink.

For Peter Stemkowski, it was an evening of roller-coaster emotions. "I remember sitting on the bench and thinking, `boy, I'll sure never forget *my* first NHL game!'" he smiles. "On the other hand, it was absolutely incredible to be out there. My only brush with Maple Leaf players had been walking past them every so often in the Gardens' lobby after a Marlie practice. I had played many games there but suddenly, everything looked brighter, the guys on the ice looked bigger, and the speed of the game was much quicker than in Junior `A'. I'd been playing with teenagers — some of us shaved; most of us didn't — and there I was on the ice with guys who had `5 o'clock shadows'.

"And just the glamour of having the stands full. I was used to small rinks in Junior, like Kitchener, London and Peterborough and now, here I was, sitting in a full Maple Leaf Gardens on the bench next to Frank Mahovlich. I mean, I grew up looking at this guy... listening to Maple Leaf games on radio back in Winnipeg. He was the `Big M', and there was Bower... and Baun... and Keon. Then, all of a sudden, I'm out on the ice with them.... it was amazing!"

For the sake of posterity, Stemkowski did make the NHL summary in his first game. The Leafs got caught with too many men on the ice at 17:03 of the second period — "that's a joke, it seemed like we were three men *short* all night," says Shack — and Imlach sent Stemkowski over the boards to serve the penalty.

"I guess he figured I knew where everything was, including the penalty box," Stemkowski laughs. "But that was okay. I figured that if I couldn't score a goal or get an assist, I may as well take a penalty so the folks back home knew I was in the game. I had a few shifts that night but my name only shows up in the penalty stats."

Murray Oliver's name shows up frequently in the *scoring* stats. In his fifth NHL season, Oliver, then 25, centred a line with the veteran Bucyk and the rookie Dornhoefer. The unit accounted for ten points — Oliver scoring twice and setting up two others.

"As the score mounted for us, all I remember thinking is `we're not this good!'" recalls Oliver, who would later play for the Maple Leafs (from 1967-70). "I mean, the whole night was just crazy. Our line was going really well. I played with Bucyk through most of my years in Boston and we had a good chemistry. Tom Williams was usually our other winger and we used to be called the `BOW' Line for our initials.

"But that night in Toronto, Dorny was playing well with us. Like a lot of the guys back then, it was a special experience because I had my family in the stands from Hamilton. And I had a pretty good night, which wasn't a rarity for me in Toronto. I used to get pumped up to play in the Gardens."

Milt Schmidt enjoyed having Oliver on that team, but says, "Murray would have been a Hall of Fame candidate if he were a bit bigger (than 5-9, 170). He had loads of talent and a sound work ethic, but he wasn't the prototypical Boston Bruin-type player. He sure was slick around the net, though."

The jubilant Bruins skated off the ice after the final bell backslapping themselves in disbelief. "Yeah, we were all pretty euphoric," Boivin remembers. "Our G.M., Lynn Patrick, was in Los Angeles that night scouting a Western League game, and when he heard the score, he made a bunch of phone calls thinking 11-0 was a misprint. He thought maybe it was 1-0.

"We bussed to the airport and took a chartered flight back to Boston and all of the guys were whooping it up. When we landed, the men who unloaded our baggage didn't believe us when we told them the score. They thought we were fooling."

Maple Leaf reaction that night was somewhat mixed. Imlach, who surprised nobody in those days by having a conniption, didn't say a heck of a lot, but his players all remember him as a smouldering volcano, one that could erupt at any minute. "I remember sheepishly approaching him to see if I'd be accompanying the team to Chicago for the game Sunday night," Stemkowski says. "He had a big frown on his face and I wondered if he was going to chew my head off.

"Instead, he slowly looked up and said, `Naw, kid, we don't want to embarrass you anymore.' He wasn't angry at *me*, but he was quite upset with the way his veterans played. And I guess he figured we could have another rough night against the Blackhawks, who were in first place at the time. So, I went back to Junior."

Harris sat on the bench shaking his head most of the night, trying to find some humour in the debacle. Shack kept his usual shenanigans to a minimum, while peeking over at Imlach now and then. "Ooooh, was he in a brutal mood," Shack laughs. "When I think back on it, I can't believe I cracked that joke in the third period. I'm surprised it didn't set him off like a firecracker. You didn't need a lot to get Punch going."

Bob Nevin, whom Imlach would trade a month later, was among several players — including the beleaguered Simmons — who found it easier than expected to shake off the 11-0 abomination. "You sure don't enjoy being involved in anything like that but after a while, you realize it's just kind of meant to be," Nevin says. "It got to the point in the third period where it *was* rather funny because the Bruins were scoring from wherever they shot the puck... poor Donny couldn't have stopped a beachball.

"But when it was over, all we had lost was the opportunity to gain two points in the standings. It would have been the same if we had lost 1-0. Still, we were all glad we had another game the next day and not a practice. Imlach would have probably skated our asses off for three hours!"

The most extreme reaction on the Maple Leafs likely belonged to veteran centerman Red Kelly, but it wasn't what you might expect after such a disaster. Harris wrote about it in *THE GLORY YEARS*:

> "We boarded the train that night for Chicago. Things were compara-
> tively quiet on the train, except for Leonard 'Red' Kelly. Red couldn't
> stop giggling. He later explained that nothing in his entire career had
> been as funny as our 11-0 thrashing at the hands of the last-place
> Bruins."

Kelly doesn't remember his reaction that night, but when reminded of the game, guess what? He starts laughing! "I suppose Billy was right, because look at me now," he says. "That was an unbelievable night. Every time they shot the puck, it would somehow find the eye of a needle and wind up in our net. When you lose that badly, what else can you *do* but laugh. I mean, the harder we tried, the worse it got... it was like a comedy.

"I don't remember giggling on the train ride, but seeing how I'm reacting now — 30 years later — I can believe it. Usually, on the train, you'd sit around before going to bed, talking about the good points and the bad points of the game. But *that* night, what else could you do but laugh? I'd have felt ten times worse if we'd lost 3-2 or something. But, 11-0... it was hilarious!"

The three Toronto-area newspapers that weekend also took stabs at humor when reporting on the game. Under a column head **GAME WILL LIVE IN IGNOMINY**, the late Dick Beddoes wrote in the *Globe & Mail*:

> "...From this day forward, Jan. 18, 1964 will be distinguished as the date when the lamb backed the butcher into a corner in Maple Leaf Gardens and carved his initials on him with a meat-cleaver."

On the front page of the *Telegram* sports section, Hal Walker penned a typical reaction to the Maple Leaf massacre:

> "Word of the catastrophe arrived in various ways, but down at the Boulevard Club, some curlers were only mildly amused when a man grasped the public-address system mike and intoned: 'I know you won't believe this, but Boston is leading the Leafs 10-0.'
> "'...Somebody,' said a curler, 'should take the microphone away from that nut.'"

But the deed was done, and the Leafs had further business to attend to in Chicago. As they sped towards the Windy City on their overnight train, Don Simmons became the central figure in Imlach's attempt at preventative maintenance. Having yielded 22 goals in his previous three outings against the NHL's weak sisters — Boston and New York — Simmons was obviously not playing very well (though he was no more inept than any of his 'mates in the 11-0 disgrace). And depending with whom you talked, Imlach was either hoping to give Simmons a rest... or never see him again.

One thing is for certain: Imlach did not want Simmons to face the league-leading Blackhawks under any circumstances. Given the situation, however, there was precious little time to summon a replacement — which might explain why Simmons vehemently denies, to this day, any knowledge of the plot to overthrow him. "Naw, that's a lot of baloney, do you really believe that?" he asks when reminded of the story. "All I know is we had a team meeting at 2 o'clock the next day in Chicago and I was playing again that night. I went from the hotel to the Stadium and dressed for the game."

Indeed, that's the way the situation unfolded, but not before a rather exhaustive search through the Maple Leaf organization. The number-three goalie in the system that year was Gerry Cheevers — the starting netminder with Rochester of the AHL. But Cheevers had been injured and *his* back-up, Ed Babiuk, had taken over in goal for the Americans. Babiuk was not NHL-calibre, so Imlach had to look elsewhere.

He could have gone the Junior 'A' route — ala Stemkowski the night before — but Imlach chose not to summon Gary Smith from the Marlboros. Instead, he instructed King Clancy to contact Al Millar, who was starring in goal for the Maple Leafs' Western Hockey League affiliate in Denver (he would lead the WHL that season with a 2.83 goals-gainst average in 70 games). Millar was in San Francisco, where Denver had lost 4-2 on Saturday night, and was told to catch the first plane to Chicago... and be ready to face the Blackhawks. Simmons was going to get the night off.

Billy Harris recalled his version of the the scenario — 25 years later — in *THE GLORY YEARS*:

> "We had a team meeting at the La Salle Hotel the next morning in Chicago. Imlach was livid. He did something he rarely did. He blamed Don Simmons, our goaler, for the 11-0 fiasco. Punch very seldom berated an individual in front of his peers. He told Simmons he would never wear the Leaf uniform again.
>
> "...We climbed the 13 steps to the Chicago ice surface for our warm-up without a goaltender. Poor weather conditions had delayed Al Millar's arrival. ...Imalch sent (trainer) Bobby Haggert to find Simmons, (who) was having a beer and a hot dog at the concession stand. He dressed hurriedly, putting on the Leaf sweater that Imlach said he never again would, and was allowed a 20-second warm-up before the opening face-off."

"Aw, that's garbage," says Simmons. "Don't you think I'd have remembered something like that?"

Of course, the three people who could unequivocally verify the story — Imlach, Clancy and Millar — are no longer alive. However, Bob Haggert, the Maple Leafs' head trainer from 1955 to 1968, does recall much of the scenario.

"Imlach *did* call Millar up because I remember him telling me so," Haggert says. "But, I don't remember going to any concession stand in the Chicago Stadium to rush Simmons to the dressing room. And, if you think about it logically, how could Simmons *not* have been in the room that close to game time?

"I mean, if Millar was circling in a plane over Chicago, and Bower was injured, we had to have *somebody* getting ready to play goal. On the other hand, I'm surprised Don doesn't remember that Millar had been called up. I'm pretty sure everybody on the team was aware of that."

Another version was presented by hockey writer George Gross, who travelled with the Leafs to Chicago for the *Telegram*:

> "...Puck-shocked from Saturday night's 11-0 humiliation, Simmons was told yesterday afternoon that he would be replaced by Al Millar, from Denver," Gross wrote in Monday's paper. "Simmons just nodded is head. Ten minutes later, the Leaf staff was informed Miller couldn't be in Chicago in time for the game because the plane (he was on) had developed engine trouble. Simmons was then asked to play. He didn't object. He understood.
>
> "Later, he said briefly: `If you are a pro, you play when you are asked. There are 16 others on the team who count on you.'"

The United Airlines flight from San Francisco carrying Millar circled Chicago's O'Hare Field in dense fog for an hour, awaiting weather clearance to land. Ultimately, the jet was re-routed to Des Moines, Iowa, where its hydraulic fuel pump jammed. As a result, Millar wasn't even in the state of Illinois for the start of the Leaf-Blackhawks game. Ironically, Millar's only NHL experience to that point (and for all time) was a six-game stretch in 1957-58, filling in for the injured Simmons when the two played for Boston.

"I didn't feel too good after that 11-0 shellacking, but I see where an NHL All-Star team lost 16-6 a few years ago (in 1992)," Simmons says. "A lot of nights, the puck would hit the post and go wide but on that night against the Bruins, it was finding little holes all over the place. What the hell you gonna do? It happens. I sure didn't lose any sleep over it, I'll tell you that."

As for the following day, when Millar was summoned to replace him in goal, Simmons says, "I don't remember anything about that and I don't recall Imlach berating me during the team meeting in Chicago. In fact, I don't think I ever said two words to Punch, and vise versa. My opinion of the guy was that of an egotistical son of a bitch, but I give him credit for putting a hell of a hockey team together. He was an average coach but a great manager."

Simmons explains that it's always been his nature not to dwell on things, and that's why he believes the 11-0 humiliation against Boston had no lasting effect on him. "In those days, you didn't make a lot of money, you just played and had fun," he recalls. "Some nights were good and others were bad, but you took whatever came and pushed forward. As a goalie, you couldn't do anything else."

It was that laisse-faire attitude, however, that Milt Schmidt believes prevented Simmons from becoming a front-line netminder. "He was a stand-up goalie with a good glove-hand," Schmidt recalls. "But, when I coached him in Boston (in the late-50s), there were many times when he just didn't seem to be into the game. He was so nonchalant out there and I often told him to grit his teeth and get more involved emotionally. I'm glad he admitted to letting things roll off his back too easily. I think that was his downfall as a goaler."

Simmons, of course, strongly disagrees. "The position was, and still is, all reaction and reflex," he counters. "Coaching never had anything to do with it because you can't tell a goalie how to play at that level. It may be more important at a younger development stage, but not in the NHL.

"I mean, you're standing there, someone's blasting a puck at your head, and you're just trying to survive. You aren't saying to yourself 'Now what did Imlach tell me to do in this situation?' That's silly. So, if Punch felt he was going to make me a better goalie by replacing me after that 11-0 loss to the Bruins, he was badly mistaken."

In any event, the shellshocked Maple Leafs appeared to be in tough against the Blackhawks. While the Leafs were being shamed by Boston, the 'Hawks were routing New York 6-1 at Chicago Stadium—increasing their first-place lead to three points over Montreal and five points over Toronto. As well, the Maple Leafs had lost all four previous meetings in Chicago, three by shutouts (Glenn Hall had blanked them four times to that point in 1963-64). And the fans at the Stadium weren't about to allow the Leafs any reprieve from their embarrassment of the night before.

Bob Nevin, who wore number 11 on his Maple Leaf uniform, says it started during the warm-up. "I was skating around when some guy leaned over the glass and said, `Hey, Nevin, is that your sweater number or the score from last night's game?!' I thought it was a pretty good line and I ended up laughing, but I figured we might be in for another long night against the Blackhawks."

A sign hanging in the Stadium wondered if the Leafs had played "hockey or ping-pong" against Boston. Everyone seemed to be having a little fun at the expense of the two-time Stanley Cup champions.

But in the end, this night would unfold like a storybook—especially for Don Simmons. After yielding 11 goals against the NHL's worst team, at home, Simmons went to Chicago and blanked the league's *best* team, on the road. He stopped all 27 shots the 'Hawks directed his way and the Leafs got second-period goals from Billy Harris and Ron Stewart to beat Chicago, 2-0. It was the type of dramatic turnaround that long-time hockey observers say was more consistent with the six-team era.

"The guys just did a reversal," Simmons remembers. "There was no big secret involved, they just went back to playing the type of disciplined hockey they almost always played back then, and it was a fairly easy night for me. That team had a lot of pride. We got shellacked the night before and we wanted to make up for it."

The Leafs had arrived in Chicago in a bad mood and they took out their frustrations on the Blackhawk players. Defenceman Carl Brewer nearly incited a riot in the Stadium when he speared Chicago center Stan Mikita midway through the final period. Autry Erickson of the Blackhawks led a four-man gang-attack against Brewer and the riled-up fans hurled debris at the late Vern Buffey, who officiated the game.

Mostly, they threw small wooden sticks, but one creative fan released a live pigeon onto the ice, which served to delay the game two or three times. Earlier — in the first period — Eddie Shack had clotheslined Chicago's Reggie Fleming with the butt-end portion of his stick, cutting him for 23 stitches. Fleming was carted off to hospital with a concussion.

Despite his claims of a "fairly easy night", Simmons did have some anxious moments, but he came up big each time. A three-save flurry off Bobby Hull late in the second period may have been the key moment of the game. It preserved the Leafs' 2-0 lead heading into the 15-minute intermission.

"I played a lot in Chicago during my career, mainly because the goalies I backed up didn't enjoy playing there," Simmons recalls. "(Johnny) Bower never felt comfortable in the Stadium and it was the same with (Ed) Giacomin when I was in New York at the end of my career. But, the place never bothered me."

The headlines and storylines in the three Toronto newspapers on Monday highlighted the Maple Leafs' improbable weekend. Under a photograph of the Gardens' sports-timer, showing the 11-0 score in the Boston game, the front page of the Toronto *Star* ran a headline that said **MAD SPORTS WEEKEND**, beneath which was written:

"It should have been April 1st. Then, it would have been easier to explain the wacky weekend in sport. Leafs, who couldn't have beaten a fat man to a bus Saturday night, when the tail-end Bruins clobbered them 11-0 at the Gardens, Sunday scored their first win this season in

Chicago. Leafs tried to unload goalie Don Simmons, but couldn't get a replacement. Simmons served up a shutout.

Spread across the front page of The *Telegram* was a headline which read **11-0! WHAT WAS WRONG WITH LEAFS IN <u>THAT</u> GAME?** Four Maple Leaf fans were then photographed and asked for their impressions.

The sports-page headlines said it all:

<u>From the ridiculous to the sublime</u>
IT'S A MAD, MAD, MAD WORLD
LEAFS STUCK WITH SIMMONS
SO HE GIVES THEM A SHUTOUT
- Toronto *Star*

SIMMONS SHAKES SATURDAY EMBARRASSMENT,
BLANKS HAWKS AFTER BRUIN BOMBARDMENT
- *Globe & Mail*

In his daily column, *SPEAKING ON SPORT*, Milt Dunnell of the *Star* summed up the Leafs' roller-coaster weekend:

"...It was hardly cricket that Don Simmons, the unhappy stand-in for Johnny Bower, should be the favourite whipping boy of the fans. He had a bad night — but no worse than that of a dozen Leafs you might name. Toronto didn't have a big-leaguer on the ice at any time. It was the worst display by an NHL club since the war days, when any able-bodied individual who could skate was liable to be grabbed by a desperate coach en route to the rink.

"How to explain it — especially after Leafs went right into Chicago and won their first game of the season on Stadium ice? Maybe the Chicago win wasn't so surprising at that. The Torontos should have been fresh. They didn't do anything strenuous Saturday night — except pick the puck out of the net."

* * * * * *

The Bruins would astound the hockey world again only one week after dismantling the Maple Leafs. Perhaps buoyed by their mastery the previous Saturday, they went into Montreal on January 25 and clobbered the Canadiens 6-0. "That was almost as unreal as the week before," Kurtenbach remembers. "We were just flying."

In the end, however, Boston would cool off and finish dead last in the NHL standings for the fourth consecutive season. The Bruins wound up 23 points out of playoff territory and a whopping 30 points behind Toronto.

Conversely, the Maple Leafs would go on to win their third consecutive Stanley Cup in the spring of 1964, but not before Punch Imlach executed one of the biggest trades in club history. After the bounce-back victory in Chicago, the Leafs stumbled to a 2-7-4 record in their next 13 games. Firmly believing his club was not good enough to defend its championship, Imlach pulled the plug on the morning of Saturday, February 22, acquiring one of the great natural goal-scorers of that era.

He dealt veterans Dick Duff and Bob Nevin, plus farmhands Rod Seiling, Arnie Brown and Bill Collins, to New York, for star winger Andy Bathgate and journeyman Don McKenney. Though Bathgate was fast approaching the downside of his brilliant career (he was coming off a 35-goal season with the Rangers, but would never again reach 20), he was easily the best player in the deal, and Imlach was hoping his scoring touch would re-surface and spark the Leafs to another productive spring.

On the same night of the deal, the Leafs played New York at the Gardens and won, 5-2. Bathgate skated on a forward line with Red Kelly and Frank Mahovlich. The following night, in New York, the Leafs again beat the Rangers, this time 4-3, on a last-minute goal by Dave Keon. The trade seemed to be working out, big time.

In the playoffs, the Leafs got by Montreal in a memorable, seven-game semifinal: Keon scoring all three Toronto goals in a 3-1 deciding-game victory on Forum ice. Maple Leafs then went the limit against Detroit in the finals — *that* series still famous for defenceman Bob Baun's overtime goal, scored on a broken ankle, in Game 6 at the Olympia. Bathgate started the ball rolling in Game 7 back home and the Leafs breezed to a 4-0 Stanley Cup victory.

*   *   *   *   *   *

WHERE ARE THEY NOW? ...

DON SIMMONS, 63, is retired and spends his winters in a house he built on Santa Rosa Beach, Florida. His Maple Leaf days ended in June, 1965, when he was selected by New York in the intra-league draft. He played five games for the Rangers in 1967-68 and five more in 1968-69 before calling it quits. A year later, he started his own business, *Don Simmons Sports*, in Fort Erie, Ont., where he spends his summers. The store caters solely to goaltenders and is now operated by his sons.

ANDY HEBENTON, 65, finished his career with Portland of the Western Hockey League in 1973-74, retiring after seven productive seasons with the Buckaroos. He then started a cement company, *A & L Construction*, and he still lives in Portland.

ORLAND KURTENBACH, 58, was the original captain of the Vancouver Canucks, when that city entered the NHL as an expansion team in 1970-71. He retired after the 1973-74 season and coached the Canucks from 1976-78. He is currently an insurance broker in South Surrey, B.C., having recently sold a golf driving range.

LEO BOIVIN, 62, played 19 years in the NHL, retiring as a member of the Minnesota North Stars after the 1969-70 season. He later went on to scout for, and briefly coach, the St. Louis Blues and he recently retired after 11 years as Quebec-area scout for the Hartford Whalers. Elected to the Hockey Hall of Fame in 1986, one of the game's all-time hardest and cleanest body checkers now lives in his hometown of Prescott, Ont.

GARY DORNHOEFER, 51, was selected from Boston by Philadelphia in the 1967 expansion draft and he went on to play 12 years for the Flyers. His rugged approach fit perfectly with the "Broad Street Bullies" image, and he was a key member of the Flyers' Stanley Cup teams in 1974 and '75. After retiring in 1978, Dornhoefer worked for several years as a colour analyst with *Hockey Night In Canada*. Living now in Voorhees, N.J., he does colour commentary on the Flyers' TV games.

MURRAY OLIVER, 57, concluded his 17-year NHL career with Minnesota in 1974-75. He coached the North Stars for 39 games in 1981-82 and '82-83 and stayed on after that as a scout. He still makes his home in Edina, Min., but is currently the Director of Pro Scouting for the Vancouver Canucks.

JOHNNY BUCYK, 58, scored 556 goals during a brilliant 23-year career with Detroit and Boston, and was being chased during the 1993-94 season by Jari Kurri of Los Angeles for ninth on the all-time NHL goal-scoring list. He was captain of the Bruins' Stanley Cup teams in 1970 and

'72, retiring after the 1975-76 season. He still makes his home in Boston and has been the Bruins' radio colour analyst for the past 14 seasons. He was elected to the Hockey Hall of Fame in 1981.

MILT SCHMIDT, 76, was a great center-iceman for the Bruins between 1936-37 and 1954-55, playing on the famed "Kraut Line" with wingers Bobby Bauer and Woody Dumart. He coached the Bruins from 1954-61, then again from 1962-66, and was the club's general manager from 1967-72. In May, 1967, he pulled off the most one-sided trade in NHL history, acquiring Phil Esposito from the Chicago Blackhawks. Schmidt was the original general manager of the Washington Capitals in 1974-75, and he also coached the team briefly in his two years there. He is currently assistant manager of the *Garden Club* (working with former Bruin Don Marcotte), a private club catering to 600 members during the hockey and basketball season, at the Boston Garden.

EDDIE SHACK, 57, was the wackiest hockey player of his era, and maybe of all time. "The Entertainer", as he was known, would do practically anything to get a rise out of the crowd, his teammates, and his coaches, but we must not forget that he scored more than 20 goals a season for five different NHL teams — Toronto, Boston, Los Angeles, Pittsburgh and Buffalo. Shack played from 1958 to 1975 and has spent the ensuing years promoting and selling various products, ranging from garbage.bags, to Christmas trees, to doughnuts. Eddie still makes his home in Toronto.

BOB NEVIN, 56, went on to captain New York in the late-60s and early-70s, after being dealt to the Rangers by Punch Imlach. He was traded to Minnesota for Bobby Rousseau in May, 1971, and finished his NHL career with Los Angeles from 1973-76. Strangely, his best season was his second-last in the NHL (1974-75), when he set career highs for goals (31), assists (41) and points (72) with the Kings. Nevin lives in East York, Ont., and does some bartending at *Soupy's Tavern* in downtown Toronto. He also plays a lot of hockey for the Maple Leafs' alumni team.

BILLY HARRIS, 59, was a role player for the Maple Leafs from 1955-65 and he wrote a wonderful book about his experiences with the Stanley Cup champions of that era. *THE GLORY YEARS* is both good reading and a valuable reference point. Harris also played with Detroit, Oakland and Pittsburgh in the NHL, retiring after the 1968-69 season. He went on to coach in the World Hockey Association with the Toronto Toros and was an assistant coach with Edmonton when the Oilers joined the NHL in 1979. Billy lives in Etobicoke, Ont., is very popular on the banquet circuit, and plays a lot of alumni hockey.

BILL FRIDAY, 61, was a flashy NHL referee from 1960 to 1972. He then jumped to the WHA as its senior referee and stayed with the league throughout its entire seven-year existence (1972-79). He was the WHA's referee-in-chief in its final four years. Now retired, Friday lives in Hamilton during the summer and spends the winter months on a golf course in Titusville, Fla. He still officiates a number of NHL alumni games.

*   *   *   *   *   *

GAME SUMMARY
Boston 11 at Toronto 0
January 18, 1964

BOSTON
Goal- Johnston
Defence - Johnson, Mohns, Green, Boivin, McCord
Forwards- Oliver, Dornhoefer, Bucyk, Kurtenbach, Prentice, Hebenton, Leiter, Kennedy, Gendron, Toppazzini

TORONTO
Goal- Simmons
Defence- Stanley, Baun, Horton, Brewer, Brown
Forwards- Pulford, Shack, Nevin, Keon, Duff, Armstrong, Harris, Kelly, Stewart, Mahovlich, Stemkowski

Referee- Bill Friday
Linesmen- Dave Smith,
Matt Pavelich

First Period
1. Boston, Dornhoefer 3 (Bucyk, Oliver) :53
2. Boston, Hebenton 6 (Kurtenbach, Prentice) 6:20
3. Boston, Oliver 14 (Bucyk, Boivin) 9:02
4. Boston, Prentice 14 (Kurtenbach) 9:28
5. Boston, Hebenton 7 (Prentice) 14:51

6. Boston, Prentice 15 (Kurtenbach) 19:54

Second Period
7. Boston, Hebenton, (Leiter, Prentice) 12:27

Third Period
8. Boston, Oliver 15 (Bucyk, Green) 2:11
9. Boston, Prentice 16 (Hebenton) 6:17
10. Boston, Bucyk 8 (Oliver, Dornhoefer) 7:04
11. Boston, Gendron 2 (Kennedy, McCord) 15:47

Shots on Goal

Boston 15	10	13	38
Toronto 7	9	10	26

Attendance- 14,011

... Leafs in Spring ...

MAY 1, 1993
Somewhere Along Highway 401

The sun was low in the western sky as I made the long drive to Detroit for the third time in two weeks. Susan and I had moved into our new house in Thornhill just the previous day and I felt somewhat guilty leaving her with the hundred or so boxes that required unpacking. As I motored along the westbound 401, I rhetorically asked myself why in the world I was making this trip.

Just two nights earlier, the Red Wings had vehemently avoided elimination, pounding the Maple Leafs 7-3 at the Gardens to square the division semifinal at three games apiece. With so much credibility at stake, the Wings couldn't possibly blow the series on home ice... could they? The prevailing sentiment I'd left behind in Toronto was that the Leafs had done themselves proud, but were now poised for the execution.

Somewhere between London and Chatham, I was listening to the radio when an FM rock station played Neil Young's ballad "Long May You Run". And I had an instant blast of deja vu. Ironically, I had purchased that album on the afternoon of the Maple Leafs' Game 7 showdown with the New York Islanders 15 years earlier. I listened to the title track over and over again that day, with so many of the same thoughts swirling through my mind about the hockey game later that night.

"There's no way the Leafs can beat the Islanders," I kept on telling myself — preparing for the inevitable.

Well, we all know what happened, thanks to Lanny McDonald.

Now here I was, a decade-and-a-half later... the Maple Leafs were embarking on a Game 7 situation for the first time since Lanny's goal, and "Long May You Run" was on the radio. Could it be an omen?

*   *   *   *   *   *

The press box at Joe Louis Arena was evidently an afterthought in the building's grand scheme. Tucked away behind the last row of seats, writers and broadcasters play "What's My Line" as they try and decipher one skater from another. The white dots are the Detroit players, while the coloured dots are the visitors.

As a result, there was little disappointment in being relegated to the "auxiliary" press location for the Maple Leaf-Red Wing series. It was roughly the same distance from the ice as the main box, but in the corner, and among a sea of rabid Detroit fans. Mark Hebscher of Global TV sat with me throughout the series and even he seemed timid in that section of fanatics (if it's possible for Hebscher to be timid).

We were surrounded by tumultuous celebration during the first two games of the series, as Detroit skated rings around the Maple Leafs. When we left to do our post-game work after the second match, none of the locals were expecting to see us again till the following season. To be honest, the feeling was mutual.

But much had changed by the time we re-appeared for Game 5, six days later. The early series haughtiness had been replaced by a thick aura of apprehension: the type that goes with being a Detroit Red Wing fan come playoff time. When the Wings have a one-goal lead in the third period at Joe Louis Arena, there's a foreboding anxiety in the building. You can almost sense defeat in the air, as the quiet Detroit fans wait for the proverbial shoe to drop. And, it usually does.

In this particular series, that shoe was a clodhopper.

The Red Wings systematically blew a 4-1 lead and lost Game 5 on an overtime goal by Mike Foligno. An atmosphere of resignation had gripped the arena by the time regulation play expired. The Leafs had every bit of momentum, and the extra period lasted just more than two minutes: an outcome that surprised nobody in the building.

The setting and environment was almost identical four nights later in the deciding seventh match. With regulation time rapidly perishing, Detroit held a 3-2 lead, but the clock seemed to be standing still. And while Doug Gilmour's tying goal at 17:17 of the third period brought an overwhelming sense of relief to Toronto fans, it appeared to have been ordained by a higher authority.

Still, the series winner by Nikolai Borschevsky at 2:35 of the first extra period thoroughly stunned Joe Louis Arena. Having retreated to the press room at the end of regulation, I watched the decisive play unfold from the tunnel area next to the Detroit bench. And I'll never forget how three or four Red Wing players shouted, in perfect unison, "Oh SHIT!" when Borschevsky's tip-in eluded Tim Cheveldae.

While the euphoric Maple Leaf players poured onto the ice (even coach Burns had an ear-to-ear grin), it seemed as if rigor-mortis had set in on the Detroit bench. The losers sat paralysed with gloom and I recall how Steve Yzerman leaned on the boards — the colour drained from his face — shaking his head in absolute disbelief.

I also remember the beleaguered Cheveldae skating morosely to the bench — glancing over his shoulder at least a half-dozen times — as if to affirm that Borschevsky's puck had indeed gone into the net.

All that seemed to be missing, from my standpoint, was a rendition of "Long May You Run" on the Joe Louis P.A. system.

FINALLY, A PLAYOFF TRIUMPH!

Maple Leaf Gardens / Los Angeles Forum
April 8-11, 1975

When the Maple Leafs opened their 1974-75 season against the NHL's new expansion team from Kansas City, the club's ultimate objective was to end the longest playoff drought in its 58-year history.

Not since defeating Montreal in the 1967 Stanley Cup Final had the Leafs won a playoff series. In the ensuing seven years, they had missed the post-season tournament three times (1968-70-73) and had lost first-round match-ups against Boston (1969-72-74) and the Rangers (1971). One more futile spring would break the dubious seven-year mark — shared by Maple Leafs teams of 1952 - 1958.

Avoiding that record seemed like a genuine possibility just the year before, as the Maple Leafs rebounded from a dreadful season more quickly than anyone could have imagined. The frugality of owner Harold Ballard had seemingly destroyed the franchise in one fell swoop. Treating the up-start World Hockey Association with ill-advised disdain, Ballard practically challenged the new league to steal some of his better players. The WHA accepted... with glee.

Ballard ignored the admonishing of general manager Jim Gregory — locked away his riches — and suffered a first-degree burn. In the space of one off-season (the summer of 1972), a total of five players jumped ship and signed with WHA teams.

The most damaging loss was world-class goaltender Bernie Parent, who joined Miami (later Philadelphia). But the young Maple Leaf defence corps crumbled with the defections of Brad Selwood, Rick Ley and Jim Dorey to New England. Dorey had been traded to the Rangers for Pierre Jarry late in the previous season, but only after making *his* WHA intentions known.

Up front, the Maple Leafs lost a pair of useful centremen. Neither Jim Harrison nor Guy Trottier were prolific scorers, but they had other endearing qualities. Both were excellent penalty killers and Harrison played with a controlled mean streak. Trottier had a burst of speed that frequently came in handy. Ballard, however, refused to lay out the cash that would've kept the two players in Toronto.

Not able to withstand such a grievous loss of personnel, the 1972-73 Maple Leafs finished with the third-worst record in the 16-team NHL, behind even the expansion Atlanta Flames.

The club started the 1971-72 season with a goaltending tandem of Jacques Plante and Bernie Parent — among the two finest in hockey history. But Parent's defection in '72 laid too much onus on the 44-year-old Plante, who received inadequate support the following year from newcomers Ron Low and Gord McRae.

On the blueline, the Maple Leafs were in a shambles.

Compounding the WHA predicament was a career-ending neck injury suffered by veteran Bob Baun only five games into the '72-73 season. A collision with Mickey Redmond of Detroit at the Gardens forced Baun to quit hockey. The incumbent defenders (Jim McKenny, Brian Glennie, Mike Pelyk, Joe Lundrigan, John Grisdale, Larry McIntyre, and Dave Fortier) were generally bereft of quality and experience. It thus came as little surprise that the Leafs permitted a total of 279 goals: by far, the most-ever to that point in franchise history.

Only the savvy of general manager Gregory — a man never accorded the respect he deserved — rescued the club from years of doom.

A shrewd combination of draft picks, free-agent signings and trades in the summer of 1973 re-constructed the depleted roster.

With a playoff spot unattainable, Gregory traded Plante to Boston late in the '72-73 season for goalie Ed Johnston and the Bruins' first-round draft choice. With that pick, Gregory chose Ian Turnbull, an alluring defence prospect from Ottawa of the OHA. With his *own* draft choice, third overall, he grabbed high-scoring winger Lanny McDonald of the Medicine Hat Tigers. Bob Neely was chosen in between.

Chief scout Gerry McNamara returned from a trip to Sweden highly recommending that Gregory sign defenceman Borje Salming and left-winger Inge Hammarstrom. The general manager complied. When Parent returned to the NHL after only one season in the WHA — and insisted on playing in Philadelphia — Gregory traded him to the Flyers for Doug Favell and a first-rounder (Neely). He added further goaltending depth by peddling no-names McIntyre and Murray Heatley to Vancouver for Dunc Wilson.

Having suffered through a justifiable chain of stomach ailments, John McLellan was mercifully relieved of his coaching responsibilities and replaced by one-time Maple Leaf icon Red Kelly (from Pittsburgh). And Gregory's coup de grace was purchasing the ever-popular Eddie Shack from the Penguins: fresh off a 25-goal season. The "Entertainer" had last worn a Toronto jersey in 1967.

The massive re-tooling worked superbly, as the 1973-74 Maple Leafs engineered a 22-point improvement and qualified for the playoffs by a comfortable 10-point margin over Buffalo. Unfortunately, they drew the powerful Boston Bruins as a first-round opponent and got blown away in four consecutive games. Phil Esposito, Bobby Orr and Co. went on to the Stanley Cup final that spring, losing in an upset to Philadelphia. The Toronto streak without a playoff victory reached seven years.

Ironically, less became expected of the Maple Leafs the following season, as they kind of wobbled through 1974-75. The club had lost Paul Henderson and Mike Pelyk to the WHA, and traded winger Rick Kehoe to Pittsburgh for unproven Blaine Stoughton. But it seemed to have made quality additions in veteran forwards Bill Flett and Gary Sabourin; defencemen Rod Seiling and Dave Dunn.

As well, center Darryl Sittler had blossomed into the star player everyone figured he'd be when the Leafs drafted him from London of the OHA in 1970. Left-winger Errol Thompson became a threat up front with 25 goals, while rookie Dave (Tiger) Williams came up from the farm to provide unabashed toughness: a missing ingredient prior to his arrival. All of the elements seemed to be in place for a continued improvement.

However, nothing clicked for the Maple Leafs until late-February of 1975, when the club laid a 9-2 pounding on the Minnesota North Stars in Bloomington. An incredible spat of timely goals (against generally weaker opposition) followed — propelling the Leafs on an undefeated string of nine games (7-0-2) that came to an unceremonious halt during an 11-3 pasting by Buffalo at the Gardens.

During the streak, the Maple Leafs scored two goals in the final minute of play to avoid an embarrassing home-ice loss to Washington. The expansion Capitals, who would win only eight of 80 games, lost 5-4. Sittler scored in the dying seconds to nip Detroit, 4-3, at the Gardens and a microcosm of the unbeaten streak occurred during its final game: a 4-4 home-ice tie against Philadelphia, Mar. 15.

While skating to the bench for a line-change in the third period, Rod Seiling routinely dumped the puck into the Flyer zone from 115 feet away. Amazingly, it took four hops and bounced over the stick of Bernie Parent — the NHL's best goalie — into the Philadelphia net, erasing a 4-3 deficit. But the Sabres brought everybody back down to earth with an eight-goal thrashing the following night.

The hot streak coincided with the emergence of Tiger Williams as a legitimate NHLer. Selected by Gregory in the second round of the 1974 draft (31st overall), Williams ploughed through his first training camp with fire and brimstone — despite an injury caused by (of all things) lacing his skates too tightly before a workout. Tiger had a reputation to uphold as the tough kid from out west, where he performed remarkably with the Junior 'A' Swift Current Broncos the previous year — scoring 52 goals and amassing 310 penalty minutes.

At training camp with the Leafs, Williams acted cocky to the point of being obnoxious. On his very first shift, he attacked Ian Turnbull and flailed away at the Maple Leaf defenceman, soon to be his teammate. An unforgettable TV interview with Tiger had the word "fuck" beeped out so many times, it sounded like a *Roadrunner* episode. Williams took on all comers during the exhibition games, but didn't fare too well in his scraps, or in the goalscoring department. The Maple Leafs were counting on him to provide both elements.

An alleged sucker-punch by Keith Magnuson of Chicago ended his quest to start the regular season in Toronto. Magnuson corked Williams near the Blackhawk bench and knocked him cold. Tiger staggered to the penalty box in the *Twilight Zone* and had to be helped to the Maple Leaf dressing room. Two days later, he was dispatched to the club's top farm team in Oklahoma City. "He not only can't skate, he can't fight," were the words of Jim Gregory upon Tiger's demotion.

But Williams hadn't made it that far on innate skill. He was a roughneck who compensated for his natural shortcomings with bare-faced enthusiasm, and it eventually led him back to the NHL. The absence of a legitimate "policeman" hastened Tiger's recall.

A soft Toronto team reacted with alarming passivity one night to a blatant spear by Bobby Clarke of Philadelphia on Seiling. The Buds were easily pushed around and the losses piled up. In a Dec. 30 game at Pittsburgh, Shack took an unmerciful beating from Penguins' defenceman Bob Gassoff and no one intervened on his behalf.

Maple Leaf management had finally seen enough and King Clancy told Gregory it was time to promote Williams. Tiger joined the Leafs the first week of January and played his inaugural NHL game at the Nassau Coliseum against the New York Islanders — Jan. 7, 1975 — skating on a forward line with Darryl Sittler and Gary Sabourin.

Tiger's first NHL fight occurred in the Maple Leafs' next road game, eight days later, at St. Louis. On a face-off, Williams took a hard shot to the snout from veteran Blues' defenceman Barclay Plager. He responded by dropping his gloves and the two players engaged in a lively scrap. His legend established, Tiger didn't spend another moment in the minor leagues for the next 10 years.

Three nights after the game — on Sat. Jan. 18, at Montreal — Williams scored his first of 241 NHL goals: the winner in a 5-3 victory over the Canadiens. He took a pass from Ron Ellis on a two-on-one and "roofed" one past Ken Dryden. He was in the NHL to stay.

When the regular-season ended with a 4-4 tie in Boston, Apr. 6, the Maple Leafs had regressed by eight points from the previous year. They qualified as the 12th (and final) team under the NHL's new playoff format. That was the year the NHL disbanded the East-West arrangement, splitting into two conferences and four divisions. The Norris and Adams divisions made up the Prince of Wales Conference, while the Patrick and Smythe divisions comprised the Clarence Campbell Conference.

The four division winners (Montreal, Buffalo, Philadelphia and Vancouver) received first-round byes. The second and third-place teams in each division were then aligned 1-through-8 based on points attained during the season. They paired off during a best-of-three preliminary playoff round (home-away-home). That group of teams appeared like so:

LOS ANGELES	105 points
BOSTON	94 points
PITTSBURGH	89 points
NEW YORK RANGERS	88 points
NEW YORK ISLANDERS	88 points
ST. LOUIS	84 points
CHICAGO	82 points
TORONTO	78 points

As a result, these were the preliminary playoff match-ups in 1974-75 (teams with home-ice advantage in CAPITAL letters):

LOS ANGELES vs. Toronto
BOSTON vs. Chicago
PITTSBURGH vs. St. Louis
NEW YORK RANGERS vs. New York Islanders

Having to meet Los Angeles in the opening round seemed to be an almost-certain pathway to yet another winless Maple Leaf springtime. The Kings had enjoyed the finest season in their eight-year history — riding an air-tight defensive system and the spectacular goaltending of Rogatien Vachon to 105 points. It remains a team record for one season and was good enough for fourth place in the overall NHL standings.

Los Angeles compiled its terrific record (three more points than any season in the Wayne Gretzky era) without the presence of a bonafide superstar. Marcel Dionne was still playing for Detroit. The Kings' top forward line of Butch Goring, Bob Nevin and Dan Maloney had a bit of everything, but the 37-year-old Nevin — in his 16th NHL season — led the club in scoring with 31 goals and only 72 points. That wasn't much when compared with the top four point producers in 1974-75: Bobby Orr (135), Phil Esposito (127), Dionne (121) and Guy Lafleur (119).

A second-line unit of Gene Carr, Mike Murphy and Tom Williams was solid but unspectacular. The late Juha Widing (26 goals) and veteran Bob Berry (25 goals) contributed offensively but the remaining cast of skaters were journeymen like Don Kozak, Vic Venasky, Mike Corrigan and Frank St. Marseille.

The Kings had little offensive savvy on the blueline. Bob Murdoch supplied a bit of oomph with 42 points from his defensive position, but his teammates were strictly stay-at-home types. Terry Harper, Sheldon Kannegeiser, Larry Brown, Dave Hutchison and Neil Komadoski *combined* for 13 goals during the regular season and Harper led that group with a paltry 26 points.

The Kings did have a true star in net, as Vachon enjoyed a monster season with a 2.24 goals-against average and six shutouts in 54 games. He received more than adequate support from back-up Gary Edwards, who had a 2.34 average in 26 appearances, losing on only three occasions.

Vachon had played on a trio of Stanley Cup winners in Montreal (1968-69-71) before his trade to Los Angeles for Denis Dejordy, Noel

Price, Dale Hoganson and Doug Robinson on Nov. 4, 1971. And despite the 105-point season, he maintains the 1974-75 Los Angeles club was a mere shadow of the teams he played for in Montreal.

"We didn't have a lot of depth with the Kings," he says. "The only reason we were so successful that year is we believed in the defensive system of (coach) Bob Pulford and played it to a `T'. Our scheme was to allow the first shot from the point, have the defence clear the front of the net, and receive help from two forwards always coming back deep.

"When we got out of that system, we couldn't compete. The Montreal teams I played for could adjust to any situation."

Los Angeles easily had its way with Toronto during five regular-season meetings in 1974-75, outscoring the Maple Leafs 24-7. Toronto did not score a goal at The Forum, losing 4-0 and 8-0. All indications pointed to a very one-sided playoff victory for the Kings.

"We went into that series feeling we would definitely beat the Leafs," acknowledges Mike Murphy, later an assistant coach to Pat Burns; then a 30-goal shooter with the Kings. "We respected the players on their team — guys like Dave Keon and Ron Ellis, who had won Stanley Cups — but we played them so well during the regular season, nobody figured we'd lose the series."

However, the Kings entered the playoffs at less-than full strength — both physically and emotionally.

Center Butch Goring, their offensive sparkplug, almost lost his right eye in a freak accident with Denis Potvin of the Islanders and had to miss the final month of the regular season. In a Mar. 4 game at The Forum, Goring pushed Potvin off balance while forechecking the sophomore defenceman. The plastic tip on the heel of Potvin's skate came up and hit Goring in the eye, shattering his orbital bone. While Goring returned for the playoffs, he was suffering from double vision in the upper and lower portions of the eye.

As well, the father of robust winger Dan Maloney had taken ill on Apr. 6 while the Kings were in Oakland for their final regular-season game. A diabetic, Mr. Maloney died of heart failure the next day and his son was in an understandably sombre mood to start the playoffs.

The series began in Inglewood, Calif. on the night of Tue. Apr. 8, 1975. The opener started at 11 p.m. Toronto time and coincided with the telecast of the 1975 Academy Awards, also taking place in Los Angeles. The Canadian Broadcasting Corporation had national TV rights for the Oscars: one of the most watched television events of the year. As a result — and for the first time since the advent of TV — hockey fans in

Toronto were not able to view a Maple Leaf playoff game on CBC.

In a last-minute step, Maple Leaf Gardens decided to show the game on its large, closed-circuit screen. But the announcement came so late that a very small audience showed up. A side-bar story in the Toronto *Sun*, entitled **"ON THE BIG SCREEN..."**, recounted the setting:

"A young and shrill crowd of about 4,000 made more noise than usual sellouts at Maple Leaf Gardens for the opening of the Leafs-Kings playoff game, televised on closed-circuit from Los Angeles.

"The gathering was mostly male, and mostly in the early 20s, and everybody yelled at anything that moved on the big screen.

"The floor covering the ice surface was filled with some 1,800 people and the rest were scattered through the golds and reds. All seats were $6."

A Toronto *Star* report said that 7,609 fans had attended the closed-circuit telecast of the hockey game.

The smallish Gardens crowd, and the thousands of fans listening to the game on radio in their homes, went to sleep disappointed in the wee hours of Wednesday morning, as Los Angeles beat the Maple Leafs 3-2 in overtime. It was a heart-wrenching loss for the Leafs, who had tied the game with 1:30 left in regulation time on a goal by Ron Ellis.

But an error in judgement by Leaf defenceman Jim McKenny cost the visitors the game. McKenny went in deep and tried to win a race for the puck to the left of the Los Angeles net. But, Kings' defenceman Larry Brown beat him there and fed a pass to center Gene Carr, who sped away on a partial break down the left side — McKenny's defencemate, Dave Dunn, the only man back.

Carr held the puck long enough for Mike Murphy to catch up and sent a cross-ice feed that Murphy rapped into a vacant Toronto goal at 8:53 of the extra period. The 12,426 fans at The Forum went home happy and relieved.

"McKenny pinched in and Carr and I had pretty much a two-on-one," Murphy recalls of the winning goal. "The Leaf goalie, Gord McRae, came out to challenge Carr and I just broke for the net. Gene made a great pass and I had a six-by-four staring me right in the face. There was no way I could botch it up."

Bob Berry had opened the scoring for Los Angeles at 14:31 of the first period, flipping a rebound off the backboards over McRae. Kings' right-winger Don Kozak had taken the initial shot. But, the Leafs tied it up with their first goal of the season on Los Angeles ice just 1:09 later. It was a play hotly disputed by the Kings, who felt that Inge Hammarstrom had not kept the puck onside at the L.A. blueline. With a sweeping motion, Hammarstrom sent it to Blaine Stoughton, who fed Dave Keon behind the Kings' net.

Coach Bob Pulford rushed to the boards to argue with the linesman and while the crowd booed vociferously, Stoughton got into position to fire Keon's return pass over Vachon's right shoulder.

Carr re-gained the lead for Los Angeles at 16:25 of the second period with a low backhand shot that fooled McRae and the Kings held that 2-1 advantage until the dying moments of the game. With less than two minutes left, however, Darryl Sittler carried the puck into the Kings' zone and passed to Tiger Williams near the front of the net. Williams looked very cool for a rookie, as he dropped the puck to Ron Ellis in the slot, and the Maple Leaf veteran slapped it past Vachon at 18:30, sending the game into overtime.

The Maple Leafs had difficulty accepting the loss afterwards.

"If they think we gave them trouble tonight, wait till we get them in Toronto," an angry Rod Seiling told hockey writer Red Burnett in the Toronto *Star*. "We'll be back here Friday (for Game 3)."

Regarding his mistake on the overtime winner, McKenny explained: "I tried to help (Dave) Keon out in the corner and got trapped. I got away with the same play shortly before and we almost got a goal. It was a gamble that didn't pay off."

Maple Leaf coach Red Kelly, forever the optimist, sounded much like Seiling during his post-game oration.

"We are not out of it," he told Burnett. "All we have to do is work hard and we'll beat them two straight. Overall, our team played very well and worked their heads off. (Gord) McRae was good in goal. I knew he would be. I have a lot of confidence in that young man.

"One mistake cost us in the end. We got sucked in and that's what happens in overtime. You can't make a mistake and survive. This is the first time we've played well here and at least we're getting closer."

The star of the game for Los Angeles — with his second-period goal, and his assist on the winner — was Gene Carr. A prolific scorer in Junior with Flin Flon, Carr had been the fourth overall selection (by St. Louis) in the 1971 amateur draft. It turned out to be a grave error by the Blues, as Carr was a failure, offensively, during his NHL career. The Blues quickly gave up on him and he later played for the Rangers, Los Angeles, Pittsburgh and Atlanta.

Carr's best season was 1977-78, when the KIngs traded him to the

Penguins along with Dave Schultz, for Syl Apps and Hartland Monahan. In 75 games that year, he had 19 goals and 37 assists for 56 points... all three totals representing career highs.

And to think, St. Louis could have drafted any of the following players ahead of Carr: Richard Martin (Buffalo), Steve Vickers (New York Rangers), Terry O'Reilly (Boston), Craig Ramsay (Buffalo), Larry Robinson (Montreal) and Rick Kehoe (Toronto). Ouch!!

Regardless, Carr was the man of the hour during that first playoff game against the Maple Leafs in 1975, and he commented on setting up Murphy's overtime winner.

"I was winding up with a shot as I crossed the Toronto blueline but I sensed that (Dave) Dunn was going to take me," he explained. "I pulled back to complete a fake, then passed to Murphy. It had to be a hard pass because I was afraid Dunn might reach it with his stick. He played me very well and Murphy did a great job of fielding the pass."

The clubs flew to Toronto for Game 2 Thursday night and were both facing a conundrum in the event of a Maple Leaf victory. The third and deciding match had been scheduled by the NHL for Saturday afternoon back in Los Angeles, but Kings' general manager Jake Milford figured that very few people would show up at The Forum for a hockey matinee, regardless of the game's significance.

As a result, he re-scheduled the potential decider for Friday night, just 24 hours after the middle game in Toronto. Such an arrangement was unheard of during the regular season, as clubs had at least one day — usually, two or three — to recover from long trips to the opposite coast. But, Milford was looking out for Number One.

"We won't draw bees on a Saturday afternoon," he explained. "It means the teams will have to fly back from Toronto on Friday morning."

Game Two of the preliminary round series — Apr. 10, at Maple Leaf Gardens — established the brief legend of Blaine Stoughton in Toronto. Acquired from Pittsburgh for Rick Kehoe in September, 1974, the second-year right-winger kept the Leafs alive by scoring an overtime goal to send the series back to Los Angeles. It was his lone moment of glory in a short Maple Leaf career, but it somehow remains so easily recallable by Toronto hockey fans who saw the game.

Inge Hammarstrom carried the puck over the Los Angeles blueline and passed to Dave Keon. Kings' defencemen Larry Brown and Terry Harper backed in, expecting Keon to shoot. But the veteran Maple Leaf center dropped the puck to a wide-open Stoughton in the high slot and it was game over. Hammarstrom went to the net and partially screened Vachon as Stoughton's hard shot found the left corner at 10:19 of the first extra period. Maple Leafs won the game, 3-2.

Again, it was Toronto that had to come back in the third period. With Jim McKenny serving a penalty, Mike Murphy scored his second goal of the night at 4:05 to break a 1-1 tie. He took a pass from Carr and drilled a low shot that hit McRae's pad and trickled into the net.

Less than five minutes later, however, the Leafs tied it up again on a goal by Dave Dunn. Vachon stopped Keon's long shot but allowed the rebound to dribble in front of him. Dunn quickly moved in and scooped the puck up under the crossbar at 8:45. Ron Ellis had two glorious chances to end the game in regulation time for the Maple Leafs, but Vachon stymied him on both occasions.

Unlike the overtime session in Game One, the extra period of Game 2 was played at a fast, wide-open pace. Butch Goring almost won the series for Los Angeles when he raced down the right side and beat McRae with a 45-foot slapshot. But the puck deflected off McRae's right skate and missed the net by three feet.

Stoughton ended the evening two minutes later.

Darryl Sittler had opened the scoring for Toronto in the first period, while Murphy's first goal of the night was the lone marker of the middle frame.

There had been much criticism over the deal that brought Stoughton to Toronto. Chosen by the Penguins in the first round (7th overall) of the 1973 draft, Stoughton spent the majority of his rookie season with Hershey of the American Hockey League. He scored only five goals in 34 games with Pittsburgh during the second half of the schedule. Gregory acquired him for a player (Kehoe) who had scored 33 goals in a Toronto uniform just two years earlier. The trade seemed not to make a lot of sense and the critics grew in number when Kehoe outscored Stoughton 32-23 during the 1974-75 regular season.

But all of that was momentarily forgotten when Stoughton extended the Maple Leaf-Los Angeles series with his overtime goal. "How many winners has Kehoe scored for Pittsburgh in their playoffs?" he asked in defiance after the game. He then commented on his goal, saying, "It was really the only decent chance I had all night. Dave (Keon) made a super play for me. All I had to do was pull the trigger."

Vachon remembers having no chance on the play. "Stoughton was in a perfect position and he had a good shot. I was a bit sidetracked by Hammarstrom but I doubt I would have made the save, even if I had seen it clearly. Blaine knew how to drill the puck pretty good."

Had Stoughton not been so young and irresponsible, he might have enjoyed a brilliant career in a Maple Leaf uniform. The record clearly shows that after spending three seasons in the WHA, he returned to the NHL with Hartford in 1979-80 and scored 56 goals, tying Charlie Simmer of L.A. and Danny Gare of Buffalo for the league lead. He followed up with seasons of 43, 52 and 45 goals for the Whalers, finishing his NHL career in 1983-84 with a total of 258.

But his hard-living ways had caused the Maple Leafs to give up on him after only two seasons, and he defected to Cincinnati of the WHA — scoring 52 goals his first year there (1976-77).

"Looking back on it, I regret not staying in the NHL — no doubt about it," Stoughton says nowadays. "Unfortunately, I wasn't committed to the game during my two seasons in Toronto. I was a young guy, making some decent money, and I enjoyed life a little too much. I stayed out late at night, drank excessively, and never worked hard enough at my conditioning. I only did what came naturally to me on the ice and that wasn't nearly enough for the Maple Leafs."

Stoughton played 43 games for the Leafs in 1975-76 and scored only six goals. Kehoe, meanwhile, had another solid year in Pittsburgh with 29 goals and 76 points. The trade was a disaster for Toronto and Maple Leaf management simply did not believe Stoughton when he made promises to get his act together during the off-season.

"I didn't like the feeling I was getting from the Leafs so I went to the WHA," Stoughton recalls. "I wound up signing a three-year deal with Cincinnati and doubled my salary (to $100,000), so it wasn't all bad. But in retrospect, I should have stayed in Toronto, signed a one-year contract, and proven myself at the NHL level. If I had scored 40 or 50 goals there, who knows what opportunities would have come my way.

"There's no doubt in my mind I could've had a big year in Toronto. I had re-committed myself in the summer of 1976 and that's why I played so well when I got to Cincinnati. But the Maple Leafs wouldn't believe me when I told them I started living properly and our negotiations went nowhere. It was just poor timing.

"However, I took something with me from Toronto that proved to be very beneficial. It was the influence of Darryl Sittler. Watching him made me change my work ethic. Darryl played hard, kept himself in shape during the off-season and was a real level-headed guy. Dave Keon was also very good to me, but Sittler is the player I admired the most."

The Maple Leafs and Kings had precious little time to travel back to

Los Angeles for the deciding game of their preliminary series, less than 24 hours after the conclusion of Game 2. Harold Ballard anted up $15,000 to charter an aircraft and the Leafs flew back to California overnight, arriving in L.A. at 3 a.m., local time. The Kings slept in Toronto and caught a commercial flight home the next morning, which had them flying almost five hours across North America on the very day of the deciding match.

"I suppose the team that wins will have chosen the best approach to getting to California," said Kings' defenceman Sheldon Kannegeisser. "It seems pretty dumb that we have to play back-to-back games in the playoffs in cities more than 2,000 miles apart."

The travel decisions were influenced by economics. Ballard, who had lots of money but rarely spent it, chartered a Boeing-727 for 15 grand. Flying commercially cost the cash-strapped Kings $11,000 less. The Los Angeles organization was so money conscious, it couldn't even afford to hire a scout to prepare an advanced report on the Leafs.

The Kings were a concerned lot heading into Game 3. Finishing with a 27-point edge on the Maple Leafs during the regular season made them overwhelming favourites to win the series, but the teams were dead even and the Leafs were beginning to gain an edge physically. Veterans Dan Maloney and Dave Hutchison were the henchmen for L.A., but Maloney's fiery spirit had waned with the death of his father.

"I didn't sleep well for a few days after Dad passed away and it probably affected my play," Maloney remembers. "You don't like to admit that you're not yourself, especially during an important time of year like the playoffs. I played as well as I could, but I guess the Leafs recognized that I wasn't up to speed. We had a close-knit team in Los Angeles and if something bad happened to one guy, everybody felt it."

The decision to move Game 3 to Friday night paid off handsomely at the box office, as all 16,005 seats at The Forum were sold. The rubber-match began at 10 p.m. Toronto time and was carried nationwide across the CBC television network. The Kings' strategy to start the game was obvious, but it proved to be a futile waste of energy.

Although the Keon-Stoughton-Hammarstrom line had done most of the scoring damage for the Maple Leafs, Los Angeles coach Pulford evidently felt he had to try and upset Darryl Sittler. Just four seconds after the opening face-off, Gene Carr provoked Sittler into an exchange of high sticks and the two players received minor penalties. At the 3:21 mark, Tiger Williams and Mike Murphy started shoving, and Carr again went after Sittler. All four players went to the box and the Kings were succeeding in keeping Sittler off the ice.

With the teams playing three-on-three, however, Maple Leafs landed the first important blow by opening the scoring. Center George Ferguson — in his third year with the Leafs — took a pass from Dave Dunn and motored around defenceman Larry Brown. He then beat Vachon with a high shot to the glove side at 4:55, giving Toronto a 1-0 lead. Playing the same defensive system as Los Angeles — and receiving timely saves from Gord McRae — the Maple Leafs nursed their one-goal advantage into the late stages of the second period, then added to it at the 14:34 mark.

Hammarstrom intercepted a stray Los Angeles pass in his own zone and broke away down the left side. His shot skipped past Vachon and the Leafs took a 2-0 lead into the second intermission.

The third period of that game in L.A. will always be remembered for a brief but ugly stick-swinging exchange between Tiger Williams and Dave Hutchison. It sparked a personal feud among the two players that ended when they became teammates in Toronto 3 1/2 years later. And it all resulted from a calculated manoeuvre on the part of Williams.

Only 42 seconds into the period, Vachon skated 25 feet in front of his net to corral a loose puck. Williams dashed towards him with a full head of steam and rudely bowled over the Los Angeles goalie. He made no attempt at all to avoid Vachon and was immediately accosted by an irate Carr. Williams and Carr tangled in a lengthy bout and afterwards, Carr lost his temper with linesman Leon Stickle, whom he jostled on his way off the ice. He received a game-misconduct for his actions.

When order had finally been restored, Hutchison left the Kings' bench and skated over to Williams, who was seated in the penalty box. He yelled something at the Maple Leaf winger, who then stood up, and the two players engaged in a quick, but frightening stick duel. They somehow deflected all of the blows with their lumber and managed not to connect bodily.

As Hutchison was restrained, the night's most bizarre incident occurred. A spectator sitting behind the penalty box scaled the glass and jumped Williams from behind. Initially surprised, Tiger quickly gained the upper hand and pummelled the dimwitted fan, sending him scurrying back over the glass for his life. The atmosphere in The Forum deteriorated and an angry cluster of fans moved in on Williams as he was escorted to the Maple Leaf dressing room.

"A lot of people were trying to get at me as I was coming off the ice," Tiger remembers. "A big, black policeman shoved me into the room and locked the door. He couldn't have been a pound under 300. A bunch of fans poured down through the back of the portable stands and were banging on the dressing-room door. The cop pulled out his handgun, put it on his knee, and said, `Don't you worry, boy. If one motherfucker comes through that door... look out!

"`There ain't no hockey pucks inside this thing.'"

To this day, Williams has no hesitation assuming responsibility for the entire incident. He admits he could have avoided Vachon, had he so desired, but it wasn't in his plans.

"He came out of his crease to field the puck and in those days, when you wandered too far, you were fair game," recalls Tiger, who says he would *not* have barged into Vachon if today's rules for protecting goalies had been in place. "Our team always played well when something happened back then and I felt it was time to stir up the pot. So I ran him over. Vachon was their MVP and I was hoping to upset him.

"By skating so far out of his net, he made it easy on me. It was a bad choice on his part. Timing is what counts most in hockey and if I *wouldn't* have hit Vachon, we might have experienced a let down. It happened just at the right time. We were up 2-0 and suddenly, I had all the L.A. guys focused on me. They became more interested in killing me than winning the game and that's exactly what I was hoping for."

Vachon remembers bracing himself for Williams' assault. "Tiger was an aggravating guy to play against and there was a lot of intimidation in hockey back then," he says. "He definitely could have gone around me on that race for the puck, but that's the way he played the game. His sole purpose some nights was to bother the goalie.

"He'd stand in front of the net and screen you and if he was behind the goal, he'd give you a little shot on the ankle while skating back into the play. He was also good at delivering elbows now and then, ala Gordie Howe."

However, the stick-swinging incident was provoked by Hutchison.

"Pulford sent him off the bench to get me," says Williams. "That's the way Pully used to coach. Hutchy skated over and yelled something, then took a swipe at me with his stick. I returned the blow and away we went. The disadvantage I had was that the penalty box in L.A. dropped down five or six inches and Hutchy was already four inches taller than me. He came over, we whittled our sticks down to toothpicks for a few seconds, and that was the end of it."

Hutchison vehemently denies taking any instructions from Pulford.

"Tiger's nuts," he says. "Pulford never said a word to me... he didn't *have* to say anything. As a player, I knew what was going on and what had to be done. We were using four defenceman during that game and it was my turn to go on with Larry Brown. If I had been on the ice when Tiger ran Rogie, I would have fought him right then. But I was on the bench and my blood really boiled.

"I remember thinking back to an incident earlier that season at Montreal when Guy Lapointe ran Rogie. I went after him and pounded him out. I was so mad, but Rogie said to me, `Don't worry, Hutch, these things happen now and then.' Still, I couldn't accept someone roughing up our MVP and when Tiger did it, I had to respond.

"I skated by the penalty box and told him he was going to get it from me but-good the next time we were on the ice. I think he might've felt kind of trapped in there and we took three or four whacks at each other's sticks. He put his stick up first. If he hadn't, I would have skated by and challenged him on the next shift."

Before Williams could collect himself, the fan climbed over the glass and jumped on his back. "I ended up beating the shit out of him," Tiger accurately recalls. "The guy was a season-ticket holder and the funny thing is, I met him when I played for Los Angeles in 1986. He was a bit of a wing-nut and he did crazy things like that now and then; the Forum security people used to have a lot of trouble with him."

When asked if he recalled the fan's name, Tiger replied, "Yeah, `Joe Stupid!'"

Darryl Sittler remembers being astonished by the incident.

"Tiger was pounding the hell out of the guy and the next thing you knew, he was climbing back over the glass. It was probably the dumbest thing he had ever done in his life and he was lucky to get out of there before Tiger hurt him badly."

Almost forgotten during the 18-minute delay was the fact that a rather important hockey game still had to be decided.

Realizing the desperate situation they were in, the Kings began to open up and take the play to the Maple Leafs. They didn't generate many shots on goal but they had some quality chances. Gord McRae stood tall in net and made a pair of terrific saves off Goring and Murphy at the midway point of the period, preserving the 2-0 Toronto lead. Finally, Los Angeles connected, as Don Kozak jammed Bob Berry's relay past McRae, but only 6:51 remained in regulation.

From that point on, the Maple Leafs frustrated the Kings by icing the puck practically every time they gained control, chewing important seconds off the clock. Los Angeles never posed a serious threat and the

Maple Leafs finally won their first playoff series since 1967.

The players poured off the bench and raced towards McRae, mobbing their unlikely hero. Nicknamed "Bird", McRae had not distinguished himself in his two cracks at becoming the Leafs' No. 1 goaltender. He played 11 games during the brutal Leaf season of 1972-73 and allowed almost four goals per outing. His 20-game stint during the 1974-75 campaign was a bit more respectable — with a 3.22 average — but McRae showed no signs of developing into a clutch playoff performer.

"To this day, I still can't explain why everything fell into place for me during that series with Los Angeles," McRae admits. "I remember being very nervous in those games and not feeling particularly sharp or confident in my abilities. It was a low-scoring series and the Kings were a defensive team. I only made five or six tough saves but they all came at important times. It was surely the high point of my career."

In hindsight, McRae says he never should have played professional hockey. He disdained the lifestyle of a high-profiled athlete.

"It wasn't for me," he admits. "I got by with some hard work and a little bit of skill. Temperament-wise, I should have done something else. I didn't like the exposure of being a hockey player in Toronto. Even when I was a bench-warmer at the end of my career, I couldn't go into a grocery store without being recognized. And I never enjoyed performing in front of so many people each night.

"Other guys revelled in that kind of atmosphere but it grated on my nerves. I was more suited to be a school teacher."

McRae became known as "Bird" during his season with Charlotte of the Eastern Hockey League in 1970-71. "I was sitting in a park one morning just contemplating life and watching the pigeons," he recalls. "One of my teammates (defenceman) Bob Shupe came by and started calling me the `Bird-man.' For some reason, the name stuck."

McRae's time in Toronto was made even more miserable by Maple Leaf owner Harold Ballard. Despite a front-page photo in the Toronto *Star* the day after eliminating Los Angeles — which showed Ballard hugging the Leaf goalie and planting a kiss on his right cheek — McRae says the head-honcho never paid much attention to him.

"My personality wasn't flamboyant enough for Harold and we had kind of a frosty relationship," he recalls. "I don't remember him going out of his way to speak with me very often. I wasn't Darryl Sittler."

What the goalie *does* remember is how Ballard removed his bearded face from the 1977-78 Maple Leaf Christmas card, transposing a cleanly-shaven McRae in its place. And not too neatly, we might add. "Bird" wound up with an elongated neck.

"Yeah, that was rather humiliating, but it just sort of fell in line with our relationship," he says. "Harold allowed Bill Flett to wear *his* beard in the team photo a few years earlier, so I couldn't understand why he objected to mine."

McRae hung around through '77-78 — playing 18 games for Roger Neilson that season — then finally decided it was time to pack it in.

"I don't think the Maple Leafs ever truly believed I could play regularly in the NHL," he says. "If you look back, every time I had the chance to become the starting goalie, they went and brought in somebody else. In 1973, it was Ed Johnston, Doug Favell and Dunc Wilson. Even after my playoff showing against Los Angeles in '75, they signed Wayne Thomas and he took the No. 1 job. And when Thomas faltered in '76, they brought up Mike Palmateer.

"I suppose I had to be cranked over the head to get the message that I was spinning my wheels. But finally, it sunk in."

Meanwhile, Williams and Hutchison became close friends when Hutchison joined the Maple Leafs for the 1978-79 season. He was traded by Los Angeles to Toronto with Lorne Stamler, for Brian Glennie, Kurt Walker, Scott Garland, a draft choice and future considerations, June 14, 1978. Heading into free-agency at the end of the 1977-78 season, Hutchison appeared targeted for Chicago, but Williams recalls that he wanted to play for the Maple Leafs.

"I was over at Darryl Sittler's place one afternoon that summer (1978) taking a sun-tan on his deck when the phone rang," Tiger says. "It was Hutchy on the other end. He and Darryl both played Junior in London and went back a long way. Hutch was upset at (his agent) Allan Eagleson because Eagle appeared to be leading him to Chicago to play for Bob Pulford, his former coach. Pulford and Bobby Orr were with the Blackhawks and both were Eagleson clients.

"Darryl phoned Jim Gregory and the Leafs worked out a trade with the Kings. Hutchy and I hit it off right away."

The two players eventually discussed their stick-swinging exchange in Los Angeles, but not until the season was underway.

"We never mentioned it for two or three months," Williams recalls. "It was no big deal. He was on my side then and I couldn't have given a shit what he or I did in the past. We laugh about it more now that we're out of the game."

After stunning the heavily favoured Kings, the Leafs had very little left for their quarterfinal series with the defending champions from

Philadelphia. The Flyers manhandled the Leafs physically and swept to a four-game triumph — winning the series on an overtime goal at the Gardens by defenceman Andre (Moose) Dupont.

Still, the lengthy playoff drought was over and the Maple Leaf teams of the mid and late-1970s provided Toronto hockey fans with some memorable moments. Ironically, it took one of the city's most honoured and decorated hockey executives — George (Punch) Imlach — to unravel the whole process once again. And he did it in record time.

*   *   *   *   *   *

WHERE ARE THEY NOW?...

DAVE (TIGER) WILLIAMS, 40, played 5 1/2 years for the Maple Leafs and became one of the most popular athletes in Toronto. His feisty, no-nonsense approach gained him legions of followers in both Toronto and Vancouver, where he played for 4 1/2 seasons after Punch Imlach traded him in Febraury, 1980. He was a key member of the Canucks team that went to the 1982 Stanley Cup final, losing to the New York Islanders. Williams later skated for Detroit, Los Angeles and Hartford, retiring after the 1987-88 season. He averaged more than 283 penalty minutes in his 14-year career and still stands way atop the all-time leader board in that category with 3,966 minutes: 923 ahead of former Montreal, New York and Boston tough guy Chris Nilan. Tiger lives in Vancouver and is part-owner and coach of the Vancouver *Voodoo* entry in the Roller Hockey International circuit.

DAVE HUTCHISON, 42, was a rugged, uncompromising defenceman with Los Angeles, Toronto, Chicago and New Jersey between 1974 and 1984. He began his pro career in the WHA with the Philadelphia/Vancouver Blazers before joining the Kings for the 1974-75 season. Hutchison averaged 220 penalty minutes during his 10-season career, several of which were cut short by injuries. He played on the so-called Maple Leaf "goon squad" of 1978-79 with other noted scrappers like Williams, Dan Maloney and Pat Boutette. The Leafs traded him to Chicago in January, 1980 for Pat Ribble. Since retiring from hockey, Hutchison has worked for *Remax*, selling residential real-estate in his home-town of London, Ont.

DAN MALONEY, 44, was a boisterous left-winger in the NHL from 1970 to 1982 with Chicago, Los Angeles, Detroit and the Maple Leafs.

He was to be avoided in the corners and had a temper that occasionally got the better of him. In late-1975, while playing for the Red Wings, he was charged with assault by the Ontario Attorney General's office after treating Leaf defenceman Brian Glennie like a sack of potatoes. Few players in the game back then were more feared for their fighting ability. Maloney went to the Leafs in March, 1978, in a controversial trade with Detroit for left-winger Errol Thompson and a boat-load of high draft choices. He coached the Maple Leafs for two years (1984-85 and 1985-86) and later became head coach of the Winnipeg Jets. He now lives in his hometown of Barrie, Ont. and co-owns an establishment, *Dr. J's Nightclub*, with two of his brothers. He is also an advance scout for the Stanley Cup-champion New York Rangers and would like to get back into coaching at the NHL level.

MIKE MURPHY, 44, scored 238 goals in a 12-year NHL career with St. Louis, the Rangers and Los Angeles between 1971 and 1983. A fine leader of men, he was captain of the Kings from 1975-81. After retiring from hockey, he became an assistant to Los Angeles head coach Pat Quinn and he coached the Kings by himself for 69 games in 1986-87. He later spent two years as an assistant in Vancouver before being named head coach of the Canucks' International League affiliate in Milwaukee for the 1990-91 season. Murphy joined the Maple Leafs as an assistant coach in July, 1991, and spent three seasons with the club. In August 1994, he moved on to the New York Rangers as an assistant to new head coach Colin Campbell. With his wealth of NHL experience, he could likely handle a head-coaching position elsewhere in the league — something he desires greatly. Are you listening, GMs?

ROGATIEN VACHON, 49, was one of hockey's better goaltenders in the mid and late-1970s but his efforts were often overshadowed by fellow netminders Ken Dryden and Bernie Parent. He began his NHL career with Montreal in 1966-67 and was branded a "Junior `B'" goaltender by Maple Leaf coach Punch Imlach during the '67 playoffs. Right again, Punch. Vachon played on Stanley Cup-championship teams in 1968 '69 and '71 and was deemed expendable by the Canadiens upon the rapid development of Dryden. He went to the Kings, where he enjoyed his finest NHL seasons, and later signed a lucrative free-agent contract with Detroit. He finished his 16-year career with Boston in 1982, posting a lifetime goals-against average of 2.99 in the regular season, and 2.77 in 48 playoff games. He was general manager of the

Kings from 1984 to 1991 and played a role in bringing Wayne Gretzky to Los Angeles. He spent the 1993-94 season as Special Assistant to Chairman and former Kings' majority owner Bruce McNall.

BLAINE STOUGHTON, 41, had a pair of tenures in the NHL, playing for Pittsburgh and Toronto (1973-76), and then Hartford and the New York Rangers (1979-84). He scored 196 goals for the Whalers in a four-year span beginning in '79, when he shared the NHL lead in goals (56) with Charlie Simmer and Danny Gare. He connected 52 times in 1981-82 and finished his career with 258 goals. Between NHL stints, Blaine skated for Cincinnati, Indianapolis and New England of the WHA, popping 52 goals for the Stingers in 1976-77. He now lives in the Cincinnati suburb of Westchester, Ohio, and is an assistant coach to former Leaf defenceman Joel Quennville with Hartford's American Hockey League affiliate, the Springfield Falcons.

DARRYL SITTLER, 44, is the all-time leading scorer in the history of the Toronto Maple Leafs. He hasn't worn a Leaf uniform since 1982, but he remains atop the club's career point list with 966: 58 ahead of Dave Keon. Sittler began his tenure with the Maple Leafs in 1970-71 and was named team-captain in 1975 at the tender age of 25. He had a year unlike any other in 1976, when he set an NHL record that still exists with 10 points in one game against Boston, tied another mark with five goals in a playoff game against Philadelphia, then scored the winning goal for Team Canada in the inaugural Canada Cup tournament. He later played for Philadelphia and Detroit — retiring after the 1984-85 season — and is still among the top 30 point producers in NHL history. Sittler finished his career with 484 goals and 637 assists for 1,121 total points. He added 74 points in 76 playoff games. He now lives in the Buffalo suburb of East Amherst, N.Y. and is Special Consultant to Maple Leaf president and general manager Cliff Fletcher.

GORD McRAE, 46, played goal on and off for the Maple Leafs between 1972 and 1978. His fine performance in the 1975 preliminary playoffs against Los Angeles enabled the Leafs to upset the heavily favoured Kings and win their first post-season series since the 1967 Stanley Cup victory over Montreal. Nicknamed "Bird" for his alleged pigeon-watching tendencies, McRae retired after the 1977-78 season and got involved in a myriad of activities. He went back to school at Michigan Tech and earned a degree in geological engineering. He then moved to Lafayette,

Louisiana (just west of New Orleans) and worked for *Tenneco Oil*. He was transferred to Englewood, Colorado — a suburb of Denver — and later earned a degree to teach mathematics. He still lives in Englewood, and drives one hour north to Longmont, Colorado six days a week to operate his latest venture — a *Meineke Discount Muffler* shop.

... Leafs in Spring ...

MAY 22, 1993
Loews Hotel, Santa Monica, Calif.

Never has a group of people been so bummed out in such a beautiful setting. The Maple Leaf players and staff wore long faces on a perfect Saturday afternoon, less than 24 hours after falling behind Los Angeles two games to one in the Campbell Conference final. The fact they were encircled by an absolute paradise seemed not to register.

The Loews Santa Monica Hotel is pretty much the last place you'd expect to find a hockey club challenging for the Stanley Cup. Perched on an embankment that veers off the Pacific Coast Highway, its lavish back-patio rises above a typically crowded and trendy California beach. Down below and across a narrow street, the bronzed beauties of southern Cal hone their bodies to perfection — tanning blissfully in the white sand. A few steps to the north, the famed Santa Monica Pier — a small community unto itself — juts into the Pacific Ocean.

The setting is sure different from the more spartan arrangement at the Los Angeles Airport Marriott, where the Leafs had stayed during the regular season. Still, the mood was decidedly sombre.

Poolside lounge chairs were monopolized by Maple Leaf players and staff members. Bill Watters and Darryl Sittler had returned from a jog to nearby Venice Beach and were working on their tans. Pat Burns emerged from the hotel with a growly look on his face — a product of the previous night's loss, and the incessant kibbitzing from the L.A. media about his rotund figure.

A benign little feud had developed between Burns and his Los Angeles counterpart, Barry Melrose. It stemmed from an incident late in the series opener at Maple Leaf Gardens. Doug Gilmour had brilliantly engineered a three-goal Toronto uprising in the third period that broke open a 1-1 tie. He capped his dominating performance by sending Kings' rookie defenceman Alexi Zhitnik flying with a smartly timed hip-check just inside the Los Angeles blueline.

The sight of Zhitnik soaring through the air and landing almost head-first incensed L.A. tough guy Marty McSorley, who sought revenge on Gilmour moments later with a wicked elbow-smash to the noggin. That brought Maple Leaf captain Wendel Clark onto the scene, and the two roughnecks had it out. A large pile-up developed, delaying the game for more than 10 minutes.

In the midst of the on-ice war, Burns began shouting accusations at Melrose for "sending" McSorley out after Gilmour. As the mercury soared in the highly agitated Leaf coach, Melrose glared back with a smug grin on his face — occasionally puffing out his cheeks to razz Burns about his weight. Burns did not take well to the insulting jab, and he quickly advanced towards Melrose, only to be intercepted by assistant coach Mike Kitchen and a Gardens' security officer.

In its wisdom, the Los Angeles media picked up on the Melrose taunt and when the Maple Leafs arrived in California for Game 3, radio shows and newspapers were cascading with frivolous little contests.

"GUESS PAT BURNS' WEIGHT" blared a headline, offering an all-you-can-eat buffet for the lucky winner.

The shenanigans peaked when a radio station delivered several-hundred doughnuts to Burns' room at the Loews resort. A group of Maple Leaf wives on the trip gathered up the tasty treats and magnanimously distributed them to the street people of Los Angeles.

Unforgettable to this reporter is the image of an annoyed Burns repeatedly insisting that he hates doughnuts while answering media queries on the morning of Game 3.

HITTING ROCK-BOTTOM

The Misery of 1984-85

There is one alarming number from the past 30 years that applies to more than just the period examined in this anthology. It transcends the modern-day history of the Maple Leaf franchise and remains a bold-face blemish in the club's record manual.

It appears on Page 180 of the 1993-94 Maple Leaf *Yearbook* under the heading **FEWEST POINTS, SEASON (80 GAMES)**. The number is 48.

A half-decade of stale, uninspiring hockey culminated in the Maple Leafs hitting rock-bottom during the 1984-85 season. Since the advent of the center-ice red line 51 years ago, which began hockey's so-called modern era, no Maple Leaf team has performed worse. The '84-85 outfit tied a club record for fewest victories in one season (20), and set new marks for most losses (52) and fewest points (48).

To underscore such mediocrity, the Maple Leaf teams Pat Burns has coached the past two NHL seasons have *each* more than doubled the point accumulation of the 1984-85 club. Yes... it was *that* bad.

The warning signs of a total collapse had been prevalent since the beginning of the decade. Particularly in the defensive zone. High draft choices who may have blossomed with care, were instead rushed into the Maple Leaf line-up for quick-fix purposes. Managerial imprudence was staggering, and the predictable results followed.

Vincent Tremblay, Bob McGill, Fred Boimistruck, Jim Benning, Craig Muni, Ken Wregget, Allan Bester and Todd Gill were all victims of the ruinous strategy. Only Muni and Gill can be considered survivors. There was some misfortune as well. Gary Nylund, a monstrous defenceman chosen third overall in the 1982 draft, tore up his knee before he ever pulled on a Maple Leaf uniform. Dubbed a "can't miss" prospect by the hockey establishment, there's no telling how good he may have otherwise been.

The defensive stability prevalent in the late-70s began to erode at an alarming pace. The 1977-78 Maple Leafs, under the guidance of Roger Neilson, permitted only 237 goals during the 80-game schedule. The 1983-84 Maple Leafs allowed 387 in the same number of games. All of the elements were in place for the club's worst season ever.

Ominous signs began to appear during the summer. American-born defenceman Al Iafrate, who the Maple Leafs had selected fourth overall in the '84 draft, was charged with dangerous driving and disorderly conduct in a one-week span. Both incidents were reported by the Toronto media, but downplayed significantly by Gerry McNamara, the Maple Leafs' general manager. When Iafrate signed his first pro contract, the club eschewed a formal press conference, thus avoiding any potential fallout from the rookie's brush with the law.

Owner Harold Ballard and veteran goalie Mike Palmateer were busily trading insults as the club convened for training camp. Ballard decreed that Palmateer should retire after a rash of knee ailments. The goalie had rebounded from surgery to play well during the 1982-83 season, but his level of performance dropped significantly the following term. He entered 1984-85 in the final year of his contract, and with rookies Bester and Wregget in camp, Ballard decreed the future was bright.

Training camp began at the Quinte Sports Centre in Belleville, as Maple Leaf Gardens was pre-booked. Two days into the session, promising rookie Steve Thomas, a prolific Junior scorer with the Toronto Marlies, broke his wrist. It wasn't big news at the time.

Another coaching shuffle had materialized in the off-season when Mike Nykoluk's contract was not renewed. In his 2 1/2 years behind the bench, the easygoing Nykoluk fashioned an abysmal winning percentage of .402 — the lowest (to that point) of any man who had coached at least 100 Maple Leaf games. He may also have had the least-*talented* teams in Maple Leaf history, but he was more renown for his celebrated quarrels with *Globe & Mail* sportswriters than anything pertaining to hockey.

Assuming the lead role for 1984-85 was Nykoluk's assistant — 34-year-old Dan Maloney. And promoted from the farm to assist Maloney was John Brophy — once among the wildest and most notorious brawlers in the history of the game. Together, they attempted a soft-soap approach with a young Maple Leaf team that badly lacked confidence.

"A basic style of play must be engrained in the players; their reactions to situations automatic," Maloney explained. "The way to do that is through repetition. The things we're doing now are the things we'll be doing in February because that's the way a team learns."

The Ballard-Palmateer feud came to a boil when Palmateer refused to practice the morning after playing 30 minutes of the Maple Leafs' exhibition opener in Quebec. The goalie figured his wonky knees were no longer up to the task. Though it was not a unique request by a veteran netminder, it represented an attitude Maloney could not accept. Angered by Palmateer's decision, Ballard announced he would never again play for the Maple Leafs. Palmateer attempted to retrieve his equipment from the Gardens, but was refused entry to the building.

The scenario was a familiar one during the Ballard era. Players who had provided the Leafs with years of loyal service were ultimately given the cold-shoulder treatment by Ballard. Dave Keon, Norm Ullman, Darryl Sittler and Lanny McDonald come to mind.

A standout Junior goaltender with Lethbridge of the Western Hockey League, Wregget was the Maple Leafs' fourth selection (45th overall) in the 1982 amateur draft. Wisely, the Leafs allowed him to remain in Lethbridge for two seasons but when they promoted him to the NHL — and Palmateer wore out his welcome — he shared the goaltending duties with an equally raw Allan Bester. Therefore, the Maple Leafs embarked on the 1984-85 season with a pair of 20-year-old netminders who, between them, had played a grand total of 35 games at the big-league level.

"The Leafs have had great goaltending in the past and hopefully, Ken and I can continue that legacy," Bester announced. "Anytime during the season, they can send one or both of us down, so we're both working hard to play well and stay with the team the entire season."

Wregget had loftier expectations. "Right now, being in my first year, my goal is to build a good foundation and be consistent. I want to build my confidence and, eventually, I'd like to see my name on the plaque with guys like Johnny Bower. That would be my ultimate goal."

The Maple Leafs went into 1984-85 season with a youthful roster full of questionmarks. The players included:

GOAL
Allan Bester, Ken Wregget.

DEFENCE
Jim Benning, Todd Gill, Gaston Gingras, Al Iafrate, Gary Leeman, Bob McGill, Gary Nylund, Bill Root, Borje Salming, Bill Stewart.

CENTER
Russ Courtnall, Dan Daoust, Bill Derlago, Peter Ihnacak.

RIGHT WING
Miroslav Frycer, Rick Vaive, Stewart Gavin.

LEFT WING
John Anderson, Jeff Brubaker, Jeff Jackson, Jim Korn, Walt Poddubny, Greg Terrion.

The most obvious area of concern was in goal, where the 20-year olds would share the duties. There was some potential, but precious little quality on defence. Borje Salming's best years were behind him and Iafrate was the only member of the younger set for whom stardom was predicted. The rest would become journeymen, and only Todd Gill would survive to one day play on a contending Maple Leaf team.

There appeared to be some scoring ability up front, where Derlago, Courtnall, Frycer, Vaive, Anderson and Poddubny all had a touch around the net. But depth was a problem and injuries had to be avoided.

The regular season began on a promising note as Miroslav Frycer's overtime goal gave the Maple Leafs a 1-0 victory in Minnesota. It was the club's first shutout in almost three years. Two nights later, Leaf publicity director Stan Obodiac — his frail body ravaged with cancer — dropped the ceremonial first puck to open the home schedule. And the Leafs won again, defeating Buffalo 4-3. At the time, nobody knew that only 18 victories would follow in the remaining 78 games.

Continuing with their foolhardy pattern, the Leafs threw Iafrate to the wolves, playing the raw 18-year-old on a regular defence shift. He was initially paired with veteran Bill Root, but then saw action with the unsteady Bob McGill — a blatant prescription for failure.

"The thing you've got to do with Iafrate's ability is put him in a situation where he can test it," said Maloney. "I've used him in some really key situations and he's handled them well." Of course, Iafrate should have been testing his abilities back in Junior hockey, where he had played only 10 games for Belleville the previous year. But nobody in the Maple Leaf organization concurred.

"I don't know if I've made it yet," Iafrate told reporters early in the season. "Right now, they're just testing me. They're putting me on the powerplay and giving me a chance. I'm just trying my hardest and they're going to put me where they think I'll develop the fastest.

"All the writers and everyone said I wasn't going to make the team but I'm giving my best effort. I was nervous in the opener at Minnesota but I hit somebody and that kind of shook the butterflies out."

With a 2-3-0 record after five regular-season games, a foreboding event took place at the Gardens on Saturday, October 20. Quebec came to town and demolished the Maple Leafs 12-3. The Nordiques pumped 53 shots at a defenceless Ken Wregget and scored six third-period goals to blow the game wide open. The Stastny brothers (Peter, Anton and Marion) had a field day, combining for eight scoring points.

An early season feud developed between Maloney and Leaf captain Rick Vaive, whom the coach felt was not demonstrating the necessary qualities of leadership. It would flare up intermittently during the balance of the campaign.

Vaive was benched during a late-October home game against Calgary. The Maple Leafs fell behind 5-1 midway through the third period, but Miroslav Frycer (at 15:00) and Bill Derlago (at 15:16) scored to make it close. With momentum on their side, and the Gardens' crowd into the game, the Leafs still had time to do further damage. But Maloney kept Vaive on the bench and Calgary won, 5-3.

The three-time 50-goal shooter brushed past reporters after the game, declaring, "I've got nothing to say." When asked why he refused to play his captain, Maloney responded, "There's enough pressure on him already. I don't want to add to it."

Meanwhile, Palmateer continued to sit around and collect his huge salary ($220,000 U.S. per year). "Gerry McNamara told me to go home, leave my gear at Maple Leaf Gardens, and wait for their call," the 30-year-old goalie said in late-October. "There have been no additional exchanges between the Leafs and myself. Of course, the money makes it easier, but I want to play. Hanging out is no fun at all."

Palmateer was unable to figure out why the Maple Leafs reacted so strongly to his request for a day off after playing. "Any goalie with my history of knee problems would receive the same privilege," he said. "I came to training camp in good shape, my legs were fine, and so was my attitude. Then they pulled this stunt.

"Maybe Harold had something to do with it, but I hope not. I've broken just about every bone in my body for you-know-who. I've spent a lot of my summers with this organization in a cast, working hard to be ready for the next season."

The Maple Leafs' early season record dropped to 3-8-1 after a trio of losses on the road. The trip began with a heart-breaking defeat in St. Louis. The Blues jumped to an early 3-0 lead and held a seemingly comfortable 5-2 advantage after the second period. Bill Derlago scored early in the third and the Leafs fought back to tie the game when Russ Courtnall and Borje Salming beat Mike Liut in the final three minutes of regulation. But, a lucky bounce enabled Brian Sutter to win it for St. Louis at 1:08 of the overtime period.

Three nights later, in Los Angeles, the Leafs outshot the Kings 10-9 in the first period but again fell behind 3-0. They Kings went on to a 7-0 romp. "We had opportunities in their end and just couldn't finish them off," sighed Maloney. "They had opportunities in our end and they capitalized." Maloney made a goaltending switch for the first time — replacing Bester with Wregget in the second period.

The Maple Leaf defence yielded 54 shots in the road-trip finale at Minnesota while suffering a gut-wrenching loss to the North Stars. Jim Benning, Jim Korn and Rick Vaive gave Toronto a 3-1 advantage after two periods, as Wregget stopped 33 of 34 Minnesota shots. But, the Stars out-gunned the Leafs 20-8 in the third frame and scored four unanswered goals to prevail, 5-3. Brian Bellows counted the winner at 6:17 and Steve Payne clinched the victory into an empty net at 19:43.

A winless homestand of five games followed that loss to the North Stars and the Maple Leafs dropped to 3-11-3 on the season. The string of home games started promisingly when Miroslav Frycer scored a tying goal against Vancouver with one second left in regulation time. Three nights later, Steve Larmer scored a third-period goal to give Chicago a 4-4 tie with the Leafs. Then, it all came apart.

Dennis Maruk beat Bester with 3:43 remaining in the third period and Minnesota won a Sunday night shootout, 7-6. Los Angeles came in three nights later and handed the Leafs another late set-back. Marcel Dionne (at 13:45 of the third period) and Brian MacLellan (at 17:11) lifted the Kings out of a 3-2 deficit. It happened yet again when the Jets were in town the following Saturday. Morris Lukowich and Robert Picard scored goals in the latter half of the third period for a 5-3 Winnipeg victory.

One of the few highlights of the season came two nights later, when the Maple Leafs turned the tide against Montreal. Courtnall and Derlago beat Steve Penney with late third-period goals and the Leafs won 6-4 at the Forum. But that victory was the lone bright spot in a dreadful span of 21 games (Oct. 26 to Dec. 9) that saw Toronto compile a record of 1-15-5. And the streak included one of the great collapses in Maple Leaf history.

A pair of second-period goals by Miroslav Frycer gave the Leafs a 6-2 lead heading into the final 20 minutes at Joe Louis Arena, Dec. 4. But, the roof caved in on Toronto, as Detroit poured five unanswered goals past Wregget in the third to come from behind and win, 7-6. Winger John Ogrodnick tied the game at 14:17, then won it with 43 seconds left on the clock. The following day, the Leafs signed free agent netminder Tim Bernhardt, a castoff from the Calgary Flames, and Wregget was demoted to the club's top farm team in St. Catharines.

Bester joined him a few days later as Rick St. Croix was promoted from the minors. The youngsters were simply facing too many shots for their well being, and management saw the fragile confidence of both men eroding. With the club going nowhere fast, it made a lot more sense to play a couple of journeymen in goal. Not so much would be expected of them and Wregget and Bester would be allowed to develop in a less-pressured environment. The Leafs were 4-19-5 with the second-worst record in hockey when they finally won a game, beating Philadelphia 6-3 at home on Dec. 12. St. Croix played net, defeating his former team.

As Christmas approached, hockey observers seriously began to wonder if the 1984-85 Maple Leafs would become the worst club in franchise history. Stan Fischler penned a column in *The Hockey News*, entitled **THE WILTED LEAFS**. In it, he wrote:

> "Having been a devoted Maple Leaf fan from age 10 through my young adult life, I take the plight of the current Toronto Make Believes very seriously. So seriously, in fact, that I am now wondering whether they qualify for a special niche in hockey history. Is this, in fact, the worst team in Maple Leaf history?
>
> "Perhaps I should put it another way: Can anyone name a Toronto sextet more enfeebled than this one?"

Fischler went on to examine three previous editions of the club. The 1945-46 team had been an enigma, coming off a Stanley Cup victory the year before. It won only 19 of its 50 games, but Fischler pointed out: "...it finished only five games under .500, which was not too bad. That team was light years ahead of the contemporary contemptibles."

The 1957-58 Maple Leaf team, coached by Billy Reay, finished in last place with a 21-38-11 record in 70 games. "Still," Fischler wrote, "the club also had significant quality including Frank Mahovlich, George Armstrong and Bob Baun. No comparison. They were definitely better than today's Make Believes."

The closest facsimile may have been the 1981-82 edition under Mike Nykoluk, which set a franchise futility mark of only 20 victories in 80 games. The club's leading scorer that season, John Anderson, failed to average even a point-a-game. And the team yielded goals by the bushel. "It would be difficult," Fischler wrote, "to discern the difference between that Toronto defence (Salming, Manno, Benning, Boimistruck, McGill) and the chorus of Saturday Night Live."

Other journalists liberally took pot-shots at the Maple Leafs. Jay Greenberg, a Philadelphia hockey writer who would one day work briefly in Toronto, wrote a satirical piece for *The Hockey News*, looking ahead at the year 1985, month-by-month. In his prediction for February 25th, Greenberg deadpanned: "Toronto losing streak reaches 33 games with a 16-2 loss to Chicago. The late Conn Smythe replaces Dan Maloney as coach. `We're dead anyway,' says owner Harold Ballard. `Why not?'"

A Christmas-time rumour had the Maple Leafs making a blockbuster trade with the New York Rangers. Borje Salming, Jim Korn and either Bill Derlago or John Anderson would go to New York for Mike Allison, Mike Rodgers and Willie Huber. Leaf GM Gerry McNamara wouldn't comment.

On New Year's Day, 1985, the Maple Leafs were dead last in the NHL overall standings with a 6-26-5 record.

They closed out 1984 by losing 5-4 at home to Chicago, as Steve Larmer of the Blackhawks scored a lucky goal with less than a minute to go in regulation time. On Jan. 2, at the Gardens against Pittsburgh, the Leafs lost 2-1 to the Penguins on a goal credited to Wayne Babych. However, Borje Salming accidentally nudged the puck into his own net on the play. The other Penguin goal came on a first-period penalty shot by Warren Young. "That was harder than losing 10-1," said Bill Derlago.

At the conclusion of that game against Pittsburgh, coach Maloney charged up into the gold seats behind the Leaf bench to confront a fan who'd been taunting him. The fan called Ballard the following day and suggested that the owner discipline his coach for leaving the area of the bench. Ballard replied that Maloney should have punched him in the mouth, and threatened to cancel the fan's season tickets.

Meanwhile, the club's misfortune continued to mount as Derlago, one of its few reliable forwards, injured his shoulder in the Dec. 29 game against Chicago. He was hit from behind by Troy Murray and had to undergo surgery. "It's just bad luck," said Derlago, who made a habit of suffering injuries around the New Year. "I've been in the best shape of my life this season. It's just one of those things."

At the time of his injury, Derlago was tied with Miroslav Frycer as the Maple Leafs' leading scorer with 32 points. He was second on the club with 17 goals and was on pace to match his career-high of 40, set two seasons earlier. Still, trade rumours involving Derlago swirled around the city, including the supposed mega-deal with New York.

"I don't want to move, I've been traded once before," he said, referring to the deal that brought him to the Maple Leafs along with Rick Vaive, for Tiger Williams and Jerry Butler in February, 1980. "I like Toronto and I'd like to stay here. Maybe I could say that I don't think about a trade, but I'd be lying."

Without Derlago in the line-up, the Leafs embarked on yet another prodigious slump, going 1-11-0 between Dec. 14 and Jan. 13. The two lengthy skids produced a shocking number. In the 33 games between Oct. 26 and Jan. 13, the Maple Leafs' record was:

2 - 26 - 5

During a 5-3 loss to the Bruins, Jan. 9, an usher at the Gardens disrobed in the corridor near the penalty benches, then heaved his jacket and tie onto the ice in protest of another brutal Leaf effort. As the Buds flew west for a mini two-game road trip to Vancouver and Los Angeles on Jan. 12, they stood a distant last in the NHL overall standings at 6-30-5 for 17 points, eight behind the Canucks.

Then suddenly, and without warning, things began to click. Only temporarily, but enough to give the players and the fans a small taste of success. The Maple Leafs won both games on their western trip: 5-3 at Vancouver and 4-3 in Los Angeles. Then they came home and hammered St. Louis 6-1 in a game marred by a bench-emptying brawl. The three-game win streak was the high-water mark of the season.

The melee started at 18:37 of the third period when Leaf captain Rick Vaive tangled with Blues' tough guy Perry Anderson. It turned ugly when the Leafs responded to Dwight Schofield of St. Louis pairing off and pummelling the much-smaller Dan Daoust. Toronto heavyweights Gary Nylund and Jeff Brubaker left the bench to help Daoust and the players on both teams spilled onto the ice.

Anderson, Schofield and Rob Ramage of the Blues were given majors and game-misconducts along with Jim Korn and Bob McGill of the Leafs. Brubaker received a double-minor and game-misconduct for being first off the bench and even the goalies — Mike Liut and Tim Bernhardt — got minor penalties for leaving the crease.

For the first time all season, the fans at Maple Leaf Gardens made some noise (other than groaning). "It's great to get two points, and to get this place screaming and yelling is a great feeling as well," said Vaive, who was booed during the Leafs' winless homestand prior to the western trip. "The fans seemed to like the brawl and perhaps that's what we needed to get them going. All in all, it was a great night."

From Jan. 13 to Jan. 30, the Maple Leafs fashioned their best streak of the season, with a 5-2-2 record in nine games. It coincided with the emergence of Bernhardt as the club's No. 1 goalie. Rick St. Croix had been the designated starter when Bester and Wregget were sent down but St. Croix pulled a hamstring muscle and had to be replaced in the Boston game, Jan. 9. Bernhardt quickly seized the opportunity. He allowed only 20 goals in a seven-game span: a remarkably low number for the defensively porous Maple Leafs of that season.

"If you put too much pressure on yourself, it may backfire," said Bernhardt, who had played six games for Calgary in 1982-83. "I'm just trying to make the most of this chance."

The 5-2-2 "hot" streak actually positioned the Maple Leafs well within striking distance of fourth-place Detroit in the Norris Division — and the most absurd playoff spot in professional sports history. On Feb. 1, the Leafs trailed the Red Wings by only seven points with two games in hand. Mercifully, they would not get any closer.

The Maple Leafs continued to make news *off* the ice with their Neanderthal policies. Following a 4-1 loss to the Islanders, Jan. 24, Maloney barred female reporters Helene Elliott and Joni Dattilo from the club's dressing room at the Nassau Coliseum. League rules provided for equal access to all reporters, or alternative arrangements for females, neither of which Maloney considered. Elliott protested to NHL president John Zeigler, who promised to study the complaint.

Another off-ice controversy surrounded veteran left-winger Walt Poddubny, who refused a demotion to the minors on Jan. 29. Acquired from Edmonton in March, 1982, Poddubny flourished in his first full season with the Maple Leafs, scoring 28 goals on a line with Peter Ihnacak and Miroslav Frycer. But he missed large portions of the next two seasons with injuries and was again hurt in December, 1984. Upon recovering from that knee ailment, he was asked by Leaf management to go to St. Catharines of the AHL. But the Leafs gave him no assurance as to the length of his stay in the minors, and he refused to report.

Poddubny was placed on recallable waivers and reportedly claimed by three teams, including Detroit. Poddubny's agent, Gene McBurney, announced that the next move was up to the Maple Leafs.

"There are a number of things that can come about, but Walter definitely wants to play with the Leafs," McBurney said. "He has no deep or abiding love with any other city. And he's never had a problem with management in Toronto. He thinks quite highly of Dan Maloney and Gerry McNamara, both of whom stuck by him when he was injured for much of last season."

Poddubny soon began to consider reporting. "I want to play for the Leafs, of course," he said. "I want to go down for a couple of weeks and then, hopefully, the Leafs can use me. There's no animosity on my part towards management. I never expected to walk back into my old job. I would have liked to have been spotted, but I can see management's view. I'll go down and there'll be no more doubts (about his injury)."

Sophomore Gary Leeman replaced Poddubny on the line with Ihnacak and Frycer and began to play very well. But Frycer openly lobbied for Poddubny's return. "I feel very bad because he's one of my best friends in Canada," said the Czech-born winger. "It always takes time to play with a new guy. I've been playing with Peter for three years and I know him from Czechoslovakia. I prefer having Walt on the line with us. We were great together.

"Right now we're talking together and telling (Leeman) what he should do. Hopefully, it will work out."

Poddubny finally did report to the minors and, typically, suffered a broken thumb in only his third game with St. Catharines.

A satisfying victory in Pittsburgh closed out the month of January for the Maple Leafs. The two clubs traded goals all night long and it appeared that Pittsburgh would prevail when Doug Shedden beat Bernhardt for a 5-4 Penguins' lead with 4:34 left in regulation time. But, John Anderson re-knotted the score at 17:42 and Dan Daoust took passes from Vaive and Anderson to pump the winner past Roberto Romano with only 16 seconds remaining on the clock.

The Maple Leafs followed the Pittsburgh victory with a 3-3 tie at Washington: Mike Gartner sending the game into overtime with a third-period goal for the Capitals. Then came three consecutive losses — to Minnesota, Washington and Chicago — before another spurt of competence set in. And against Montreal, no less.

The Leafs and their fans enjoyed by far the most memorable weekend of a very forgettable season with back-to-back wins over the Canadiens, Feb. 9-10. Leafs smoked the Habs 6-2 in Montreal on Saturday night, although Bernhardt had to stand tall in the face of an 18-shot barrage in the third period. Frycer led the way with a goal and an assist while Leeman chipped in with three helpers.

Vaive and Anderson scored goals late in the first period to give the Leafs a 2-0 lead in the Sunday night re-match at the Gardens. But Mario Tremblay and Mike McPhee replied in the second period to knot the count. The third frame was scoreless, but Vaive won it for the Leafs at 3:38 of overtime — taking Daoust's pass to beat Steve Penney for his team-leading 27th goal of the season. Bernhardt was again spectacular in goal, facing 43 Montreal shots.

However, the honeymoon was a short one. The Leafs followed up the Montreal sweep by losing games to St. Louis and New Jersey. "We might have had a bit of an emotional let-down," admitted Leaf winger Stewart Gavin. "We were really up for the games against Montreal. Several of players are ex-Montrealers as well as (assistant coach) John Brophy. If I could market that feeling, I'd sell it. Everytime we go onto the ice, we try our best. But, sometimes, our best is not enough."

Could there possibly have been a more profound understatement during the entire 1984-85 season?

An accurate barometer of the Maple Leaf woes came in the form of constant player shuffling, through either injury or incompetence. Here, for example, is a list of Toronto player transactions in the one-week period between Feb. 22 and Mar. 1:

GASTON GINGRAS, D, RECALLED FROM ST. CATHARINES OF AHL AND TRADED TO MONTREAL TO COMPLETE EARLIER TRADE FOR LARRY LANDON, RW, CURRENTLY WITH ST. CATHARINES. TODD GILL, D, RETURNED TO WINDSOR OF OHL. JEFF JACKSON, LW, SENT BACK TO HAMILTON OF OHL. BILL STEWART, D, AND STEVE THOMAS, RW, RECALLED FROM ST. CATHARINES OF AHL. BILL ROOT, D, AND WES JARVIS, C, RETURNED TO ST. CATHARINES. AL IAFRATE, D, AND BILL DERLAGO, C, BACK FROM INJURY LIST. JIM KORN, D, SIDELINED INDEFINITELY WITH SHOULDER SEPARATION. STEWART GAVIN, RW, OUT WITH CHARLEY HORSE.

All of that in seven days! Harold Ballard must have been pleased with program sales that week.

Detroit began to play some better hockey under coach Nick Polano in the first half of February and a 7-4 victory over Chicago, Feb. 16 at Joe Louis Arena, pushed the Red Wings into third place in the Norris ahead of Minnesota. The Leafs then went into Detroit and won a hockey game that would have loomed larger if not for the Wings' renaissance.

Toronto rallied in the third period for a 4-2 triumph, Feb. 23. Trailing 2-1 heading into the third, the Leafs got a goal from Borje Salming at the 5:04 mark. Then, with just 1:58 left in regulation time, defenceman Jim Benning took a pass from Salming and beat goalie Greg Stefan with a low shot through the legs. Greg Terrion clinched the comeback victory with an empty net marker in the final minute. It was the Maple Leafs' 15th victory of the season but they still trailed fourth-place Minnesota by eight points and third-place Detroit by 10 for the final playoff spot in the Norris Division.

The Maple Leaf improvement, while not dramatic, made enough of an impression on one of their media baiters to warrant a pseudo-apology. Jay Greenberg of the Philadelphia *Daily News* penned a column for Mar. 22 issue of *The Hockey News* entitled **EVEN THE BEST WRITERS MAKE THE ODD MISTAKE.** In it, he wrote:

> "I laughed at the Toronto Maple Leafs for passing over bright up-and-comers like Doug Carpenter and Mike Keenan to promote Dan Maloney to their coaching job. I figured they probably couldn't get anybody else to take it.
>
> "Then I heard that Maloney has taken a patient, teaching approach from the beginning of training camp. And now I see that it's starting to pay off. The Leafs still have a long way to go, but they have been much more competitive since mid-January.
>
> "You can now count four recent high No. 1 picks on their roster — Russ Courtnall, Jim Benning, Gary Nylund and Al Iafrate. So maybe Toronto is finally starting to come back."

But the Maple Leafs quickly fell out of even remote contention for a playoff spot by embarking on a 2-7-0 skid after the Detroit victory. The Red Wings gained revenge on Mar. 6 at the Gardens, defeating the Leafs 5-3. Detroit's big gunner that night was former Leaf captain Darryl Sittler, who had two goals and an assist. It was sweet revenge for Sittler, who had suffered a broken cheekbone in the Red Wings' previous visit to Toronto when checked into the glass from behind by defenceman Jim Korn. He broke a 3-3 tie at 6:52 of the third period, then set up Dwight Foster for the empty net clincher.

"It's nice to get an opportunity to play, and play well," Sittler said. "You try to be ready when the chance comes... I wanted to prove to people that I can still play."

The events of Mar. 15-16 were a microcosm of the sorry Maple Leaf year and served to establish an all-time franchise record for defeats in one season. On a five-game losing streak, the Leaf players were in foul moods during a Friday morning practice session at the Gardens. At one point, captain Rick Vaive told coaches Maloney and Brophy to "Fuck off", which led to some additional skating drills for Vaive and his linemates Derlago and Anderson.

Philadelphia was at the Gardens the following night and the coaches decided to enact some disciplinary measures. As the Flyers romped to an easy win, Vaive sat on the bench and seethed. He dressed for the game but did not see a single, solitary shift. Anderson and Derlago sat with Vaive until the 15-minute mark of the opening period, when they finally got onto the ice. While hurtling over the boards, Anderson took a comical pratfall, which brought howling laughter from the stands. It was the only semblance of entertainment for the paying customers all night long.

In blasting the Leafs 6-1, the Flyers handed Toronto its 46th loss of the season — most-ever by a Maple Leaf team — breaking the mark set just the year before under Mike Nykoluk. Towards the very end of the game, the fans began chanting, "We want Vaive!", which prompted Maloney to crack afterwards, "He just went from the most unpopular to the most popular player in one game." Vaive had been booed by Gardens' patrons throughout most of the sorry Maple Leaf season.

Maloney addressed the Vaive benching after the game, saying, "I think tonight served its purpose. He wasn't going to play tonight." When asked if he had told Vaive of his decision prior to the game, the coach replied, "No." Then he added, "That's enough about him."

Vaive insisted he had nothing to say about the matter, but did admit he had never previously been benched for an entire hockey game. Meanwhile, Anderson was disappointed at the fan reaction to his tumble off the bench. "My feelings were hurt," he admitted. "I didn't get this far in my career by not trying. I came here tonight to play."

Reports later surfaced that the roots of the Maloney-Vaive feud were quite deep — dating back several seasons, when they were Maple Leaf teammates. They didn't get along then, and Leaf management had apparently asked Vaive to surrender his captaincy earlier in the '84-85 campaign. Vaive refused, thus putting the onus on management to take the "C" away from him, and relations went downhill from there.

The Maple Leafs were finally bounced from playoff contention when Minnesota beat Vancouver 5-3 on Mar. 25. Ironically, elimination came on the heels of another victory over the Red Wings in Detroit. Adding emphasis to its worst season ever, Toronto practically conceded its final five games — allowing 35 goals — and assured itself of the No. 1 selection in the 1985 entry draft.

A fitting epitaph of the Maple Leafs' rock-bottom season was authoured by the man who saw them the most during the Harold Ballard years: Toronto *Star* hockey writer Frank Orr wrote in his *Hockey News* column of April 5:

> This season, the Maple Leafs plumbed new depths by finishing absolutely, totally, dead last among the 21 NHL teams, losing more games than any roster in the history of the club.
>
> "But as always, the men who own and operate the Leafs spouted the usual baloney. Owner Harold Ballard said he had great faith in the men who operated the team and was sure that Stanley Cup contention was a couple of years in the future.
>
> "The truly strange happening on the Toronto scene — the Leafs' No. 21 finish isn't strange; it was very predictable — is the way the club devours its captains. It started with Dave Keon in the mid-70s, continued with Darryl Sittler in the mid-80s, and now involves Rick Vaive: the team's best player and wearer of the `C' since Sittler's departure.
>
> "...Now Vaive, too, is finished with the Leafs — a guy who scored 50 goals in three consecutive seasons.
>
> "Old folks like to talk about Leaf tradition, but when they do, just go along with it. There's no such thing as Leaf tradition. Close to 20 years has passed since the team meant anything at all and that places a dent in any positive tradition they may have had.
>
> "The only tradition the Leafs have now is mediocrity and chaos."

... Leafs in Spring ...

MAY 27, 1993
Great Western Forum, Inglewood, Calif.

This night stands alone as the most rousing and spectacular Maple Leaf game I've covered in more than a decade in the media business.

It will long be remembered for Wayne Gretzky's overtime goal that spared the Kings elimination and sent the '93 Western Conference final back to Toronto for a seventh and deciding match. The evening, though, would never have been so utterly spellbinding if not for the exploits of Wendel Clark. It may have been his finest hour in nine years of donning a Toronto uniform.

The Maple Leafs were hoping to crown the Kings and advance to the Stanley Cup final for the first time in 26 years. Two night earlier, in Toronto, Glenn Anderson had scored an overtime winner to lift the Leafs into a 3-2 lead in the best-of-seven affair. A fourth victory, on Forum ice, would create a Toronto-Montreal quarrel for the coveted mug.

It was a game Los Angeles dominated for 40 minutes. The Kings had a wide edge in puck control and quality chances and they began to solve Felix Potvin in the second period, scoring three goals in 8 1/2 minutes to assume a 4-2 lead. McSorley, Darryl Sydor and Luc Robitaille did the damage and Los Angeles appeared to be very much in command.

The Maple Leafs had precious few scoring opportunities throughout the night, and did not pose a threat in the opening half of the third period. There was no prelude, offensively, to Clark's surprise goal at the 11:08 mark — a partially screened snapper from the high slot. It was a harmless-looking rush, and one of the few times the Maple Leafs had crossed into the L.A. zone. But, Toronto was suddenly within a goal of the Kings and almost half the period remained to be played.

The Leafs showed a bit more life after Clark's goal, but Kings' netminder Kelly Hrudey snubbed all of their advances and L.A. still had its 4-3 lead with less than two minutes to go in regulation time.

Then the game really got interesting.

Sitting in the press box at the Forum, you could feel the same kind of trepidation as in Detroit. In Los Angeles, the hockey media is situated directly at center ice — in the second tier of seats — and literally among the spectators. With no girders built into the roof, the Forum has never embodied a conventional press facility, as in Maple Leaf Gardens. Therefore, the scribes and talking heads are surrounded by the paying public — which creates a heightened awareness of the atmosphere during a sporting event. And the L.A. fans watching Game 6 wind to a close practically trembled with anxiety.

The Kings of 1992-93 were not renown for their defensive aptitude and a one-goal lead meant little — so long as time remained on the clock. The Maple Leafs weren't an explosive scoring club but the '93 playoff outfit had an uncanny flair for the dramatic, which thoroughly rationalized what happened in the game's dying moments.

Pat Burns pulled Felix Potvin and replaced him with a sixth attacker. Mindful of his club's lack of offensive zip, he did so with more than 90 seconds remaining in regulation — providing his charges with plenty of time to organize a desperation assault.

The strategy, however, worked almost immediately.

Todd Gill spun around near the left-wing boards in the L.A. zone and feathered a pass to Gilmour in the corner. Incredibly, the blazing-hot Clark cruised in unmolested from the point and Gilmour sent him a perfect feed. Clark whipped one of his patented wrist-shots past Hrudey before the Kings' goalie could even flinch and 16,005 spectators let out the loudest collective groan you'll ever hear.

It was 18:39 of the third period and the Maple Leafs had tied the game, 4-4. Clark became the first Leaf to record a hattrick in 1992-93, as he had also scored Toronto's second goal early in the middle frame.

But the comeback was effectively nullified by the Leaf player who, ironically, had experienced the greatest amount of Stanley Cup glory. Right-winger Glenn Anderson came to the Maple Leafs prior to the 1991-92 season, after playing a key role on all five championship teams in Edmonton. Known *considerably more for his offensive skills than his on-ice rationale, Anderson took the most ill-timed and dimwitted penalty of his career when he squashed defenceman Rob Blake into the glass.*

The indisputable boarding infraction occurred with only 13 seconds left in regulation, allowing Los Angeles to start the overtime period with a man-advantage. And spectator apprehension shifted squarely to those in support of the Maple Leafs. With good reason.

Led by the line of Gretzky, Robitaille and Tomas Sandstrom, the L.A. powerplay had been clicking spectacularly — counting all three goals in the Kings' second-period uprising. Anderson was either not paying attention, or he suffered an enormous brain cramp. Either way, his foolish penalty harboured disaster for the Maple Leafs.

I remember talking with Jim Proudfoot of the Toronto Star in the Forum press room during the intermission. And we both seemed to agree that in spite of Toronto's gallant comeback, the overtime would simply not last very long. Neither of us realized, however, that the most heated controversy of the series would unfold soon after the puck was dropped — and it would involve the eventual winning goal-scorer.

Just 39 seconds into the extra period, Gretzky accidentally — but without question — high-sticked Gilmour in the neck area: cutting the Maple Leaf center for eight stitches. To this day, no reasonable excuse has been offered by referee Kerry Fraser for not observing the rulebook and ejecting Gretzky from the game with a five-minute major. The play appeared to take place in full view of the three officials: Fraser and linesmen Ron Finn and Kevin Collins — both of whom were empowered to recommend a suitable penalty call.

While the vast majority of referees would consciously refrain from penalizing Gretzky in a similar circumstance, Fraser is not among them. Love him or hate him, the man has balls. But he cowered in the incident with Gilmour, choosing to overlook the obvious — perhaps envisioning the spectacle of a Maple Leaf series victory with Gretzky planted in the box. Worse things have happened, of course, but not this time.

Instead of cooling his heals for five minutes (and maybe the entire summer), the Great One scored the game-winning goal. He took Robitaille's pass and neatly lifted the puck over a sprawling Potvin from point-blank range at 1:41 of the overtime period. The ensuing eruption from the L.A. audience sounded more like relief than joy.

After the game, Melrose brazenly told reporters, "We're going to Montreal" — boldly forecasting a Game 7 victory in Toronto and a trip to the Stanley Cup final. And he was right. Another monstrous effort by Gretzky finished off the Maple Leafs two nights later and broke a lot of hearts on Carlton Street.

Burns could not fight back tears in his post-game media session. "Don't be mad at this team," he said. "My guys never quit."

The disappointment in Toronto was soon replaced by a sense of joviality and pride for a team that had rekindled past glories. And to these eyes, the defeat ultimately could not — in any way — detract from the wonderment of that exhilarating Game 6.

QUINN VS. ORR...
CRUNCH!!

Boston Garden
April 2, 1969

The most recent image Maple Leaf fans have of Pat Quinn is not a pleasant one. It's a television close-up of the smiling Vancouver Canucks' coach, at his bench in the Pacific Coliseum. The source of his jubilation is forward Greg Adams, who has backhanded a rebound past Felix Potvin early in double-overtime — dispatching Toronto from the Western Conference final in five games.

Pat Quinn, who began his NHL career in Toronto, is going to the Stanley Cup final. His former team is going home.

For woebegone Maple Leaf fans watching on TV, that scene took place in the wee hours of May 25, 1994. It was hardly relevant, at the time, to reflect upon another TV image, a full quarter-century earlier, in which Quinn had brought joy and excitement into the livingrooms of Maple Leaf faithful... while sparking and fuelling one of the great hockey riots of all time.

On opening night of the 1969 Stanley Cup playoffs, Quinn delivered the most memorable, and likely the most punishing open-ice body check of the early expansion era in the NHL. A rookie defenceman with the Maple Leafs, Quinn decimated the great Bobby Orr — hockey's premier star of the time — and he did it in front of Orr's adoring fans at the Boston Garden. The thunderous check had no impact whatsoever on the fortunes of that inferior Maple Leaf team, but it elevated Quinn to cult-like status among followers of the blue and white.

To this day, whenever Quinn visits Toronto with his Vancouver club, he is frequently reminded of that startling moment in Boston more than a generation ago. "No one would likely even remember that I played the game if not for that hit," he says, rather modestly. "But I always get asked about it by Maple Leaf fans and there are some kids that probably weren't even born yet who claim to have seen it happen."

The situation unfolded in Game One of an East Division quarterfinal series in which the Maple Leafs were decided underdogs. Having rebounded from missing the playoffs the previous spring, the 1968-69 club finished fourth in the East by a comfortable seven-point margin over Detroit.

Norm Ullman and Paul Henderson, acquired from the Red Wings a year earlier in an unpopular trade for Frank Mahovlich, both prospered in their first full seasons in Toronto: Ullman scoring 35 goals; Henderson 27. Veterans Dave Keon, George Armstrong and Ron Ellis also managed to exceed the 20-goal mark, while the additions of Quinn and Jim Dorey beefed up the blueline. So Toronto was indeed an improved hockey club.

But, Boston was a different story altogether. After seemingly endless years of mediocrity in the 1960s, the Bruins had been instantly transformed into a physical and talent-laden powerhouse. For a period of three insufferable seasons, diehard Bruin fans anxiously awaited the arrival of Orr — the Junior-hockey icon in Oshawa — around whom the nucleus of a contending team was promised. Under rookie coach Harry Sinden, Orr flashed his expected brilliance in 1966-67, but the Bruins were still woefully shy of accomplished scorers to halt a seven-year playoff drought.

All of that would change, however, with a gargantuan trade on the afternoon of May 15, 1967. In the most lamentable decision in hockey history, Chicago general manager Tommy Ivan concluded that his team had gotten maximum use out of Phil Esposito, the lanky centerman from Sault Ste. Marie, who'd been benched by coach Billy Reay through most of the Blackhawks' 1967 playoff loss to the Maple Leafs.

Mortified by that semifinal upset, Ivan sought to reverse the chemistry of his underachieving hockey club by dealing talented puckhounds Esposito, Ken Hodge and Fred Stanfield to Boston, for center Pit Martin, promising defenceman Gilles Marotte and unheralded goalie Jack Norris. Within only weeks of the following season, it would become the worst trade in the annals of hockey.

Esposito stuck it in Ivan's ear in 1967-68, blossoming into the prolific center the Chicago boss figured he would not become. Scoring a career-high 35 goals, Espo finished a scant three points behind Art Ross Trophy winner Stan Mikita of the Blackhawks. Hodge and Stanfield combined for 45 goals and the Bruins made the playoffs for the first time since 1959. Conversely, the 'Hawks plummeted 14 points in the standings and finished fourth in the East, four points behind Boston.

But, the 1968-69 NHL season really emphasized just how enormous a mistake Ivan had made. Esposito exploded offensively, becoming the first player in NHL history to reach the 100-point plateau. Centering a forward unit with Hodge and Ron Murphy, Esposito scored 49 goals and set up 77 others for a surrealistic 126 points, easily winning the Art Ross Trophy. Hodge scored 45 himself (and 90 points), while Stanfield chipped in with 25. Boston finished second to Montreal in the East with 100 points, their highest total ever. Chicago finished last and missed the playoffs for the first time in 11 years.

Additionally, the Bruins had become a tough, menacing team that thrived on intimidating weaker opponents, particularly in the squalid environs of the Boston Garden. Ted Green, Don Awrey, Eddie Shack, Derek Sanderson, John McKenzie, Wayne Cashman and Hodge were all adept at combining bellicosity with their hockey playing talents. Orr was no shrinking-violet either. Together, they formed the now-legendary collection known as the "Big, Bad Bruins". Few teams back then looked forward to a trip to Boston.

So, big things were expected of the Bruins as they embarked on their 1969 playoff run. In fact, Montreal appeared to be Boston's only legitimate Stanley Cup obstacle. However, the Bruins would first have to deal with an undercurrent of bad blood that had developed between themselves and the Maple Leafs. The ill feelings stemmed from a pair of incidents during the previous two regular seasons.

On November 7, 1967, at the Garden, the Bruin players responded in mob fashion to a perceived attack on Orr by Maple Leaf forward Brian Conacher. A low-impact player whose objectives in life stretched far beyond the realm of hockey, Conacher had played for Canada's national team at the 1964 Winter Olympics in Innsbruck. Often outspoken, and generally passive on the ice, he was among Punch Imlach's least-favourite players, and he saw limited action.

While killing a penalty in that game at Boston, he high-sticked Orr across the bridge of the nose. To this day, Conacher maintains it was purely accidental: a plausible claim considering his non-aggressive nature. But Orr and his Bruin teammates evidently believed otherwise, and they unleashed a gang attack against Conacher.

Those who witnessed the scene recall being astonished at how unwilling Conacher's Maple Leaf teammates were to involve themselves in the melee. The consensus is that they chickened out and left Conacher to fend for himself. Accordingly, he took an unmerciful beating.

The second incident between the Maple Leafs and Boston, just more than 16 months later, was decidedly more balanced. On March 15, 1969, a Saturday night, the Bruins were in Toronto for the opener of a home-and-home weekend series. In the third period of a game the Leafs would ultimately win, Quinn ran Orr from behind, ploughing him violently into the crossbar of the Maple Leaf net.

It was a response, Quinn maintains, to Orr jabbing away at the glove of Leaf goalie Bruce Gamble after the whistle had sounded to end play. "I guess Bobby thought the puck was still loose, but Bruce had it smothered," Quinn remembers. "He was hacking at Bruce's glove, so I came in and knocked him down, just as any defenceman worth his salt would do in that situation.

"As I was standing over Bobby, he kicked me in the stomach with his skate, so I kicked him in the ass with *mine*. And then, as I fully expected, a whole bunch of their players jumped in to help out." Quinn and Orr ultimately separated and engaged in a dandy fight.

Having pulled a groin muscle during that game, Quinn was unable to suit up for the return match at the Garden Sunday night. But, the Bruin fans were unfazed by his absence. *"We want Quinn!"* they shouted, after it was announced he would not be in the line-up. Without Quinn, the Leafs were overwhelmed by the fired-up Bruins to the tune of 11-3.

Several days later, under the headline **"CAN'T TURN YOUR BACK," QUINN SAYS OF BRUINS**, the Maple Leaf defenceman lashed out at the Boston players in an article by *Globe & Mail* hockey writer Lou Cauz.

"All they are is a bunch of back-stabbers," Quinn said. "You can't turn your back on them or they'll give it to you, and good."

About not being able to play in the Sunday game at Boston, Quinn said, "I was eating my heart out not to be out there; I've never wanted to play in a game as much as that one."

In response to the Garden fans chanting for his blood, Quinn admitted, "Sure I was tense but I never thought of being scared. There isn't anybody on the Bruins who scares me. Listen, I don't profess to be a fist fighter. But, I don't intend to take any guff from the Bruins. I'm going to play their style of game. We've got a lot of small forwards and if they're going to be hammered by the Bruins, I'm going to do the same in my end of the rink."

Concluding his verbal rant, Quinn offered up a personal wish. "I'm not going to say anything that will perhaps come back and haunt me, but I'd like to get another shot at them."

It was against that backdrop that the Leafs and Bruins readied to face each other in the Stanley Cup quarterfinals. By finishing fourth in the East Division, the Leafs and Quinn were assured of at least *four* more shots at the Bruins. The best-of-seven series would open in Boston for games Wednesday and Thursday, before shifting to Toronto Saturday and Sunday. The Maple Leafs appeared to be in over their heads, having lost all four games in Boston during the regular season. But, neither were the Bruins able to win in Toronto, losing and tying twice.

As well, a potential sign of optimism had surfaced only a week earlier, in the Maple Leafs' final Wednesday night game of the season. Having fallen behind the high-powered Canadiens, 3-0, the Leafs showed immense poise and energy in roaring back to beat Montreal, 6-4. Could they display the same kind of stubbornness against the favoured Bruins?

That question was answered rather emphatically in the first half of the series opener. And it came as an embarrassment to the Leafs, and their millions of fans watching on TV back home. Led by an impassioned Esposito (on his way to a four-goal, two-assist performance), Boston erupted for a 6-0 lead midway through the second period. After killing off an early two-man disadvantage, the Beantowners made it look easy — pouring shots past a beleaguered Bruce Gamble; then continuing their assault against the old playoff warhorse, Johnny Bower.

Coming off an eight-goal loss in their previous visit to Boston, it was painfully obvious the Leafs could not contend with the Bruins in even a respectable manner away from home. But, through the humiliation and lop-sidedness, the fact remained that in order to prevail in the series, the Leafs would have to win one game at the Boston Garden. The opener was beyond repair, but Game 2 would be played in less than 24 hours and several Leaf players (with blatant encouragement from coach Punch Imlach) figured it was time to send a message.

At 18:03 of the second period, Pat Quinn delivered that calling card, and hockey fans in Toronto have been talking about it ever since.

Bobby Orr gathered up a loose puck behind his own net and started out of his zone along the right-wing boards. Maple Leaf forward Brit Selby was hounding him from behind and the puck got caught up between Orr's skates. In an effort to regain control, Orr frantically tried to kick it back to his stick, all the while looking at the puck. With his head down, the Boston superstar was frighteningly vulnerable — his old buddy, Quinn, moving forth like a locomotive.

"Orr was great at wheeling back behind his net and picking up the puck, especially on shoot-ins," Quinn recalls. "He was then able to skate past opposing forecheckers because of his incredible speed. Well, on that particular rush, Brit Selby caught up to Bobby and directed him on an angle towards the right-hand boards. As a result, Orr was paying more attention to Brit than to me, and it was the perfect set-up... a forward putting his defenceman in a position to step up and hit.

"Bobby never saw me coming."

Quinn launched all of his 215 pounds at Orr, smashing into the star defenceman with brute force, and the two players went catapulting in opposite directions. Orr crash-landed on his back, near the boards, and his body went limp. Ken Hodge immediately skated over and propped Orr's head on one of his gloves, like a pillow. Hockey's greatest star was out cold in the middle of the Boston Garden.

The late Bob Pennington described the scene on a front-page story in the Toronto *Telegram*:

> "...Quinn hit Orr, the idol of this city, with almost sickening force. Orr lay still on the ice with his head tilting at a strange angle. For almost a minute, that seemed like an hour of nightmare, there was the terrible suspicion his neck might have been broken."

Seeing their hero in such obvious peril, and knowing it was the hated Quinn who had caused it, the Bruin fans turned instant-ugly. As the training staff attended to the unconscious Orr, Quinn coolly circled the ice in his own zone — verbal threats raining down on him from all sides. He was very much a wanted man.

Referee John Ashley, obviously predisposed by the atmosphere in the arena, decided to levy Quinn with a five-minute major for elbowing, even though television replays clearly showed Orr smashing into Quinn's shoulder. With only 1:57 remaining in the period, and the Garden crowd growing nastier by the minute, it would have seemed logical for Ashley to send Quinn to the relative sanctuary of the dressing room. Instead, Quinn skated to the penalty box... within easy reaching distance of the fans who so desperately wanted his scalp.

Meanwhile, Orr finally came to, after a 90-second blackout. As he unsteadily shuffled past the penalty box area, propped up by teammates on either side, he paused to offer Quinn a few pleasantries. As soon as Orr disappeared into the Boston dressing room, the fans in the vicinity of the box focused *their* hostilities on the despised Maple Leaf.

"A number of the people surged down and tried to get at me," Quinn remembers. "Someone smacked me in back of the head with something — I don't know what — and I turned around to protect myself with my stick. One of Boston's finest was trying to contain the mob of spectators, who had surrounded me on all sides. I swung my stick again and accidentally smashed the small pane of protective glass behind the penalty box.

"Unfortunately, the policeman caught the brunt of the glass exploding and was cut rather badly on his forehead. At that point, I realized I had to get the hell out of the box and I skated back onto the relative safety of the ice surface."

Meanwhile, other Maple Leaf players, including defenceman Mike Pelyk, swung *their* sticks over the glass in an attempt to scatter the unruly throng.

In his *Telegram* story, Pennington recounted the frenzied climate around Quinn:

> "A policeman, trying to hold back Quinn's attackers, was hurled against the glass and the broken safety glass cut him around the eyes. A woman in her sixties was hit on the head by a lunging hockey stick and helped to the first-aid room. Other women screamed, and a man shouted: 'Get that @&#%@ Quinn out of here before they kill him!'"

As the Maple Leaf defenceman skated around near the Toronto bench, the crowd began chanting, in unison, *"We want Quinn! We want Quinn!"* Ashley finally came to his senses and ushered Quinn towards the exit to the Maple Leaf dressing room — Boston policemen taking over as escorts once Quinn left the ice.

"I remember feeling a bit frightened by that entire scene," Quinn admits. "It's kind of different when you're standing in the middle of a hockey rink and thousands of people are screaming that they want to kill you. The fans were littering the ice and yelling threats at me. I was more than happy to get out of there and to the dressing room."

After a brief examination in the Garden medical clinic, Orr was taken to hospital, where he'd spend the night under observation.

"That was definitely one of the hardest body checks I ever took," admits Orr, who says he never harboured any ill feelings towards

Quinn. "Hockey's a tough game and if you get involved in the play like I used to, you're going to get hit. Patty came a long way to wallop me that night and I felt he deserved a penalty. I was trying to kick the puck up the boards, I had my head down, and he took a good run at me.

"But, hey, that's part of the game. He was a tough, physical player and I think he'd have done the same to anyone else. The little feud we had going back then made it seem like he was trying to hurt me, but I don't believe there was ever a player who intentionally did that. Not when I played, anyway."

With his innate ability to control the tempo of a hockey game, Orr was almost always a preferred target on the ice. But even with his bevy of knee ailments, he was somehow both dexterous and powerful enough to circumvent even the most menacing of opponents.

"That's not to say I didn't get hit," Orr stresses. "I carried the puck a lot and never shied away from the physical part of the game. So I got banged around pretty good, believe me. That strategy sure didn't help my problems with the bad knees, but that's the way I played and the hits came with the territory."

While the brutal check he took from Quinn may have been the most renowned of his NHL career, Orr isn't sure it was the hardest. "Heck, I got hit so many times, it's difficult to remember," he says. "But, I'd have to think it was in the top half-dozen, anyway. There were many times where I felt I could sneak by someone, and got sent flying instead. Billy Barber (ex-Philadelphia Flyer) nailed me like that in the open ice one night and hurt my knee.

"But, apart from that check by Quinn, the hit I think I'll always remember most came courtesy of Gordie Howe in my very first NHL game (at the old Detroit Olympia). I was admiring one of my pretty passes... and *WHAM!!!* Ol' number nine stopped by to say hello. I suppose Gordie wanted to let the kid know he was still around. And I remember doing a little bird-watching that night."

After belting Orr, then scurrying away from the angered mob of Bruin supporters, Quinn served his five-minute penalty and went back into the game early in the third period. Even the Boston fans had to feel that was a gutsy and courageous move. John McKenzie took an early run at Quinn, delighting the Garden crowd, but the game soon returned to its more-familiar pattern — the Bruins swarming offensively; the Maple Leafs digging the puck out of their net.

By the 12:47 mark of the third period, the score read: Boston 10, Toronto 0. On the Garden sportstimer above center ice, the evening's degradation was complete, but several of the Maple Leafs felt they had other scores to settle before the start of Game 2. As a result, the name Forbes Kennedy is still fresh on the minds of long-time Maple Leaf observers, 25 full years after his final game in the NHL.

A native of Dorchester, New Brunswick, Kennedy had risen through the Montreal organization, playing three years for the Junior Habs. But, he was sold to Chicago in May, 1956, and he began his NHL career with the Blackhawks the following season. A little pepperpot at 5-foot-8 and 185 pounds, Kennedy — nicknamed "Spud" because of his Maritime roots — never scored more than 12 goals in any one season, but he was always a willing scrapper. Sometimes *too* willing.

"When I broke in with Chicago, I actually played on a scoring line with Harry Watson and Eddie Litzenberger," Kennedy remembers. "I guess they figured that if you came up through the Canadiens' organization, you'd know how to put the puck in the net. Well, they soon found out that I wasn't another Rocket Richard, but one thing I *could* do is skate all night and not get tired.

"As a result, our coach Tommy Ivan told me to start hitting and roughing things up. He put me on a checking line with Johnny Wilson and Nick Mickoski, and the three of us later wound up together in Detroit. When you're on the checking line, it's your job to aggravate people and that's what I started doing. In fact, I never *stopped* doing it until the day I retired from hockey."

Rarely have truer words been spoken. Kennedy played parts of 11 seasons in the NHL with Chicago, Detroit, Boston, Philadelphia and the Maple Leafs. In 603 regular-season games, he managed to score 70 goals, and ring up 988 penalty minutes. Kennedy wasn't big, but he had a quick temper and he knew precisely how to earn his meal ticket.

"I had to fight to stay in the NHL," he says. "Otherwise, I'd have been out beating the bushes. It began when I played that checking role with Chicago. I'd find myself getting into one fight, then another one. And I'd win some and lose some. But, I always showed up."

Selected from Boston by Philadelphia in the 1967 expansion draft, Kennedy was a fan-favourite on that first Flyers' team.

"He was probably our most popular player," recalls Doug Favell, who played goal for the original Flyers. "He was a little guy with a choppy skating style who worked like hell on the ice, and had a lot of charisma off the ice. He always had the cigar going and he wore cowboy boots most of the time. Everybody loves a small player who is tough and that's how Forbsie was in Philadelphia."

Kennedy was a character, and his Flyer teammates occasionally enjoyed having fun at his expense. "I don't recall how we found out, but word somehow got around that Forbsie was terrified of mice," Favell smiles. "Here was a man who would fight the toughest players in hockey — guys who were twice his size — but he was scared of a wee, little mouse. Of course, once we found that out, his life was never the same."

Hardly a day went by between September and May in which Kennedy did *not* find a rubber mouse stuffed into his glove, his shoe, his socks — anywhere a mischievous teammate could fit one.

"We even slipped one into his pre-game meal a couple of times," Favell laughs. "Right between the potatoes and the vegetables. He'd be munching away unsuspectingly and we'd all be watching him with one eye. Then he'd suddenly leap up and run like hell, screaming and swearing. It was the funniest thing you've ever seen."

Kennedy also enjoyed *partaking* in various team pranks, and Favell recalls being his victim on one memorable occasion.

"We used to practice at a rink in Cherry Hill, New Jersey, but the place didn't have any dressing rooms," Favell says. "So, we would get into our gear at the Spectrum and bus over there. Well, one day, the guys did something to me and I wanted to get even. So, when we returned to Philadelphia after practice, I jumped off the bus before anyone else and ran into the Spectrum.

"There was only one entrance-door that we could use and I locked it behind me. Nobody else could get in. While the boys were standing outside and screaming for me to open up, I was enjoying a leisurely shower. I then slipped out another entrance and they never even saw me leave the building.

"Well, the next day, Forbsie came up to me with that devilish smile of his and I knew I was in trouble. That was back in the late-1960s, when a lot of men were wearing long sideburns. While Forbsie held me down, the other guys shaved off my left sideburn. I looked absolutely ridiculous, but I suppose I deserved it."

For some reason, Kennedy had a particularly wild 1968-69 season with Philadelphia and Toronto. Averaging just more than 90 penalty minutes during his first 10 years in the league, he suddenly hacked and brawled his way to a career-high (and league-leading) 219 minutes. As per usual, he took on all comers... big and small... on or off the ice.

A fracas during a game in Oakland just prior to Christmas drew the wrath of NHL president Clarence Campbell. The Flyers and Seals got into a melee and Kennedy wound up fighting several Oakland players.

When cooler heads finally prevailed, referee Bruce Hood ushered Kennedy to the penalty box without incident.

"I was standing in the box and yapping back and forth with a couple of their players: Gene Ubriaco and Carol Vadnais," Kennedy remembers. "After a few seconds, Vadnais turned to Ubriaco and said, `Don't pay any attention to him, he's just trying to sucker us into another penalty. We'll get him when he comes out.' Well, I figured there was no use in waiting for *that*, and I jumped out of the box right then and there.

"I tried to get at Vadnais for his wise-ass remark but there were too many people between us. Hood gave me a game misconduct for coming out of the box and as I was leaving the ice, (Oakland coach) Fred Glover screamed something at me. So, I made a detour over to their bench and grabbed Glover by the tie.

"I was practically choking him and was about to haul his ass over the boards when one of my teammates collared me around the neck. I fell over backwards and never got the chance to give Glover a smack. I think (Clarence) Campbell fined me a hundred bucks for that incident."

Just two weeks after the blow-up in Oakland, Kennedy was involved with Jim Dorey of the Maple Leafs in a high-sticking incident at the Spectrum. "It was the first and only time in my career that I hit a player on the head with my stick," Kennedy says. "That wasn't my style and I felt badly about it right away. But, I'll tell you what happened.

"(Gary) Dornhoefer hit a Maple Leaf player and (Mike) Pelyk took a run at Dornhoefer. So, I went in to straighten out Pelyk and we both got minor penalties. As we're skating to the box, Dorey came over and said to Pelyk, 'Why don't you *give* it to him?', wondering, I guess, why Pelyk wasn't fighting me. And I said to Dorey, 'Hey, I didn't ask him (Pelyk) to go, why don't *you* take his fucking place?'"

After serving his penalty, Kennedy got the puck and skated deep into the right-wing corner in the Maple Leaf zone. "I turned around and looked for someone in front of the net, but everyone was covered, so I waited for a defenceman to move up," Kennedy recalls. "As I held the puck, Dorey whacked me across the arms with his stick. I turned around, still holding the puck, and got whacked again. Then a third time.

"Finally, I passed the puck and went towards Dorey with my stick raised to give him a half-scare. Well, I wound up clubbing him right on top of the head. And I couldn't believe it... I felt sick. That's the last thing I ever wanted to do. When I played, I always said, `A coward uses his hockey stick.' And there I was hitting Dorey over the head.

"(Punch) Imlach sent Pat Quinn over the boards, and Quinn said to me, 'Spud, I never thought I'd see you use your stick.' And, I said, 'Well, Dorey used my arms as a fucking pin-cushion, so I used his head.' But, that was just for the sake of saying *something*. I didn't feel at all good about what I had done.

"Anyway, we had to go right into Toronto for our next game three days later, and all their guys were telling the newspapers how they were going to get even with me. So, we had a meeting before the game and I said to (Flyers' coach) Keith Allen that I wanted to be out there on the first shift... I wasn't going to back away and hide.

"It turned out that nothing happened. I think I wound up with six minutes in penalties, but all for separate fouls. There were no carry-over incidents from the previous game."

Kennedy became a Maple Leaf on March 2, 1969 — in a four-player deal between Philadelphia and Toronto. "The trainer wound up putting my locker right next to Dorey's in our dressing room at the Gardens," Kennedy recalls. "We were sitting there before my first game when Imlach walked by with a smile and said, '*You* know this guy.' I smiled back and said, 'Yup.'"

Kennedy played 13 games for the Maple Leafs at the end of the '68-69 season, setting up three goals and accumulating 24 penalty minutes. But, he'll always be remembered for his lone playoff appearance in a Maple Leaf uniform — which turned out to be his last game in the NHL.

With less than four minutes remaining in that terribly lop-sided quarterfinal game in Boston — Leafs losing, 10-0 — Imlach dispatched Kennedy on to the ice to create some havoc. "Punch was a smart coach," Kennedy recalls. "We were getting bombed and he said, 'We gotta play here again tomorrow night, boys... let's not lay down and die. Let 'em know we're still alive.' And with that, he tapped me on the shoulder."

To this day, Kennedy acknowledges that his objective at that moment was to "try and stir up a little shit". But he never figured World War Three would break out.

"I cut across in front of the Boston net and Gerry Cheevers (the Bruins' goalie) gave me a dandy two-hander, right across the ankle," Kennedy remembers. "Maybe he thought I was going after *him*, but I was just chasing the puck. Anyway, the play went up the ice and when I got to the Boston blueline, I said to myself, 'What the fuck am I doing?! We're losing 10-0... I'm not going to take that shit.' So, I turned around to go back at Cheevers."

Before he could get there, however, Kennedy was intercepted by Bruin defenceman Ted Green, who high-sticked him across the bridge of his nose. Bleeding, but undaunted, Kennedy maintained his pursuit of Cheevers and the two players began fighting. After a spirited battle, firey John McKenzie intervened on his goaltender's behalf and he also fought with Kennedy, winning a close decision over the tiring Maple Leaf. Pretty soon, Kennedy found himself surrounded by an angered flock of Bruin players — all wanting a piece of him.

Sports editor Charles (Chick) McGregor of the *Telegram* watched the brawl unfold on television, and described the scene in a column atop the sports section the following day:

"...The spectacle of Forbes Kennedy — The Disturber — wheeling and swooping like a bird of prey while the enemy lurked on all sides was one thing. But to see him then leap at Gerry Cheevers (unmasked, at last!) and knock him over, ungainly goalie pads flopping like broken limbs, was quite another.

"And then, into a melee of players, again seeking Cheevers, who was by now getting physical as well as moral support from teammates, including back-up goalie Eddie Johnston."

The part about Kennedy bobbing and weaving like a boxer stands out all these years later. "They were coming at me from all sides and I had to be ready," he recalls. "I didn't know who was going to try and hit me next. Everybody was into it."

It was during that exaggerated moment of self-preservation that Kennedy threw his final punch as a pro hockey player. And it landed squarely on the chin of linesman George Ashley.

"I never meant to hit him," Kennedy says. "All I remember is that everybody on the ice was after me, and Ashley had a different colour sweater than I did. It was simply a reaction. I was looking to my left, trying to get back at Cheevers, when somebody yelled, `Look out!' I saw another guy coming at me from the corner of my right eye and I just let 'er go. And, as soon as I did, I remember thinking, `Oh jeez, I'm in shit now!'"

Ashley tumbled over backwards in front of fellow linesman Matt Pavelich, who had a look of disbelief on his face, and at the feet of back-up goaltenders Bower and Johnston, who had paired off during the fighting.

"Kennedy and Cheevers started coming towards each other near the front of the Boston net," Ashley recalls. "Back then, linesmen were instructed to more-or-less maintain a `hands-off' policy during fight situations, because it was felt we would only further aggravate the players if we tried to manhandle them. So, I just sort of stepped in front of Forbsie and as soon as I got there, his right hand came up and caught me on the brow of my chin."

Ashley remembers being completely unaffected by the punch. "He knocked me on the seat of my pants but I don't recall feeling the force of the blow. I got up very quickly because Jim Dorey and Eddie Shack were going at it. All I remember is wanting to get some semblance of order restored."

By then, everybody in the Garden not wearing a Maple Leaf uniform wanted a piece of Kennedy. While pursuing Cheevers yet again, he found himself along the boards inside the Boston blueline. Trying to restrain him with a bearhug was Johnston, his former Bruin teammate and good friend. Not having played in the game that night, Johnston still had a towel wrapped around the back of his neck and tucked into the front of his Boston uniform.

Up until several years ago — in many NHL rinks — fans sitting at ice level between the goallines were protected by panes of plexiglass that rose only two feet above the boards (it has since been increased to four feet). As a result, a spectator in a rail (or front-row) seat back in the late-60s could easily stand up and reach over the glass. As Kennedy struggled along the boards to free himself of Johnston's grip, that's exactly what happened. And it was frightening.

"Several fans were reaching over, grabbing Forbes in a headlock, and pounding away at him," Johnston remembers. "One guy had a big ring on his right hand and he was punching at the back of Forbsie's head. I was just trying to get him away from the boards so he wouldn't have to keep on taking that extra punishment.

"We had played together in Boston and were great friends. So I was pleading with him to get away from there, but when Forbsie blew his stack in those days, there was nothing you could do."

Kennedy has vivid memories of that struggle with Johnston, but he doesn't recall being bopped on the noggin by that fan wearing the ring.

"Oh well, if he hit me on top of the head, I wouldn't have felt it," he laughs. "Of course, if my arms were loose, I could've easily gotten a hold of that guy and I'd have taken an awful whack at him. He obviously didn't care about me, so I wouldn't have been too concerned about him, either. It was the only time I ever got hit by a spectator.

"Eddie was trying to get me away from there and he was calling me `Howie' (as in Montreal legend Howie Morenz). One night, when we played together in Boston, I was killing a penalty and lugging the puck all over the ice. Well, from that moment on, Ed called me `Howie'.

"Of course, during that fight, I didn't want anything to do with him. We were like brothers. I think I said a couple of times, `C'mon Eddie, get out of here.' And he kept on saying, `Cool down, Forbsie, you're going to get yourself into big trouble.' But, I don't remember being in a mood to listen."

Johnston finally coerced Kennedy to lighten up, but John McKenzie then re-entered the picture and spoiled the whole thing.

"I was going off the ice, absolutely dead-tired, when McKenzie started yapping at me again," Kennedy recalls. "So, I gave him a push or a half-shove and he caught me on top of the head with a punch. Well, I couldn't leave the ice after *that* so I reached out to get a hold of him and he grabbed my sweater. He got his right-hand loose and nailed me with a dandy to the nose, where I was already bleeding from Green's cross-check at the start of the brawl.

"I finally got *my* hand loose and fought back, but it was just like slappin' somebody; I had nothing left. So, that's when I grabbed John by the shoulders and gave him a coco-bonk. It was all I could do to save myself. McKenzie went down to the ice and Jim Dorey said, `Give it to him now!' And I said, `Whad'ya want me to do, *kiss* him?!'

"I was beat, the fight was over, and all I wanted was to get the hell into the dressing room and sit down."

Forbes Kennedy would never again skate onto an NHL ice surface. For his self-proclaimed unintentional knockdown of linesman Ashley, he was suspended by NHL president Clarence Campbell for four games and hit with a $1,000 fine. He also set an NHL playoff record that still exists for most penalties in one game — eight — four minors, two majors, a 10-minute misconduct and a game-misconduct (Kim Clackson of Pittsburgh tied the mark in a first-round game against Boston, April 14, 1980).

Kennedy underwent two operations on his knee during the summer of 1969 and had to retire from hockey. But, he remembers the hearing with Campbell as if it happened only yesterday.

"It was held the following afternoon at the old Madison Hotel next to Boston Garden, and I can tell you that Campbell wanted my ass," says Kennedy. "I think our team was staying at the Hilton Plaza, so me and King Clancy took a cab to the Madison and went up to Campbell's suite: he had flown in from New York for the hearing.

"There were seven of us in the room: Campbell, me and King, (NHL referee-in-chief) Scotty Morrison, and the officiating crew from the previous night (John Ashley, George Ashley and Matt Pavelich). Campbell must have had 10 newspapers spread out on the desk in front of him... the Boston paper, Chicago paper, New York paper, Toronto paper, and all of them had front-page photos and stories of me punching Ashley.

"I'm sure he wanted me to see them and get nervous, but I didn't flinch. I had been reading them all fucking day, anyway; *he* didn't have to show me what happened the night before."

Campbell was a Rhodes Scholar and a lawyer by trade, and Kennedy says he played up that latter role to the hilt. "Oh yeah, he thought he was another goddamned Perry Mason," Forbes recalls. "He must have asked me at least 20 times for my version of the events that took place the previous night, hoping that I'd eventually contradict myself. He was writing things down like a lawyer but I kept repeating myself word for word... not a thing was different.

"I told him: `I went in front of the net and got slashed. I got to the blueline, then came back towards Cheevers, and got crosschecked by Ted Green. A fight broke out; I was bleeding, and my eyes were watery from the crosscheck.' Punch Imlach told me to add that watery part in; he thought it would make a better excuse for me hitting Ashley.

"Then I concluded: `With my eyes watering, things were a little blurry. The linesman came at me from the corner of my eye and I thought it was one of the Bruin players. So I let one go. It was an accident.' As I mentioned, I must have repeated that story 20 times."

After Campbell's thorough grilling of Kennedy, King Clancy stood up to cross-examine some of the other witnesses. Kennedy remembers that scene very well.

"King turned to Scotty Morrison and said, `Scotty, you were in the pressbox, did you see Kennedy get crosschecked?' Scotty said no. Then he turned to John Ashley and said, `John, did you have a penalty call on Cheevers for slashing?' John said no. King then asked Matt Pavelich if *he'd* seen either of those infractions, and Matt also said no.

"Campbell then wanted to show all of us a videotape of the whole incident but I told him I was going back to the hotel to get some rest. I said, `I've got a game tonight; there's playoff money at stake and I have a family to feed. I need my sleep.' At which point, he looked at me over top his glasses and said, `If I were you, I wouldn't plan on too many more games this year.' I told him that was fine but just in case, I still needed my rest. And I left."

Kennedy took a cab back to the Hilton and went up to see Imlach.

"I filled Punch in on what happened at the hearing and he told me to get dressed for the game that night. It was already late in the day and he didn't think the league would have enough time to send a formal telegram stating that I was suspended. So, I had a brief nap then went to the Garden and got my gear on prior to the warm-up.

"Just before we were going out on the ice, Punch and King walked in. Punch looked at me and said, `Are you ready to go?' I said I was. Then he smiled kind of sheepishly and said, `Well, you better take off your equipment, you got four games and a thousand bucks.'

"At which point George Armstrong stood up and said to King, `Some kind of fucking lawyer *you* are!' Of course, that's all Clancy had to hear."

Kennedy laughs uproariously when recalling Clancy's response to Armstrong's little dig. Here's how the story goes.

Clancy glared over at the Leaf captain and said, "Now you listen to this. I had everything won. We got in there, the tape came on, Cheevers slashed Kennedy, John Ashley put his arm up, and I yelled `CUT!' And I said, `John, I thought you told me you didn't call a penalty' (Ashley forgot that he'd called a delayed holding minor on Bruin defenceman Rick Smith). So I won that one.

"Then the tape showed Forbsie going up to the blueline, turning back, and getting hit in the nose with a crosscheck by Green. And Matt Pavelich is looking at the whole thing from five feet away. I said, `Matt, you're going to tell me you didn't see that?' He said he didn't. `Well then, you should be wearing glasses.

"`And how about you, Scotty... you didn't see that crosscheck from the pressbox?' He never said a word.

"I was sure I had it won. Every time something happened on the tape, I yelled `CUT!' and nobody had any answers for me.

"But then, the tape showed Forbsie knocking down Ashley, and all I heard Campbell say was, `CUT!!'

"I put my hat on and left the building."

George Ashley says he felt bad for Kennedy when Campbell suspended him. "I remember sitting there at that hearing, a day after my very first NHL playoff game, and thinking what kind of an eye-opener it was to have this whole thing unfold before me," Ashley recalls. "And I will always remember Clarence Campbell saying, `My God!' after seeing the tape of Kennedy knocking me down. I knew then that Forbes was finished for the remainder of the playoffs.

"And that didn't make me feel good. I don't believe that Forbes meant to hit me... it just happened in the heat of the battle. I had known Forbsie from the past and he wasn't the type of player who would even consider doing something like that intentionally. But, I suppose if you knock an official down — accidentally or not — you're likely to be suspended and that's one aspect of the game that hasn't changed."

*   *   *   *   *   *

The Bruins went on to a four-game playoff sweep, humiliating the Maple Leafs almost as badly in Game 2 by a score of 7-0. If you're keeping count, that means Boston beat the Leafs three consecutive times at the Garden by a combined score of 28-3 (including the 11-3 regular-season romp, March 16). The Leafs were more competitive in their two playoff home games, losing by counts of 4-3 and 3-2. But close only counts in horseshoes, and the Leafs had none of *them* in the post-season of 1969.

Reacting to the altercations of Game One, the fans at Maple Leaf Gardens loudly booed Bobby Orr, Gerry Cheevers and John McKenzie. And they cheered wildly every time Pat Quinn stepped onto the ice. When the series ended, and the teams lined up to shake hands, practically every eye in the building was fixed on No. 23 in blue and No. 4 in white. Would Quinn and Orr embrace one another?

"Oh, of course we did; we were both professionals, the series was over, and there were no hard feelings," Orr remembers. "I had my head down and I got belted. If I hadn't been knocked unconscious, there would never have been such an uproar. Patty and I are great friends and I never felt he tried to hurt me. But I will admit that for the rest of my career, I was always aware when we were on the ice together."

Quinn concurs with Orr on almost everything about that incident, with one exception. "I didn't feel there should have been a penalty called on the play, and I still don't, 25 years later," he says. "Bobby wasn't looking up and it was a hard, clean check. If I'd hit any other player in any other arena, I doubt I would have been penalized. But we were in Boston and the player was Bobby Orr.

"It's one of those situations you still see today. A player will get a penalty for who he *hits* or who he *is*, rather than for the actual infraction. I suppose that's a human response from the officials."

In regards to shaking hands with Orr after the series, Quinn did so naturally. "You can't hold grudges in hockey or you'll go punchy," he says. "Bobby played great and his team won the series. At the same time, I think he realized the body-check was clean, and it was more his fault than mine that he was injured. I don't remember saying anything to Bobby when we passed each other in line, but neither do I remember thinking that we wouldn't shake hands."

Quinn still feels satisfaction from showing the "Big, Bad Bruins" that at least *he* wasn't going to be intimidated.

"They were a tough bunch of guys and their tactics scared the hell out of a lot of hockey clubs," he says. "They were gang-fighters and that's why the NHL instituted the third-man-in rule (in 1971). They were definitely the forerunner to those teams in Philadelphia in the early 70s and it's no coincidence that both organizations won a pair of Stanley Cups. It's the way you had to play to be successful during that era in hockey.

"But, the Bruins never scared me. They had beaten up Brian Conacher pretty badly in that game a year earlier and nobody stepped up to help him. One of the reasons I came to the Leafs was to make sure that never happened again."

The brawl involving Forbes Kennedy was also a sign of the times and Kennedy remembers feeling the same as Quinn did about the Bruins.

"They never bothered me and neither did the type of situation that unfolded that night," he says. "I knew a lot of those players from my days in Boston and we were great buddies away from the rink. But they sure as hell weren't going to run roughshod over me on the ice. Guys like myself, Dorey, Quinn, Rick Ley... we were aware of the atmosphere in the rink that night after Orr got clobbered. But, we laughed at situations like that. If they wanted to fight us, we were ready."

However, Kennedy's Boston ties did affect him on one occasion during that donnybrook. "After Ted Green crosschecked me in the face, we piled up in the corner and Ley got a hold of Teddy's arms from behind. Rick pinned his arms, turned him around to face me and said, `Go ahead, Forbsie, slug him.' He was right there, wide open for a smack. But, I couldn't do it... no way. I'd known Teddy for a long time and he wouldn't have hit me if that situation had been reversed.

"He gave me an awful whack across the nose with his stick, but he knew I was going after Cheevers and he was protecting his goalie. I would have done the same thing to him."

When recalling his little dance along the boards with Ed Johnston, Kennedy laughs at a line Johnston came up with several weeks later.

"Somebody asked him about the fight, and what went on when he was trying to pull me away from the boards," Kennedy recalls. "Well, I was a guy who enjoyed having a drink or two after a game and Ed remembered that one of the fans threw a cup of beer at me from five or six rows up in the seats. And he told this reporter, `Yeah, he was having a rough time that night, but when the fan threw the beer, Forbsie just turned around and opened his mouth.' I thought that was a great line. I mean, what are friends for, huh?"

Joking aside, Kennedy was very fortunate not to have been badly injured in that brawl with the Bruins, and the fans.

"It was the wildest night I can recall from *my* playing days," says Brit Selby, who came to the Maple Leafs with Kennedy from Philadelphia. "There was an uglier incident when I was playing with the Flyers, and Larry Zeidel and Eddie Shack (of Boston) had a horrific stick-swinging duel (in a neutral-site game at Maple Leaf Gardens, March 7, 1968, after high winds had torn a hole in the roof of the Spectrum).

"But I never remember hockey fans being in as surly a mood as the folks in Boston that night. It was kind of scary."

The four-game sweep by Boston signified the end of a largely glorious era in Maple Leaf history. Scant moments after the series ended, Leaf president Stafford Smythe walked into the dressing room and fired general manager/coach Punch Imlach. The man who had led the Maple Leafs to four Stanley Cups in the 1960s was gone, making room for the new regime of general manager Jim Gregory and coach Johnny McLellan.

*   *   *   *   *   *

WHERE ARE THEY NOW? ...

PAT QUINN, 52, is the president and general manager of the 1993-94 Western Conference-champion Vancouver Canucks. He dropped his coaching portfolio after the Canucks lost the Cup Final to the New York Rangers. A rugged defenceman, he played in the NHL with Toronto, Vancouver and Atlanta between 1968 and 1977. He has since been a fairly accomplished coach in the big league with Philadelphia, Los Angeles and the Canucks. While coaching the Flyers in 1979-80, his team strung together a 35-game unbeaten streak, longest in NHL history. Philadelphia did not lose a game between Oct. 14, 1979 and Jan. 6, 1980. The Flyers made it to the Stanley Cup final, losing to the Islanders, and Quinn was named coach-of-the-year.

BOBBY ORR, 46, is the greatest defenceman in NHL history and one of the top half-dozen players who ever lived. Joining the Boston Bruins in 1966 at the age of 18, he quickly revolutionized hockey by creating an entirely different role for defencemen. Using his incredible skating and playmaking skills, he opened up a whole new realm of strategy and only a set of wonky knees prevented him from being, undisputedly, the greatest player of all time. He played with Boston and Chicago from 1966 to 1978, winning the Norris Trophy as the NHL's top defenceman in eight consecutive seasons. He's the only defenceman in NHL history to win the Art Ross Trophy as league scoring champ (1969-70 and 1974-75), an inconceivable accomplishment prior to his arrival. And his overtime goal against St. Louis to give Boston the 1970 Stanley Cup — with the startling photo of Orr flying through the air — may be the most famous in NHL history. Orr went back to Boston after his playing days and has done publicity work for a number of companies, including *Planter's* and *Nabisco*. He is on a pedestal with Ted Williams and Larry Bird among favourite sons in Boston sports history.

FORBES KENNEDY, 59, made it through 13 years of professional hockey with the guts, determination and courage of men much bigger than him. Only 5-foot-8, he was among the NHL's most rugged players with Chicago, Detroit, Boston, Philadelphia and Toronto, from 1956 to 1969. A native of the Maritimes, he lives in Charlottetown, P.E.I. and has coached Tier 2 Junior hockey for most of the past 20 years — currently coaching the Charlottetown Abbies of the Nova Scotia-P.E.I. Junior A League. During the summer, he works for the *City of Charlottetown* in the Recreation Department.

DOUG FAVELL, 49, was an original member of the Philadelphia Flyers, splitting the goaltending chores with Bernie Parent from 1967 to 1971. Parent was traded to the Maple Leafs in February, 1971, but he jumped to the WHA a year later. When he came back to the NHL in 1973, he wanted to play in Philadelphia, so the Flyers traded Favell to Toronto. Favell played two-plus seasons in a Maple Leaf uniform then finished his career with the Colorado Rockies between 1976 and 1979. While in Denver, he started a wholesale/brokerage car business that he still operates in St. Catharines called *International Gallery of Cars*. Favell was a goalie coach with the Buffalo Sabres from 1987 to 1991 and he currently lives near St. Catharines in Jordan, Ont.

GEORGE ASHLEY, 52, was an NHL linesman from 1967 to 1971, and says he only got knocked on the seat of his pants *once* during that span. He currently lives in Guelph, Ont. and over the past 20 years, has worked for *Canada Post* as a letter carrier.

EDDIE JOHNSTON, 59, played goal in the NHL with Boston, Toronto, St. Louis and Chicago between 1962 and 1978. He was the Bruins' top goaltender during their lean years in the early to mid-1960s, and he shared the netminding duties with Gerry Cheevers on Boston's Stanley Cup-championship teams of 1970 and 1972. He has since been a general manager and coach in the NHL with Chicago, Pittsburgh and Hartford. He is currently the Penguins' head coach, having replaced Scotty Bowman for the 1993-94 season.

BRIT SELBY, 49, won the Calder Trophy as the NHL's rookie of the year with Toronto in 1965-66. It was his crowning achievement during an otherwise unspectacular pro hockey career in the NHL and WHA between 1964 and 1975. Selby played for the Maple Leafs, Philadelphia and St. Louis and later saw action with Quebec, New England and the Toronto Toros in the WHA. During the off-seasons in his playing days, he earned his teaching certificate and has been in that profession for the past 18 years. Currently living in Toronto, he teaches history and economics at *North Toronto* Secondary School.

... *Leafs in Spring* ...

APRIL 28, 1994
Chicago Stadium

One of these days, I'll be able to tell my grandchildren that I attended the final hockey game ever played at Chicago Stadium.

By then of course, 1800 W. Madison Street will have been converted into a parking lot to accommodate the adjacent United Center — new home of the Blackhawks for the 1994-95 season. But the ghosts of the Stadium will remain, long after it becomes a pile of rubble.

Knowing this would be my last chance to see the venerable arena, I brought my videocam to Chicago for the first of two trips during the 1994 Western Conference quarterfinals. Recalling that more than 20,000 fans used to cram into the Stadium for hockey games, what struck me the most upon approaching the building was its compact dimensions. Shaped like a giant loaf of bread, it stood as a shrine amid one of America's most notorious slums. Venturing beyond its fenced-in boundary — known menacingly as the "Compound" — was akin to a death wish.

But the west side of Chicago wasn't quite so intimidating during daylight hours. The taxicab driving me to the pre-game workouts entered the neighbourhood on a hazy springtime morning, and the enormity of the United Center, still under construction, was unmistakable: its distant roof rising above treelines across the street. The Stadium, itself, was dwarfed by the new arena: the contrast *most apparent while standing on the 103rd floor of the Sears Tower in downtown Chicago, two miles east.*

*   *   *   *   *   *

The media entrance to Chicago Stadium was on the west side of the building, at Gate 3 1/2, and beneath the ominous fire-escape stairwells protruding from its facade. The arena was unremarkable from the inside, with three tiers of padded seats, coloured licorice-red. Dominating the Stadium's east end — behind the goal defended twice by the Blackhawks — was the esteemed organ loft: its canopy adorned by a slogan which read:"**REMEMBER THE ROAR**". Indeed, it was one loud building.

But, a pall had been cast over the twilight days of the Stadium. Two weeks earlier, anthem singer Wayne Messmer had been shot in the throat by some lunatic while leaving a Chicago nightclub. Thankfully, he survived the attack, but was obviously unavailable to perform his stirring renditions in person. A recording of Messmer had to suffice but even it managed to whip the Stadium crowd into its usual frenzy.

During the '94 playoffs with the Maple Leafs, I did live radio shows from our broadcast locations in Chicago, San Jose and Vancouver. They would take place late in the afternoon, two or three hours before the game. The Chicago Stadium broadcast booth was suspended from the roof, on the south side of the building. It was a privilege to watch a game from there, as it hung directly over center-ice and was easily the best vantage point in the arena. The regular press box was behind the goal opposite the organ loft, and its sightline was far less appealing.

But reaching the radio/TV facility presented broadcasters with a cardiovascular challenge unlike any other rink in the NHL. Upon asking a security guard for directions, I was instructed to turn left at an opening in the lobby 25 feet away, and "keep climbing". The Stadium had been built before escalators were invented and its legendary owners — the Norris and Wirtz families — were not exactly spendthrifts. A fresh coat of paint every couple of years kept the old joint looking adequate and not a nickel more was spent modernizing the arena.

Therefore, reaching the broadcast booth required a fair amount of exercise: more than the vast majority of us media folk engage in on a daily basis. Attaining the summit effected a strange mixture of feelings and emotions: sort of a cross between Sir Edmund Hillary and a heart-attack victim.

Bob Cole of Hockey Night In Canada agreed to join me for a chat during one of my radio shows but I made the mistake of putting him on the air only seconds *after he arrived in the booth. The poor guy gasped and wheezed through his first answer before I came to my senses and took a commercial break.*

Worse than the climb were the seedy bathroom facilities at either end of the walkway.

If you're a man, peeing wasn't a major problem, so long as you could tolerate lining up in front of a trough like a herd of cattle. However, experiencing a relaxed and pleasurable evisceration was next to impossible in stalls without doors.

*   *   *   *   *   *

The Leafs finished off the Blackhawks and closed out 65 years of hockey history at Chicago Stadium with a 1-0 victory in Game 6 of their Conference quarterfinal. A shot by Dave Ellett bounced into the net off Mike Gartner's posterior at 14:49 of the first period, and that was all the Maple Leafs needed. Incredibly, it was Toronto's third 1-0 triumph of the series.

In the Chicago Sun-Times the next morning, columnist Jay Mariotti capsulized a city's disappointment:

"The finish was all wrong. If this was the very end, then 65 years of ice madness should have been funnelled into one festive, chaotic night. It should have been a time for all 3,675 pipes of the Barton organ to blow through the ceiling and walls. It should have been a time to rattle the foundation one last time, to see if the place actually can move along a city block. Alas, it was too quiet in the Stadium, too tense, too big a letdown. The Hawks couldn't score.

"...Sixty-five years of echoes will have to suffice."

Legendary goalie Terry Sawchuk stones his former teammate Gordie Howe in front of the Toronto net. Sawchuk's record of 103 career shutouts still stands.

Maple Leaf rookie Brian Spencer battles along boards with Bryan Campbell of Chicago, December 12, 1970. That same night, Spencer's father was shot and killed by RCMP officers in Prince George, B.C. in a bizarre attempt to force a local television network to continue coverage of the game.

Jim Dorey jostles with Phil Esposito in front of goalie Marv Edwards during Maple Leaf-Boston game in 1969-70.

New York's Vic Hadfield whistles puck past Maple Leaf goalie Bernie Parent while Bob Baun stumbles in quarterfinal playoff game, Apr. 8, 1971. Later on, Hadfield would toss Parent's mask into the crowd.

*Dave (Tiger) Williams struggles with Pittsburgh defenceman
Dave Burrows at Gardens, Oct. 20, 1976 while Penguins'
Dennis Owchar looks on. Moments later, Williams would club
Owchar over the head with his stick, drawing weapons charge
from Ontario Attorney General's office.*

*The dismal eighties. Team owner Harold Ballard (above) became a
focal point for complaints about the team's continuous losing ways.
But despite these protests, attendance never wavered.*

Two of the familiar faces directly responsible for the resurgence of the Toronto Maple Leafs in the 1990s: above, Head Coach Pat Burns, acquired from the Montreal Canadiens and (facing page) team captain Doug Gilmour, acquired from the Calgary Flames.

7

THE TRIUMPH OF BURNS AND GILL

Montreal Forum
January 9, 1993

"You know, I thought about this game a lot last summer but in the season, I didn't start thinking about it until maybe two weeks ago. And from then on, no one would let me forget it."

Those were the words of Maple Leaf coach Pat Burns moments after the most emotional and exilharating victory of his career, thus far, in the National Hockey League. As if games between the Leafs and Montreal aren't melodramatic enough, the only Forum meeting of the two rivals in 1992-93 took on epic proportions. And all because of the guy behind the Toronto bench.

The Maple Leafs and Canadiens are the two most storied and decorated franchises in NHL history. Since the League was formed back in 1917, there have been 76 Stanley Cup challenges among a group of 39 different franchises. Either Toronto or Montreal has prevailed in 36 of those challenges — for 47 percent of the take. Only twice, however, has the same man coached both clubs.

Dick Irvin guided the Maple Leafs to one Stanley Cup victory and six appearances in the finals between 1931 and 1940. He then took over behind the Montreal bench for 15 seasons and had his name engraved on the mug three more times. Travelling in the opposite direction, Pat Burns became the second coach to handle both teams when he arrived in Toronto amid profound astonishment on May 29, 1992.

While the Leafs were in the market for a new head man, there had been no speculation whatsoever concerning the availability of Burns, whose contract had expired with the Canadiens. By Montreal standards, Burns had been practically a failure behind the bench — guiding the club to its apparently righteous spot in the Cup final only once, and losing (to Calgary in 1989). The Montreal hockey media, with its French and English solitudes, ultimately identified Burns as a one-dimensional coach, whose mildly successful teams were an antidote for insomnia.

Never mind three first place finishes in the Adams Division; a 115-point season and NHL coach-of-the-year honours in 1988-89. He was strictly defensive-minded and his teams were renown for underachieving come springtime. Unless you win it all in Montreal, you're a bum.

It's no wonder, therefore, that Burns felt he had hit a wall after five years in the Canadiens' organization. His coaching record would have spawned lavish praise in practically all other NHL cities, yet he endured mostly criticism as the Cup drought mounted in Montreal. Burns also found himself at the mercy of the French tabloids, whose infantile banter is enough to drive anyone close to the edge.

When his agreement with Serge Savard expired, he began to look elsewhere — unbeknownst to much of the hockey establishment.

"Yeah, I felt I needed a change," Burns admits. "I wasn't happy in Montreal and didn't feel I had any long-term future there. I was spinning my wheels with the Canadiens and it was time to move on."

Burns had extensive negotiations with the Los Angeles Kings, who were looking for a coach to replace the deposed Tom Webster. But when agent Don Meehan discussed the Maple Leaf coaching vacancy with Cliff Fletcher, and ascertained profound interest, he hurriedly guided Burns in Toronto's direction. Within 48 hours of first contact, his client became the 21st coach in Maple Leaf history, replacing Tom Watt.

When he arrived in town, Burns found himself inundated with a request that quickly grew familiar. "The first day I got to Toronto, all I kept hearing was, `You gotta get rid of that Todd Gill' — people were telling me that on the streets," Burns remembers. "And I said to myself, `Why? What's wrong with the guy?' Of course, people would always bring up the Troy Murray thing, but I thought Todd Gill was an honest player and deserved a chance to play for me."

Ah, the Troy Murray thing.

If Todd Gill has a dart-board in his basement, chances are that Murray's photo adorns the front of it. Rarely, if ever, has an ill-fated moment in Maple Leaf history been so hugely magnified as Gill's lurid

blunder in Chicago on Apr. 2, 1989. Requiring a victory over the
Blackhawks to make the playoffs, the Leafs lost 4-3 in overtime when
Murray picked Gill's pocket from behind. An unsteady defensive ca-
reer thus took a seemingly irreparable turn for the worse.

The videotape of his giveaway became more familiar than the
Zapruder film and Gill fell into disfavour with even the most die-hard
of Maple Leaf supporters. After hitting rock-bottom, it took the arrival
of Burns almost four years later to resuscitate his career... and a scintil-
lating goal in a hype-filled match against the Canadiens to finally
eradicate the lingering ghosts of Troy Murray.

*   *   *   *   *   *

When the 1992-93 NHL schedule came out, the game of Jan. 9 was
circled by just about everybody interested in Toronto and Montreal. It
would be the Maple Leafs' lone visit to the Forum during the regular
season and would mark the return to Montreal of Pat Burns. As the only
game of nine scheduled that night north of the border, it would also be
televised coast-to-coast on *Hockey Night In Canada*.

Burns had not left Montreal with an abundance of hard feelings —
at least, not towards Canadiens' management. "I had five pretty good
years there and was treated very well," he recalls. "My contract was
over and I felt I needed a change. If I had't left on my own, I don't
believe Serge Savard would have fired me, but he wasn't unhappy to
see me go either. The fans and media had fallen off the Pat Burns
bandwagon and it was a mutual parting of the ways."

For Cliff Fletcher, it was a blessing. The Maple Leaf boss had
acquired his cornerstone player in Doug Gilmour the previous January
but the hockey club badly needed some stability behind the bench. Tom
Watt coached the Leafs for the better part of two seasons, having taken
over from the idiosyncratic Doug Carpenter twelve games into the
1990-91 campaign. A dedicated and knowledgable hockey man, Watt
injected a measure of defensive acumen during his time behind the
bench. Fletcher, however, wasn't convinced he could adequately "sell"
the goods and on May 4, 1992 — a month into the off-season — he re-
shuffled Watt's duties and announced the Maple Leafs would be hiring
a *new* head coach.

The most qualified individual already on the Toronto payroll was
assistant coach Mike Murphy, who'd been with the team for two seasons. And Murphy clearly wanted the top position. But Fletcher offered

him only a mild endorsement — saying he'd strongly consider Murphy while exploring the entire coaching market. As the weeks passed, it became clear that Fletcher wasn't sold on the former Toronto Marlboro winger. Rumoured replacements from outside the organization began to materialize with Barry Melrose gaining frequent mention. A former Leaf defenceman, Melrose would guide Adirondack to the American Hockey League title and he seemed clearly in line for a promotion to the NHL.

But Fletcher's search came to an abrupt conclusion when Burns left the Canadiens. A telephone enquiry from agent Don Meehan was all the Maple Leaf GM needed. The new coach had landed right in his lap. As a result of this hasty arrangement, the hiring of Burns came as a major surprise to everyone in Toronto. The story broke around noontime on May 29 and within hours, Burns was standing at a podium in the Gardens' Hot Stove Lounge adorned in a leather Maple Leaf jacket.

Looking like someone who had just won a lottery, Fletcher spoke in glowing terms about the credibility of his new man. Indeed, Burns came to Toronto with indisputable credentials at varied levels of coaching. Formerly a policeman in Hull, Que., he took over that city's Junior 'A' club in 1983-84 and had the Olympiques in the Memorial Cup tournament three years later. The Canadiens hired him to coach their Sherbrooke AHL affiliate in 1987-88 and Burns was elevated to the Montreal job the following season — replacing Jean Perron.

In his rookie year with the Canadiens, Burns guided the club to the second-best record in the NHL. Montreal won 53 games, lost only 18, and finished with 115 points — winning the Adams Division title by an ample 27-point margin over Boston. The Habs swept Hartford in the first round of the playoffs, brushed past the Bruins in a five-game division final, then ousted Philadelphia for the Wales Conference title — the deciding game of *that* series gaining renown for goalie Ron Hextall's attack on Montreal defenceman Chris Chelios.

The Canadiens met Calgary in the Stanley Cup final and took a 2-1 lead in the best-of-seven series when Ryan Walter scored at 8:08 of the third overtime to win Game 3. However, the Flames rebounded to win the ensuing three matches and became the first-ever visiting club to parade the Stanley Cup around the hallowed ice at the Montreal Forum. Fletcher — the Calgary GM — had bested his future employee.

Burns would never get closer to the holy grail in Montreal. The Canadiens finished with 93 points the following season — three more than the eventual Cup champions from Edmonton — but were bounced from the Adams Division final by the Bruins in five games. They were ousted in the same playoff round by Boston in 1991 and '92: suffering a four-game sweep in the latter series. It was time for Burns to move on.

"I don't feel like I underachieved in Montreal," the coach says. "After I came to Toronto, I kept hearing that my teams actually went further than they should have based on their level of talent. I don't know if I agree with that but I *do* know one thing: coaching hockey in Montreal is probably the toughest job in professional sports. There is no acceptance of anything beyond winning and no team in any sport comes out on top *all* the time.

"When we lost to the Bruins in the 1992 playoffs, I figured it might be my final game in Montreal. Never in my life — as a cop or a coach — had I felt so absolutely drained, physically and emotionally."

The hockey environment was far more submissive in Toronto, where each season began with an aim to merely qualify for the playoffs. Maple Leaf fans in the '70s and '80s were clearly appeased by the attainment of that menial objective, and advancement beyond the first round — as in 1987 — generated the degree of euphoria Montreal fans reserve for a *Stanley Cup* celebration. In no way could expectations be compared.

The Maple Leafs of the pre-Burns era had missed the playoffs in six of 11 years, including the two seasons prior to his arrival. With Fletcher at the controls, and Gilmour the trigger-man down below, Burns could take his new club in only one direction. How *quickly*, nobody knew, but the organization seemed to finally be on the correct path.

As Burns maneuovered the Maple Leafs through the early stages of 1992-93, two factors became apparent: a) the excellent performance of Gilmour in the previous season's stretch drive was no fluke. The Maple Leafs had truly landed an individual who encompassed all the qualities of a franchise cornerstone. Not since Darryl Sittler had the Leafs iced a player of that nature, and comparisons between the two men promptly began to materialize. And, b) the Burns-led Maple Leafs were showing clear signs of defensive composure. For years, the Toronto zone had been in virtual disarray. No apparent method existed for maintenance of that critical territory and the consequences were frightful. But Burns supplied his troops with a system that minimized defensive gaffes, and those who deviated from the system found themselves in the press box.

A lack of scoring balance prevented the Maple Leafs from making serious headway in the standings and the club hovered around the .500 mark for the first half of the season. As the much-anticipated clash with Montreal approached, Toronto seemed headed towards its customary ambition: a playoff spot. Leafs had distanced themselves in the Norris Division by a fairly comfortable margin over both the St. Louis Blues and the expansion Tampa Bay Lightning.

The game in Montreal would be isolated for obvious reasons, with Burns as the focal point. A profound anxiety began to swell inside the Maple Leaf coach as the day neared, but he tried very hard to maintain perspective. "We play Tampa Bay nine times and the Canadiens twice," he told Michael Farber of the Montreal *Gazette*. "That's eighteen points versus four. Who should I worry about?"

While Burns tried to downplay the Montreal encounter, the media began its own speculation. Wrote Farber: "Asking any man to project his feelings onto a blank screen of a new experience is unfair. But Burns' emotions always had such a free rein on that cop face of his that the question of 'How will you feel?' is inevitable."

The Canadiens had replaced Burns with veteran Jacques Demers, who was out of coaching for several years after being fired by Detroit. A more jovial fellow, Demers had apparently lightened up the atmosphere in the Montreal dressing room and comparisons between he and Burns were rampant in the days preceding the Maple Leafs' visit. Indeed, on the very morning of the game, there appeared a headline in the *Gazette* that read: **DEMERS SAYS BURNS DOESN'T LIKE HIM**.

Burns was quoted in a Montreal tabloid as saying, "Jacques Demers doesn't want to lose this game." For the media, it was a battle between the Burns scowl and the Demers smile. The comments of the two coaches reflected their personalities. "I think the main thing Pat doesn't like is that I get along with the media," Demers said. "That's because I was *in* the media (as a radio broadcaster for the Quebec Nordiques). I'm not a media suck. It's just part of my job."

Said Burns: "You have to be a prick once in awhile if you're going to win games. You can be the nicest guy in the world and keep getting jobs, but I don't know that you'll win."

With the coaching squabble as a backdrop, Burns prepared for his return to Montreal. "I knew there would be a media onslaught," he says. "That's why I was thrilled that we had a game the night before. If there had been a two or three-day build-up to the Montreal thing, we might have all gone off the deep end."

As it was, the Maple Leafs played San Jose at the Gardens on Friday — whipped the Sharks 5-1 — then chartered to Montreal in the middle of the night. "Getting there at two in the morning cut down on all the hype and shit we'd otherwise have to face," Burns recalls. "Everything was pretty much quiet in the city by the time we arrived and that was a blessing. Also, the fact we played the night before — then had to travel — allowed me to cancel the morning skate. That kept the players away from the crossfire."

Instead of going to the rink, Burns spent much of the day Saturday entertaining family members. "I stayed pretty close to the hotel," he recalls. "There was a lot of hype not only in Montreal but across Canada for that game, and I knew the atmosphere would be different. I had a lot of family coming to see me and I didn't want the players being distracted by my situation. I spoke to Wendel about it and told him it was going to be a bit of a zoo.

"He and Dougie talked to the players and everybody handled it very well. I wanted the guys to get some rest and be ready for one of the toughest challenges in hockey: winning a game in the Montreal Forum. I didn't want them getting caught up in the side show."

On that Saturday in January, 1993, Todd Gill was the longest-serving Maple Leaf. He had been with the organization for almost a decade but had rarely entered a circumstance like the one in Montreal. "Going to the Forum was always special for the Maple Leafs," he says. "I was born very close to Montreal (Brockville, Ont.) and the Habs were the team I watched on Saturday nights in my youth. The first NHL game I played was at the Forum and it was one of the most incredible moments of my life. So going into Montreal always had the same affect on me.

"But the day Pat went back was completely different. The former coach of the Canadiens was now behind our bench and I think it had an impact on all of us. With a lot of my family members in the crowd, I wanted to win the game as much for myself as for Pat. But knowing that Pat wanted it so badly made the whole thing more exciting."

Gill had some trouble sleeping that day and he spent part of the afternoon wandering around the lobby of the Sheraton Centre. He also kept one eye on his coach. "I just remember Burnsie pacing back and forth like you don't often see him," Gill recalls. "You could tell he was jittery and wanted to get on with the show. In fact, I remember being rather nervous *for* him."

The anxiety swelled within Burns as the day progressed and he took a cab to the Forum several hours before the game.

"That's when it really hit me," he recalls. "When I got out of the taxi, there were hundreds of people outside the building and a horde of media surrounded me. I was definitely nervous at that moment — more so than I'd been in my entire coaching career."

The butterflies were natural considering the situation but Burns insists that revenge was not a factor. "It wasn't a matter of getting even with anybody, or showing the Canadiens' organization that I could beat them," he says. "What made me nervous was all the media attention and wondering what kind of reception I'd get from the fans. As far as the game was concerned, it was a one-shot deal against a club that wasn't even in our Conference.

"We had a chance to pick up two points just like any other game, and that's how I wanted the players to approach it. I asked them to play well and win it for themselves... not me."

Rarely does Burns make an appearance in the pre-game warmup but he emerged from the dressing room for a few minutes in Montreal. Less than half an hour later, the ice had been cleaned and it was show time. The visitors' dressing room at the Forum is on the opposite side of the players' benches and Burns knew he'd have to walk across the ice. It was a moment in time he had pondered for many weeks.

"That walk seemed like an eternity and I can still remember every second of it," he says. "I looked straight ahead of me and saw people sitting behind the bench area that I knew from my days in Montreal; the same faces were in the same places. I looked up above me into the booth where Serge Savard sits during games and I had a funny feeling in my stomach and head that said, `Y'know, I gave five years of my life to these guys and now here I am on the other side.'

"I remember the fans booing a bit — not wildly, or anything — but enough for me to hear. There was no heckling or name-calling: at least not that I could make out. When I finally got to the bench, one of the usherettes I knew said, `Welcome back.' I then looked over to my left, behind the Montreal bench, and my old trainer Eddy Palchak and all the guys were there. We had a little smile between us."

After the national anthem, the moment Burns had been longing for was finally upon him. And he could feel the relief. "Once the puck was dropped, all the butterflies went away," he recalls. "From then on, it was just like another hockey game and we were flying in the first two periods. The guys were really pumped up that night."

Indeed, the Maple Leafs dominated the initial 40 minutes, bolting to a 4-0 lead by the 16:23 mark of the middle frame. Wendel Clark opened the scoring at 5:44 of the first period, beating Patrick Roy through the five-hole with a wrist shot. Roy then looked shaky trying to clear the puck up the boards, and Doug Gilmour pounced on his errant feed to make it 2-0 Leafs (on the powerplay) at 8:56 of the second.

Less than five minutes later occurred perhaps the most memorable goal by a Maple Leaf player during the entire 1992-93 season, and most definitely, the signature moment of Todd Gill's NHL career.

Emerging from the penalty box after serving a minor, Gill sped forward and took Gilmour's pass at the center-ice red line. He motored in on goal with defenceman Patrice Brisbois giving him plenty of room down the right side. With a step on Brisbois, Gill cut across in front of the net, switched to his forehand, and deftly flipped the puck over Roy's left shoulder at 14:13, putting the Leafs in front 3-0.

"I remember sitting in the penalty box and praying for Montreal not to score," Gill says. "We were only up by two goals at that point and I didn't want to be the guy who started their comeback. When I came out of the box, the play was right in front of me and Dougie had the puck. I turned up ice and he put it right on my tape. Dougie and Wendel were with me on kind of a three-on-two, so Brisbois gave me lots of room to the outside. I cut in and put 'er up on Roy and I'll tell you, it was one awesome feeling.

"To beat a defenceman like that and then flip the puck over the best goalie in the world was the most exciting personal moment of my career, bar none. I knew my family was in the building and as I skated back out to the blueline with my arms raised, I looked over at Burnsie who was pumping his arm in celebration. Dave Ellett was the first to greet me and I ended up giving him a head-butt by accident. But he was as excited as I was. It was an incredible moment in my life."

It was also a moment of vindication for Gill — a cleansing, if you will, of all the dirt he'd been dragged through during more than eight tumultuous seasons in a Maple Leaf uniform. He could see the triumphant image of Troy Murray melting before his eyes. And his thoughts were very much focused — for a brief moment, anyway — on the man who had tormented him most during his stormy NHL career: ex-Leaf coach Doug Carpenter.

Considered to be among the brightest coaching prospects in the game, Carpenter made it to the NHL with New Jersey in 1984-85. He guided the Devils for three seasons and the club failed to qualify for the playoffs. Early in his fourth season, he was fired and replaced by Jim Schoenfeld, who not only took New Jersey to the *playoffs* for the first time in 1988, but all the way to Game 7 of the Stanley Cup semi-finals. The Devils were finally ousted by the Bruins, in Boston.

A year later, Harold Ballard made what turned out to be the final significant decision of his ownership tenure (and his life) when he hired Carpenter to replace George Armstrong as Maple Leaf coach. The Leafs showed marked improvement in 1989-90 — bettering their point-total of the previous year by 18 — and finishing at the .500 level for the first time in 11 seasons. They did so, however, with a surge of offence, scoring a team-record 337 goals. Defensively, they were still raw, and St. Louis made them pay in the opening round of the playoffs, romping to a lop-sided victory in five games.

The move forward had been exciting and dramatic, but the tell-tale sign was a late-season slump and the quick playoff exit. A number of Maple Leaf observers figured that Carpenter had taken the Leafs as far as he could and they were proven correct early in the following season. The Leafs staggered out of the gate at a 1-10-1 clip and Carpenter took the fall after an 8-5 loss in St. Louis, Oct. 25, 1990. Ballard dumped him in favour (naturally) of assistant coach Tom Watt, who remained in charge until Burns came on the scene almost two years later.

Carpenter was a peculiar man who kept his players and the media off balance. His mood-swings were unpredictable and he was generally a difficult person to communicate with. From Todd Gill's standpoint, he was *impossible* to tolerate, and Gill credits the appointment of Watt with saving his NHL career.

"It's all in the past now but I will admit that, to this day, I have no respect for Doug Carpenter," Gill says. "Neither as a person, nor a coach. He had no respect for me, either, so it was definitely a two-way street."

According to Gill, his problems with Carpenter began before the two even met one another. "A couple of friends from my home town ran into Doug at a marina a few days after he was hired by the Leafs and they asked how he thought I'd fit in with the team," says Gill. "And, Doug's response was, `Well, he's not going to get a Maple Leaf jersey handed to him *this* year.' They couldn't believe he would say something like that before even *meeting* me for the first time."

Actually, Carpenter's response to the query was hardly unique. "Are the Leafs finally gonna get rid of Todd Gill?" was a question posed almost annually at the start of training camp. A second-round draft choice from Windsor of the OHL in 1984, Gill quickly developed a propensity to cough up the puck at the most inopportune moment. He had skills that were mandatory for an NHL player — primarily, as a skater. He was smooth on his feet, with an impressive burst of speed.

But he simply had the "Yips" with the puck. Anyone who watched the Maple Leafs with even remote interest understood *that*. As a result, the only transgression by Carpenter in his response to Gill's marina pals may have been blatant honesty. It's quite logical to suggest they would have received a similar retort from just about *anybody* connected with hockey back then. Gill was a hanger-on, at best.

"I thought my first two seasons in the NHL were fairly decent but it went downhill after that," Gill acknowledges. "We were losing as a team and the finger was pointed mainly at our defence and goaltending. We had forwards who could score but we obviously didn't have a system to keep the puck out of *our* net. And I think that in the NHL, you *need* that system: not just a goalie and two defencemen trying to keep things in order themselves.

"With Tom Watt and Pat Burns, we've had a defensive arrangement that helps out the guys playing along the blueline and it's made every one of us more reliable. I can take a run up ice without feeling that if I *do* lose the puck, it'll create a dire circumstance. Someone is always there to back me up and as a result, I'm not afraid to hold onto the puck a bit longer.

"Earlier in my career, I'd make a rush and get caught up ice. Then to compensate for *that* mistake, I'd make another rush and get caught again. Then a third time. It had a snowballing effect and I was out of control most nights. But, again, there was no defensive system to back me up. I was basically on my own.

"Nowadays, we *have* that system and it's awfully comforting. Too bad Al Iafrate or Borje Salming aren't still playing for us. They could both skate like the wind."

Doug Carpenter's final image of Gill before taking over as coach of the Maple Leafs was the same image *we* all had: his giveaway to Troy Murray that cost Leafs a shot at making the playoffs on the final night of the 1988-89 regular season. The Blackhawks were two points up on Toronto as the clubs prepared to meet at Chicago Stadium. But the Leafs were two up in the victory column and would make the playoffs ahead of Chicago in the event of a tie. The game went into overtime deadlocked 3-3 with the Maple Leafs needing to score; the Blackhawks looking to hold on for their lives. With less than a minute to play, Gill ambled into his own zone to retrieve the puck.

"I played left-wing in that game on a line with Tom Fergus and Craig Laughlin," he remembers. "The puck was dumped in and both our defencemen were changing on the fly. I was the closest man to the puck, so I went back to get it and I turned up-ice thinking the defencemen who were coming *on* would skate in behind me.

"As a result, I actually thought that Troy Murray was one of my teammates coming off the bench and getting back into position. You can imagine, then, how surprised I was to have my stick lifted and the puck taken away from me. I almost died when I saw it was a Chicago player and we all know what happened. Troy beat Allan Bester with a great shot and we were out of the playoffs."

Gill's folly was the last straw for a legion of Maple Leaf rooters who wanted him removed from the picture. He read and heard some of the most disparaging remarks of his NHL career. Yet he insists the donation to Murray did not largely effect his mental well-being.

"It wasn't so much how it effected me but rather how it effected everyone's perception *of* me," he explains. "Everybody remembered that giveaway and it hurt their confidence in me more than it did my own. And I think it took that goal in Montreal almost three years later to erase all the bad memories and have people say, `Y'know, maybe this guy isn't as bad a player as we've thought all these years.' In between, though, I had some pretty rough times."

Gill and Carpenter were like oil and water. When the latter took over as coach, he told Gill he planned only to use him on defence, not at left-wing, where Gill had toiled for 35 games the previous season. Gill sat out a stretch of eight games, during which the Leafs played rather well. But after a two-game skid, he approached Carpenter about getting back into the line-up.

"He told me the only way I was going to dress was in the event of an injury," Gill recalls. "So, the next game, Ed Olczyk and Gary Leeman both got hurt and what did he do? He called up a couple of guys from the minors. I went in to see him and he said, `Listen, I told you from the start I wasn't going to play you at forward, only on defence.' And I said, `Christ, Doug, I'll play *goal*, just get me in there.' But he repeated himself and I walked out."

After sitting out 17 games, Gill finally did dress and guess what? Carpenter started him at forward. "I couldn't believe it," says Gill. "I was perfectly healthy and had missed more than a month of the season because my coach said he'd never use me anywhere but on defence. Of course, I didn't care where I played, as long as I was in there.

"But a few days later, he came up to me in practice and said I'd be sitting out again. And I just cracked."

Gill and Carpenter had a good, 'ol fashioned shouting match on the ice at Maple Leaf Gardens. "Doug said, `Who the fuck are you yelling at me, I'm your fucking coach,'" Gill recalls. "And I said, `Well at least you could be a man and not lie to me.' We went back and forth and said

`Fuck you' a couple of times, at which point Doug said that I'd never get back into the line-up.

"I told him fine, I was going up to ask (general manager) Floyd Smith for a trade. He thought it was a good idea. So I asked him, point blank, if he would stand in the way of a deal and he said no."

Gill and Smith had an amiable relationship and the general manager promised to try and move the disgruntled veteran prior to the NHL trade deadline, three weeks later. "I thought I was being up-front about the whole thing," Gill says. "Rather than acting on my own and going behind Carpenter's back, I told him flat out that I would ask for a trade and he agreed it would be best for both of us. Floyd said he'd move me — told me not to mention anything to the media — and I went home to tell my wife that within three weeks, we'd be going to new city."

Of course, the deal never did materialize and Gill blames it on Carpenter. "About a week after the deadline passed, I heard that he had gone up to Floyd and told him not to trade me, even though he promised not to stand in the way," Gill says. "Around that time, Al Iafrate went down with a knee injury and Tom Kurvers broke his thumb, so I started playing again. But I had lost every ounce of respect for Doug."

As you might imagine, the day Carpenter was fired a few months later was not the saddest of Gill's life. "For some reason, he was out to get me, there was a vendetta on his part," says Gill. "I tried to respect his job and his decisions and he treated me like a dog. He thought he was a lot smarter than he actually was but, hey, he's long gone and I'm still here."

Gill's fortunes went instantly uphill when Watt became head coach. "Tom was the assistant coach during all the shit I went through with Carpenter and we did a lot of extra skating together," Gill recalls. "And I think he realized that I honestly wanted to win and be a part of the team. I had a pretty good year in 1990-91, playing with Rob Ramage as my partner, and I learned the defensive part of the game from Watt. He showed confidence by putting me on the ice in the final minutes of close games and it was exactly the tonic I needed."

With his self-esteem growing, Gill was finally able to put the Troy Murray debacle behind him. "You know, the funny thing about my situation back then was that other players on our team were making as many or more mistakes than I was — especially on defence," he says. "But mine always seem to be under the microscope. It seemed like people were just waiting to say, `Well, it's time for him to hand the puck to somebody.' Even people who stood by me and wanted me to do well, never really thought I would.

"But you know what? It doesn't bother me anymore. When I scored that big goal in Montreal, I'd be lying if I said I didn't feel like rubbing it into a few people. I took my share of bullshit, even if a lot of it was justified. Nowadays, when people ask me to compare my good seasons to the feeling I had when I made that mistake with Troy Murray, I tell them the Murray giveaway is in the past, it'll always be there, but I prefer to look to the future.

"Tom Watt gave me a chance to prove I could play defence. When Pat came along, he allowed me to combine it with my more natural offensive abilities and things really took off. I owe them both a great deal."

Despite the admonishing of Maple Leaf fans when he first came to Toronto, Burns says he never had any preconceived notions about Gill. "I remember feeling kind of bad for Todd when people belittled him," the coach admits. "He's a good, honest kid and I liked him from the first time we met. That's not to say I'm not hard on Todd — he gets his licks like everybody else. I was on him from the start because of some work habits in practice, but only to make him a better player.

"I thought that by putting some added pressure on him, it would help. Some players don't handle pressure well, but Todd does. He'll respond to a challenge and he needed it back then."

As a result, Burns admits that he feels particularly happy when Gill has a good game. "Oh, definitely. He was a bit of a project for me and it's very gratifying to see him play well. He deserves it, too. I remember he had back spasms in my first training camp with the team (1992) and missed the first few games of the season. When he came back, everyone else was into the flow and he had no choice but to get in there as well. And he did a super job for us.

"And I really admired the way he performed in the playoffs that season. He worked like hell in the St. Louis series and must have lost eight or nine pounds. But I kept putting him out there against the Blues and then in the next series with Los Angeles. He really wanted to play and it was very satisfying from a coach's standpoint. It's not something you think about while it's happening, but afterwards — over the course of the summer — you look back and say, `Geez, that guy really gave it all he had.' I remember feeling that way about Todd.

"And man, did he score a gorgeous goal that night in Montreal! I was so excited for him and the team at that moment."

*   *   *   *   *   *

The Maple Leafs gave Pat Burns quite a homecoming present when they knocked off the Canadiens, 5-4, on his return to the Forum. But the game developed into quite a nail-biter for the Leaf coach. Just more than two minutes after Gill's picturesque goal, Doug Gilmour deflected another shot past Patrick Roy and Toronto led 4-0. However, Benoit Brunet put Montreal on the board with 45 seconds remaining in the second period and the Canadiens stormed the Maple Leaf zone in the third frame.

A pair of goals by Mike Keane shaved the Toronto lead to 4-3, but Mark Osborne scored on a wrist shot at 17:39 to restore a comfortable margin. Still the Habs wouldn't quit and ex-Leaf Vincent Damphousse connected 30 seconds after Osborne to set up a frantic last two minutes of play. And Burns can still feel the anxiety.

"Yeah, I was damned concerned," he recalls. "I'm sure the Montreal players were given a pretty good lecture by Jacques (Demers) after the second period. The Canadiens don't handle losing very well, especially at home, and I warned my players that they weren't dead. I told them to go out and win the game not for me, but for the team."

Gill remembers an unmistakable sign that his coach was a bit more impassioned than usual. "Burnsie isn't normally much of a talker but as we were leaving the dressing room for the start of the second period, he was very intense," Gill recalls. "The *look* he gives you on the way out is usually enough to tell what's on his mind. But when I walked by him that night — I'm always the last guy to leave the room — he gave me a shot in the ribs and said, `C'mon Giller, I need you.' That's the first time he ever did something like that and it gave me an instant shot of Adrenalin.

"I said to myself, `Fuck, this is *big*' then went out and had maybe the best 20 minutes of my career. We were all so pumped up."

Otherwise, Gill says that Burns pretty much stayed away from the players during the two intermissions. "He really doesn't have a set routine," explains the veteran defenceman. "If we're botching up, he'll come into the room and let us know rather loudly. He can go from one extreme to the other in a matter of seconds. Like he'll be talking to us about something positive on the ice then a negative will cross his mind and he'll start ranting and raving. But a few seconds later, he'll be back on the positive. I don't remember him being too visible during our game in Montreal that night."

The Maple Leafs hung on for the 5-4 victory and Burns released his emotions when the siren roared out to end the game. He pumped his right arm in a windmill fashion then hugged assistant coach Mike Murphy. On the ice for the game's final seconds, captain Wendel Clark skated to the bench, reached over the boards, and shook hands with his ecstatic coach. If he had tried to downplay the event beforehand, Burns left no doubt that he was enjoying one of the best moments of his career.

"Yeah, I was happy but I think it was more relief than joy," he says. "I was glad it was over and even more excited that we had the two points. That's what I was hoping for the most. Nowadays, when I go back to Montreal, it isn't quite the same. I still get that special feeling, but it doesn't compare to how I felt on that first trip to the Forum.

"It's tough to rank significant games in my career, but that one is definitely in the top three."

Adds Gill: "Everyone knew he was thrilled at the end of the game. He gave us all a tap on the way to the dressing room and that's all he really had to do. There was no need for any speeches that night."

It had been one triumphant evening for Burns and Gill.

... Leafs in Spring ...

MAY 9, 1994
Fisherman's Wharf, Monterey, Calif.

This day was an absolute bonus in my travels with the Maple Leafs —
mostly unexpected, but blissfully welcomed. After three solid weeks of the playoff
grind, everyone needed a day to just forget about hockey and Pat Burns made that
possible by cancelling the Maple Leafs' workout between Games 4 and 5 of the
San Jose series.

The previous night, the Leafs had bombed the Sharks 8-3 to square their
Western Conference semifinal at two games apiece. So, instead of practising at
the San Jose Arena early in the afternoon, the Maple Leaf players relaxed at the
Fairmont Hotel and were later bussed into San Francisco for a dinner at
Fisherman's Wharf. With no workout to attend, I sent back enough post-game
material the previous night to last all of Monday and decided to escape the hockey
environment, myself.

Jetting into San Jose was neither convenient nor economical. So, Toronto
media who were not on the Maple Leaf charter flew non-stop into San Francisco,
rented cars at the airport, and made the 45-minute drive south along U.S. 101.
Once in San Jose, cars were hardly a necessity as we could walk from the hotel
to the Arena in roughly 15 minutes.

By its own standards, the new San Jose Arena is a palace. However, it
becomes a Taj Mahal when compared to the squalid environs of Maple Leaf

Gardens. For years, I allowed sentiment to intervene whenever talk surfaced about a prospective new arena in Toronto. How could the Maple Leafs play anywhere but the Gardens? The two are intertwined like bread and butter. However, that affection dissipated like a gas leak the very moment I walked into the San Jose facility.

Here was a clean and handsome building with amenities that Maple Leaf supporters could hardly fathom. Two tiers of seats — separated by a walkway, and rising more vertically than in most new arenas — were ringed at the top by exquisite SkyBoxes: not at all like the unsightly "prison cells" that dangle from the north and south end at the Gardens.

Each of the 17,310 seats was upholstered in a pleasant corduroy-like material with individual cup holders and ample leg room. The chairs were wide enough to accommodate even the most voracious eaters and would not require a semi-fetal contortion as in Toronto. Fans were also treated to a scoreboard with sharp replay images, and were spared the clapping Mickey Mouse-like hands that we so frequently endure on Carlton Street.

During a Leaf practice in San Jose, I approached Cliff Fletcher and offered to torch the Gardens in return for a new rink, and judicial immunity. He said he'd look into it.

As mentioned, the Monday after Game 4 provided all of us with an opportunity to flee the hockey environment, if only for a few hours. I made a pledge to simply get into the car and drive as far as a tank of gas would take me. I started out north along Interstate-880, the Nimitz Freeway, looking for the stretch of road that collapsed during the 1989 Bay Area earthquake. The "Cypress" structure — connecting I-880 to the San Francisco-Oakland Bay Bridge — pancaked during that devastating tremor, killing 41 motorists on its lower tier.

I had driven that exact route, myself, going into San Francisco for dinner with media friends while covering the '89 baseball playoffs between the Blue Jays and Oakland. When I heard initial reports of the freeway collapse not 10 days later, I knew precisely the area they were referring to. And it haunted me for a few moments.

Driving now through Alameda County, past the Oakland Coliseum, I came upon the anticipated detour. I swung onto the Bay Bridge and decided to catch the baseball matinee between the Giants and Colorado Rockies.

Purchasing a ticket off some fast talker outside Candlestick Park, I vowed to stay until the early afternoon cloud dissipated. Barry Bonds smacked a grand-slam deep to right in the third inning — at which time blue skies began to emerge. As promised, I bolted.

The remainder of the day was delightfully relaxing. I drove west towards

Half Moon Bay then turned onto the Pacific Coast Highway. With the ocean's deep-blue majesty to my right, I cruised southward through picturesque towns like Pescadero, Santa Cruz and Pacific Grove. Late in the afternoon, I stopped briefly on the shores of Monterey and walked around Fisherman's Wharf — having to remind myself a couple of times that I was in northern California to cover a hockey series.

"MR. GREGORY, YOUR TROUBLES ARE OVER!"

Detroit Olympia
October 28, 1976

When Harold Ballard let Bernie Parent escape to the World Hockey Association in 1972, the Maple Leafs lost the most critical element to success in the game — goaltending stability.

Like a baseball team without pitching, or a football club minus a top quarterback, a hockey team simply cannot prosper without competent netminding. The best teams in NHL history, regardless of their talents up front, have all been strong in goal.

Edmonton's prolific Oilers of Gretzky, Messier, Kurri, Anderson and Coffey dazzled opponents with unprecedented puck-movement wizardry in the 1980s. Still, they would not have won Stanley Cups without the splendour of Grant Fuhr.

The "Firewagon" Montreal teams that won a record five consecutive titles between 1956 and 1960, featured the offensive tenacity of Rocket Richard, Jean Beliveau and Bernie Geoffrion. They could skate like the wind and score in bunches. But, they also had Jacques Plante: hockey's best goalkeeper of that era, and one of the top half-dozen of all time.

We recall, more recently, the brilliance of Bryan Trottier, Mike Bossy and Denis Potvin on the New York Islander teams that won four

Stanley Cups in the early 1980s. Still, has the game ever seen a better "money" goalie than Billy Smith?

Parent may have been the closest facsimile.

When he left to join the WHA, the Maple Leafs lost any legitimate hopes of regaining their past glory. For four seasons, they employed a cast of unproven beginners and re-cycled veterans that included Plante, Ron Low, Gord McRae, Eddie Johnston, Doug Favell, Dunc Wilson, Pierre Hamel and Wayne Thomas.

Quite a roll-call for a club which had relied, essentially, on one man — Johnny Bower — through the entire decade of the 1960s.

Something clicked briefly during the 1975-76 season with Thomas: a 28-year-old Montreal chattel who had not seen a minute of action the previous year. When Ken Dryden left hockey for one season to study law, Thomas moved up from the Canadiens' farm team in Halifax. He shared the netminding chores with Michel (Bunny) Larocque and Michel Plasse during 1973-74: playing the majority of games (42), and compiling a tidy 2.76 goals-against average.

Larocque, however, appeared in all six playoff games that spring, as the Habs were first-round victims of the New York Rangers. And when Dryden returned the following year, Larocque assumed full-time backup duties. Thomas was part of the Montreal roster but actually sat in the press box for all 80 regular-season games.

"That was a brutal experience," he recalls. "I tried not to get nervous about the situation, but I'd been around long enough by then to realize a goaltender can lose his edge pretty fast. I began to wonder: 'What happens if I've lost mine?'"

The Maple Leafs obviously weren't concerned and they rescued the beleaguered netminder from Montreal, giving the Canadiens their first selection in the 1976 amateur draft.

Toronto was searching for that elusive stability between the pipes after yielding an all-time franchise record of 309 goals in 1974-75 — a whopping 79-goal increase from the previous year. The performances of Doug Favell and Dunc Wilson withered: Favell's average ballooning from 2.71 to 4.05, and Wilson's from 2.89 to 3.70. Thomas came in and leapt ahead of both men to assume the number-one position.

His goaltending was part of an exciting Maple Leaf resurgence in 1975-76. Darryl Sittler became the first Toronto player to amass 100 scoring points in a season and he set an NHL record with 10 points in one game against Boston. Lanny McDonald finally emerged as a scoring threat in his third NHL campaign, popping in 37 goals, an increase of 20 from the previous year. And Errol Thompson flourished as the left-winger on the big line with 43 goals.

Borje Salming (57 points) and Ian Turnbull (20 goals) developed into mainstays on the blueline.

Thomas appeared in 64 games — the most in one season by a Maple Leaf goalie since Bower's 66-game allotment in 1959-60. He compiled a 28-24-12 record with a respectable 3.19 goals-against average and wound up excelling in the playoffs. The Maple Leafs knocked off an explosive Pittsburgh team in the best-of-three preliminary round, then extended Philadelphia to the limit in a boisterous seven-game quarterfinal.

Sittler scored a record-tying five goals in Game 6 of that series, all of them against his illustrious former teammate — Parent.

Five months later, in September, Sittler bagged an overtime goal against Czechoslovakia to win the first Canada Cup tournament.

The Maple Leafs embarked upon the 1976-77 season full of youthful exuberance and with no apparent concerns in goal.

Then, something went awry.

The Leafs gained just a single victory in their first nine games (1-5-3) for the worst start in franchise history. They played abysmally in their own end of the rink and Thomas failed to make the timely stops that had been his forte the previous year.

Typical of the Leafs' plight was a pair of home games three days apart against Los Angeles and Philadelphia in which they blew 4-0 leads each night and had to settle for unsatisfying draws. Leafs suffered a key injury when Errol Thompson broke his wrist against the Kings. And, the early season frustration boiled when Tiger Williams broke his stick over the head of Pittsburgh defenceman Dennis Owchar, cutting him for 22 stitches, and spilling a ghastly pool of blood on the Gardens' ice.

But the real enigma was Thomas, who seemed to be fighting the puck at every turn. Although he was the victim of numerous defensive lapses, he bore little resemblance to the poised, self-assured netminder of the previous year. Something was wrong, and the Leafs knew it.

Back-up Gord McRae replaced Thomas for a dismal 5-3 loss at home to Minnesota, which proved to be the breaking point. The club clearly needed a shot of morale that only competent goaltending would provide. It could have merely switched to McRae: hero of the 1975 playoff upset of Los Angeles. But he had proven to be a short-term remedy, if at all. Instead, management decided to dip into its farm system and promote the top minor-league prospect in the organization.

Mike Palmateer, 22, had once again earned the number-one position with the Dallas Blackhawks: the Central Hockey League affiliate shared by Toronto and Chicago. A fifth-round draft choice by the Maple Leafs in 1974, he was infinitely familiar to hockey people in Toronto, having worked his way up through the Marlboro system.

A smallish but fiery competitor, Palmateer backstopped one of the finest Junior 'A' clubs *ever* to a Memorial Cup victory in 1972-73: that Toronto team featuring future NHLers Mark Napier, Bruce Boudreau, Wayne Dillon, Mark Howe and Bob Dailey. He languished in the minors for the first two years of his career, and craved a shot at the big time.

That chance finally came around 11 p.m. (Central) on the night of Oct. 27, 1976 — moments after the Maple Leafs' embarrassing loss at the Gardens to Minnesota.

"Our Dallas club was in Oklahoma City for a game with the Blazers when the phone rang in my hotel room," Palmateer recalls. "It was (Leaf general manager) Jim Gregory calling from Toronto. Said he needed help in goal. I knew where he was coming from because I'd been following the Maple Leaf results in the paper. Thomas was in a slump and they were giving up a lot of goals. It was exactly the situation I was hoping for."

Gregory chuckles when remembering that phone-call.

"Yeah, the first thing Mike said was, `I've been *expecting* to hear from you.' He sure didn't lack confidence for a young guy."

After their defeat against Minnesota, the Maple Leafs travelled to Detroit for a meeting the following night with the Red Wings. Palmateer stayed over in Oklahoma City and flew up to Detroit the next day. When he arrived at the Olympia — a heavy equipment-bag strapped over his shoulder — he casually sauntered up to the Maple Leaf general manager and said, "Mr. Gregory, your goaltending troubles are over."

Then he went out and proved it.

"I was so excited that day," Palmateer remembers. "And I really *was* expecting to hear from the Leafs. In fact, I felt I could've made the team in my rookie season (1974-75). I saw that Doug Favell, Dunc Wilson and Gord McRae were the goalies and I said, `Piece of cake, I can beat those guys out.' But, I never got the chance."

Instead, Palmateer split his freshman year between Saginaw of the International League and Oklahoma City of the Central League. With the Blazers, he played 16 games and compiled an excellent 2.78 average. He spent the entire 1975-76 season in Oke City — Thomas excelling with the Maple Leafs — and his average rose to 3.61 in 42 starts.

"That took patience, and I didn't have a lot of it," Palmateer says about his second year in the minors. "I knew I was good enough to play in the NHL and it was the only place I wanted to be."

Palmateer arrived at the Maple Leafs' 1976 training camp having to compete with Thomas, McRae and Pierre Hamel: a perennial Leaf farmhand who had been his goaltending partner in Oklahoma City. The first true indication of Palmateer's ability to excel at the NHL level happened during a pre-season game at Kalamazoo, Mich. — Sept. 23, 1976.

He sprawled, flopped and dove all over the place to make 47 saves in a 2-1 Maple Leaf victory over Detroit. The only puck that eluded him was a screen-shot by veteran Danny Grant, on the powerplay, at 12:26 of the third period. He was particularly sharp in the second period, when the Leafs were outshot 20-6 by the Red Wings.

With the Leafs and Blackhawks sharing the Dallas farm team, there was room for only one Toronto goaltender on the Central League roster. Mike Veisor of the Blackhawks would take the other spot. The second Leaf cut would have to play for Saginaw of the International League — *two* rungs below the NHL — and Palmateer was doing everything his power to at least assure he wouldn't be *that* man.

"I might have to spend some time in the minors, but hopefully not down there," he said after the game in Kalamazoo. "The IHL is just like a Junior circuit. It's hard to get up for games. In the Central League, it's much easier because you know if you do well, you'll get a chance to move up to the big team.

"Both `Frenchie' (Hamel) and I are hoping the number-two job with the Leafs is still open. All we can do is our best."

Alas, Palmateer got only half his wish. Prior to leaving for Denver and their season opener against the Colorado Rockies, the Maple Leafs reduced their roster to 22 players by returning five prospects to the minors. Palmateer was among them, but at least he went to Dallas. Hamel was loaned to Oklahoma City of the CHL. Incumbents Thomas and McRae would start the season with the big club.

The season opener proved to be an indication of things to come for the Leafs, who were beaten 4-2 by the first-year Rockies. Adding salt to the Maple Leaf wound was Doug Favell, who stoned his ex-teammates in goal for Colorado. Leafs returned to Toronto for their home opener with Boston and fell behind, 2-0, less than two minutes into the game. When they rallied for a thrilling 7-5 win over the Bruins, nobody figured it would be their only victory of the month.

Nor did anyone foresee the demise of Wayne Thomas.

"That was a very disappointing juncture of my career," Thomas says when recalling his dreadful start to the 1976-77 season. "I had come to the Leafs from Montreal with a winning attitude and I think I helped pass it on to the Toronto players in my first year. Having to beat out Doug Favell and Gord McRae for the number-one spot was a real test for me. But, I wound up having my best season and the team was successful, too, pushing Philadelphia to seven games in the quarterfinals.

"Then, I got lazy. I thought the starting job was all mine and I'd have it forever, without putting in the mental and physical preparation for the season. For the first time in my career, I was going to camp as the number-one man and I let up, figuring everything was automatic. I took it nice and easy over the summer — resting on my laurels — and it turned out to be the biggest mistake I ever made in hockey."

The leisurely off-season impacted on Thomas, who simply couldn't get out of the gate in the '76-77 campaign. The decline in his overall performance was of grave concern to everyone in the Leaf organization, including captain Darryl Sittler.

"Wayne was a bit of a 'Good-time Charlie,'" recalls Sittler. "He was enjoying himself a little too much off the ice, running around with guys like Ian Turnbull and George Ferguson. And I think he lost focus on why he'd been so successful the year before."

After practice one day, Sittler pulled Thomas aside and politely read him the Riot Act.

"He basically told me to get off my ass and start putting out," Thomas recalls. "He said the team needed me and the guys still believed in my ability, but that it was obvious I didn't have the same attitude as the previous year. Darryl was the kind of guy who could say that to you because he led by example.

"He was the perfect captain — playing and practising hard all the time. I appreciated his concern but, looking back, I suppose it didn't have much of an effect on me."

Thomas effectively lost his starting job with the Leafs during a 5-2 victory by the New York Islanders, at the Gardens, Oct. 23, 1976. He was no less effective than the injury riddled line-up in front of him that Saturday night but, again, he failed to make a timely save. Leafs were without Errol Thompson, Borje Salming, Claire Alexander and George Ferguson for the game, and the stress of losing caught up with Maple Leaf coach Red Kelly afterwards.

The normally taciturn red-head barked at a broadcast reporter to "Get that mike away from my face. It's driving me up a wall."

Kelly decided to start McRae in goal for the Maple Leafs' next game, at the Gardens against Minnesota, four nights later. The North Stars weren't exactly tearing a swath through the NHL with their 3-5-1 early season record, and the coach looked upon the game as yet another potential turning point.

The Leafs played a spirited, physical match but still wound up on the wrong end of a 5-3 final — the result of North Star tallies by ex-Leaf Pierre Jarry and Bill Hogaboam in the third period. With the club starting a three-game road trip in Detroit the following night, Kelly had seen enough.

"We're going to need a superb effort in goal to get us turned around, so we're bringing up Mike Palmateer from Dallas to play against the Red Wings," he announced. "We simply have to make changes. We can't continue to give up five goals a game.

"Palmateer played tremendously and stopped more than 40 shots in an exhibition game against Detroit at Kalamazoo. He's capable of coming up with big games and this is what we need.

"He may turn things around for us."

Upon arriving in Detroit from Oklahoma City late the following afternoon, Palmateer met briefly with reporters. "I got the call at 11 o'clock last night and had to find the trainer from the Dallas team to get my equipment from the rink," he explained. "It was 2 a.m. before I got to bed and I had to be up at 5 to catch a flight here.

"I had a 1.75 goals-against average in the Central League and I felt I might get a chance with the Leafs if they didn't start to win. I think I can help them get back on track."

A few hours later, at the Olympia, Palmateer won his NHL debut. His self-confidence was evident from the moment he stepped between the pipes, and the troops rallied in front of him to play their best game of the season. Second-period goals by Bob Neely and Sittler broke a 1-1 tie and sent the Leafs on to a 3-1 victory over the Red Wings. It was the first time all season that Toronto had yielded less than four goals in one game, and it snapped a seven-game winless streak.

The shot that beat Palmateer came off the stick of Danny Grant — the same player who had scored for Detroit in the exhibition game at Kalamazoo. Grant deflected Terry Harper's long pass behind Palmateer at 8:08 of the first period, exactly one minute after Tiger Williams had opened the scoring for Toronto. But the rookie netminder was flawless after that, turning aside 24 Red Wing shots.

"We were aware what Palmateer was doing in the Central League," said a relieved Kelly. "I thought last week if we didn't cut down on the goals against and didn't start winning, I'd have to make a change. I waited until after the Minnesota game and if we had beaten the North Stars, we wouldn't have called Palmateer up."

Surrounded by reporters after the game, an exhausted but happy Palmateer said, "This was a big night in my life — a chance to show that I could do in the NHL and get my foot in the door. I wasn't too nervous, but then I'd had a rather hectic 24 hours and was a little tired. That helped me relax."

Almost two decades after that landmark game — played in a fabled arena that no longer exists — Palmateer revels in the nostalgia.

"It all happened so fast," he remembers. "With all the excitement, I didn't sleep the whole night before that Detroit game and I travelled most of the day to get there. I didn't have a lot of time to think, and that probably helped.

"Yes, the story about me telling Jim Gregory that his goaltending troubles were over is true. I had been fairly cocky beforehand, saying that I'd do the job if given the chance, and I honestly believed what I said to Gregory. It was an opportunity I'd been dying for and there's no way I was going to give them an excuse to send me back down."

That same night in Detroit, Palmateer revealed one of his numerous idiosyncrasies — singing behind his goal-mask. "I was humming my usual tunes in the nets," he told reporters. "Songs, commercials... anything that popped into my head."

From Detroit, the Leafs moved on to Minnesota for a re-match with the North Stars and won again, 5-1. While the Red wings hadn't tested Palmateer severely, this game was a different story. The Leafs came out in a coma and were blasted 15-1 in shots in the first period. But only Lou Nanne's powerplay drive eluded the rookie, whose acrobatics served to awaken his slumbering 'mates. Lanny McDonald scored twice and Borje Salming had four assists in a lop-sided Maple Leaf victory.

"Woosh, we're on a winning streak!" said a buoyant Kelly after the game. "Palmateer kept us in there until we got untracked. It was just a great performance."

The final stop on the three-game road swing was Richfield, Ohio — home of the Cleveland Barons (formerly the California Golden Seals). The 18,544-seat Richfield Coliseum was practically empty as only 3,488 fans showed up to see the Maple Leafs win their third consecutive game in front of Palmateer, 6-3 over the Barons. Again, the rookie was solid in goal, making a series of tough stops that showcased his reflexes. On one flurry, he stuck his pad out to block a hard shot by Mike Fidler, then recovered to make a high glove-save on Rick Hampton.

In the second period, with Leafs ahead 5-2, Palmateer showed his willingness to challenge opposition shooters when he charged 35 feet out of his net to thwart Wayne Merrick of Cleveland on a breakaway. Such forays would occasionally cause heartbeats to increase on the Maple Leaf bench, but would become Palmateer's trademark.

"Sure it was a big gamble," he said. "But I started to skate out as soon as he got the pass to move into the clear. He was looking at the puck and I don't think he saw me until I was right on top of him. It's not a move I plan to make often, but it seemed like a good idea at the time."

Flying from Cleveland to Toronto, Palmateer remembers feeling very much a part of the Maple Leaf team — even though he'd been in the NHL for only five days.

"Starting out with three victories was obviously a big confidence boost," he says. "But I really never felt overwhelmed by the situation because I knew I belonged in the NHL. I was thrilled to be there, don't get me wrong, but I wasn't in awe of anybody. I had played *against* guys like (Ian) Turnbull in Junior, so it was no big deal.

"Of course, I got involved in the tier-one card game right away," he laughs. "With Lanny, Jack Valiquette and Claire Alexander. Flights went by quickly with those guys."

Palmateer's NHL debut at the Gardens was a forgettable experience. St. Louis brought the rookie goalie and the entire Leaf team back to earth with a 6-2 pasting that Red Kelly labelled "our worst game of the season." Palmateer actually played well, keeping the Leafs in the match for the first period-and-a-half, as his 'mates reverted to the careless brand of defensive hockey that plagued Wayne Thomas. The Blues scored three goals in the third period to pull away from Toronto.

"We were lousy," said Kelly. "For the first time this season, I felt the team almost quit. When St. Louis started pulling ahead in the third period, it seemed like we just gave up. Palmateer played well and kept us in the game for as long as it was close."

The Gardens loss was both disappointing and ironic for Palmateer, who had spent much of his youth at the famous building on Carlton St. Ascending through the Marlboro minor-hockey system, he practised at the Gardens on Saturday mornings from the time he played Peewee (on a team sponsored by Shopsy's restaurant).

"It was my home since I was 12 years old," he says. "At the lowest level, our practices would start at 6:45 a.m. and they'd be a half-hour later as we moved up through Minor-Bantam to Bantam and so on. That was during the late-60s and I'll always have great memories of chasing the Leafs around for autographs.

"They would usually skate around 10:30 or so, and sometimes I'd have breakfast in the Gardens and wait for them to arrive. Then I'd run from player to player. Frank Mahovlich was my hero. Meeting him for the first time was a real thrill.

"So, playing there in the NHL obviously meant a great deal to me and I think I was quite nervous before my first home game."

The Leafs rebounded from that horrible effort against St. Louis and continued to prosper with Palmateer in goal. He was outstanding in a 2-2 tie at Los Angeles, as the Kings outshot the Maple Leafs 42-28. Three nights later, in Vancouver, Palmateer blocked all 30 Canuck shots to record his first NHL shutout — a 3-0 Toronto victory.

"He's a little guy who's always coming up big," praised Red Kelly. "He's got great poise for a young man and he hasn't played a bad game since he's been with us."

The signature moment of Palmateer's entire career, however, may have been his second home game as a Maple Leaf — Wed. Nov. 17, 1976. He followed up his whitewashing of Vancouver with yet another shutout, but this was an entirely different story.

Palmateer turned in one of the truly memorable goaltending efforts in Maple Leaf annals — stymieing the Montreal Canadiens — whose 1976-77 outfit was arguably the finest in NHL history. A dazzling array of acrobatics enabled him to block 39 shots for a 1-0 Toronto victory that Maple Leaf fans still talk about.

That was the year the Habs compiled an astonishing 60-8-12 record for 132 points, the most-ever in one season, and easily captured their second of four consecutive Stanley Cups. Palmateer would be the only netminder to blank them during that incredible season. His performance ended a streak of 192 games in which Montreal had scored, dating back to a 3-0 loss at the Forum to Philadelphia more than two years earlier.

"That night was an absolute dream," Palmateer remembers. "I recall that everything bounced right and the guys played almost a perfect game in front of me. Of course the classic hockey rivalry between Montreal and Toronto made it all the more special. I was a Leaf fan growing up and my brother was a Canadiens' fan, so I may have rubbed it into him a little bit that night.

"What I remember most, however, is my father. I looked up at him when I skated out as the game's first star and he was glowing. That meant more to me than the shutout."

Lanny McDonald's goal at 8:26 of the first period, on passes from Sittler and Turnbull, was the only scoring play of the night. He beat Ken Dryden with a wrist shot to the glove side. "You couldn't ask for anything better than what Palmateer did tonight," Sittler said after the game. "Dryden was great, too. But right off the bat — when Steve Shutt had that excellent chance — Palmateer stopped him. That's what you need to win big games."

Montreal's Guy Lafleur wasn't as impressed with the rookie goalie, telling reporters, "He played well, but we missed too many chances and made him look good."

Dryden, however, had praise for his up-start opponent. "It's the first time I've seen him and he sure has a lot of confidence," said the veteran goalie. "He's smart and quick on his skates. It's obviously an honest shutout. He earned it."

Upon reflection, Palmateer's superb effort against Montreal is less of a shock than it seemed to be at the time.

"The tougher the challenge, the better Palmy played," remembers Sittler. "He thrived on the satisfaction of doing well and he backed up his cockiness on the ice. He wanted to play against the best teams and beat them. He'd challenge you in practice and was one of those guys who just loved performing — he always had that boyish smile on his face.

"He could also switch the momentum of a game with one big save — not unlike Felix Potvin nowadays. Felix doesn't have Mike's personality but the two of them were very similar on the ice."

Dryden remembers some conflicting emotions as he watched Palmateer stone his Montreal teammates from the other end of the ice. Primarily, he was anxious at being on the wrong end of the score. Secondarily, he recalls a begrudging sense of admiration for his rookie counterpart.

"I think there's a little bit of fan in every player so part of my reaction that night was, `Geez, this kid is playing really well,'" says Dryden. "Afterwards, I remember thinking that we'd really been through something special; I mean, 1-0 games don't happen very often. So, while the down-side was losing, it was certainly an exciting night."

The Montreal teams of that era were light years ahead of the Maple Leafs (and everyone else) in terms of skill and depth. But the Toronto-Montreal rivalry often served to narrow that gap.

"There was always an electric atmosphere when we played in Toronto and that feeling would heighten if the game stayed close," Dryden says. "The Leafs usually played well against us, even when they weren't very good. And when Palmateer came into the league, they developed into a formidable opponent.

"That 1-0 game had all the ingredients of a classic. Everyone in the Gardens realized we were capable of erasing a one-goal deficit and I believe that most people thought we'd eventually score. But Palmateer was playing tremendously and as the game wore on, you could sense that the fans were starting to dream a little.

"It wasn't just that Mike was *making* the saves, as much as the *way* he was making them. There he was, a rookie, playing against a team that hardly ever lost, and he was winning every challenge... charging out of his net to confront our best shooters. I remember thinking, `How dare you come into the league and not just play so well against us, but with that in-your-face style.' It really was a terrific performance."

Palmateer's smug, devil-me-care attitude served him well during games and frequently materialized off the ice.

"He would sit and eat hand-fulls of popcorn in-between periods," Sittler remembers. "I don't know how he did it. If that was me, I'd be burping up all over the place, but it never seemed to bother him."

The former goalie laughs when recalling his peculiar habits.

"Yeah, I never had a problem wolfing down a hamburger or eating fried shrimp with hot-sauce between periods," he says matter-of-factly. "If I was hungry, what the hell? It wouldn't affect my performance."

At other times, the impulsive, carefree side of Palmateer's nature would lead to trouble. Such was the case in March, 1978, when he lost a dangerous amount of blood after horsing around in his apartment at the Town Inn Hotel on Church St.

The official version of the incident — the one that appeared in the Toronto papers — was that Palmateer put his arm through a window while hanging drapes.

"It was really a crazy thing," he told James Christie in the *Globe & Mail*. "The accident happened at about 10:30, after I came home from the sportsmen's show. I stepped up on a wobbly wooden chair and was reaching for the drapery track when one of the legs gave way.

"I cut myself a little. It was a small cut, but deep I guess. I figured I would let the trainer fix it at practice (the following day) and put a bandage on it myself.

"I went to bed and a couple of hours later, I woke up very weak. The bandage came off and I must have lost a couple pints of blood. I was going to wait until morning but I couldn't stop the bleeding.

"I called a policeman friend who came over with an ambulance and I spent about a half-an-hour in the hospital being stitched up."

The *unofficial* version of the incident is that Palmateer and several friends got fairly juiced up and began clowning around in the middle of the night. The horseplay got out of hand and ended with the Leaf goalie smashing his forearm through the window.

Jim Gregory was summoned in the wee hours of the morning.

"Mike must have hit an artery because blood was spurting all over the place with every one of his heartbeats," recalls the former general manager. "The apartment was really a mess and I remember telling him, `You better die tonight because if you don't, I'm going to kill you.'"

After returning from hospital, Palmateer and Gregory discussed how they would handle the incident with the media. Palmateer came up with the curtain-hanging scenario and Gregory went along with it. He told the Toronto *Sun*: "Mike had an accident while adjusting the drapes in his apartment. He fell off a chair and his arm went through a window. He was with some friends at the time and after they left, Mike felt dizzy and had the cut attended to."

Predictably, the media became very sceptical when the story broke. They checked with police about reports of a disturbance in the building and described the apartment as "looking like a tornado had hit." To which Palmateer replied, "If it did, it only hit the one window."

To dissuade any further investigating, Palmateer donned his full equipment and somehow took part in the Maple Leafs' practice just hours later at the Gardens. Leaf owner Harold Ballard was asked about the incident and said, "I don't know anything more about it. All I know is that Mike was off duty at the time and that he's at practice today. If you go out at night and have a few drinks when you're not working, does your boss give you hell the next morning?"

However, Ballard later told the Toronto *Star* that more than one window had been broken and some furniture had been damaged in the apartment. He said Palmateer was not alone when police were called and there had been complaints of noise in the building. The Leaf owner said he would fully investigate the incident before deciding on any punitive action against his young goalkeeper.

Nothing further came of the story and Palmateer played goal later that night at the Gardens in a 6-2 loss to the New York Islanders. To this day, he loathes talking about the incident.

"I'd rather not discuss it. It wasn't a proud moment," he says.

Another controversial incident with Palmateer occurred during the 1977 quarterfinals against Philadelphia. In the second period of Game 4 at the Gardens, he clubbed Gary Dornhoefer over the head with his stick during a goalmouth skirmish. Dornhoefer was knocked cold.

"That was an accident," Palmateer says. "I was watching the play and we were jostling back and forth. He gave me a little shot and my stick came down as a reaction. I would never have hit him in the head on purpose. If I could've broken his leg or ankle... maybe. But not his head. I was horrified when it happened."

The Maple Leafs wound up getting three fairly good seasons out of Palmateer. Between 1976-77 and 1978-79, he played in 171 regular-season games and gave up around three goals per outing. Despite having to face Montreal in '78 and '79, he fared just as well in 24 playoff matches. Like most of his Maple Leaf teammates, he suffered amidst the turmoil of Punch Imlach's second regime and was dealt to Washington in June, 1980 for defenceman Robert Picard.

He re-joined the Leafs for the 1982-83 season and played in 53 games. But his wonky knees soon landed him in poor stead with Ballard and the two had a bitter divorce the following year. Still, most Leaf fans and other hockey observers remember Palmateer for his flashy style of play during the peak moments of his not-so lengthy career.

"Palmy believed in himself and that attitude carried right through the entire team," says former Leaf defenceman Brian Glennie. "He was a reflex goalie with a very cocky demeanour and it served him well during games. I know there were many times when he saved *my* ass."

Adds Ken Dryden: "Palmateer was more than self-confident; he was brash, and he had a certain flair about him that brought out the best in his on-ice performance. It was the right combination of style and personality and those two elements have to fit together. His did.

"He was small, gymnastic, unpredictable — a goalie who was spectacular in all of the good senses and some of the bad. He played a game that was verging out of control but, for the most part, it worked for him. I think at times, he did a bit more than he needed to and got into trouble on the ice. But there was a purpose in almost everything else and he had the type of personality that was well-suited for the Maple Leafs of that era.

"They were making a breakthrough with a bunch of players who probably didn't realize how good they were. Then Palmateer came around and his play said, `Of *course* we're good. In fact, we're better than you think we are.' When you start out in a situation like that, it's fun. And Mike's performance helped make it fun for everybody."

* * * * * *

WHERE ARE THEY NOW?...

MIKE PALMATEER, 41, played goal for the Maple Leafs and Washington Capitals between 1976-77 and 1983-84. He finished his career with a 3.53 goals-against average in 356 regular-season games and a 3.03 mark in 29 playoff matches. He'll always be remembered around Toronto for a spectacular performance in the 1978 quarterfinals, as the Maple Leafs upset the New York Islanders in seven breathtaking games. When his career ended, Palmateer opened up a restaurant that bared his name in Aurora, Ont. He recently moved to St. Petersburg to work for *Sutton Group/Gulf Coast Realty*, one of the largest real-estate companies in the Bay Area of Florida.

WAYNE THOMAS, 47, attended the University of Wisconsin and came up to the NHL with Montreal in 1972-73. His career essentially featured one very good season — with the Maple Leafs in 1975-76. He played in 64 games that year and his netminding heroics almost led the Leafs to a stunning playoff upset of Philadelphia. His downfall with Toronto is documented in this chapter and after leaving, he played parts of three seasons with the New York Rangers, retiring after the 1980-81 campaign. Thomas later became an assistant coach with Chicago and St. Louis. His tutelage of young Curtis Joseph is said to have helped dramatically in the development of one of hockey's best current-day goalies. He moved on to the San Jose Sharks for 1993-94 as assistant to head coach Kevin Constantine and director of hockey operations Dean Lombardi.

KEN DRYDEN, 47, was a member of six Stanley Cup-championship teams with the Montreal Canadiens between 1970-71 and 1978-79. His sudden and spectacular rise to prominence with the 1971 Habs will be marvelled at as long as the game is played. The rookie from Colgate University spent all but the final weeks of that season tending goal for Montreal's AHL farm team: the Voyageurs. The Canadiens called him up and he played in six late-season games, posting a superb 1.65 average. His performance level accelerated through the playoffs, enabling Montreal to shock the explosive and record-breaking Boston Bruins of Bobby Orr (102 assists) and Phil Esposito (76 goals). After an easy semifinal victory over the Minnesota North Stars, Dryden and the Canadiens stymied Chicago in the finals and Montreal won a very unexpected Stanley Cup. Dryden was on the ice for Team Canada when Paul Henderson scored his famous goal to beat the Russians in 1972. He later authored perhaps the finest hockey book of all time ("The Game"), and helped narrate several television specials, including a 20th anniversary reflection of the Canada-Soviet summit. Dryden earned his law degree while playing hockey and currently lives in Toronto.

BRIAN GLENNIE, 48, was a big, hulking defenceman with Toronto and Los Angeles between 1969-70 and 1978-79. A product of the Marlboro Junior system, he played nine seasons for the Maple Leafs and was noted for his ability to deliver hard open-ice bodychecks. He was also a member of the 1972 Team Canada squad that played the Soviets. The Leafs traded him to the Kings in June, 1978 in the deal that brought fellow defenceman Dave Hutchison to Toronto. Glennie suffered a mild heart-attack several years ago but is currently doing well. He is retired and lives in the Muskoka region of Ontario.

... Leafs in Spring ...

MAY 11, 1994
San Jose Arena

Like most of us, Doug Gilmour is a person of varying emotions. He can be altogether engaging, aloof, belligerent and jocular — sometimes in the course of a few hours. He is therefore a perfect captain.

The belligerent Gilmour is normally reserved for NHL adversaries. He rarely reveals any bellicose tendencies off the ice. He did blow up at a small group of reporters, including myself, for what he perceived to be unjustifiable laughter during a gruelling practice midway through the 1993-94 season. The Maple Leafs had been embarrassed the previous night by lowly Tampa Bay: losing 2-1 at the Gardens to extend a three-game winless streak. And Pat Burns was in a foul mood.

The coach ordered all pucks removed from the Gardens' ice surface and he skated his charges into virtual exhaustion for one full hour. It was both painful to watch and monotonous to sit through. As the torture wound to a close, the players staggered over to the boards for a drink. At that very moment, a cameraman from CFTO television (Channel 9) told an outrageously funny joke about Lorena Bobbit. Those of us surrounding him in the gold seats burst into side-splitting laughter.

Peering up from the Leaf bench, and obviously irritable from all the skating, Gilmour assumed that we were chuckling at the scene on the ice. And he *unleashed a vitriolic stream of profanities that would have embarrassed a sailor, let alone an unsuspecting media huddle. This was not the Doug Gilmour we had come to know and admire and, typically, he apologized a few days later.*

During the Maple Leaf-San Jose Western Conference semifinal, the real Gilmour surfaced on more than a few occasions, several of which I witnessed first-hand. I saw the final moments of Game 3 from ice level, at the gate leading to the Toronto dressing room. The Sharks had badly outplayed an alarmingly lacklustre Maple Leaf team and were leading 5-2 with 38 seconds left in regulation time when a melee developed not 15 feet in front of me.

Despite playing on a strained right ankle that required freezing, Gilmour had been among a small core of Leaf players who seemed to care about the proceedings. And with less than a minute to go in a game that was far beyond salvaging, he found himself entangled with a much larger opponent in Sandis Ozolinch. Valiantly struggling to fight the San Jose defenceman, Gilmour was nonetheless in a predicament, and Mike Gartner intervened on his behalf.

After being separated from Ozolinch, Gilmour resisted the urgings of linesman Kevin Collins to leave the ice and was loudly insulting a group of Shark players as Collins nudged him towards the exit. At that moment, an Arena security officer mindlessly reached over and began to assist Collins. Of course, he had no business interfering with the game and Gilmour — after blinking his eyes in amazement — tore a strip off the feebleminded guard, who recoiled from the verbal assault.

As he stormed off the ice, Gilmour made an indelible statement: another playoff game loomed in less than 48 hours and a highly improved effort would be compulsory. As per usual, he had shown the way — this time without results. Over his dead body would it happen again.

Gilmour and Wendel Clark steamrolled the Leafs to a five-goal rout of San Jose in Game 4 but two nights later, the Sharks regained control of the series with another 5-2 victory. Watching the dying moments from ice level once again, it was a more-subdued Gilmour who barged towards the dressing room while his teammates consoled Felix Potvin. He seemed to be in a hurry, but just as he turned the corner, Gilmour abruptly stopped and pivoted in his tracks. He then waited for his mates and as each one passed by, he offered a tap of encouragement — as if to say, "C'mon guys, we can still do it." Once again, he became the story.

More than an hour later, after most of the Maple Leaf players had left for the hotel, I stubbornly pursued the elusive Gilmour, who was apparently still in the Arena. He wasn't in the main dressing room, in the shower, or in the trainer's room. But nobody had seen him leave the building. Saddled with grievous deadline restrictions, Toronto scribes relented in their search for Gilmour — all

*except Steve Simmons of the Sun. He and CFTO reporter Suneel Joshi stayed
behind with me.*

*Having exhausted all reasonable options, I decided to check out an ante-
room across the hall from the Maple Leaf quarters. By then, every other inch of
the Arena had been scoured. After a tenuous knock, I went into the room and
turned to my right. And there — sitting by himself, watching TV — was
Gilmour. A lesser man would have told me to get out of his hair, and with some
justification, but the Maple Leaf sparkplug generously invited me, Simmons and
Joshi for a chin-wag.*

*He carefully explained why he had purposely greeted each of his teammates
as they left the ice and insisted, rather convincingly, that the Maple Leafs would
bounce back at home and win the series.*

I left the room feeling good about their chances.

9

THE NIGHT "FLIPPER" FLIPPED

Maple Leaf Gardens
October 16, 1968

There was nothing remarkable about the pre-game atmosphere at the Maple Leafs' home opener of the 1968-69 NHL season.

A typically stoic audience had filed into the Gardens to watch the Leafs play Pittsburgh, three nights after edging the Red Wings, 2-1, at the old Detroit Olympia to begin the regular season. Polite applause rained down as the 48th Highlanders bagpipe unit marched through the annual ceremony of ushering in the new hockey campaign on Carlton Street.

The Maple Leafs appeared first, deftly avoiding the red carpet that stretched from the penalty box gate towards center ice. Clad in their predominantly blue home uniforms, they were soon joined by the Penguins, decked out in their white road duds, with the powder-blue shoulder piping and dark-blue pants. For the 38th consecutive hockey season, it was showtime at Maple Leaf Gardens, but surely no one in the fabled arena had any inkling of the history that would unfold before the night was over.

Nobody, perhaps, except the muscular rookie defenceman who, moments earlier, had been nervously pacing the floor of the Maple Leaf dressing room. At 21 years of age, and following a tumultuous ascent through the Junior and minor-pro leagues, James Robert Dorey had made it to the NHL. As he circled the south end of the Gardens' ice with his new teammates — sporting the number '8' on his Maple Leaf jersey — Dorey pondered the reputation he had garnered on his way to the big league. He was there for his brawn, not his brains, and there existed a hungering to prove he belonged.

That obsession had flared spontaneously in the Detroit opener. Having been deposited unceremoniously into the Red Wings' bench by a thunderous bodycheck, Dorey instinctively began flailing away in self-defence. Upon opening his eyes to see with whom he was jostling, Dorey found himself face-to-face with the man known universally as "Mr. Hockey" — none other than Gordon Howe.

"The Red Wings were making a line change and I got bounced right through the door of their bench," Dorey remembers. "I quickly realized I wasn't a welcomed guest and began battling for my life. Gordie was trying to keep me at arm's length and he had a look on his face that said, `Who the hell is *this* nut?' I wasn't penalized, but I do recall being asked to go back to my own bench."

The zany incident served as a precursor to an altogether refined strategy by GM/coach Punch Imlach. The Maple Leafs of 1968-69 were coming off one of the most abysmal seasons in club history. The NHL had doubled in size and the Leafs were sectored in the new East Division with the other five established teams. The six expansion clubs comprised the West Division. In a galling turn of events, the defending Stanley Cup champions staggered through 1967-68, playing sub-.500 hockey in the 24 games against the fledgling newcomers. In so doing, they actually missed the playoffs — marking the fourth time in franchise history they had gone from champs to chumps.

They were also among the "softest" teams in the NHL, and were easily pushed around by some of the less-talented, but aggressive players the expansion clubs were forced to employ. It was the first time in Imlach's decade behind the bench that his Leafs failed to qualify for the post-season, and he was not a happy man.

At the same time the '67-68 Maple Leafs were floundering, the club's farm team in Tulsa, Oklahoma was running roughshod through the Central Hockey League. Sporting a pack of hooligans like Dorey Pat Quinn, Doug Barrie, Mike Pelyk, Gord Nelson, Randy Murray, Nick Harbaruk and Ken Campbell (averaging 122 penalty minutes apiece), the Oilers brawled their way to the CHL championship — winning the Jack Adams Trophy in four consecutive games over Fort Worth.

The wildest games, however, were those in which inter-state rivals

Tulsa and Oklahoma City engaged. They finished with the two best records during the regular season and then battled through an exhausting, seven-game semifinal — Oilers prevailing, 6-4, in the deciding match. Oke City was Boston's CHL affiliate, with bruisers like John Arbour, Barry Wilkins, Barry Gibbs, Wayne Cashman and Ross Lonsberry. All-out war ensued when the two clubs met.

"There were stretchers," Dorey recalls. "I remember Lonsberry being carried off the ice after me and Quinn hammered him. We beat 'em in the alley and on the ice. Nobody wanted to go near us."

The Tulsa players even fought among themselves. Campbell and another tough forward, Len (Comet) Haley, engaged in a school-yard melee on the night of teammate Gerry Meehan's stag. "They got into a wild argument over a blackjack game and drove to a nearby school off Route 66," remembers Mike Pelyk. "A bunch of us followed them there in another car and they just hammered the living shit out of each other. Then they went back to the party."

Dorey and Barrie had a donnybrook hours after Barrie was traded to Tulsa late in the season. "He chopped me in a game at Omaha one night — broke his goddamned stick right over my head," Dorey recalls. "When he came to our team, the guys had a gathering at Pat Quinn's apartment. I went up to Barrie and said, `Dougie, you're welcomed on this hockey club but I want you to come outside with me for a moment.'

"We got out there and I told him, `I'm not happy with what you did and I want to see you handle yourself as well *off* the ice as you did when you clubbed me from behind.' We went at it tooth-and-nail, I got it off my chest, and we went back into Pat's place as pretty good friends. That's the kind of group we had in Tulsa."

That rambunctious, all-for-one tenacity caught the attention of Imlach and he reinforced the '68-69 Maple Leafs with members of the Central League champions. Dorey, Quinn and Pelyk all made the jump to the NHL, as did Tulsa goalie Al Smith. Rugged defenceman Rick Ley, a Junior 'A' star with Niagara Falls the previous year, was also added. The Leafs were suddenly cream-puffs no more.

Actually, Dorey had long been a topic around the Imlach household, thanks in large part to Punch's wife Dorothy (or Dodo). Columnist Jim Proudfoot of the Toronto *Star* penned an article on Dorey for the February, 1969 issue of *Hockey World* magazine, in which he outlined Mrs. Imlach's role.

"...Toronto scouts discovered Dorey in Kingston and shifted him to their Junior `A' affiliate at London, Ont. for the 1965-66 season. He spent two years there with London Nationals and during that period, his biggest booster was Mrs. Dodo Imlach, wife of Leafs' manager-coach.

"Mrs. Imlach used to attend Nats' games to keep an eye on son Brent, who played with them while attending college in London. When she'd come home, though, she'd be talking only about Dorey."

Imlach kept a close eye on the rugged defenceman and Dorey was thrilled to make the '68-69 Leafs with his buddies: Ley, Quinn and Pelyk. "We were brash kids who fit in with the temperament of that era," Dorey explains. "It was the late-60's, America was at war with Vietnam, and it was the `in' thing to be tough. You didn't talk trash, you *did* trash. That was the deal back then."

Indeed, on the very afternoon of the Maple Leafs' 1968-69 home opener, in another part of North America, there occurred one of the more infamous demonstrations of the turmoil-filled decade. At the Olympic Games in Mexico City, Afro-American sprinters Tommie Smith and John Carlos of the U.S.A. finished one-two in the 200-metre final. While standing on the podium during the medal ceremony, the two athletes raised their right and left arms, respectively, and clenched their fists in a black-unity salute.

The fascist-type display appalled even the most rebellious of on-lookers and two days later, both men were banished from the U.S. team and ordered to leave the Olympic village. It was against that back-drop that the Maple Leafs began their '68-69 home schedule on the night of Wednesday, October 16.

For almost two full periods, the opener was an ordinary affair between a couple of ordinary hockey teams. The Pittsburgh Penguins were starting their second NHL season, having joined the loop as part of the six-team expansion. They had missed the playoffs in their inaugural campaign by the narrowest of margins, finishing two points behind fourth-place Minnesota in the West Division.

Like their expansion brethren, the Penguins were practically devoid of accomplished personnel — forwards Lou Angotti, Ken Schinkel and Val Fonteyne, and defenceman Leo Boivin being among those with established credentials at the NHL level. Others, like Wally Boyer, Billy Dea and Earl Ingarfield were journeymen types: generally quick afoot, but small, and ineffective in the rough going. Boivin and rookie John Arbour did provide some muscle along the blueline.

As the game wound towards the conclusion of the second period,

Pittsburgh held a 1-0 lead on Dea's first-period tally and a couple of patterns had developed: Les Binkley was especially sharp in goal for the Penguins, and Jim Dorey was suffering through an exasperating first night at the Gardens.

Referee Art Skov showed precious little tolerance for the rookie's aggressive style and had penalized Dorey on three separate occasions — for interference at 2:49, and cross-checking at 13:06 of the first period, and then for tripping at 13:38 of the middle frame. Dorey took the penalty barrage as a personal affront and he began to swell with anger and resentment. Forever a ticking time-bomb, the young defenceman was now a raging bull just waiting for someone to wave the red cape. That someone turned out to be Ken Schinkel.

A 15-year veteran of the pro hockey ranks, Schinkel played parts of six seasons for the Rangers between 1959 and 1967, having distinguished himself as a reliable goalscorer with Springfield and Baltimore of the American Hockey League. Like many of his co-horts in the NHL's West Division, new growth provided a ticket to the big league. Drafted from New York's roster in round eight of the 1967 expansion lottery, Schinkel performed admirably for the Penguins during their initial campaign.

In fact, his standout achievement of the season helped to make NHL history. On October 21, 1967, Chicago arrived in Pittsburgh and Penguins' coach George (Red) Sullivan assigned Schinkel the dubious task of checking Blackhawks' superstar Bobby Hull. Incredibly, not only did Schinkel keep Hull off the scoresheet, he wound up netting three goals himself in a 4-2 Pittsburgh victory. The Penguins thus became the first of the expansion clubs to defeat an established foe.

Schinkel's low penalty numbers implied that he generally kept his nose clean on the ice, but he wouldn't recoil from a challenge. He was also adroit enough to seize an opportunity when it arose, and that fortuitous skill produced an ugly, history making fracas with the Maple Leafs.

Less than two minutes remained in the second period when Schinkel gobbled up the puck in the neutral zone. He bore down on the beleaguered Dorey, who bumped Schinkel slightly, with his stick in an upraised position. Realizing that Dorey could do little right that evening, Schinkel took an exaggerated pratfall, and up went the arm of referee Skov, who assessed the rookie his fourth minor penalty of the game.

Visually confronted by a now-seething Dorey, Schinkel scoffed uncharacteristically at the incensed rearguard, basically laughing in his face. Unable to withstand anymore disparagement, Dorey snapped, and bolted after the Penguin forward.

"Jimmy took so many dumb penalties that night that I couldn't resist goading him into another one," Schinkel remembers. "He was doing a lot of running around, trying to impress the fans, and when I got Skov to call that penalty, I looked at Dorey and said, `Rook, I think you've got lots to learn.' I then turned around, unaware that he would fly off the handle, and he jumped me from behind."

Dorey is quick to verify Schinkel's version of the incident. "I lost it," he admits. "Went right off the deep end. I was having a bad game and the penalty totals were adding up. We should have been burying a club like Pittsburgh and I was making it hard for the whole team. The fans were booing me and I simply got tired of being the scapegoat. When Schinkel took that dive, then gave me the horse laugh, I said, `Fuck it, let's go!'"

Dorey grabbed Schinkel and twisted him around, forcing the Pittsburgh player to lose his balance. As Schinkel fell to his knees, Dorey essentially tried to punch his lights out but Schinkel managed to entangle himself in Dorey's sweater. With a passive opponent seemingly at Dorey's mercy, the Gardens' crowd booed the antics of the tormented rookie. The Penguins then poured onto the ice in defence of their prone teammate.

As both benches emptied, Dorey and Schinkel disengaged and nothing further might have developed had it not been for Maple Leaf goalie Al Smith. Subbing that night for Bruce Gamble, the mercurial Smith sprinted from his goalcrease at the south end of the Gardens and grabbed Penguins' forward Keith McCreary. As the other players paired off — dancing and tugging in the center-ice area — Smith took a good whack at McCreary... and the war was on again.

"A lot of the goalies in the NHL back then liked a scrap and I was the same," Smith recalls. "Guys like Gary Smith, Doug Favell, Gerry Cheevers and Ed Giacomin — we all got involved in fights. In that situation against Pittsburgh, I was wrestling with McCreary and I didn't like the way he was tugging at my sweater. So I spun around and tried to smack him, but I was only able to clip his arm. Still, he lost his balance and I jumped on him."

Smith had come up through the Maple Leaf system, playing 22 games with the Junior 'A' Toronto Marlboros in 1965-66. He split the netminding chores on the championship team in Tulsa with Serge Aubry and was essentially the Maple Leafs' third goalie.

"Al was a shit disturber," says Dorey. "In that flare-up with the Penguins, I had pretty much calmed down and wanted to get off the ice — it had been a lousy night. But, my old pal John Arbour came towards me and Smitty began egging me on. He said, `Jimmy, here's another guy who needs taking care of. You can't leave the ice — it's like a bar fight.' So, I said, `okay' and I wound up knocking Arbour on his ass."

Arbour and Dorey had been teammates briefly with the Junior 'A' Niagara Falls Flyers in 1963-64. "He was my big brother that year," Dorey says. But Arbour then moved up to Oklahoma City of the Central League and became the bitter enemy of the Tulsa gang. While the Oilers and Blazers battled for top spot in the 1967-68 regular season, Arbour compiled the second-highest penalty total in the CHL with 224 minutes (Bryan "Bugsy" Watson of Houston had 293). Arbour was not overly big (5-11, 195), but toughness was never a problem.

"I caught Arbour with a couple of lefts, but I don't think he was expecting it," Dorey says of the Pittsburgh brawl. "I remember thinking he was coming over as a peace-maker, probably to calm me down, but I wound up clobbering him anyway."

Arbour has a slightly different version. "I don't recall much about that fight — I used to get into so many of them — but I doubt I was coming towards Dorey to make peace," he says. "I wasn't a real smoothy when I played, and fighting was definitely my job on the Penguins with all those small teammates. So I'm pretty sure I challenged Jimmy that night. We were both rookies in the NHL and when you're first there, if you're supposed to be a tough guy, you'd better do your job."

Not to be outdone, Smith went after McCreary for the second time and he later caught Billy Dea with a surprise punch. Every time the ruckus seemed to be fizzling out, either Dorey or Smith re-kindled the fire.

"I just remember turning around and seeing Smitty bolting towards me at a hundred miles an hour," McCreary recalls. "Why he was after *me* I don't know, but I think he picked on the wrong guy: I almost choked him to death."

McCreary was an average goalscorer but a true leader type who would later become the first captain of the Atlanta Flames. He was not a fighter, per se, but he often found himself having to stick up for his smaller Penguin 'mates.

"I remember the Rangers coming to Pittsburgh in our first season there and they had a pretty tough team," McCreary says. "Our coach, Red Sullivan, told the newspapers that he wasn't worried about guys like Orland Kurtenbach, Vic Hadfield and Reggie Fleming because the Penguins had *me* on their side.

"Well, you just knew after the Rangers read that, I'd be in for a little trouble that night. I wound up fighting all three of those bruisers and I was barely alive after the game. I went into Sully's office the next morning with one eye closed, unable to lift my arm, and I said if he ever again told that kind of thing to the press, I'd be coming over the desk at *him*!"

When the Penguins and Maple Leafs finally cooled down, and Art Skov totalled up his penalty count, Jim Dorey had established a new NHL record for penalty minutes in one game. Heading into the '68-69 season, the mark had been 37 minutes, shared by the afformentioned Reggie Fleming, and former Boston Bruins' defenceman Don Awrey.

Fleming first established the standard while playing for the Chicago Blackhawks. On October 19, 1960, at the old Madison Square Garden, Fleming touched off a wild fracas by swatting Ranger goalie Jack McCartan during a third-period skirmish in the goalcrease. It was not a popular move as only months earlier, McCartan had backstopped the U.S. hockey team to an astonishing gold medal at the Winter Olympic Games in Squaw Valley, California. But Fleming wasn't much for sentiment and he sliced open McCartan's chin.

That brought Rangers' Eddie Shack onto the scene and he got into it with Fleming. When all was said and done, Reggie wound up with 37 minutes: a minor penalty, three majors, one 10-minute misconduct, and a game misconduct.

Fleming's record endured for more than seven years, and was equalled by Don Awrey on the night of December 3, 1967. The Bruins were hosting Montreal and Awrey sparked a brawl late in the first period when he butt-ended Ralph Backstrom of the Canadiens in the solar-plexus. Backstrom crumpled to the ice in agony and Dick Duff of Montreal tried to get at Awrey — Duff pushing linesman Walt Atanas out of the way. It was a bold move by Duff, but Awrey cleaned his clock.

With two Montreal players now prone on the ice, the benches emptied — Canadiens' defenceman Terry Harper leading the way. Awrey took Harper out with one punch. Earlier in the game, he had fought with Bryan Watson of Montreal. In total, he finished with a minor, three majors, a 10-minute misconduct, and a game misconduct: 37 minutes in all, matching Fleming's record.

But Dorey was able to take it just a step further against the Penguins. He ran up four minor penalties, two fighting majors (for his scuffles with Schinkel and Arbour), a 10-minute misconduct, and a game misconduct for a new record of 38 minutes. Dorey's total of eight penalties (later upped to nine) was also a new mark — the old one being seven — shared by George Boucher of the Ottawa Senators (January, 1927) and Ted Green of Boston (December, 1965).

Thirteen days after the Toronto-Pittsburgh brawl, the NHL office in Montreal increased Dorey's total to 48 minutes when it realized the Maple Leaf defenceman had not been assessed an automatic 10-minute sentence for receiving two fighting majors in one game.

*   *   *   *   *   *

Jim Dorey's landmark outburst against the Penguins was merely the tip of the iceberg in a turbulent professional hockey career that spanned 11 years and two leagues. A highly intense performer, Dorey remained forever focused on his role as an enforcer, and it landed him in hot water on numerous occasions during his four-year tenure with the Maple Leafs.

Only 10 days after the fracas against Pittsburgh, Dorey met up with the Boston Bruins for the first time. They were the "Big, Bad Bruins" of Awrey, Shack, Green, Ken Hodge, Wayne Cashman and Derek Sanderson. On October 26, 1968 — a Saturday night at the Gardens — Dorey and Shack went at it, as did Sanderson and Leaf defenceman Tim Horton. Perhaps surprised to be challenged so physically by the Maple Leafs, who had been pushovers the year before, Bruins' coach Harry Sinden spewed venom at reporters after the game.

"We'll kick the shit out of them when they come to Boston," he woofed. "I've been hearing how tough they are. Well, we'll see just how tough they *really* are. Last year, they were nothing."

That next meeting took place at the Boston Garden on November 24, a Sunday night. A sign hanging from the Garden balcony said "GET DOREY!" but a re-match with Shack late in the first period was the only incident of the night. Boston won, 7-4.

It seemed, however, the wide majority of Dorey's early career problems, both on and off the ice, involved the Penguins. Following that late-November loss in Boston, the Maple Leafs flew to Pittsburgh for the first meeting between the teams since the brawl on opening night in Toronto.

Sometime in the wee hours of Tuesday morning (November 26), thieves broke into the Maple Leaf dressing room at the Civic Arena and stole Dorey's shin and elbow pads. When it was coyly suggested to Penguins' general manager Jack Riley that someone was plotting to force Dorey out of the following night's game, Riley quipped, "Don't look at me. I would have stolen his skates as well."

On Tuesday afternoon, the Penguins held their weekly fan lunch-eon at the Igloo Club in the Civic Arena. Riley and coach Red Sullivan were on hand, along with Penguin players Earl Ingarfield, Jean Pronovost and Dunc McCallum. Maple Leaf invitees were Imlach, assistant gen-eral manager King Clancy, Dorey and Horton. After eating lunch, Sullivan stepped up to the microphone for his weekly question period with the fans.

Anticipating that someone would quickly address the subject of the brawl in Toronto, the Penguins' coach turned to Dorey and deadpanned, "Tell me, Jim, did Schinkel hurt you when he belted you in that fight?" Knowing full well that Schinkel never had a chance against Dorey, the sardonic question was either a stab at humour by Sullivan, or an attempt to embarrass the Maple Leaf rookie.

Before Dorey could reply, however, Imlach bolted out of his chair — impervious to any humour on Sullivan's part — and snarled, "I'll tell you what, Red. I'll let you see the TV tapes of the game and if you see Schinkel hit Dorey even once, I'll pay you a hundred dollars."

Sullivan doesn't recall that exchange more than a quarter-century ago, but says his objective would not have been to try and humiliate Dorey in front of the Igloo Club audience.

"Naw, he was a tough kid and I was just horsing around — playing it up for the fans. In fact, if anything, I was probably trying to get under Punch's skin, and it seems like I did."

During the pre-game warmup the following night, several fans hurled wisecracks at Dorey but the game itself moved along without incident until the waning moments of the second period. As he battled for the puck in the neutral zone with Penguins' center Lou Angotti, Dorey stumbled sideways. Angotti's stick accidentally caught him un-der the right eye and Dorey fell to the ice clutching his face — blood squirting between his fingers.

Dorey was helped off the ice and rushed to Divine-Providence Hospital at the behest of Penguins' team doctor, Paul Steele, who put two stitches in Dorey's eyeball. The Maple Leaf rookie had suffered a severe corneal abrasion, with bleeding in the interior chamber of the eye. With patches over both eyes, Dorey was given permission to return home with the Leafs following the game. He was immediately trans-ferred to Toronto General Hospital.

The sports headline in the Toronto *Telegram* the next day said, **THEY FINALLY GOT TO LEAFS' JIM DOREY**. On the plane ride home from Pittsburgh, Dorey discussed the incident with reporters.

"I don't remember how it happened," he told the *Telegram's* George Gross. "I don't know if it was a skate or a stick... I've never experienced anything like that before. I felt a very sharp pain and in the hospital, they told me I had an abrasion of the eyeball. I saw spots. I hope it will clear up soon."

The Pittsburgh Civic Arena was also the scene, a year later, of the night Dorey officially received the nickname "Flipper". Never confident at passing along the ice in the defensive zone, Dorey would almost always raise the puck a few inches. By doing so, he'd invariably drive his teammates and coaches crazy, but he took that fetish a step further against the Penguins.

Standing behind his own net while attempting to organize a rush, Dorey noticed Mike Walton streaking into the clear at center ice. With haste now a factor, he actually tried to flip the puck *over top the Leaf net* and out towards Walton. Instead, he hit goalie Bruce Gamble in back of the head, and the puck went into the Maple Leaf net for a Penguins' goal.

"Yeah, I K-O'd poor Brucie," Dorey laughs. "He was moving back and forth in the goalcrease, trying to figure out what I was going to do, and he screwed up my timing. I saw `Shakey' bursting into the clear but I couldn't get the puck over Bruce's head. From that moment on, I've been known as `Flipper'".

On January 5, 1969, the Maple Leafs were in Philadelphia for a Sunday night encounter with the Flyers. In the first period, Dorey got into a wild scrap with Brit Selby, who three years earlier — while with the Leafs — had won the Calder Trophy as the NHL's rookie of the year. Selby clipped Dorey in back of the head with his stick. Dorey ignored the play as it swung into the Flyers' zone and turned to immediately challenge Selby. Dorey won a close decision but got the worst of it, as Selby apparently tried to gouge his eye.

Flyers' broadcaster Stu Nahan, calling the game for TV station WKSB in Philadelphia, let his emotions get carried away as Dorey jawed with Selby. "Shut up Dorey! Get in the box, you punk," Nahan hollered into his microphone, in full ear-shot of the entire press box. Flyers' team president, Bill Putnam, was rather embarrassed by Nahan's outburst and he told the broadcaster to cool it.

The game was tied 2-2, late in the third period, when Flyers' tough guy Forbes Kennedy also decided to club Dorey over the head. For that little deed, Kennedy received a five-minute major, but the Maple Leafs were unable to break the deadlock with a man advantage in the final 4:46 of play. After the game, the various combatants discussed their run-ins.

Described by *Globe & Mail* hockey writer Lou Cauz as "a mess of scratches, bruises and stitches", Dorey talked about the fight with Selby. "He hit me a couple of times but I did okay," he said. "What bugged me was his scratching. He was clawing away at my eye when I knocked him down. I think I'm going to grow some nails myself."

Over in the Philadelphia dressing room, Kennedy expanded on *his* altercation with Dorey. "He tried to elbow me and I hit him with my stick. It all happened so fast. Anyway, I've been reading his press clippings on how tough a guy he is and I wanted to find out for myself."

There was no fallout when the Flyers paid a return visit to the Gardens the following Wednesday. But the next night, in Boston, Dorey got into it again with the Bruins.

At 8:50 of the first period, a scuffle broke out behind the Toronto net. John McKenzie of the Bruins began trading punches with defenceman Pierre Pilote, whom the Leafs had acquired from Chicago (for Jim Pappin) the previous May. Dorey tried to get involved, but was intercepted by Bruins' defenceman Dallas Smith, who might have had second thoughts. Dorey pulled Smith's sweater over his head and administered quite a pounding.

A wild cheer then engulfed the Garden as Bruins' goalie Gerry Cheevers made a mad dash the length of the ice and jumped on Dorey. Another uncontrolled hassle ensued and when the situation cooled, referee John Ashley gave Dorey a fighting major, misconduct, and a game misconduct. Enraged at such a stiff sentence, Dorey had to be restrained from accosting the official. When he left the ice, he placed his hand across his throat and gave Ashley the "choke" sign.

Fights with Lou Nanne of Minnesota and Craig Cameron of St. Louis in February put Dorey in position to break the Leafs' single-season record for penalty minutes by one player. It fell before a TV audience on both sides of the border on March 2, 1969. The Leafs hosted Chicago in a Sunday afternoon game televised by CBS in the United States. A cross-checking penalty at 7:50 of the first period raised Dorey's penalty minutes to 178 — one more than the total amassed by defenceman Carl Brewer in the 1964-65 season.

That same day, Dorey became teammates with Forbes Kennedy and Brit Selby, his antagonists during that wild game at Philadelphia. The

Flyers traded the duo to the Maple Leafs for forwards Gerry Meehan, Bill Sutherland and Mike Byers.

On the final Saturday night of the '68-69 campaign, the New York Rangers were in Toronto and Dorey tried to lure Ranger defenceman Arnie Brown into a scuffle midway through the third period. However, Brown backed off when Dorey assumed a boxing stance. "That's the dumbest play I've ever seen," said Brown, after the game. "It was obvious what he was trying to do."

Not so obvious, however, when Dorey explained his side of the incident. "I just wanted to get something started out there. I was after my bonus for 200 minutes," he joked.

Well, you know what they say about true words spoken in jest. Dorey finished his rookie season with *exactly* that total. It placed him second in the league, behind only Kennedy's 219 minutes.

Dorey toned it down a bit during his sophomore campaign as he was plagued by injuries. He dressed for only 46 games in 1969-70, but was front and center once again after another blow-out late in the season. This particular tantrum occurred at the Met Center in Bloomington, Minnesota and it closely resembled Dorey's record outburst against the Penguins.

The Leafs were in Minnesota on March 1, 1970, for another one of those Sunday afternoon games televised by CBS. The North Stars were in a horrible funk, not having won a game in their previous 20 attempts, dating back to the middle of January. A generation later, that streak remains as the longest without victory in the history of the franchise, now located in Dallas.

The accounts of that game, and its rather surprising result, were eloquently and emotionally described by the late Red Burnett in the Toronto *Star*.

"BLOOMINGTON, Minn. — There's nothing as inexcusable as the actions of a player who tries to cover the inept work of himself and his teammates as they stumble to a humiliating defeat, by starting an uncalled-for hey-rube.

"That was the Jim Dorey story here yesterday afternoon. Minnesota North Stars were making Maple Leafs look like fugitives from a county league en route to an 8-0 win when Dorey staged a third-period temper-tantrum.

"He blew his stack after referee Bill Friday handed him a minor penalty for interference. Instead of going to the box, he cross-checked

Claude Larose, captain of the home side, to the ice. Then he took a punch at Larose — and missed.

"...Players left both benches to join the fray. Leafs' Terry Clancy and Barry Gibbs staged the best brawl while thrashing around on the ice, with linesmen Pat Shetler and Neil Armstrong trying to pull them apart.

"Just when it looked as if everyone had cooled out, Dorey made a second run at the taunting Larose. This time Shetler was hit on the mouth by a Dorey punch as he tried to push the Leaf away.

"...Dorey added to his crime by tossing a chair on the ice as he headed to the dressing room.

"This was a `bush-league' act and perhaps general manager Jim Gregory and coach John McLellan, who agreed it was stupid, should send him to the bushes to cool out. There's no room in the NHL for this kind of showboating."

The 8-0 loss to a team struggling so horribly — all of it captured on national television — was the element that fuelled Dorey's temper. The Maple Leafs were losing 6-0 when the incident flared. "I don't know what got into that guy," Larose said after the game. "He started it all after getting a minor penalty. I was expecting nothing when he cross-checked me to the ice. What was he trying to prove? They were dead as far as the game was concerned."

Five days after the incident, NHL president Clarence Campbell suspended Dorey for six games, primarily for belting Shetler.

"It is my opinion that Dorey's action in striking the official was completely without justification, or excuse," said Campbell. "If it were not for the fact that this is Dorey's first misconduct of this kind, the suspension would have been longer."

Campbell mentioned that Dorey used abusive language as he tried to order Shetler out of the way. The league report said that CBS videotapes of the game refuted Dorey's notion that he'd been unfairly restrained by Shetler. It said the punch that struck the linesman was thrown with Claude Larose well out of range. Shetler received cuts on the inside of his mouth and required two stitches to close a wound on his lip.

Dorey was coming off an injury in that Minnesota game and he remembers being unable to hold up his end of a resolution. "We were flying to Minneapolis after our Saturday night home game (against Los Angeles) and I told (Leaf radio broadcaster) Ron Hewat that I was going to change my style; not react to situations so quickly," Dorey recalls. "So what happens? I go snaky and get suspended for six games. So much for *that* promise.

"I shouldn't have hit Shetler but he had me all wrapped up, and Larose was killing me. He hit me with so many lefts, I was begging for a right. When I finally got loose, I couldn't get to Larose so I cold-cocked Shetler. And I guess I wasn't satisfied with Shetler laying on the ice, so when I skated off, there was a chair next to our bench and I threw it in the direction of (referee) Bill Friday. I remember not being too happy with the way we played that day."

Dorey occasionally misplaced his combativeness and wound up clashing with his own teammates. Those who have known him for a long time will tell you of two primary examples. The first occurred during the Christmas break in 1971 and it happened in full view of roughly 12,000 screaming youngsters at Maple Leaf Gardens.

Back in the '60s and '70s, the Dominion grocery store chain would sponsor an open practice each year — usually on Boxing Day — so the fans could get a free and rare glimpse of the Maple Leafs working out. After going through their drills, the players would split up into squads and engage in a scrimmage — Blues vs. Whites.

Well, during the 1971 open practice, Dorey was on the White squad and he began trading punches with Blues' defenceman Rick Ley. At first, the fans and players thought the two were horsing around, but it soon became apparent they were quite serious about the whole thing. After two or three minutes, several teammates moved in to separate the pair and Dorey stomped off the ice clutching his right hand in pain. Inside the dressing room was Maple Leaf defenceman Jim McKenny, nursing one of his frequent hangovers.

"I didn't see the start of the fight because I was in the room having a Coke... I was still a bit dehydrated from the previous evening," McKenny recalls. "I remember stepping outside and seeing a bit of the fight and everybody thought it was a put-on at first. But then we noticed that Ley had a cut above his eye and the thing was serious.

"I went back and sat down and a few moments later, Jimmy and Rick came into the room. And before you knew it, the whole mess started up again. Dorey said, `Fuck you' and Rick said, `No, Fuck *you!*' After a few more exchanges like that, they started throwing sticks at each other and the training staff had to come in and settle things down."

When the practice ended, the rest of the team came into the room and a number of the players made plans to go for lunch at the old

Carriage House Hotel on Jarvis Street. As they were walking over, McKenny saddled up alongside Ley and began causing mischief.

"Rick was my close buddy on the team and I started kidding him about the fight, saying things like, `Geez Rick, I think you got the best of him but you know, a lot of the other guys are saying Flipper had the edge.' He looked at me all upset and said, `What the fuck you talkin' about, I gave it to him twice.'

"Well, we got to the Carriage House and sat down to have a few pops. Jim walked in a few minutes later and within 15 seconds, they were going at it yet again. And this was the best one of all. They were screaming and yelling and throwing chairs at each other... it was quite the scene."

It turned out that during the initial scuffle on the ice, a Dorey punch had connected with one of Ley's upper teeth and Dorey severed a tendon in his right hand. Having already missed a chunk of the season with a separated shoulder, the hand injury would keep him out of action for another month.

"Oh, did I get shit from Jim Gregory," Dorey recalls. "I don't even remember what started the fight; I think we were both just suffering from hangovers. I used to kid Rickey now and then about not being a real sharp dresser and maybe he had enough of me that day. All I know is that it never lingered on. We were always the best of friends."

When the World Hockey Association was formed for the start of the 1972-73 season, Dorey was part of a mass exodus from the Maple Leaf team. Owner Harold Ballard scoffed at the exorbitant salaries being offered by the WHA clubs, never believing the league would get off the ground. That miscalculation cost him the services of five important players, and it ripped apart the core of a young, promising defence unit.

Dorey was traded to the New York Rangers (for Pierre Jarry) in February, 1972, but he had his mind set on the WHA. He defected to the New England Whalers along with Ley and Brad Selwood. Hard-working centerman, Jim Harrison, bolted to the Alberta Oilers and standout goaltender Bernie Parent signed with the Miami Screaming Eagles, who died before their first scream. Parent settled instead on the Philadelphia Blazers.

Paul Henderson, Dave Keon, Guy Trottier, Mike Pelyk and Bob Baun were other members of the 1971-72 Maple Leafs who later jumped to the WHA and Ballard came very close to losing a young Darryl Sittler, which would have been the biggest calamity of all.

In that first WHA season at New England, Dorey got into another celebrated ruckus with one of his teammates. During a game against

Alberta at the Edmonton Gardens, he actually engaged in a brief fight with Whalers' centerman John French. The Northlands Coliseum was still under construction, and the old Edmonton rink had a two-tiered players bench. French takes it from there.

"The whole thing stemmed from Jim's hesitation to pass the puck," he explains. "I was on the ice with linemates Larry Pleau and Tim Sheehy. Flipper made a great play at our blueline and intercepted a pass. If he had moved it up to one of us, we'd have had a three-on-nothing breakaway. We were all yelling for the puck, but Jim wouldn't pass.

"When he finally did, one of us went in offside. Our coach, Jack Kelley, made a line change and the three of us skated to the bench all pissed off. But Jack didn't change the defence pairing. Flipper got the puck and he circled back in our zone. I yelled at him, `Would you move the goddamned thing!' and a few seconds later, there was a faceoff in front of us.

"I was on the bottom of this double-tiered bench and Larry Pleau was sitting up behind me. Flipper and I were jawing at each other and when the play started, he skated over and took a swing at me. Right in the middle of the game. Fortunately, I ducked, but Larry was leaning over trying to catch his breath and wound up getting clobbered right between the eyes. Jimmy then turned around and skated back into the play."

Al Smith, Dorey's old brawling partner with the Maple Leafs, handled most of the netminding chores for New England in 1972-73. On that night in Edmonton, however, back-up Bruce Landon was in goal and Smith was resting on the bench.

"I can still see Flipper carrying the puck behind our net and yelling all the way over at Frenchy, `You stupid asshole, don't be screaming at *me!*' Jim was a good player but he couldn't pass worth a shit. He was kind of muscle-bound and maybe that had something to do with it. But in all the years I spent in hockey, I never saw another player take a swing at a teammate during a game."

Like French, Dorey laughs about the incident today. "I just had enough of his yapping that night," he says. "We were at the end of a long road trip and my nerves were frayed. Frenchy was a decent guy but he hardly ever shut his mouth in those days. He was a bit too big for his britches and I decided to give him a smack. There was a little tension between us for a few days, but the incident soon became something humorous."

The wide majority of Dorey's fistic encounters, however, were undertaken on *behalf* of his teammates. On New Year's Eve, 1974, the Whalers sent Dorey to the Toronto Toros as compensation for a prior deal involving Wayne Carleton. With players like Frank Mahovlich, Wayne Dillon, Vaclav Nedomansky and Paul Henderson, the Toros were a fairly talented club, but not overly aggressive. However, Dorey and Larry Mavety were added in the second half of the season, and some bad blood began to flow.

Toronto played the San Diego Mariners in a WHA quarterfinal in April, 1975: San Diego prevailing 4-2 in a bizarre series in which the home team lost all six games. The Mariners had some loonies in Jamie Bateman, Ted Scharf, Mike Rouleau and Kevin Morrison, and the series turned out to be fairly wild.

Hockey fans in the Toronto area with good memories (and bouts of insomnia) might recall watching Game 4 on local TV. The Global Television Network — a realtively new entity back then — carried the game from San Diego on a Wednesday night, starting at 11:30 Eastern time. Predictably, the fireworks began early and Dorey was the central figure in a wild and frightening incident.

The San Diego Sports Arena had been built nine years earlier, primarily to house the Gulls of the Western Hockey League. Despite being a large and beautiful rink, it had one Neanderthal feature — wire-fencing, not Herculite glass, surrounded the playing surface, only semi-protecting the crowd from the action... and vise versa.

A ruckus broke out in the Toronto end of the rink — involving players and fans — and Dorey led several teammates over the wire-screen and in among the spectators. Bedlam ensued. The sight of the players climbing that school-yard-like fence was preposterous, to say the least. But Dorey never shied away from a threat.

Humour, some of it unintentional, played a large role in Dorey's career — usually *off* the ice. "He was funny even when he tried not to be," says Jim McKenny. "If he had a bad game, he'd walk out of the Gardens on Wood Street and there'd be a thousand kids wanting his autograph. But he'd leave the building with a towel over his head so nobody could recognize him. He was quite hard on himself."

Dorey seemed to be forever suffering from back problems and he'd try all kinds of potential remedies. During a Maple Leaf exhibition game at Halifax prior to the 1971-72 season, he came off the ice with a kink in his upper back. The training staff was busy with another player, and Dorey needed some prompt attention. Looking around, he spotted a rather portly usherette standing in the corridor between the players' benches. He went over and laid down at her feet, asking her to walk on his back.

"She was a big moose," recalls Mike Pelyk, who was watching in amazement from the bench. "At least 200 pounds. Most of us couldn't believe what we were seeing. But Flipper got up after a few moments and seemed to feel much better."

Dorey laughs when recalling that scene. "Well, nobody was paying any attention to me when I got back to the bench so I had to look after myself," he says. "I called the usherette over and said, `I think it would work if you got on top of me and walked around a bit.' She was a big, beefy woman and that's why I chose her. I needed someone who could put a lot of pressure on the area and she sure as hell did that!"

The unpredictable side of Dorey could surface almost anywhere, anytime. When the Leafs failed to make the playoffs in the spring of 1968, the Rochester Americans held several of their late-season matches at the Gardens. Dorey and McKenny were members of that team and the coach was Joe Crozier.

"We were playing really lousy one night and Crozier came into the dressing room all pissed off," McKenny recalls. "He was giving us shit, left and right, and when he quieted down for a moment, we heard this whizzing sound coming from the back of the room near the showers. Crow stood silent for a few seconds and then he went over to investigate the noise.

"When he poked his head around the corner, there was Flipper *styling his hair*. He had the dryer on full blast and was making himself beautiful. Crow looked at him and said, `What the fuck are you doing?!' And Flipper replied, `Gotta keep myself looking good for those lucrative endorsement deals, coach.' The rest of us almost died laughing and it turned out to be exactly what we needed to break the tension."

During his playing days, Dorey had a peculiar obsession about the sticks he'd use for a game. He'd spend hour upon hour working on his sticks and he'd number them, one through four, in order of preference. He would then hand them to trainer Guy Kinnear for safe keeping, with specific instructions on how they'd be deployed.

"I can still see Flipper walking around in the dressing room before the pre-game warmup wearing only his skates, gloves and a jock-strap," Pelyk laughs. "He would take each stick individually and get the feel of it... hold the shaft, test the blade, lean on it to see how much `give' it had. It was a ritual he went through prior to every game, without fail."

Of course, any player with that type of fetish would be prone to hijinx and Dorey was no exception. Prior to Game 3 of the 1969 quarter-finals against Boston — at the Gardens — Pelyk and McKenny got a hold of Dorey's sticks. They removed the tri-coloured wrapping from the top of the heal, cut through the wood with a hacksaw, then carefully put the wrapping back on.

"We went out for the warmup and all the guys were waiting for Flipper to take his first shot," McKenny recalls. "Of course, when he did, the stick busted in half and he went over to the bench to ask `Gunner' (Kinnear) for his `number-two' stick. Naturally, that one broke as well, and we nearly went into hysterics when he threw the stick over the glass and almost impaled George Armstrong. After the third stick broke, Flipper knew he'd been had.

"When we got back into the dressing room, he went crazy. He started throwing rolls of tape and banging his broken sticks over a garbage can. It was a riot."

Dorey wasn't beyond pulling the odd prank, himself, and he played a leading role in a raunchy episode during his second year at New England. Once again, the Whalers were in Edmonton, and Al Smith remembers it well.

"We had a `Kangaroo Court' on the team that year to keep the guys on the straight and narrow, and I was the judge," Smith says. "We had a session scheduled for late in the season and the manager of the Edmonton Inn, where we stayed, let us have a meeting room on the second floor. We really played it up big-time... I wore a wig, and we had a chair and table set up like a witness stand.

"The court session began and Flipper mentioned that something was bothering him. I said, `Okay Mr. Dorey, please come forth and tell me of your complaint.' Jim was holding a paper bag and he stepped onto the witness stand. He then looked at me and said, `Your Honour, my complaint is about my roommate, Larry Pleau. He's a wonderful guy, but he's got a problem that makes him repugnant to live with on the road.'

"He then reached into the bag, pulled out some wax-paper, and unwrapped about a five-inch turd! A big, ugly piece of crap. And god, did it stink! Within seconds, we all ran out of the room, gagging. The stench went right through the entire second floor of the hotel and we had to pay a porter about 12 bucks to go up there, wrap the thing, and get rid of it."

Dorey shakes his head when reminded of that episode is quick to pass the blame. "It was Pleau's idea, Larry was into that kinky stuff," he says. "And it was *his* turd, also. I don't know why I let myself get talked into that one, because it was pretty crude and distasteful. But we sure got the reaction we were looking for."

* * * * * *

Jim Dorey's record accumulation of 48 penalty minutes in one game lasted for more than ten years. It was finally broken by a *couple* of players during a wild melee between Philadelphia and Los Angeles on March, 11, 1979, at the Spectrum. Frank Bathe of the Flyers received 55 minutes in the brawl while the Kings' Randy Holt got tagged for 67 minutes: receiving a minor, three majors, two 10-minute misconducts, and three game misconducts.

Defenceman Russ Anderson of the Pittsburgh Penguins also surpassed Dorey's total with a 51-minute accumulation on January 19, 1980. Anderson went off the deep end in a game with Edmonton at the Civic Arena. Holt, Bathe and Anderson remain one-two-three in the NHL record book.

Dorey has some mixed emotions when reflecting on his tantrum against the Penguins in 1968. "On one hand, I realize I was doing my job," he says. "Sure, I lost my temper, but I thought Art Skov picked on me a little too much and I still don't believe I deserved that fourth penalty on Ken Schinkel. I think what also set me off was a flashback I had about getting kicked out of a Bantam hockey game one year.

"I was playing for Kingston against Peterborough in a very important game for me, because a lot of Junior `A' scouts were on hand. An altercation started and I was basically an outsider. But I got ejected from the game because of my reputation. So, when Schinkel laughed at me that night at the Gardens, it triggered some pent-up emotions.

"I also believe that incident clouded the rest of my career. I was an enforcer-type player on the ice but I wasn't just an uncontrollable hothead. Every team I played for used me on the powerplay and I think my physical approach gave my teammates some extra room to manoeuvre.

"Yet, I did Don Cherry's `Grapevine' TV show last year and we never got around to the subject of playing hockey. All we did was talk about that Pittsburgh brawl.

"I lasted 11 years in pro hockey and I'd like to think it wasn't all by accident."

* * * * * *

WHERE ARE THEY NOW? ...

JIM DOREY, 47, accumulated 553 penalty minutes in a four-year NHL stint with the Maple Leafs and New York Rangers. He added 617 minutes during seven years in the WHA with the New England Whalers, Toronto Toros and Quebec Nordiques — retiring after the 1978-79 season. Living in Kingston, he briefly ran that city's Ontario Hockey League team in he late-1980s and is currently a respected employee of the *All-State Insurance Company* of Canada.

MIKE PELYK, 47, was a hard-nosed defenceman with the Maple Leafs from 1968 to 1974, then again from 1976 to 1978. Not blessed with unlimited talent, he compensated by playing a tough, physical game. He also skated for Vancouver and Cincinnati in the WHA. He still lives in Toronto and works for the shopping-center division of the *Bramalea Ltd.* real-estate company.

KEN SCHINKEL, 62, was a smooth-skating right-winger with New York and Pittsburgh between 1959 and 1973. Never a big goalscorer, he reached the 20-goal plateau only once — with the Penguins in 1969-70. After retiring, he coached the Penguins on and off until 1977. He then scouted for Pittsburgh until 1989, when he joined the Hartford Whalers as Director of Player Personnel. He later became assistant general manager, and is currently the Whalers' chief scout. He still lives in Pittsburgh.

AL SMITH, 49, bounced around between seven cities during a 15-year professional career from 1965 to 1981. He had his busiest NHL seasons with Pittsburgh, playing goal in 46 games in both 1969-70 and 1970-71. He also played in the NHL with Detroit, Buffalo, Hartford and Colorado. He spent four years with New England of the WHA. His career came to an unceremonious end when he sucker-punched American hockey hero Jim Craig during a game at Colorado in 1980. Craig was playing for Boston after backstopping the U.S. to that miracle gold medal victory at the Winter Olympics in Lake Placid. Smith currently lives in downtown Toronto and you may unknowingly bump into him one day, as he drives a taxi for a living.

JOHN ARBOUR, 49, was a tough, journeyman defenceman who played professionally in eight different cities between 1965 and 1977. He broke in with Boston but was sold by the Bruins to Pittsburgh with Jean Pronovost in May, 1968. He also played with Vancouver and St. Louis in the NHL. He jumped to the Minnesota Fighting Saints of the WHA in 1972 and later played with Denver, Ottawa and Calgary in that league. He now lives in Fort Erie, Ont. and owns a restaurant called *Marco's Pizzaria.*

KEITH MCCREARY, 54, came up through the Montreal organization and was selected by Pittsburgh in the 1967 expansion draft. He played five years for the Penguins, scoring a career-high 25 goals in the 1968-69 season. Atlanta chose him from Pittsburgh's roster in the 1972 expansion draft and he captained the Flames for three years, before retiring in 1975. His older brother, Bill McCreary, played four years with St. Louis after the 1967 expansion. Keith was a prime mover in the 1991 to 1994 pension-fund dispute between former NHL players and the league. The oldtimers prevailed. He now lives in Toronto and runs his own insurance company, *McCreary and Associates.*

GEORGE (RED) SULLIVAN, 65, played center with Boston, Chicago and the Rangers between 1949 and 1961. He then coached New York for three years before Emile Francis replaced him in 1965. Sullivan then became the first coach of the Pittsburgh Penguins in 1967. He guided the Pens for two years and was replaced by Red Kelly for the 1969-70 season. He coached the Washington Capitals during part of their futile first season in the NHL (1974-75), along with Jim Anderson and Milt Schmidt. He later worked for the NHL's Central Scouting Bureau and he retired in 1993 after eight years as a scout with the Philadelphia Flyers. He currently lives in Douro, Ont. — a 15-minute drive east of his native Peterborough.

JIM MCKENNY, 48, was frequently touted as a replica of Bobby Orr when he played Junior 'A' hockey with the Toronto Marlboros in the mid-1960s. As it turned out, he wasn't much better than *Frank* Orr. Blessed with more-than average talent, McKenny's care-free attitude and affinity for the bottle marred what may have been a brilliant career. He was a regular defenceman with the Maple Leafs between 1969 and 1977 and was sold to Minnesota in May, 1978. He played 10 games for the North Stars in the 1978-79 season before calling it quits. He is now a well-known and jocular sportscaster on CITY-TV, Channel 57, in Toronto.

JOHN FRENCH, 44, was owned by Montreal, California and Minnesota but he never played a game in the NHL. Instead, he spent six years in the WHA with New England, San Diego and Indianapolis between 1972 and 1978. A left-winger with a scoring touch, he twice netted 24 goals for the Whalers and he scored 25 for San Diego in 1975-76. Several years after his hockey career ended, he moved to Centerville, New Brunswick (one hour north of Fredricton), and is currently credit and collections manager for *Thomas Equipment*, a subsidiary of the McCain Foods group.

AUTHOR'S NOTE

In the process of researching material for this chapter on Jim Dorey, I had several long conversations with ex-NHL and WHA goalie Al Smith. Dorey and Smith were teammates with Tulsa of the Central Hockey League, Toronto of the NHL, and New England of the WHA.

Regarding the record-setting brawl between the Maple Leafs and Pittsburgh Penguins (October 16, 1968), newspaper accounts strongly imply that Smith played a prominent role in "fanning the flames" of the incident—particularly with his unprovoked assaults on Keith McCreary and (especially) Billy Dea. This claim was supported in my conversations with Dorey, who referred, somewhat playfully, to Smith as a "shit disturber" (a classic example, some might say, of the pot calling the kettle black).

Several days after talking to Smith, I received a letter at my radio station that left me wondering why the former goalie never pursued writing his own book. After a follow-up chat, yet another letter arrived at THE FAN-1430 three days later.

Described in a friendly manner by many of his former hockey teammates as "slightly off-the-wall", that depiction shone through brilliantly in his correspondence with me. And so, with Al Smith's permission, I share with you portions of those two letters.

```
February 21, 1994

Dear Howard:

Better to leave the ironies to the Gods, Howard,
I hope you are not intending to slander me by
indicating that I have spent ten years driving a
```

cab because I went around suckering guys in fights. That is a lie. My life has been slandered enough by its own events without making up new ones.

I suckered one guy in my life, John Arbour, and it was in St. Louis with 17,243 screaming fans. We then played them the next night (in Pittsburgh). In the first period of that game, Scotty Bowman sent out Plager, Plager, Picard, etc. to right the slight.

Damn silly to fight a goalie, or a goalie who fights, but besides the shameful J.C. Tremblay, Gerry Odrowski and Jim Craig, I fended myself against (Vic) Hadfield, (Pierre) Bouchard, (Jim) Harrison, (Curt) Brackenbury, (Reggie) Fleming, Hextalls (Dennis and Bryan), and others.

The fact is, I've been suckered a few times in my lifetime, and that could make for cab-driving material. But, to say that I went around suckering guys in fights is a lie — so don't say it or I'll get Carl (Brewer) after you, and you know how Carl likes to go to court.

I do not read these books, but kids do, and who knows, I might live to see my grandchildren. I suckered nobody.

If you are indicating that because I suckered guys and was part of that 48-minute fiasco (against the Penguins), I then ended up in the WHA and (later) driving a cab, you shall have to explain that conspiracy of righteousness to me.

Elsewise, great luck with your book and ...while we are at it, Howard, I never gave the finger to Seymour or Northrup (Knox, owners of the Buffalo Sabres, where Smith played briefly in 1975-76 and 1976-77). In fact, I have never given the finger to anyone in my entire life and that includes ten years of driving a cab.

Best Regards,
AL SMITH

Smith's letter obviously refuted testimony from teammates — including Jim Dorey — so I phoned him moments after receiving it to discover just how much "tongue-in-cheek" material it contained. The second letter arrived within 72 hours.

February 24, 1994

Dear Howard:

Not to turn this into the Sabine letters or anything (possibly the Labine letters), but this is the last note from me on the 48-minute, one-punch fiasco with Pittsburgh. The denial phase is over in me and I accept the revolutionist's approach by you that I went around "suckering guys in fights."

Since I provided you with evidence to the contrary in my first letter, your investigation of the incident reveals that there was one other punch thrown (besides those thrown by Dorey), and it was me suckering Billy Dea. As a result, I accept your visceral charge.

I shall accept your revision if you accept mine. It was me who suckered Billy Dea and thus threw the only other punch in a fight that put Dorey — with pictures and ink — in Sports Illustrated. The only time I was in S.I., other than on a list of the most over-rated goalies, it was concerning my fight with Jim Craig, the great Olympian goalie from Boston.

The reporter asked me about fighting Craig, who, incidentally, I did not sucker, and I said, "Yeah, wasn't it horrible? It was like beating on the American flag."

Under these terms, I accept your stern hand of revision.

Best Regards again,
AL SMITH

... Leafs in Spring ...

MAY 23, 1994
Cypress Mountain, West Vancouver

It was a brilliantly sunny afternoon on the west coast of Canada as the country celebrated Victoria Day.

Trailing the Vancouver Canucks 3-1 in the Western Conference final — and quickly running out of gas — the Maple Leaf players had been given the option of practising by coach Burns.

Many of them chose to loaf around the Westin Bayshore Hotel and a small group — including Burns, Doug Gilmour, Wendel Clark, Dave Ellett and Todd Gill — made themselves available to the media at poolside. Basking in the midday sun, they spoke bravely about scaling improbable heights and seemed content in the knowledge that no one truly expected them to rebound against Vancouver. The atmosphere was altogether relaxing.

That night, the Maple Leaf publicity department hosted the Toronto media for dinner at The Cannery — a popular and trendy fish-house with a breathtaking view of Vancouver Harbour. I ate with Ken Daniels of CBC and Lance Brown of CFTO. Daniels had flown in from Toronto that day and was on his last legs by the time dinner ended. So Lance dropped him off at the Westin and the two of us drove across the Lion's Gate Bridge to Cypress Mountain, northwest of the city.

Lance sweet-talked the provincial park Ranger into allowing us a few moments at the look-out, which had been closed to the public for the night. And what a treat it was. Several-thousand feet below us — and four or five miles in the distance — glowed the yellowish lights of Vancouver, stretching far to the south. The view was similar to that from a descending aircraft, but with an eerie absence of noise. Beyond us was a metropolitan community of 1.5 million people, but all we could hear was a slight wind ruffling through the mountain trees.

Rarely are spring evenings on the Canadian west coast this clear. The light from a full moon reflected brilliantly off the waters of the Burrard Inlet and Strait of Georgia. Twinkling on the western horizon were the lights of Vancouver Island: 40 miles in the distance. Perhaps the serenity overcame me, as I had a sudden and indomitable desire to urinate. With Lance being the lone possible spectator, I climbed upon a cobblestone ledge and did my business.

Begrudgingly, Lance confessed to a similar impulse — urgently joining me on the ledge. And there stood the two of us, like a pair of monuments, peeing down on the lights of Vancouver... an implication, perhaps, of a Maple Leaf season going down the drain.

"DON'T GIVE IT BACK!"

Madison Square Garden

April 8, 1971

Almost a quarter century has passed since winger Vic Hadfield of the New York Rangers presented fans at Madison Square Garden with the most unique souvenir in hockey history. To long-time Maple Leaf fans, however, it happened only yesterday.

"I'm reminded about it all the time," says Hadfield, who operates a golf driving range in Woodbridge, Ont., just west of Toronto. "There isn't a day that passes at the golf center in which some Leaf supporter in his 30s or 40s doesn't ask me about it. I just can't live it down."

The "it" he refers to dates back to the second game of a playoff quarterfinal series in 1971 between the Maple Leafs and Rangers. More specifically, to a spontaneous and bizarre reaction on Hadfield's part to an emotional flare-up late in the game. The not-so innocent victim was Maple Leaf goaltender Bernie Parent, who wound up losing roughly $150 worth of equipment. Without his consent.

* * * * * *

The new Maple Leaf regime of general manager Jim Gregory and coach John McLellan spent a full season spinning its wheels after taking over the club from the deposed Punch Imlach.

A decade of autocracy ended when Imlach was fired by Maple Leaf president Stafford Smythe after the 1969 quarterfinal sweep by Boston. The transition of power was not at all smooth, as the 1969-70 Toronto outfit plummeted to the depths of the Eastern Division and missed the playoffs by a whopping 21 points. On-ice quandaries seemed endless.

Aging veterans George Armstrong, Bob Pulford, Tim Horton and Floyd Smith slowed to a crawl all at once. Offensive kingpins Norm Ullman (60 points) and Paul Henderson (20 goals) had sub-par years. The young Leaf defence corps ran into a stream of injury problems. And the netminding duo of Bruce Gamble and career minor-leaguer Marv Edwards proved only adequate. An influx of new blood was essential and Gregory went to work on his inaugural Maple Leaf house-cleaning.

Before the first puck was dropped in 1970-71, he peddled Horton, Pulford, Murray Oliver and Brit Selby in separate deals, acquiring Guy Trottier, Denis Dupere, Gary Monahan and Bob Baun. He purchased veteran goalie Jacques Plante from St. Louis, where the 41-year-old had played superbly after returning from a three-year retirement. Selected eighth overall in the 1970 entry draft was highly touted center Darryl Sittler from London of the Ontario Hockey Association. Winger Billy MacMillan was added from the Canadian national team.

Young forwards Brian Spencer (1969 draft choice) and Jim Harrison (acquired from Boston) brought aggressiveness to the table.

The club even sported an entirely new uniform design, featuring a modified Maple Leaf emblem, and shoulder-piping that extended all the way down the arm to the sleeve. The re-tooling and re-polishing worked as desired, with the 1970-71 Maple Leafs playing much-improved hockey from the very outset. The club was dominant in the friendly confines of Maple Leaf Gardens, compiling a 24-9-6 home-ice record. A mediocre 13-24-2 mark on the road, however, prevented the Leafs from challenging for a higher ranking in the division.

A major adjustment was made to begin the stretch drive of the regular season. In a three-way transaction that involved Philadelphia and Boston, Leafs acquired goalie Bernie Parent from the Flyers in exchange for Bruce Gamble and Mike Walton. Philadelphia then peddled Walton to the Bruins for Rick MacLeish and Danny Schock.

The goaltending tandem of Plante and Parent was second to none, and appeared to give Toronto a legitimate shot at post-season fulfilment.

The Maple Leafs finished a solid fourth in the East, posing no threat to the teams ahead of them, nor feeling any heat from the rear. Third-place Boston was 15 points better while fifth-place Buffalo sat 21 points below. Veteran centers Norm Ullman (85 points) and Dave Keon (76 points) enjoyed their most productive NHL seasons while the ageless wonder — Plante — turned in the chintziest goals-against mark of any season in his brilliant career: an incredible 1.88 in 40 games.

However, there appeared to be a competitive imbalance in the East Division. First-place Boston smashed a deluge of team and individual records while rocketing to 57 victories and 121 points. Phil Esposito bagged an outrageous total of 76 goals: 18 more in one season than any player in league history. Even more preposterous was Bobby Orr's 102 assists from his defence position.

Boston led the NHL with 399 goals as a team — 108 more than its nearest competitor, Montreal. As the playoffs began, there seemed to be no plausible argument against the Bruins whizzing to their second championship in as many years.

The predicament facing the Maple Leafs was an opening-round match-up with the *second*-best team in the regular season. After floundering through the mid-1960s, the New York Rangers had developed into a Stanley Cup contender, but simply couldn't overcome any of their East Division rivals. They lost opening-round playoff battles to Montreal in 1967, Chicago in '68, Montreal in '69, and Boston in 1970.

New York enjoyed its most productive season ever in 1970-71, placing second in the overall standings with 109 points. The Rangers did it, primarily, with defence and goaltending, allowing the fewest number of opposition scores (177) during the 78-game regular schedule. Ed Giacomin (2.16 goals-against average) and Gilles Villemeure (2.30) shared the Vezina Trophy, playing behind a solid five-man defence unit of Brad Park, Jim Neilson, Rod Seiling, Tim Horton and Arnie Brown.

Up front, the Rangers could throw two excellent scoring lines on the ice. Jean Ratelle, Vic Hadfield and Rod Gilbert would become known the following season as the "G-A-G" line, for their propensity to score a *Goal-A-Game*. There was the "Bulldog" line of Walt Tkaczuk, Dave Balon and Bill Fairbairn — Balon leading the '70-71 Rangers with 36 goals. A third unit of Pete Stemkowski, Bob Nevin and Ted Irvine provided New York with excellent balance in the forward ranks.

"Even though Boston set so many records, I think the Rangers truly believed they could win the Stanley Cup that year," recalls former Leaf center Jim Harrison. "We knew we had a real job ahead of us if we were going to beat them in the first round of the playoffs."

New York had bested the Maple Leafs in five of six regular-season encounters, including all three at Madison Square Garden. But, Toronto had won the final meeting between the clubs — 3-1 at home on Mar. 20 — to gain a springboard of momentum. With the calibre of goaltending each team possessed, most expected a low-scoring playoff series.

Such was not the case in the opener at New York, as both Plante and Giacomin were shaky. A 4-2 lead more than halfway through the game was a fairly secure circumstance for the 1970-71 Maple Leafs, who could protect advantages as well as any club in the league. Dave Keon and Paul Henderson had each scored twice, to offset New York goals by Hadfield and Gilbert.

But on this night, Plante would let it slip away.

Bob Nevin took advantage of a mistake by Leaf defenceman Jim Dorey and beat the veteran goalie with three seconds remaining in the middle period. It gave New York some much-needed life heading into the third and Rangers were dominant over the final 20 minutes. They outshot the Leafs 13-6 and received unanswered goals from Hadfield and Tkaczuk to win the hockey game, 5-4. Strangely, the Maple Leafs had folded.

"When a team gets four goals in a Stanley Cup playoff — make that a National Hockey League game — it should win," a dejected Plante told Red Burnett in the Toronto *Star*. "I wasn't sharp. I was a half-second slow and shaky. I guess I was away too long." Plante had missed the final four games of the regular season with an infected nose.

The goal by Nevin was the turning point. Dorey should have frozen the puck along the boards in the Ranger zone and killed off the final seconds. Choosing instead to dump it into the corner, his pass was intercepted by Dave Balon, who quickly fed Nevin behind the net. The former Leaf tried to pass it in front, but the puck caromed in behind Plante off the stick of Maple Leaf defenceman Bob Baun.

"It was a lack of experience," Leaf coach John McLellan said about Dorey's blunder. "The Rangers were flat at that point but the goal gave them a lift and you saw the result in the third period. They really put it to us. It was a tough game to lose."

The decision was quickly made to replace Plante with Bernie Parent for the second game of the series, the following night. "The old fellow (Plante) had his first bad game in our goal," admitted Maple Leaf vice-president King Clancy. "But, this thing is far from over. They'll have much more trouble with Parent."

Clancy's prediction proved to be accurate as the Maple Leafs were thoroughly dominant in Game 2. Goals by Garry Monahan and Henderson, 48 seconds apart late in the first period, gave Toronto an all-important 2-0 lead. Keon scored early in the second while ex-Leaf Horton finally beat Parent with 3:49 remaining in the middle frame. Henderson's second of the night (and fourth of the series) at 11:35 of the third, put the game out of reach. It also served as a spark for an emotional fire that had been smouldering all night long.

The Rangers, don't forget, were fully expecting to advance beyond the opening round of the playoffs for the first time in 21 years. With Game 2 having slipped from their grasp, they were now facing a two-game furtherance in Toronto, where the Maple Leafs had fashioned one of the best home-ice records during the regular season. New York, in fact, was fortunate not to be emerging from *its* home lair with a two-game deficit and obviously believed a statement had to be made in the dying moments.

"Parent was playing great in goal and I'll always remember how Bob Baun was dominating the blueline for Toronto," says Emile Francis, the Rangers' general manager and coach back then. "Walter Tkaczuk must have hit Baun a hundred times in the first two games. We had to go after him because he was so tough.

"And Davey Keon was playing phenomenal hockey for the Maple Leafs as well. I was using just about everybody on my bench to try and slow him down. As the second game wound to a close, I think a lot of us were concerned we might lose the series."

As the Ranger frustration mounted, the game evolved into a savage exchange of cheap shots and the atmosphere in the Garden — both on the ice and in the seats — began to erode. There had been earlier bouts between Ted Irvine and Brian Spencer, Vic Hadfield and Bob Baun, and Hadfield and Jim Harrison that proved to be merely the undercard on this night. Toronto refused to give an inch, even with its three-goal cushion, and tempers were operating on borrowed time.

The anticipated eruption finally occurred at 15:18 of the third period. And so many Maple Leaf fans remember it to this day.

The melee began with Harrison and Hadfield squaring off for the second time near the boards in the Maple Leaf zone. Strong and balanced on his skates, Hadfield quickly gained the upper hand and pounded the Maple Leaf centerman with his right fist. Watching the one-sided affair from his goalcrease was Parent, who could stand it no longer.

He rushed towards the skirmish like a mutinous tag-team partner and collared the unsuspecting Hadfield from behind. That course of action brought an immediate response from Giacomin, who dashed the full length of the ice to confront his Maple Leaf counterpart.

Giacomin yanked Parent away from Hadfield and the two netminders tangled. As they shimmied towards the dasher, Hadfield re-emerged and pulled off one of the most outlandish and memorable stunts in hockey history. With deft precision, he stripped Parent of his goal-mask and flung it over the glass. It struck a policeman on the shoulder and wound up in the lap of a female fan seated in the expensive pews.

Initially surprised by the intriguing souvenir, the spectator soon passed it behind her and it continued to be fed backwards, row by row, until the mask vanished into the upper reaches of the Garden mezzanine.

And the Maple Leaf goalie didn't have a spare.

"I couldn't believe it," says Jim Gregory, who watched the game from the Garden press box. "The incident happened right across the ice from where I was sitting with King Clancy. Hadfield flipped the mask over the boards and we saw it get passed from the front-row seats right up to the top. After a half-minute or so, King said he was going to try and get it back, and I told him he was crazy.

"But he took off, and I watched as he walked across the rotunda in the first level, then to the second and third levels on the other side. He finally realized he was risking his life up there and he came back a few moments later empty handed."

As the mask made its way to the upper levels, the Garden public-address announcer implored the crowd to return it. The fans responded, in unison, with a defiant chant of, *"Don't give it back! Don't give it back!"* It would be their only measure of victory on the night.

"It's amazing how clearly I remember that incident," says Parent. "Hadfield was all over poor Harrison and nobody on our team was doing anything about it. So, I decided to go over and help out. I didn't plan on fighting Vic, I just wanted to pull him off Jimmy.

"That's when Giacomin came flying towards me from the other end of the ice. He pulled me away from the fight and we started jostling.

"Within a few seconds, Hadfield got loose and I'll never forget how he just reached up, yanked the mask off my face, and threw it into the crowd. It happened so suddenly. I can still see the people throwing it to each other higher up into the stands.

"I remember panicking because I realized I didn't have another mask. And there was still almost five minutes left in the game."

Meanwhile, the rumble continued on the ice as players from both teams milled about, looking annoyed. A third fight broke out between Brad Park and Darryl Sittler. Linesmen Pat Shetler and Claude Bechard finally restored order and referee Lloyd Gilmour sent Hadfield, Park, Harrison and Sittler to the penalty box.

The game was further delayed when Parent balked at McLellan's suggestion that he play the remaining four minutes and 18 seconds without his mask.

"I told him, `No way, Jose,'" Parent remembers. "I wasn't going back in there bare-faced. I never played without a mask in my career, even back in my early days with Boston (1965-67). I didn't feel good about coming out of the game, but I wasn't going to risk getting hurt.

"Jacques Plante went in for the final few minutes."

After a short warm-up session for the veteran goalie, play finally resumed. But not for long. Hockey writer Gerald Eskenazi described what next happened in the New York *Times*.

> "Plante saw only 34 seconds of action when, suddenly, Ted Irvine of the Rangers and Jim Dorey began pummelling each other. Glen Sather then tackled Leafs' Ron Ellis and pulled his sweater over his head. The sight aggrieved Plante and he tried to aid his teammate. Along came Giacomin again, this time throwing a body check against the new goalie that nearly squashed the 42-year-old Plante into the protective glass.
>
> "Then the benches emptied, as did the penalty box, and 40 players were squeezing, holding, elbowing and cursing one another. Fans fought in the stands. One grey-haired man sitting in a $12.50 loge seat dared Parent to come up and fight him. A boy with the fan waved a rubber chicken at the goalie.
>
> "And when they had the chance, the Maple Leaf players held up four fingers, and then one finger (to signify the lop-sided score)."

Brian Spencer was the first combatant from either team to leave the players' bench and he did so in response to Park breaking loose from the penalty box. Sittler also re-joined the fray. Dorey, Sittler, Irvine and Park were all banished by referee Gilmour. The remaining 4:08 of regulation time was contested without incident and the Maple Leafs skated off with a well-earned 4-1 victory to square the best-of-seven quarterfinal at one game apiece.

Gilmour assessed a total of 160 penalty minutes — 14 less than the existing record for one playoff game, set the previous year in a quarter-final match between the Rangers and Boston.

The by-play in the dressing rooms afterwards was almost as heated as the two on-ice battles. Most of the talk centred around Hadfield's confiscation of Parent's mask.

"That was the most childish thing I have ever seen," fumed King Clancy. "Imagine a man doing a thing like that. Those masks cost $150 and the Rangers will have to pay for a new one."

Added Jim Gregory: "I'm holding the Rangers responsible for that mask. We'll send them a bill. We didn't bring a second mask for Parent because you could drop a building on the one he wore tonight and not break it. But if the guy who has the mask returns it, I'll get him two tickets for Saturday's (third) game and pay his way to Toronto."

Such was the Maple Leaf concern over Parent losing his facial protection. He had performed infinitely better in Game 2 than Plante had in the opener and less than 48 hours remained till the resumption of hostilities on Carlton St. That is why the 68-year-old Clancy risked life and limb clamouring after the mask among the Garden linch-mob. As columnist Jim Proudfoot recounted in the Toronto *Star*:

> "...Clancy sprinted around the mezzanine and offered to fight all 17,250 in the building for the mask. He was led away by three members of the Garden constabulary and later popped up at the Leaf bench, where he loudly debated with another segment of the audience."

"Geez, I just charged over there and then discovered I was all by myself among several-hundred hostile New Yorkers," Clancy told anyone who would listen. "So, I showed them I'm a pretty good sprinter. There wasn't a soul I knew in that mob and I didn't have Charlie with me."

The latter reference was to Charlie Conacher, the great Maple Leaf of the 1930s who often rode shot-gun for Clancy, settling many of the disputes the hot-headed (but very small) Irishman had instigated.

Emile Francis could have told Clancy a thing or two about New York hockey fans. By 1971, he had been the Rangers' G.M. and coach for more than six years and had witnessed a variety of spectator incidents.

"But I never saw a player throw a mask into the crowd," he admits. "I suppose the closest example happened one night when we were playing in Montreal. Arnie Brown and Claude Larose got into a fight and Larose yanked the sweater right off Arnie's back. He then threw it into the seats. But a goalie-mask? That was the first and only time."

Ironically, it was Francis himself who had been the central figure in the most famous encounter with Ranger fans. He was G.M., and George (Red) Sullivan was still the coach when Detroit and the Rangers played a Sunday night game at the old Madison Square Garden, Nov. 21, 1965. New York was leading 2-1 near the midway mark of the third period when the Red Wings broke into the Ranger zone. Norm Ullman took a pass from Parker MacDonald and fired a quick shot that Ed Giacomin blocked. The rebound went to Floyd Smith and Giacomin appeared to stop his shot as well. However, the red goal-light behind Giacomin flicked on, signalling a Detroit score.

"If the puck had gone in, I'm sure the Red Wing players would have raised their sticks and skated over to congratulate Smith," reasons Francis. "Instead, they all turned up-ice as we carried the puck into their zone. All of a sudden, (referee) Art Skov looked back, saw the light on, and blew his whistle. Here we were, going towards the Detroit goal, and he stopped play — just like that.

"Skov went over to check with the goaljudge then he skated to the timer's bench. A few seconds later, I looked up at the scoreboard and, bingo, a `2' went up beside Detroit. So with that, I took off."

Seated at rink-side, Francis dashed towards the area behind the glass where goaljudge Arthur Reichert was located and he demanded an explanation. By the time he got there, the five Ranger skaters on the ice were gesticulating wildly in Reichert's face.

"In the old Garden, there wasn't much room between the glass and the front-row seats," Francis remembers. "I had to kind of squeeze in sideways, but I finally got to where he was sitting."

In his 1970 book, *STRANGE BUT TRUE HOCKEY STORIES*, Stan Fischler described what happened next:

> Francis bulled his way past the spectators surrounding Reichert. "I was watching that play clearly," Francis shouted, "and that puck never crossed the red line."
>
> Reichert stared Francis in the eye and replied, "I've got two witnesses here to prove I'm right."
>
> "I don't give a damn about witnesses," screamed Francis. "You're the guy who makes the decision and you just made another rotten one." Suddenly, a burly spectator who was sitting near Reichert yelled at the Ranger manager, "Bug off Francis, that puck was in."

"I told the fan to mind his own business, that I wasn't talking to him," Francis recalls. "So, I went to talk to Arthur again and all of a sudden, the fan stood up and confronted me. Well, I figured I'd better get the first punch in, so I let him have it. But I didn't realize he had two buddies sitting with him on the other side of the goaljudge.

"The three of them jumped me and started working me over pretty good. Luckily, Vic Hadfield climbed over the glass and came to my aid and he was followed by four or five of my other players. Someone opened up the gate and we cleaned out that whole end of the rink in about ten minutes. It was a hell of a scene."

Francis and the three spectators all had to be stitched up in the Garden hospital. "The police brought them in and they said they were sorry, they didn't realize it was me," Francis recalls. "Yeah, sure. You know how sorry they were? Three days later, I got a letter in my office saying that I was being sued for a million bucks. When the cops had asked me if *I* wanted to press charges, I said, `Naw, forget it.'

"Obviously, those three fans weren't willing to do the same."

The case went to court in New York seven years later and testimony lasted for 28 days, at which point the judge asked the jury to go and bring back a final verdict.

"The jury walked out in front of me and as the last fellow passed by, he stuck out his hand and wished me good luck," Francis remembers. "Well, the judge ordered them all back into the box and put that guy on the stand. He asked him what he was doing and the fellow explained that he was a Ranger fan and was wishing me luck for the next hockey season.

"The judge declared the whole thing a mis-trial."

The case went to court again a year later and the three fans were awarded $90,000 in damages. A Madison Square Garden insurance policy covered the payment. When it all ended, Francis was again approached by the three spectators.

"After eight years, and suing me for $90,000, these guys had the gall to come up and ask me for my autograph," Francis laughs. "I told them to get the hell away from me and not even come close."

By comparison, the incident five-and-a-half years later, in which the fans relayed Bernie Parent's mask up to the cheap seats, was tame. But it still had quite an effect on the participants.

Hadfield — still aggravated from the loss — showed no remorse for his odd behaviour. "Parent jumped me from behind when I was beating Harrison so why should I care about his damned mask," he growled.

In another corner of the dressing room, Giacomin talked about his two rink-length dashes, and the $200 in fines he'd be paying the NHL. "That's nothing," he said. "The boss (Francis) probably would have fined me $500 if I *hadn't* gone. When Parent and Plante got into it, I had to go just to keep it even."

Despite losing his only mask, Parent wound up chuckling about the fight with Giacomin. "He had my head and he was choking me... I could hardly breathe," Bernie explained. "I kept telling him it was okay to let me go and then you know what he did? After choking me for five minutes, he let me go and as I'm gasping, he reached over and unhooked my leg-pad. What a dirty trick that was."

The Maple Leafs flew back to Toronto after the game and the race was on to have a new mask ready for Parent's use in Game 3. Plante woke up early Friday morning and called his partner, Marc-Andre Beaudin, at their mask-manufacturing plant in Magog, Que., about 80 miles north of Montreal. Many of the goalies in the NHL were wearing the new mask that Plante and Beaudin had created. Larger and more-encompassing than the original models, it offered better protection for the throat and temple areas. It was also liberally ventilated.

Parent still had the mask he wore during his three-plus years in Philadelphia, but he'd gotten use to the Plante design and didn't want to switch back.

"I phoned my partner at 7 o'clock this morning and he knew right away what I was calling about," said Plante on Friday. "He had to call two plant workers away from their homes because the production line was halted for the (Good Friday) holiday.

"The three of them will have to work all day to make the mask. They'll have the mold all ready, but there is a lot of work involved in making a hand-crafted goalie mask.

"I hope it's ready and in Toronto by our skate tomorrow morning because there is always a bit of filing to do — you know, it might press a little too much on the cheekbone and Bernie would have to file it down a bit. Also, he could take it home during the day and adjust the straps the way he wants them."

Parent remembers waiting somewhat impatiently at his home for the new mask to arrive from Montreal. Around noon on Friday, the doorbell rang, but it wasn't Plante's manufacturing company.

"There was a little kid, about 10 years old, standing at my door and he wanted to give me *his* goalie mask," Parent smiles. "He came over because he watched the game on television and knew I lost mine in

New York. He was hoping his could be used as a replacement.

"Of course it couldn't, but I got that kid two tickets for the game later that night and I felt like buying him tickets for every game the rest of my career. I don't think I'll never forget that moment."

In 1971, the 26-year-old Parent was still three seasons away from establishing himself as the best goalie in the world. Born in Montreal, he was scouted in his early 'teens by the Boston organization — placed on the infamous "reserve" clause by the Bruins — and transferred to the Niagara Falls Flyers of the OHA for his Junior hockey apprenticeship.

Twice, he led the Ontario circuit with the lowest goals-against average and he back-stopped the Falls to a Memorial Cup title over the Edmonton Oil Kings in 1964-65. That Niagara club featured a number of players who would eventually graduate to the NHL — including Parent, top scorer Jean Pronovost, Derek Sanderson, Bill Goldsworthy, Gilles Marotte and fellow netminder Doug Favell.

The following season, Parent made the Bruins as a rookie and split the goaltending chores with veteran Eddie Johnston. He played in 34 games and finished with a 3.69 goals-against average on a team that missed the playoffs for the seventh consecutive year.

Bobby Orr arrived from Oshawa the next year (1966-67) and rookie coach Harry Sinden took over from Milt Schmidt behind the bench. Bruins again failed to qualify for the playoffs, but promising days were just around the corner.

Parent saw less action at the NHL level, as ex-Maple Leaf farmhand Gerry Cheevers became the primary back-up to Johnston. In 18 games with Boston, Parent had a 3.64 average.

When the NHL doubled in size for the 1967-68 season, the existing clubs were allowed to protect only one goalie apiece. Others had to be made available for the expansion draft to stock the six in-coming teams. The Bruins protected Cheevers and later filled with Johnston, leaving Parent and Favell up for claim. Ironically, both players wound up with the Philadelphia Flyers.

Parent was taken second overall in the draft of goaltenders, after Los Angeles had grabbed veteran Terry Sawchuk from Toronto. The Flyers then chose Favell in the second round, ninth overall, after Minnesota's selection of Gary Bauman from the Montreal organization.

Philadelphia ended up with easily the most competent goaltending tandem in the new West Division. Parent and Favell evenly split the 74-game schedule in the Flyers' inaugural season, allowing only 179 goals: the third-best total in the NHL (behind Montreal and Toronto). Philly won a season-long battle with Los Angeles and St. Louis for first place in the new division, but was eliminated by the veteran-clad Blues in a heated seven-game quarterfinal.

During the 1968-69 and 1969-70 seasons, Parent clearly emerged as the Flyers' number-one goaltender: playing in 118 regular-season games while Favell saw action in only 34. An Achilles-heal rupture requiring surgery sidelined Favell for much of the '69-70 campaign, but Parent had already established himself as one of the NHL's better netminders.

Unfortunately, the Flyers were not nearly as proficient as a team. They made the playoffs in '68-69 but were bounced again by St. Louis in the opening round, losing four straight.

The following year, they tied an NHL-record 24 games and were edged out for the final playoff spot in the West by the Oakland Seals, who had the same number of points (58), but five more victories. And it was during that 1969-70 season that Jim Gregory felt he might be able to wrest Parent away from the Flyers.

"Philadelphia wasn't having much playoff success and I figured it might be the right time to try and swing a deal," Gregory recalls.

The Maple Leafs' goaltending situation was unstable. Johnny Bower finally called it quits at 45 years of age and Marv Edwards — a career minor-leaguer who had left hockey for eight years — made the club as back-up to Bruce Gamble.

Edwards had played sparingly with Buffalo of the American Hockey League in the late-1950s and he retired after the 1958-59 season. He resurfaced with Portland of the Western League in 1967-68 and his NHL experience upon joining the Maple Leafs consisted of one game with the Pittsburgh Penguins in '68-69.

Gamble and Edwards clearly were not going to lead the Maple Leafs to the Promised Land and Gregory knew it. So, he began making inquiries with Philadelphia about Parent.

"I talked a number of times with (Flyers' general manager) Keith Allen, but he had no interest in dealing Bernie," Gregory remembers. "I kept trying for almost two years before giving up on the idea. It never got to the point of discussing players because Keith wouldn't even consider a trade for Parent."

As a result, Gregory signed Jacques Plante away from St. Louis for the 1970-71 season but knew he had to get younger in goal. Gamble was beginning to fade at 32 years of age and there was no heir apparent in the Toronto organization.

Murray McLachlan, a 22-year-old University of Minnesota grad, held down the number-one spot with the Leafs' Central League affiliate in Tulsa, but was unimpressive in a couple of outings with the big club. The Maple Leafs were shallow between the pipes.

It was midway through the '70-71 season that Gregory received a surprising, but most-welcomed telephone call.

"We were in Montreal for a game with the Canadiens (Jan. 30, 1971) and John McLellan and I had adjoining rooms in the Sheraton Mount Royal Hotel," Gregory remembers. "It was late in the afternoon and John was ready to leave for the Forum when the phone rang. He answered and said it was for me. Keith Allen was on the other end wondering if I still had any interest in Bernie Parent.

"Well, I nearly fell off my chair! I was extremely interested in Parent and we consummated a trade in 15 minutes. We sent Philadelphia Gamble and Mike Walton, a pretty good goalscorer. It turns out the Flyers wanted young Rick MacLeish from Boston and they immediately sent Walton to the Bruins.

"I ran over to the Forum and told McLellan about the deal. He couldn't believe it."

Parent recalls being far less enthused about the trade.

"It was a big let-down for me and my wife," he says. "Not because we were going to Toronto — we both knew it was a beautiful city. But, being traded for the first time was tough to accept. Carol and I aren't together anymore but she was a Philadelphia girl and she wasn't anxious to leave her home town. And I thought I had really established myself with the Flyers. The trade to the Maple Leafs came as quite a shock."

However, it quickly turned into a blessing for Parent. During a season-and-a-bit in Toronto, the French-Canadian goaltender worked and studied with his boyhood idol, Plante. And, to this day, Parent credits that 14-month period for the astounding success he later enjoyed during his second stint in Philadelphia.

"Playing with Jacques changed my whole career," he says. "During the early years in Philadelphia, my work habits were only fair and even though I played well for the Flyers, I never really understood my full potential. When I came to Toronto, I saw this 42-year-old man working like hell during practice, challenging his teammates, and getting angry when shots beat him.

"I looked at the guy and said, 'Why does he have to bother?' He had done just about everything possible in the game — winning Stanley Cups and Vezina Trophies — yet he still had the same competitive fire as during his peak years with Montreal. And I realized that if I wanted to be as successful, I had to show the same kind of dedication.

"At the time, I'd say that I applied myself maybe 50 percent in practice. Jacques showed me that I had to improve my attitude. Before I had any chance of helping a team win the Stanley Cup, I would have to work 50 percent harder. That's what I learned from Plante."

Playing with one of his genuine heroes became an instant thrill for Parent, who learned many aspects of the game from Plante.

"He taught me how to read the different players in the league," Parent remembers. "Nobody ever studied the game as closely as Jacques, and he knew the opposition shooters inside and out. He showed me how my defenceman would react to a left-hand shot as opposed to a right-hand shot and it helped me anticipate their tendencies.

"His concentration was incredible and he was a fun guy to be with two or three days between games. But the night before — and the day of a game — he was all business, and you just had to respect him. People remember Jacques being quite moody, but that was his way of preparing to play. Even at such an advanced age, he was better than most of the other goalies in the NHL."

Parent played 65 regular-season games in a Toronto uniform during the 1970-71 and 1971-72 seasons, allowing roughly 2.6 goals per outing. He became a more refined goaltender under Plante and his stock began to rise immeasurably.

His contract with the Maple Leafs was set to expire at the end of the '71-72 campaign, which coincided with the advent of the World Hockey Association. The Miami entry in the new league made an overture to Parent's agent that Leaf owner Harold Ballard scoffed at.

Ballard figured the WHA was merely a pipedream that had not the slightest chance of materializing. It turned out to be a dreadful blunder. Parent was making $25,000 with the Maple Leafs. Miami offered him $125,000 to jump to the new league. When apprised of the interest from Florida, Ballard laughed out loud and, despite warnings from Gregory, called Parent's bluff. He contemptuously told the star goalie to accept the "phantom" proposal.

The Maple Leafs whipped Vancouver 7-1 at the Gardens on Saturday night, Feb. 26, 1972 and had four days off until their next game, at St. Louis. On Sunday morning, without informing Ballard, Parent went to Toronto International Airport and caught an Air Canada flight to Miami. He inked a lucrative contract with the Screaming Eagles later that day and the club held a splashy news conference to announce it.

The signing sent shock waves through the unsuspecting and terribly naive NHL. After weeks of rampant speculation, a player had actually defected. One of hockey's brightest young stars had left his team in the middle of the season, flown south, and boldly announced he was joining the WHA for 1972-73.

It came at a time when rumours circulated that Bobby Hull was considering an offer from the Winnipeg Jets to leave Chicago. Not even the most liberal-minded hockey fans believed *that* was possible, but it took on added credence after Parent's move.

And, of course, Hull later defected.

"In that situation, I really had no other choice," Parent says. "Gregory wanted to negotiate with us, but Ballard would have nothing to do with it because he believed the WHA would fold before it started. I wasn't anxious to leave the NHL but how could I turn down that kind of money? It was a 400 percent increase from my Toronto salary."

Ballard's obstinance cost him a front-line goaltender and five other prominent members of his young hockey club. There may have been some slight vindication when it turned out that the Miami franchise was indeed barking up a tree. It never got rolling but Parent stayed in the WHA and took his services to the Philadelphia entry.

He appeared in 63 games for the WHA Blazers in 1972-73 and made the second All-Star team with a 3.61 goals-against average. Coached by his former Bruin teammate, John McKenzie, the club played at the 9,000-seat Philadelphia Civic Center and Parent will never forget the zany incident that occurred prior to the Blazers' very first game. It cast an immediate aspersion in his mind about the WHA's credibility.

The New England Whalers were in town to kick off Philadelphia's home schedule on Friday night, Oct. 13, 1972. Along with Parent, the Blazers had signed popular Derek Sanderson away from the Boston Bruins. As an opening-night souvenir, the club handed each fan a bright-orange puck with the WHA emblem on it.

Following the pre-game warm-up, the Zamboni at the Civic Center hacked open a 15-foot gash in the ice surface that arena workers simply couldn't repair. They determined the game would have to be postponed.

"We were sitting in our dressing room wondering how we would tell the fans that the game was cancelled," Parent recalls. "Sanderson stood up and said he would go out, take the rink-side microphone, and explain the situation. As soon as he started talking, the fans began pelting him with the bright-orange pucks. They almost killed the poor bugger."

Spending a year in the fledgling league emphasized to Parent what he already knew: there was only one place to play hockey.

"On the ice, we are actors," he explains, "and we have to perform to the utmost of our abilities. Well, trying to perform in front of 800 people is very difficult. The intensity and noise from a crowd gets the players excited and helps us `act.' That's what was missing in the WHA.

"You could fit 9,000 people in the Philadelphia rink, so if we had 5,000 on some nights, it was alright. But I remember playing in much-larger arenas with less than a thousand spectators watching.

"It was impossible to motivate myself. I just couldn't do it."

Philadelphia stumbled through a disappointing inaugural season — finishing third in the East Division with a 38-40-0 record. Parent left the club in Cleveland after the opening game of a first-round playoff series with the Crusaders. Cleveland prevailed 3-2 after 10 minutes of overtime and Parent couldn't take it anymore. His WHA rights were dealt to the New York Golden Blades in May, 1973, but he had long decided by then that his future was back in the NHL.

"That isn't to knock the WHA," Parent says. "That league was damn good for hockey. A lot of players like myself took a chance by leaving the security of the NHL, and people said we were crazy. But, salaries went way up, and everybody is richer today as a result."

Upon announcing his intentions to return to the NHL, a conflicting story arose. And it remains rather muddled more than two decades later.

The Maple Leafs owned Parent's NHL rights and any player back then who returned from the WHA had to deal with the club he had left. Parent insists that his attempt to re-join the Leafs was blocked by Ballard, who was still furious over his defection.

"Harold didn't want me back," Bernie says. "He was still mad at me for leaving. So, the Leafs traded me to the Flyers."

Such was not the case, according to Gregory.

"No, we tried to get Bernie back but his wife wasn't interested in returning to Toronto," says the former Leaf G.M. "Harold actually had no problem re-signing him for the same money he was making in the WHA. We were basically forced into consummating a deal with Phila-delphia."

The trade had two parts and turned out rather miserably for the Maple Leafs. Gregory dealt Parent's NHL rights back to the Flyers on May 15, 1973 along with the Leafs' second-round choice (defenceman Larry Goodenough) in that summer's amateur draft. Toronto received the Flyers' first choice in the same draft (defenceman Bob Neely) and a player to be named later. Obviously having to re-coup some goaltending, that player became Parent's ex-partner, Doug Favell, who joined the Maple Leafs on July 27, 1973.

Favell teamed with veterans Ed Johnston and Dunc Wilson to provide the Leafs with decent netminding in the 1973-74 season.

But, Parent went off into the stratosphere.

Returning to Philadelphia at the absolute peak of his career, he backstopped the Flyers to consecutive Stanley Cup championships and carved his niche among the top half-dozen goalies who ever lived.

He played 73 of the Flyers' 78 games in his first season back with the club and posted a remarkable 1.89 goals-against average to go along with 12 shutouts. He had a 2.02 average in 17 playoff matches as the Flyers up-ended Atlanta, the Rangers and Boston to become the first of the expansion teams to win the Stanley Cup. Fittingly, Parent was named winner of the Conn Smythe Trophy as playoff MVP.

His goal permittance was equally as remarkable the following year: 2.03 in 68 regular-season games (including 12 more shutouts) and 1.89 in 15 playoff encounters as the Flyers won their second Cup, defeating the Buffalo Sabres. Again, Parent earned the Conn Smythe Trophy.

Maple Leaf fans can only imagine what *their* club may have been able to accomplish had Ballard not dared Parent to join the WHA.

* * * * * *

Vic Hadfield deals with his numerous golf-club inquiries in a good-natured manner. He really has no other choice.

"Maple Leaf fans are always reminding me about the mask incident," he says. "Nobody remembers it in New York, but I can't get away from it around Toronto. I've gained some kind of legendary status."

Hadfield has no problem discussing the incident, but he does so with a touch of reticence. "Really, it's a little embarrassing when I look back on it," he says. "I guess we all do things we're not proud of and that was one of them. But, it happened in the heat of battle and I often joke with Leaf fans that Bernie was lucky his head still wasn't attached to the mask.

"He came into that fight I was having with Harrison and tried to pull me away. The mask was right there. I just grabbed it and threw it up into the seats. I don't really know *why*, it was pretty much a reflex move. I didn't stop and think about it.

"But I do remember saying to myself at the time, `Oh Geez, what have I done now?' I knew it wasn't exactly a normal reaction."

Harrison had all but forgotten the incident, but it came back to him in vivid detail when discussing it for this anthology.

"Hadfield and I went at it that whole series," he says. "I played on a line with Darryl Sittler and Brian Spencer and it was our job to try and slow down the Ratelle-Hadfield-Gilbert unit. It was the only possible way we could win the series and I wasn't afraid of Hadfield. We had fought earlier in that game but in the second battle, he got the best of me. He was one hell of a tough customer.

"Bernie and I had become good friends during our time in Toronto so it never surprised me that he came out of his net to help. That's the kind of teammate he was. Unfortunately, it cost him his mask."

Hadfield and Parent have joked about the incident on several occasions in the ensuing years. "Yeah, I'll run into Bernie at a golf tournament now and then," Hadfield says. "We'll come towards each other, our eyes will meet, and we'll both break out laughing because we know exactly what the other guy is thinking. We'll then call each other a few names and continue on our way."

Says Parent: "It's a hell of a lot more funny now than it was a the time, I can tell you that."

New York ended up winning that quarterfinal series in six games. Parent's new mask arrived on time for him to play in Game 3, and the Maple Leafs won for the second and final time in the series. Rangers eliminated Toronto at the Gardens on Bob Nevin's overtime goal. The ex-Leaf scored on a long shot from outside the blueline that somehow beat Plante through the five-hole. Jacques did the splits, but too late.

At least he had his mask.

*   *   *   *   *   *

WHERE ARE THEY NOW?...

VIC HADFIELD, 54, played 16 seasons in the NHL with the Rangers and Pittsburgh Penguins. In 1971-72, while playing left-wing on the famed "G-A-G" line with Jean Ratelle and Rod Gilbert, he became only the sixth player in NHL history (and first-ever Ranger) to score 50 goals in one season. Traded to Pittsburgh for defenceman Nick Beverley in May, 1974, Hadfield enjoyed his second and third-most productive NHL seasons — scoring 31 and 30 goals for the Penguins. He retired from hockey early in the 1976-77 campaign. Currently living in the

Toronto area, he operates a golf driving range in nearby Woodbridge, Ontario.

BERNIE PARENT, 49, deserves mention alongside Glenn Hall, Terry Sawchuk and Jacques Plante as one of the best goaltenders who ever played the game. He spent 14 seasons in professional hockey: one of them in the WHA. He skated with Boston, Philadelphia and the Maple Leafs during his NHL career. No goalie could touch him in the mid-1970s, when Parent helped the Flyers win consecutive Stanley Cups. His career came to an abrupt end midway through the 1978-79 season when he suffered a serious eye injury in a game at the Spectrum against the New York Rangers. He currently splits his time between several vocations. He's been the Flyers' goaltending instructor for the past 14 seasons. He is also senior vice-president of *Rosanio, Bailets and Talamo* — an advertising, marketing and public-relations firm in Cherry Hill, N.J. Parent spends the summer months on a boat in Cave May, N.J. — 20 miles south of Atlantic City. On Sept. 25, 1984, he became the first member of the Flyers to be inducted into the Hockey Hall of Fame.

JIM GREGORY, 59, took over from Punch Imlach as general manager of the Maple Leafs for the 1969-70 season and held the job for ten years. Ironically — and tragically — he was replaced by the very same Imlach after the 1978-79 campaign. During his decade with the Leafs, Gregory twice built the club to respectability. He was responsible for drafting players the calibre of Darryl Sittler, Errol Thompson, Rick Kehoe, Ian Turnbull, Lanny McDonald, Dave (Tiger) Williams, Mike Palmateer, Doug Jarvis and Randy Carlyle. Perhaps his major fault was that he traded away much of that talent while it still had plenty to offer. Having to work for the tight-fisted Harold Ballard didn't help. Gregory's budget precluded the assembly of a front-line hockey department. He didn't have enough scouts, and was never accorded the capital to prevent such players as Bernie Parent from defecting to the WHA. Most people agree that Gregory was clearly a better hockey executive than he proved to be under Ballard. "He was one of the top men in the game," says Parent. The NHL has always thought highly of the Port Colborne, Ont. native as Gregory, for years, has been the league's vice-president of hockey operations, working out of its Toronto office.

EMILE FRANCIS, 68, played, coached and managed in the NHL for 31 years. He was a goalie with Chicago and the Rangers between 1946 and

1952. He made 54 appearances for the Blackhawks in the 1947-48 season, but played in just 95 NHL games in total, posting a 3.76 career goals-against average. Something about him must have been quick, because he was nicknamed the "Cat" during his brief playing career. Francis is best remembered for his years as G.M. and coach of the Rangers (1964-75). In the early 70s, he guided New York to consecutive seasons of 109, 109 and 102 points, and the Rangers advanced to the 1972 Stanley Cup Final, losing to Bobby Orr and the Boston Bruins. Francis later went on to manage St. Louis and Hartford through the 1988-89 season. He is currently retired and living in Hartford. He did some broadcast work for the *Madison Square Garden* Network during the Rangers' drive to the 1994 Stanley Cup championship.

JIM HARRISON, 47, was one of the six Maple Leaf players Harold Ballard allowed to escape to the WHA in 1972. A rugged center-iceman, Harrison broke into the NHL with Boston in 1968-69. He played sparingly for the Bruins and was traded to Toronto for winger Wayne Carleton in December, 1969. He skated for the Maple Leafs through 1971-72, scoring a career-high 19 goals in his final year. He jumped to Alberta of the WHA in '72 and blossomed into an offensive threat with 39 goals and 86 points. He later played for Cleveland before coming back to the NHL with Chicago in 1976. He retired as a member of the Edmonton Oilers in the 1979-80 season with 67 career NHL goals. He currently lives in Kelowna, B.C. and his activities have been curtailed by back injuries suffered during his NHL career. He underwent three back operations and has very limited feeling in his right leg. Harrison is actively seeking insurance compensation from the former Alan Eagleson empire.

... *Leafs in Spring* ...

MAY 24, 1994
Pacific Coliseum, Vancouver

The turmoil above the portable seats stood in great contrast to the misery down below. As loud bursts of fireworks hailed Vancouver's annexation of the Western Conference championship, Pat Burns sauntered gloomily towards his office beside the Maple Leaf dressing room — the shock of an overtime elimination painfully etched on his face.

Seconds earlier, Greg Adams of the Canucks had sent the Leafs into summer. He backhanded a rebound past Felix Potvin at the 14-second mark of double-O.T. — earning Vancouver a spot in the Stanley Cup final and touching off pandemonium in the Pacific Coliseum.

Burns seemed in a hurry to escape all the chaos, until he realized his players were still on the ice, consoling one another. He opened the door to his office then quickly changed his mind and went back to the entrance of the dressing room. There he stood, awaiting his charges, who filed silently and forlornly past him for the final time. And he shared in their anguish — gently tapping each player in appreciation of an honest yet futile effort.

Having retreated to the bowels of the Coliseum during the first overtime, I watched Adams score the series winner with Don Cherry and Ron MacLean in the Hockey Night In Canada studio next to the Maple Leaf dressing room. Given his druthers, Cherry would have preferred a Toronto victory but he found comfort in his choice of Adams –- on the air — to be the overtime hero. As the

Canucks celebrated, he listened anxiously to his TV monitor, and then grumbled an indignity at Bob Cole for not reminding viewers of his premonition.

The Maple Leafs had gone down, but not without a fight. Summoning one final burst of energy, they bolted to a 3-0 advantage in the first period and seemed likely to send the series back to Toronto. During the intermission, I walked past Pierre Dorion: the club's scouting director who would so tragically die of a heart attack only a few weeks later.

"That's better," I offered in response to the three-goal outburst.

"Oh, it's not over yet, Howie," he said. "We've got to score the next goal. If they get one early, we're in trouble."

Pierre sure knew his hockey.

Murray Craven started Vancouver rolling with a backhander at 1:34 of the second period and the Maple Leafs began a slow fade.

By the end of the period, the Canucks had obliterated the Toronto lead and the series pattern began to unfold.

Adams delivered the final blow just more than two hours later.

*   *   *   *   *   *

Several days after the defeat in Vancouver, during a meeting with his boss, Pat Burns told Cliff Fletcher of an ominous suspicion.

Unless dramatic changes were made, the coach believed his club would have much difficulty qualifying for the playoffs in 1994-95.

From the midway point of the '93-94 campaign, the Leafs had played .500 hockey and had staggered unimpressively through the playoffs. The club was particularly shallow up the middle, where Doug Gilmour — bad ankle and all — often centred the first, second and third-line units. Too grave a decline existed between the club's few reliable scorers and the remainder of the forward cast. Offensive responsibilities had to be disseminated more evenly on a legitimate Stanley Cup contender.

Additionally, the Maple Leafs were an aging club with a number of players approaching their twilight years. Neither was there a genuine influx of ready made talent in the farm system. Clearly, alterations would have to be affected through the trade market.

With that in mind, the Maple Leaf hierarchy — smarting from the sudden loss of Dorion just days earlier — journeyed to Hartford for the 1994 NHL draft meetings. Rumours circulated about a deal between the Leafs and Quebec involving Sylvain Lefebvre and Mike Ricci. I went to Hartford for the radio station assuming that something newsworthy would transpire. The time was right for Fletcher to pull the trigger.

*   *   *   *   *   *

The floor of the Hartford Civic Centre was typically abuzz with activity as the 26 NHL teams finalized their draft agendas.

My press location was in the very first row of the media section. A narrow walkway and a four-foot steel fence was all that separated me from the actual drafting area. GMs, coaches and scouts were accessible and mostly cooperative with reporters who simply approached the fence. While loitering at the separation point roughly 40 minutes prior to the draft, I stumbled across some valuable information.

Maple Leafs' assistant general manager Bill Watters — previously my colleague at the radio station — was chatting with his ex-business partner: player-agent Rick Curran. With all the speculation concerning a trade, Curran asked Watters if the Leafs were indeed up to something.

My ears probably should have been elsewhere at that moment, as I couldn't help but overhear Bill's response.

"Oh yeah... big! In fact, you'll be shocked when you hear it," he told Curran.

With that gem of knowledge, I immediately phoned the station and broke in during the network hour of Prime Time Sports — our nightly magazine show. Alerting hosts Dan Shulman and Jim (Shakey) Hunt of the comment from Watters (whose name I kept out of the report), I told our listeners, in no uncertain terms, to stay tuned. Hanging up, I began to scout around for some covert information, hoping to nail down details of the impending transaction. A player agent based in Toronto (not Don Meehan) indicated he might eventually have some dope on the trade and said he'd fill me in.

Calling the station back, I was informed that Wendel Clark's name was now involved in the three or four variations of trade rumours with Quebec. All of the speculative deals had Mike Ricci joining the Leafs and 1992 first-round draft choice Brandon Convery going to the Nords. While chatting on the air, and frantically trying to keep abreast of the rumours flying around my desk, I became privy to at least three "done deals" — none of which materialized.

At around 6:40 p.m., 20 minutes before the start of the draft, the agent I had previously spoken to shoved a piece of paper under my nose. It read:

```
Wendel Clark, Sylvain Lefebvre and Landon
Wilson to Quebec for Mats Sundin, Garth
Butcher and Todd Warriner. Teams will
exchange first-round picks.
```
THIS DEAL HAS BEEN MADE!!

This variation differed in many respects from all the rumbles we'd been hearing. It did not involve Ricci or Convery. Wilson, Warriner and the swap of draft choices were mentioned for the first time. However, I considered my source to be impeccable and ran with the story, saying that Quebec would officially announce the deal upon making its initial draft selection — ninth overall in the first round.

Moments later, during our final network commercial spot, someone from Reseau des Sports (RDS) — french affiliate of The Sports Network in Canada — tapped me on the shoulder. Somehow, he heard that we had announced the Clark-Sundin deal and he politely requested that I share my information. I asked to see what he had and his rumour still involved Ricci and Convery. So, I gave him the trade.

Three days later, in a Toronto Sun broadcast column, I was amused to read that RDS had broken the story across Canada.

Of course, the deal was not yet a matter of record until announced officially by the Nordiques. That occurred around 7:20 p.m. and I held my breath as NHL Commissioner Gary Bettman rattled off the names. The crowd at the Civic Centre let out a collective gasp as the enormity of the trade unfolded. Thankfully, all of my rumoured particulars were verified. It had been a rousing 90 minutes, to say the least.

*   *   *   *   *   *

Less than 72 hours after the trade — at Don Cherry's Grapevine in Mississauga, Ont. — Wendel Clark sat before a deluge of reporters.

And he cried like a baby.

The brawny former captain of the Maple Leafs spoke courageously about new challenges in Quebec but you could tell his heart was broken. Broadcasting the address live, I sat mere feet from Clark and it was both unique and sorrowful to see him reduced to a whimper.

Yet another era in Toronto hockey annals had come to an end.

TORONTO MAPLE LEAFS 30-YEAR INDEX

A THUMBNAIL REVIEW OF MAPLE LEAF HOCKEY
1964-65 to 1993-94

CATEGORY LISTINGS

(1) FIRST GAMES vs. ALL OPPONENTS
(2) FIRST-GAME RESULTS IN NEW (OR RENOVATED) ARENAS
(3) DATES OF FIRST GAMES IN 1994-95 NEW ARENAS
(4) MAPLE LEAF GENERAL MANAGERS
(5) MAPLE LEAF HEAD COACHES
(6) MAPLE LEAF TEAM CAPTAINS
(7) LEADING SCORERS, YEAR-BY-YEAR
(8) PENALTY MINUTE LEADERS, YEAR-BY-YEAR
(9) MAPLE LEAF PENALTY SHOTS
(10) ANALYSIS OF MAJOR TRANSACTIONS
(11) COMPLETE PLAYER INDEX

Since the start of the 1964-65 National Hockey League season, the Maple Leafs have faced off against teams representing 31 different locations across North America. During the era covered in this book, there have been eight separate waves of expansion and five franchise re-locations. The following, is an index listing and a brief summation of the first Maple Leaf games, both home and away, against all 31 opposition clubs over the past three decades. From 1967 on, it becomes a listing of the first-*ever* games played against teams from the post-expansion era.

DETROIT RED WINGS
[FRANCHISE DATE: September 25, 1926]

DETROIT OLYMPIA, Thu. Oct. 15, 1964
MAPLE LEAFS 5, DETROIT 3. TORONTO SCORERS: ANDY BATHGATE, RED KELLY, DAVE KEON, RON STEWART, BOB PULFORD. DETROIT SCORERS: AL LANGOIS, FLOYD SMITH, RON MURPHY. The Maple Leafs won their 1964-65 season opener by out-scoring the Red Wings 2-0 over the final 40 minutes. Ron Stewart scored the eventual winner at 44 seconds of the middle period, giving Leafs a 4-3 lead. He finished off a nice three-way passing play with Bob Pulford and Eddie Shack. Pulford added some insurance at 2:01 of the third, scoring a shorthanded goal. He took a pass from George Armstrong and beat Roger Crozier with a shot that deflected into the net off defenceman Doug Barkley. Both teams complained about the strict officiating of referee Vern Buffey, who began the game by calling Maple Leaf goalie Johnny Bower for intentionally holding the puck just 34 seconds after the opening faceoff. After a four-year retirement, Ted Lindsay was back in a Detroit uniform for the first time since his 1957 trade to Chicago. His rights were re-purchased by the Red Wings just a day earlier and he received a minute-long standing ovation prior to the game.

MAPLE LEAF GARDENS, Wed. Nov. 11, 1964
MAPLE LEAFS 3, DETROIT 1. TORONTO SCORERS: DON MCKENNEY, JIM PAPPIN, BOB PULFORD. DETROIT SCORER: BRUCE MCGREGOR. The Leafs capitalized on a tired Red Wing club by scoring twice in the third period for the win. Jim Pappin broke a 1-1 tie at the 11:10 mark when he took Bob Baun's rebound off the back-boards and beat Roger Crozier. Bob Pulford salted the victory with an empty net goal nine seconds from the final buzzer. Terry Sawchuk, in goal for the Leafs, played his first game against his former team, having been claimed by Toronto during the summer intra-league waiver draft. By winning, he ran his personal unbeaten streak in a Leaf uniform to 3-0-2, and had immense praise for his teammtes. "I had a soft night's work with Brewer, Baun, Stanley and Horton playing so well on defence," he said. "Man, did they belt those Wings!" Detroit had played to a 3-3 tie the previous night in Boston and didn't arrive in Toronto until 5 a.m. "We ran out of

gas after the first period," said coach Sid Abel. "Only great work by the kid in net (Crozier), and the fact they hit a few goalposts, kept the score down."

BOSTON BRUINS
[FRANCHISE DATE: November 25, 1924]

MAPLE LEAF GARDENS, Sat. Oct. 17, 1964
MAPLE LEAFS 7, BRUINS 2. TORONTO SCORERS: FRANK MAHOVLICH (2), RED KELLY (2), RON ELLIS, EDDIE SHACK, DAVE KEON. BOSTON SCORERS: MURRAY OLIVER, DEAN PRENTICE. Rookie right-winger Ron Ellis scored his first NHL goal as the Leafs romped to victory. He beat Eddie Johnston at 12:17 of the first period to tie the game at 1-1 after Murray Oliver had opened the scoring with a powerplay goal. Red Kelly had two goals and an assist, and continued to play very well after missing the entire exhibition schedule while representing the Canadian government at the Olympic Games in Tokyo. Kelly played on a line with Billy Harris and Jim Pappin, as well as on the powerplay with Frank Mahovlich and Dave Keon. "He looks as frisky as a colt out there," said Leaf coach Punch Imlach. "I guess Tokyo didn't hurt him." Mahovlich also had a pair for the Maple Leafs.

BOSTON GARDEN, Thu. Oct. 22, 1964
MAPLE LEAFS 2, BRUINS 2. TORONTO SCORERS: ANDY BATHGATE, BOB PULFORD. BOSTON SCORER: REGGIE FLEMING (2). The Bruins gained their first point of the young season, but coach Milt Schmidt was steaming mad at referee John Ashley after the game. With the Bruins leading 2-1, and less than ten minutes remaining in the game, Ashley threw center Bob Leiter out of the faceoff circle in the Boston zone. Reggie Fleming replaced him and was beaten easily on the draw by Bob Pulford, who scored the tying goal a few seconds later. "My guys deserved to win but that guy (Ashley) took victory away from them with a bad call," Schmidt said. "You'd think the fans paid to see those guys, not the players. They're ruining the game." When asked about a possible $500 fine for his criticism of Ashley, Schmidt said, "What for, telling the truth?" NHL referee-in-chief Carl Voss watched the game from the press box and supported Ashley's decision. "John warned Leiter several times about moving around in the circle," Voss said. "He had every reason to order him out." Veteran Dickie Moore made his debut in a Maple Leaf

uniform after his rights were acquired from Montreal in the intra-league waiver draft. Moore had taken the 1963-64 season off but decided to come back. He was on the ice for both Boston goals, as Fleming scored a pair of shorthanded markers. "I wasn't very good tonight," Moore said. "Pulford got me off the hook by scoring the tying goal. I sure didn't set the world on fire." Pulford's tying marker came on a pass from Ron Stewart in the corner. He took two whacks at the puck before getting it past Eddie Johnston.

NEW YORK RANGERS
[FRANCHISE DATE: May 15, 1926]

MADISON SQUARE GARDEN, Sun. Oct. 18, 1964
MAPLE LEAFS 3, RANGERS 3. TORONTO SCORERS: JIM PAPPIN (2), KENT DOUGLAS. NEW YORK SCORERS: LOU ANGOTTI (2), BOB NEVIN. Once a Maple Leaf farmhand, Lou Angotti was obviously upset that the Toronto club had never given him a chance to play in the NHL. And he verbalized that bitterness after scoring twice against the Leafs. "I've never enjoyed two goals more than that pair," he said. "It gave me a great deal of pleasure to take a win away from those guys." During his two seasons in Rochester (1962-63 and 1963-64), Angotti had suffered numerous injuries, including two dislocated shoulders, a dislocated arm and a broken leg. When reminded of that, he said, "That's their story. I know they never gave me a look when I was healthy." The game marked goalie Terry Sawchuk's debut as a Maple Leaf. Both he and Ranger goalie Marcel Paille stopped 30 shots. Former Leaf Bob Nevin scored the game-tying goal with 6:06 remaining in the third period. The Leafs jumped to a 3-1 lead on Jim Pappin's goal at 4:04 of the second period, at which time the Ranger fans began booing their team and shouting insults at coach Red Sullivan. Defenceman Kent Douglas was the best Maple Leaf on the ice, scoring his first goal of the season to go along with six assists after only three games.

MAPLE LEAF GARDENS, Sat. Oct. 24, 1964
MAPLE LEAFS 1, RANGERS 1. TORONTO SCORER: RON ELLIS. NEW YORK SCORER: ROD GILBERT. The Maple Leafs improved their unbeaten record to 2-0-3 on the young season, but the headline on Red Burnett's game story in the Toronto *Star* read: STANDINGS FLATTER LACKLUSTRE LEAFS. Only the alertness of goalie Johnny Bower pre-

vented them from losing. Ron Ellis opened the scoring at 9:35 of the first period on the powerplay, with Ranger defenceman Jim Neilson in the penalty box. Ellis converted a feed from Don McKenney past goalie Marcel Paille. Rod Gilbert scored the game-tying goal at 12:19 of the second period. He banged in his own rebound off the shin-pads of Leaf defenceman Tim Horton. Coach Punch Imlach was disatisfied with his club's effort and he skated his players hard for 90 minutes the following day. The Leafs missed a number of open-net opportunities against the Rangers and Imlach deemed that each miss was worth three wind-sprints across the ice. Jim Pappin did 18 of them; Frank Mahovlich and Ron Stewart 15 each.

CHICAGO BLACKHAWKS
[FRANCHISE DATE: September 25, 1926]

CHICAGO STADIUM, Tue. Oct. 27, 1964
MAPLE LEAFS 3, BLACKHAWKS 2. TORONTO SCORERS: GEORGE ARMSTRONG, ANDY BATHGATE, RON STEWART. CHICAGO SCORERS: STAN MIKITA, BILL HAY. Maple Leafs' best effort of the early season improved their record to 3-0-3 after six games. Once again, the losing side had a bone to pick with the officiating. In the dying seconds of the game, Stan Mikita of the Blackhawks threw a tantrum at linesman Matt Pavelich, who had whistled play dead as the 'Hawks were trying to remove goalie Glenn Hall for a sixth attacker. Pavelich determined that Hall was not within 15 feet of the bench — as required in the rulebook — before Mikita jumped onto the ice. Mikita and Pavelich shoved each other and launched into a chin-to-chin debate at center ice. Mikita then be-rated referee John Ashley as well, and received a pair of 10-minute misconduct penalties, with fines totalling $75. When the game ended, Chicago coach Billy Reay made a mad dash to the officials' exit but Ashley stepped between he and Pavelich. To the Toronto writers, afterwards, Reay said, "You wrote how (Reggie) Fleming speared Eddie Shack in Toronto last season. So, let's see you say how (Frank) Mahovlich speared Mikita in the second period tonight and got off with a two-minute roughing penalty. He should have had five for spearing." Ron Stewart scored the winner for the Leafs at 11:56 of the second period, jamming the puck past Hall while defencemen Pierre Pilote and Elmer Vasko tried to dig it loose with their sticks.

MAPLE LEAF GARDENS, Sat. Oct. 31, 1964
MAPLE LEAFS 5, BLACKHAWKS 1. TORONTO SCORERS: RON ELLIS (2), ANDY BATHGATE, RON STEWART, FRANK MAHOVLICH. CHICAGO SCORER: BOBBY HULL. Four nights after the controversial ending in Chicago, Leafs beat the Blackhawks again, but more convincingly. Ron Ellis, the impressive rookie from the Junior Marlboros, had two more goals, plus an assist. Ellis said he was starting to accept the advice of his veteran line-mate, Andy Bathgate, who suggested he carry the puck more and worry less about back-checking (wonder if Andy had Imlach's blessings on that one?) Bathgate had three assists on the night. "It was no contest," said a dejected Chicago coach Billy Reay. "We had a few chances, but (Terry) Sawchuk played a hot hand in goal for them." The score was tied 1-1 after the opening period, as Ellis and Bobby Hull traded goals. But, the Leafs counted twice in both the second and third periods.

MONTREAL CANADIENS
[FRANCHISE DATE: November 22, 1917]

MAPLE LEAF GARDENS, Wed. Oct. 28, 1964
CANADIENS 5, MAPLE LEAFS 2. TORONTO SCORERS: DON MCKENNEY, RON ELLIS. MONTREAL SCORERS: CLAUDE LAROSE (2), CLAUDE PROVOST, BOBBY ROUSSEAU, RALPH BACKSTROM. A weary Maple Leaf team suffered it's first loss of the season after seven games. Leafs were tired after winning in Chicago the previous night and they allowed the Canadiens to skate. "Our older fellows aren't ready for two tough games in as many nights," noted Punch Imlach. "They have to build up to the rugged schedule and our younger players, with the exception of the rookie (Ellis), couldn't take up the slack. You have to hit Canadiens to beat them and our fellows couldn't catch them to hit them." The first of two goals by Claude Larose was the backbreaker for the Leafs. Ellis had tied the score 2-2 with a shorthanded goal at 16:04 of the second period — defenceman Ted Harris in the penalty box for Montreal. But, Larose scored 35 seconds later to re-gain the lead for the Habs. Larose and Ralph Backstrom put the game out of reach early in the third. "We were up for this one," said Montreal goalie Charlie Hodge. "And when you're right, mentally and physically, things seem to break for you. One shot plopped out of my glove and was going over the goal-line when Ted Harris banged it clear. That was a big break."

MONTREAL FORUM, Thu. Nov. 5, 1964
MAPLE LEAFS 2, CANADIENS 2. TORONTO SCORERS: RON ELLIS,
CARL BREWER. MONTREAL SCORERS: HENRI RICHARD, JEAN-
GUY TALBOT. In his Toronto *Star* game story from the Forum, Red
Burnett heaped more praise on freshman Ron Ellis: "He continues to
look like the best right-winger to join the Maple Leafs since Charlie
Conacher burst on the National Hockey League scene back in 1929. Like
Conacher, this fellow is rugged and can score goals." Ellis, 19, scored a
big goal for the Leafs in the final minute of the first period, off-setting an
earlier Montreal tally by Henri Richard. Carl Brewer and Jean-Guy
Talbot traded goals late in the second period, and the third was scoreless.
Habs' coach Toe Blake also had kind words for Ellis. "He covers his wing
well and leads the team in scoring. What more can you ask? He could be
a great one." Dickie Moore of the Maple Leafs returned to the Forum —
scene of his greatest years in the NHL. But, the Montreal fans generally
ignored his presence. "I hate the sight of him in that uniform," said Blake.
"He doesn't suit blue and white. But, I have to admit he made some good
moves out there, although he was slow."

---

*For the 1967-68 season, the NHL made the bold move of doublling in size from
six to 12 teams. It was the largest, single-year expansion in the history of pro
sports, splitting the league into two divisions: East and West. Two more clubs
were added by the NHL in 1970, 1972 and 1974.*

LOS ANGELES KINGS
[FRANCHISE DATE: June 5, 1967]

MAPLE LEAF GARDENS, Wed. Oct. 25, 1967
MAPLE LEAFS 4, KINGS 2. TORONTO SCORERS: JIM PAPPIN, RON
ELLIS, BOB PULFORD, FRANK MAHOVLICH. LOS ANGELES SCOR-
ERS: BILL FLETT, ED JOYAL. The Maple Leafs' first game against the
1967 expansion teams ended on a happy note and the surprising Kings
suffered their first NHL loss after seven games. The Los Angeles players
skated out in their bright gold road uniforms with purple pants and
numbering. It marked the return to Toronto of goalie Terry Sawchuk,
whom the Kings had selected in the expansion draft. Sawchuk's bril-

liance had helped Leafs win the Stanley Cup just six months earlier and he received a huge ovation when he skated out as third star of the hockey game. Also returning was Kings' coach Leonard (Red) Kelly — also a member of the '67 Stanley Cup team. Bob Pulford broke a 2-2 tie with the eventual winner at 15:55 of the second period. Frank Mahovlich scored on Sawchuk to ice the victory with 5:46 left in the game. Despite the win, the Leafs were generally lacklustre. "It's tough to get up for games like this, but we've got to do it," admitted Dave Keon. "I mean, how many scoring chances did the Kings really have in the last 25 minutes? I'll tell you — ONE. We had the game in hand and we knew it." Gord Labossiere of the Kings had three good chances to score with the game tied 2-2 but Leaf goalie Bruce Gamble came up big each time. Sawchuk made breakaway saves on Mahovlich and Ellis.

LOS ANGELES SPORTS ARENA, Thu. Nov. 9, 1967
KINGS 4, MAPLE LEAFS 1. TORONTO SCORER: BOB PULFORD. LOS ANGELES SCORERS: ED JOYAL (2), DALE ROLFE, BRIAN SMITH. The Kings avenged their loss in Toronto and handed the Maple Leafs their first of many defeats in 1967-68 against the expansion clubs. Bob Pulford scored Toronto's lone goal at 16:03 of the second period, but L.A. was already ahead 3-0. With owner Jack Kent Cooke's Forum still under construction in suburban Inglewood, the game was played at the Los Angeles Sports Arena in front of 9,604 fans. The Kings split their early season home games between the Sports Arena and the Long Beach Arena. The story of the game was Kings' rookie goaltender Wayne Rutledge, who stopped 29 shots despite playing with no mask and a broken nose. His biggest save was on a Jim Pappin breakaway late in the first period with the Kings leading 1-0. Leaf coach Punch Imlach tried a number of strange ploys to get his team going. He pulled goalie Johnny Bower with four minutes left, only to see Ed Joyal of Los Angeles pot an empty net goal. He also used defenceman Tim Horton on right wing a few times. The victory was sweet for Kings' coach Red Kelly. "Don't forget one thing: they won the Stanley Cup and we beat them," he said. "We could have beaten them in Toronto, too. They said we will be a last-place club. So what has happened? We've played seven games against the old clubs and won three." The win left the Kings and Leafs tied atop the overall NHL standings with 17 points apiece.

CALIFORNIA SEALS
[FRANCHISE DATE: June 5, 1967 / FINAL SEASON: 1975-76]

MAPLE LEAF GARDENS, Sat. Oct. 28, 1967
MAPLE LEAFS 5, SEALS 2. TORONTO SCORERS: JIM PAPPIN (2), TIM HORTON, RON ELLIS, GEORGE ARMSTRONG. CALIFORNIA SCORERS: BILL HICKE, GEORGE SWARBRICK. Chosen by many observers to be the best of the expansion teams, the Seals were floundering late in games. And it happened again in their first visit to Toronto. "This is the fifth game in a row we've blown in the third period, you can look it up," fumed California coach Bert Olmstead, a former Maple Leaf. "Something always happens between the eighth and 12th minute and we go to pieces. I can't explain it." The Seals took a 2-1 lead into the third but yielded four unanswered goals. Jim Pappin tied it early and then Ron Ellis, Pappin, and George Armstrong poured three past Charlie Hodge in a 4:54 span midway through the period. The game marked the return to Toronto of former Maple Leaf defenceman Bob Baun as captain of the Seals. Leaf coach Punch Imlach wasn't happy with his team's effort. "We played a lousy first period," he said. "We were a little better in the second but that Hodge stopped everything. I was worried it could turn out to be one of those games." Hodge was indeed very good as the Maple Leafs outshot California 48-29.

OAKLAND COLISEUM-ARENA, Wed. Nov. 8, 1967
MAPLE LEAFS 6, SEALS 1. TORONTO SCORERS: MURRAY OLIVER (2), JIM PAPPIN (2), RON ELLIS, ALLAN STANLEY. CALIFORNIA SCORER: AUT ERICKSON. Maple Leafs began their first-ever trip to the west coast with another easy win over the Seals. Hockey writer George Gross, who covered the game for the Toronto *Telegram*, described the rather strange atmosphere in and around the Oakland arena: "Ushers wearing white gloves escorted patrons to their seats. Hot-dog sellers wore candy striped jackets and straw hats. And to top it off, someone at the box office asked for four tickets on the 50-yard line." Only 4,749 fans showed up for the game, leaving more than two-thirds of the stands empty. Celebrating his 43rd birthday, Leaf goalie Johnny Bower received a cake from Seals' owner Barry Van Gerbig. Bower blew out the candles in a pre-game ceremony at center ice. He then stymied the California players in the first period, as the Leafs were outshot 16-4 but led 1-0 on a goal by Ron Ellis. Ex-Leaf defenceman Kent Douglas, the NHL's top rookie in 1962-63, was benched by an angry Seals' coach Bert

Olmstead. "He must be 15 pounds overweight," Olmstead growled. "He is not as important to the team as he thinks he is. I benched him hoping it would hurt his feelings. I'm certainly disappointed in his play."

MINNESOTA NORTH STARS
[FRANCHISE DATE: June 5, 1967 / FINAL SEASON: 1992-93]

METROPOLITAN SPORTS CENTER, Sat. Nov. 11, 1967
NORTH STARS 2, MAPLE LEAFS 1. MINNESOTA SCORERS: BOB WOYTOWICH, ANDRE BOUDRIAS. TORONTO SCORER: RON ELLIS. Maple Leafs lost their second consecutive game to an expansion team, coming off the defeat in Los Angeles two nights earlier. And it had quite an effect on the Toronto hierarchy. In the second intermission, with Minnesota leading 2-1, Leaf president Stafford Smythe asked his North Star counterpart Gordon Ritz to show him the way to the Toronto dressing room. Once there, Smythe unloaded on his players. "You are the world's champions and you should play like champions," he roared. "Instead, you're playing like a bunch of beginners." Punch Imlach wasn't in the room. He was outside in the corridor kicking a wall in anger. "We are doing more for expansion than anybody in the world," Imlach would say after the game. "And believe me, I hate it. They should send us around the league if they want to make sure expansion is a success." Andre Boudrias scored the game winner at 17:52 of the second period. Leafs were outshot 36-14 but Bruce Gamble was brilliant in goal. Ron Ellis tied the score at 1-1 with one second remaining in the first period. "I thought that goal would kill them, that we'd romp home easy," said Leaf vice-president King Clancy. Adding insult to injury, roommates George Armstrong and Johnny Bower missed the team bus to the Minneapolis airport the next morning. They didn't hear their alarm clock and woke up when Clancy phoned them from the airport.

MAPLE LEAF GARDENS, Wed. Nov. 22, 1967
MAPLE LEAFS 3, NORTH STARS 0. TORONTO SCORERS: MIKE WALTON, WAYNE CARLETON, TIM HORTON. Bruce Gamble recorded his first NHL shutout since March, 1965, when he made his debut with the Maple Leafs and had four shutouts in eight games. Otherwise, the victory over Minnesota was anything but a thrill. "It was almost as interesting as watching an hour of soil erosion," wrote Paul Dulmage in the *Telegram*. Leafs were even better than the final score indicated. They

came flying out of the gate and had three good chances to score on Cesare Maniago in the first 30 seconds. Maniago stopped Mike Walton on a breakaway, then rebound attempts by Wayne Carleton and George Armstrong. Walton and Carleton did score later in the period. Tim Horton added one in the second. The game was played on the 50th anniverssary of the day the National Hockey League was formed in 1917.

ST. LOUIS BLUES
[FRANCHISE DATE: June 5, 1967]

ST. LOUIS ARENA, Sun. Dec. 10, 1967
BLUES 2, MAPLE LEAFS 1. TORONTO SCORER: JIM PAPPIN. ST. LOUIS SCORERS: FRANK ST. MARSEILLE, DICKIE MOORE. Making the second comeback of his NHL career, former Montreal and Toronto winger Dickie Moore scored the winning goal for St. Louis in just his second game with the club. Moore had joined the Blues the previous night in Oakland. Against the Leafs, he took a pass from Tim Ecclestone and faked defenceman Larry Hillman and goalie Bruce Gamble to pot the winner at 11:20 of the third period. "It felt great," said Moore, 36. "It's been a long time between goals." Leaf coach Punch Imlach was speechless after the loss. He stormed out of the dressing room, slammed the door, and marched away in disgust. King Clancy spoke for Imlach: "Did you ever see anything like that performance? The worst yet. Absolutely the worst." The outcome might have been different if not for the superb goaltending of Glenn Hall, who stopped Bob Pulford and Ron Ellis on clear-cut breakaways.

MAPLE LEAF GARDENS, Sat. Dec. 30, 1967
MAPLE LEAFS 8, ST. LOUIS 1. TORONTO SCORERS: FRANK MAHOVLICH (3), MIKE WALTON (2), JIM PAPPIN, GEORGE ARMSTRONG, RON ELLIS. ST. LOUIS SCORER: RED BERENSON. After beating the Penguins in St. Louis the night before, the Blues were a tired bunch and it showed. The team had awakened at 5 a.m. for the flight to Toronto, while the Maple Leafs were resting at home for three days. Seth Martin, goaltender for the 1962 world hockey champions from Trail, B.C. started in net for the Blues. But the former Smoke Eater pulled a groin-muscle and left the game with Toronto ahead 5-0 early in the second period. Rookie Don Caley replaced Martin — making his NHL debut. Leafs put this one away early, as Mike Walton scored twice, and

Jim Pappin once, in the first 3:07 of play. Frank Mahovlich scored three consecutive goals for the natural hattrick. "Leafs beat a tired hockey team," said Blues' general manger Lynn Patrick. Red Berenson ruined Johnny Bower's shutout bid with 4:31 left in the game. He fired a 20-foot backhander that deflected into the net off Maple Leaf defenceman Duane Rupp.

PITTSBURGH PENGUINS
[FRANCHISE DATE: June 5, 1967]

MAPLE LEAF GARDENS, Wed. Dec. 13, 1967
PENGUINS 2, MAPLE LEAFS 1. TORONTO SCORER: RON ELLIS. PITTSBURGH SCORERS: ART STRATTON, KEN SCHINKEL. Another loss to an expansion team finally sent Leaf coach Punch Imlach over the edge. After the game, he fined every player $100 for their inept performance. Leaf goalie Johnny Bower had to dish out an extra $75 after uncharacteristically losing his temper with referee Bob Sloan. With less than four minutes remaining in the game, Andy Bathgate of the Penguins broke down the left side and Bower came out to poke-check him. Bathgate lost control of the puck and fell to the ice, prompting Sloan to give Bower a two-minute tripping penalty. Bower sprinted out to center ice and lit into Sloan, who put his hands on his hips for a 10-minute misconduct. "That was the first time in my career that I skated after a referee and my first misconduct penalty," Bower said afterwards. "What was I supposed to do, let Andy skate in and score? It was a good sweep-check. I went for the puck, not Bathgate. It's the worst call I've seen in my career." Bathgate had a decidedly different story. "He hooked me from the side, I can still feel it," said the veteran forward. "He couldn't have gone for the puck because it rolled off my stick before he hooked me." Ken Schinkel netted the winner for Pittsburgh. Frank Mahovlich sent an errant pass onto the stick of Penguins' defenceman Noel Price and Schinkel tipped Price's shot past Bower at 8:59 of the third period. Pittsburgh goalie Les Binkley was the game's first star, having stopped Dave Keon an a pair of breakaways.

CIVIC ARENA, Fri. Jan. 12, 1968
PENGUINS 4, MAPLE LEAFS 3. TORONTO SCORERS: BRIAN CONACHER, MURRAY OLIVER, RON ELLIS. PITTSBURGH SCORERS: AB MCDONALD, BOB DILLABOUGH, LEO BOIVIN, ART

STRATTON. Following a second consecutive loss to the Penguins, Maple Leaf coach Punch Imlach repeated a familiar refrain. "We're the greatest thing to happen to expansion," he said. "We make these clubs look like champions and the fans love it." A crowd of 8,292 enjoyed the Leafs' first-ever visit to Pittsburgh. Art Stratton put the Penguins ahead 4-2 with the eventual winning goal at 1:43 of the third period. He dashed between Dave Keon and Frank Mahovlich to beat goalie Bruce Gamble. Tim Horton, celebrating his 38th birthday, was the only Leaf defenceman to play well. Veteran defenceman Leo Boivin of Pittsburgh was the game's first star, playing solidly and fighting with Bob Pulford in the dying minutes. "This was a big win for us," said Penguins' coach Red Sullivan. "It was also our best performance so far in this building."

PHILADELPHIA FLYERS
[FRANCHISE DATE: June 5, 1967]

MAPLE LEAF GARDENS, Wed. Jan. 24, 1968
FLYERS 2, MAPLE LEAFS 1. TORONTO SCORER: BOB PULFORD. PHILADELPHIA SCORERS: ED HOEKSTRA, CLAUDE LAFORGE. The story of the Flyers' first-ever visit to Toronto was 22-year-old rookie goaltender Doug Favell of Philadelphia. He stoned the Maple Leafs all night long, stopping 46 shots. He started by robbing Dave Keon from point-blank range in the first minute of the game. He then out-guessed Jim Pappin on a third-period breakaway with the score tied 1-1. "The saves on Keon and Pappin were my two toughest," said Favell, a native of nearby St. Catharines. "I was really excited before the game. I could hardly sleep last night." Claude LaForge scored the winner for Philadelphia at 11:34 of the third period when Tim Horton failed to take him out of the play. "Flyers really checked tonight and their defence was tough," said Maple Leaf Frank Mahovlich. "I hit Ed Van Impe three times and couldn't knock him off the puck." Bob Pulford scored the Leafs' only goal, beating Favell on the short side with a backhander at 3:11 of the second period.

THE SPECTRUM, Sun. Feb. 4, 1968
FLYERS 4, MAPLE LEAFS 1. TORONTO SCORER: PETER STEMKOWSKI. PHILADELPHIA SCORERS: JOHN MISZUK (2), CLAUDE LAFORGE, DON BLACKBURN. The Maple Leafs' first visit to Philadelphia capped off a perfect weekend for the Flyers, who had beaten Chicago 5-3 at home the previous night. Both games drew sellout

crowds to the Spectrum. Defenceman John Miszuk scored twice for Philadelphia — his first goal a shorthanded effort at 8:08 of the opening period. With Joe Watson in the penalty box, Forbes Kennedy chopped the puck away from Jim Pappin. Claude LaForge and Miszuk went in on a 2-on-1 break and Miszuk scored on Johnny Bower. Wayne Carleton made a nice play in the corner to set up Peter Stemkowski with the Leafs' only goal. It tied the game at 10:58 of the first. "The Flyers were skating tonight," said Leaf coach Punch Imlach. "They scored on their chances then made us do the work." Typical of the Maple Leafs' luck around the net was Mike Walton having Doug Favell at his mercy in the final minute of the game, only to shoot the puck over top the Philadelphia goal. Favell was excellent once again as the Leafs outshot the Flyers 44-36.

VANCOUVER CANUCKS
[FRANCHISE DATE: May 22, 1970]

PACIFIC COLISEUM, Sun. Oct. 11, 1970
CANUCKS 5, MAPLE LEAFS 3. TORONTO SCORERS: NORM ULLMAN, BRAD SELWOOD, DAVE KEON. VANCOUVER SCORERS: WAYNE MAKI (2), ORLAND KURTENBACH, DANNY JOHNSON, ANDRE BOUDRIAS. The expansion Canucks won their first-ever NHL game in their second home start, spoiling the Maple Leafs' 1970-71 season opener. Vancouver had lost its inaugural game, two nights earlier, to Los Angeles. This game was surprisingly no contest, as Vancouver led 5-0 before the Leafs scored their first goal — Norm Ullman finally breaking the ice at 9:07 of the third period. "I thought we were really worked up for this game but we just had no zip," said Maple Leaf coach Johnny McLellan. "Vancouver played well and checked the hell out of us. They outhustled and outbumped us too." Leafs failed to capitalize on a five-minute powerplay early in the game. The Canucks received a major for starting the incorrect line-up. Canucks' coach Hal Laycoe pencilled in Len Lunde to start at center ahead of veteran Andre Boudrias, who complained of abdominal pains. But team doctors cleared Boudrias to play and Laycoe failed to make the correction on the game sheet. Ullman scored the Leafs' first goal of the season, stealing the puck from defenceman Marc Reaume and beating veteran goalie Charlie Hodge. One fan was overheard to say, "This makes up for the football game last night," — referring to a 50-7 romp by the Argonauts over the B.C. Lions at C.N.E Stadium in Toronto.

MAPLE LEAF GARDENS, Wed. Nov. 11, 1970
CANUCKS 4, MAPLE LEAFS 2. TORONTO SCORERS: PAUL HENDERSON, BILL MacMILLAN. VANCOUVER SCORERS: RAY CULLEN (2), ROSAIRE PAIEMENT, BARRY WILKINS. The Canucks made it two in a row over the Maple Leafs in their first-ever visit to the Gardens. And Vancouver had played the night before, losing 6-3 in Boston. Ray Cullen and Paul Henderson traded goals in the first period, but Vancouver got the next three. Rosaire Paiement put the Canucks ahead to stay at 3:22 of the second period. Andre Boudrias dug the puck free from Dave Keon after a pile-up along the boards and sent Paiement in on Bruce Gamble. "(Referee) Art Skov had his whistle in his mouth and Keon thought he'd stop play," Boudrias explained. "So, he eased up and I got the puck. In this game, you never ease up." Vancouver rookie defenceman Dale Tallon made his return to the Gardens, where he had starred for the Junior Marlboros. "It feels super to win here," Tallon said. "I played only defensively tonight because I was tired from last night's game in Boston. But, I wasn't nervous." The Canucks had chosen Tallon second-overall in the 1970 amateur draft, behind Buffalo's selection of Gilbert Perreault.

BUFFALO SABRES
[FRANCHISE DATE: May 22, 1970]

MAPLE LEAF GARDENS, Wed. Nov. 18, 1970
SABRES 7, MAPLE LEAFS 2. TORONTO SCORERS: GARRY MONAHAN, MIKE WALTON. BUFFALO SCORERS: GERRY MEEHAN (2), LARRY KEENAN (2), DONNY MARSHALL, STEVE ATKINSON, PAUL ANDREA. This game will always be remembered for Punch Imlach's triumphant return to Toronto. Fired by the Maple Leafs after their 1969 playoff loss to Boston, Imlach quickly re-surfaced as general manager and coach of Buffalo's NHL expansion team and the Sabres blasted the Leafs in their first visit to the Gardens. When Imlach appeared behind the bench to start the game, the Leaf fans rose in a long and heartfelt ovation for the man who had guided their team to four Stanley Cups in the 1960s. "I was deeply touched," Imlach later said. "I've always said Toronto fans were good to me. They stayed that way and I'm grateful." While driving to Toronto for the game, Imlach received thumbs-up signals from motorists who recognized him. When legendary broadcaster Foster Hewitt dropped by to see him before the game,

Imlach said, "Have a good game, Foster. I hope you'll be able to say at the end that the final score is Buffalo 4, Toronto 1." The Sabres were even better than that, scoring the final five goals of the game to win handily. Larry Keenan broke a 2-2 tie at 6:45 of the second period and Buffalo never looked back. Veteran goalie Roger Crozier was excellent, stopping 44 of 46 Leaf shots.

MEMORIAL AUDITORIUM, Sun. Dec. 13, 1970
MAPLE LEAFS 4, SABRES 0. TORONTO SCORERS: NORM ULLMAN (2), RON ELLIS, JIM HARRISON. The Maple Leafs' first-ever visit to Buffalo has been well-documented through the years in the tragic story of Brian Spencer. A rookie with the Leafs, Spencer played in Buffalo despite the shooting death of his father just 24 hours earlier. Roy Spencer was killed by RCMP officers in Prince George, B.C. after he forced television station CKPG off the air at gun-point. He was insensed at the station's choice of showing the California at Vancouver NHL game, rather than Chicago at Toronto, where his son was playing his first Saturday night game with the Leafs. Brian was told of the shooting only seconds after emerging from a between-periods interview with Ward Cornell. Remarkably, he not only played in Buffalo the following night, but he set up the first two Leaf goals and was named first star. "My father always wanted me to be an NHL player," Spencer said afterwards. "He wanted me to be a hockey player more than anything else. That's why I'm playing." Spencer skated on a line with veterans Norm Ullman and Ron Ellis and assisted on a goal by each player as Leafs took a 2-0 lead in the first period. Bruce Gamble recorded his second consecutive shutout in net for the Leafs. Ironically, Spencer would also be killed by a gunshot blast just more than 17 years later in West Palm Beach, Fla.

ATLANTA FLAMES
[FRANCHISE DATE: June 6, 1972 / FINAL SEASON: 1979-80]

THE OMNI, Sun. Nov. 5, 1972
MAPLE LEAFS 2, FLAMES 2. TORONTO SCORERS: DARRYL SITTLER, DAVE KEON. ATLANTA SCORERS: JACQUES RICHARD, RON HARRIS. A mistake by defenceman Mike Pelyk cost the Maple Leafs a victory in their first-ever game against the Flames. His clearing attempt was gloved down by Atlanta defenceman Randy Manery, who fed Ron Harris for a slapshot that beat goalie Jacques Plante at 11:20 of the third

period. Leaf coach Johnny McLellan wasn't impressed. "Pelyk goes and throws the puck to the point," the coach complained. "He should know better." A crowd of 10,732 showed up at the Omni to see the Maple Leafs for the first time. It was sunny and 70 degrees in Atlanta and the Leafs didn't seem to have a lot of energy. "You can't go all out every time for 78 games," said Leaf captain Dave Keon. The game featured a quick but interesting boxing match between Leaf defenceman John Grisdale and former Leaf Pat Quinn, then with Atlanta. They dropped their gloves and circled one another, waiting for an opening. Grisdale unleashed a vicious right that missed Quinn. The force of the blow spun him around and he was wide open for a Quinn karate chop that sent him to the ice. Linesmen then moved in.

MAPLE LEAF GARDENS, Wed. Nov. 15, 1972
MAPLE LEAFS 2, FLAMES 1. TORONTO SCORERS: RON ELLIS, RICK KEHOE. ATLANTA SCORER: JOHN STEWART. The Maple Leafs scored two goals in 39 seconds midway through the second period to ruin Atlanta's first visit to Toronto. Ron Ellis scored the first one, deflecting Dave Keon's pass behind goalie Dan Bouchard at 10:26. Rick Kehoe then slipped behind Flames' defenceman Randy Manery and took Darryl Sittler's pass to make it 2-1 Leafs at 11:05. John Stewart had opened the scoring for Atlanta at 9:53 of the first period. Pat Quinn of the Flames got a roughing penalty midway through the third period for punching Sittler. The call, by rookie referee Peter Moffatt, upset Atlanta coach Bernie (Boom Boom) Geoffrion. "Why do they always do that to us?" he asked, in reference to the league's choice of officials. "That guy couldn't referee Midget. He gave Quinn a roughing penalty when Sittler hit our goalie. What the hell kind of refereeing is that?" Leafs outshot Atlanta 42-27.

NEW YORK ISLANDERS
[FRANCHISE DATE: June 6, 1972]

MAPLE LEAF GARDENS, Wed. Jan. 10, 1973
MAPLE LEAFS 4, ISLANDERS 2. TORONTO SCORERS: PAUL HENDERSON (2), ERROL THOMPSON, DAVE KEON. ISLANDER SCORERS: BILLY HARRIS, BRIAN LAVENDER. Paul Henderson scored his 200th and 201st career goals to give Leafs a victory in their first-ever

meeting with the Islanders. His milestone tally opened the scoring at 13:53 of the first period. Henderson drifted behind the Islander defence and took a perfect lead-in pass from Jim McKenny to beat Gerry Desjardins with a backhander. He then scored the clincher at 10:14 of the third period, on passes from Norm Ullman and Pierre Jarry. "I guess it proves I perform better with a few days' rest," Henderson said. "When you don't work Monday and Tuesday, you get a chance to recover from the bruising you took on the weekend." Dave Keon scored the winning third Maple Leaf goal for his 19th of the season, one more than his total for the previous year (1971-72). Desjardins stopped McKenny's shot from the point, but Keon pounced on the rebound. Islander rookie Billy Harris scored in his return to the Gardens, where he starred for the Junior Marlboros. Ron Low was sharp in goal for the Leafs, winning his fifth consecutive start.

NASSAU COLISEUM, Tue. Feb. 6, 1973
ISLANDERS 4, MAPLE LEAFS 2. TORONTO SCORERS: DARRYL SITTLER, RICK KEHOE. ISLANDER SCORERS: GERMAIN GAGNON, BOB COOK, BILLY HARRIS, NEIL NICHOLSON. The expansion Islanders avenged their earlier loss to the Maple Leafs, improving their puny record to 7-43-5. They would win only 12 games all season. A crowd of 10,676 watched the Leafs play on Long Island for the first time and saw former Marlie Billy Harris have another great game. Harris scored the Islanders' winning third goal at 12:47 of the second period and he added an assist on Neil Nicholson's clincher two minutes later. Harris's goal gave him 17 for the season. Only Steve Vickers of the Rangers had more among rookies (20) and Vickers would go on to win the Calder Trophy. Islander coach Earl Ingarfield, who won his first game since taking over the previous week from Phil Goyette, praised Harris. "He's doing all the things now that an NHL winger has to do," Ingarfield told Frank Orr in the Toronto *Star*. "He's scoring, making plays, back-checking and digging effectively in the corners." Added Islander general manager Bill Torrey: "Harris deserves attention in the Calder voting. He hasn't had an experienced linemate to help him and he's under pressure as the top draft choice with a big contract." Darryl Sittler had opened the scoring for the Leafs only 1:56 into the game but Toronto did not score again on Billy Smith until Rick Kehoe's marker at 15:04 of the third.

KANSAS CITY SCOUTS
[FRANCHISE DATE: June 11, 1974 / FINAL SEASON: 1975-76]

MAPLE LEAF GARDENS, Wed. Oct. 9, 1974
MAPLE LEAFS 6, SCOUTS 2. TORONTO SCORERS: LYLE MOFFAT, RON ELLIS, JIM MCKENNY, DARRYL SITTLER, IAN TURNBULL, DAVE KEON. KANSAS CITY SCORERS: SIMON NOLET, LYNN POWIS. The Maple Leafs spoiled Kansas City's NHL debut, romping to an easy victory in the 1974-75 season opener. Famed broadcaster Gordon Sinclair dropped the ceremonial first puck. Maple Leaf rookie Lyle Moffat opened the scoring with his first (of 12) NHL goals (he would score 10 with Winnipeg in 1979-80). Dave Keon notched his 350th career goal to close out the scoring with 1:10 left in the game. It was anything but entertaining, as the under-talented Scouts employed a clutch-and-grab style. "I was hoping to keep it close and we would have if some of our kids hadn't gotten over-anxious," said Kansas City coach Bep Guidolin. "They wound up out of position and took foolish penalties, paving the way for three Leaf powerplay goals." The frustration got to Scouts' winger Robin Burns (who wore No. 13 on his Kansas City sweater). He was handed a tripping penalty in the third period, and referee Bob Myers tacked on a 10-minute misconduct when Burns shot the puck away from him. "They gave it a hang of a try for Bep," said Leaf coach Red Kelly. "They stayed close to us with a flat-out effort but we skated away from them in the third period"

KEMPER ARENA, Thu. Feb. 6, 1975
SCOUTS 3, MAPLE LEAFS 2. TORONTO SCORERS: BLAINE STOUGHTON, DAVE (TIGER) WILLIAMS. KANSAS CITY SCORERS: SIMON NOLET, DAVE HUDSON, GARY COULTER. After impressive victories over Boston and St. Louis, the Maple Leafs laid an egg in their first visit to Kansas City. Kemper Memorial Arena was less than half-filled with 7,128 on hand and the Scouts improved their expansion-year record to 11-34-7. Frank Orr covered the game for the Toronto *Star* and wrote: "Since 1967, the Leafs have waged a one-team campaign to make expansion work — a program they're continuing this season." Leafs had already lost once to the Washington Capitals, a club that would win only eight of its 80 games. Leafs turned in a listless effort, especially in the second period, when Kansas City scored all three of its goals and held an 18-5 edge in shots. "I keep telling my players that if you have a system and work hard, you can accomplish a hell of a lot," said Scouts' coach Bep

Guidolin. Goalies Doug Favell of Toronto and Denis Herron of Kansas City were both sharp.

WASHINGTON CAPITALS
[FRANCHISE DATE: June 11, 1974]

CAPITAL CENTER, Sun. Oct. 27, 1974
MAPLE LEAFS 4, CAPITALS 3. TORONTO SCORERS: GEORGE FERGUSON (2), INGE HAMMARSTROM, DARRYL SITTLER. WASHINGTON SCORERS: RON ANDERSON, GORD SMITH. In their first-ever game against the Capitals, the Maple Leafs broke a six-game winless streak and rebounded from a 9-3 pounding by Chicago the previous night in Toronto. George Ferguson scored the winning goal, his second of the night, at 9:01 of the third period. He used his speed to slip behind the Washington defence, took a pass from Ian Turnbull, and beat former Leaf netminder Ron Low. Ferguson played on a checking line with Errol Thompson and Lanny McDonald. "I have a little more conficence now to move into the other team's zone and make things happen," Ferguson said. "Having wingers who check well the way McDonald and Thompson do is a big help. I know they'll cover up for me if I take a chance." Ironically, the roles would be reversed a year later. McDonald and Thompson would join Darryl Sittler on an explosive scoring unit, while Ferguson would return to his more customary defensive role. A crowd of 10,106 watched the game in Landover, Md. Washington defenceman Greg Joly, the No. 1 selection in the 1974 amateur draft, played only four shifts. "Joly simply isn't working hard enough," said Capitals' coach Jim Anderson. "For a kid making his money ($150,000/year), he just isn't putting out."

MAPLE LEAF GARDENS, Sat. Nov. 30, 1974
MAPLE LEAFS 7, CAPITALS 1. TORONTO SCORERS: DARRYL SITTLER (2), DAVE KEON, INGE HAMMARSTROM, LANNY McDONALD, CLAIRE ALEXANDER, BILL FLETT. WASHINGTON SCORER: TOM WILLIAMS. Washington's first-ever visit to the Gardens was a great tonic for an injury riddled Maple Leaf team that had won only three of its previous 19 games. Goals by Darryl Sittler and Dave Keon late in the first period erased a 1-0 Washington lead and enabled Leafs to break an 0-5-1 slump. Defenceman Claire Alexander, a former milkman in Orillia, Ont., joined the Leafs from their farm club in Oklahoma City

and scored his first NHL goal in the third period. His services were required to compensate for injuries to fellow defencemen Borje Salming, Ian Turnbull and Rod Seiling. Things looked bad early for the Leafs. While ragging the puck trying to kill a penalty, Lanny McDonald fell down and allowed Washington's Tom Williams to score on a breakaway. It gave the Capitals a 1-0 lead at 14:34 of the first period, but Sittler tied it up just more than a minute later. "There's a little more life in the dressing room tonight because it's good to see a win and score a few goals for a change," said Leaf coach Red Kelly.

For the 1976-77 NHL season, two franchises switched locations. After nine years of playing before sparse crowds in Oakland, the California Golden Seals moved to Cleveland and became the Barons. And the Scouts abandoned Kansas City after two seasons, moved to Denver, and became the Colorado Rockies. The Barons would last only two years in Cleveland before merging with the Minnesota North Stars for the 1978-79 season.

COLORADO ROCKIES
[FRANCHISE DATE: Aug. 25, 1976 / FINAL SEASON: 1981-82]

McNICHOLS SPORTS ARENA, Tue. Oct. 5, 1976
ROCKIES 4, MAPLE LEAFS 2. TORONTO SCORERS: ERROL THOMPSON, BOB NEELY. COLORADO SCORERS: LARRY SKINNER, DAVE HUDSON, NELSON PYATT, WILF PAIEMENT. A sparse gathering of 7,359 attended Denver's NHL debut, but the fans enjoyed a victory over the Maple Leafs in the 1976-77 season opener for both clubs. The story of the game was Colorado goalie Doug Favell, who the Leafs had benched the previous year, and sold to the Rockies a month earlier. He played brilliantly, stopping 39 shots. When he left the game briefly with a leg cramp in the third period, the fans gave him a standing ovation. They rose to their feet again when he returned five minutes later. "Look, I love a crowd reaction like they gave me here, who wouldn't?" asked Favell. "Having the crowd in the corner revs my engines." On any revenge factor with Toronto, Favell said, "I'm happy to play well in my first game after what happened to me last season. But, most important is that the team won its first game in the NHL." Leaf coach Red Kelly felt the altitude in Denver may have contributed to his team's lacklustre

effort. But, as Lanny McDonald pointed out, "Both teams were at the same altitude, weren't they?" The Rockies led 2-0 before Errol Thompson scored for Toronto at 17:53 of the opening period.

MAPLE LEAF GARDENS, Sat. Dec. 18, 1976
MAPLE LEAFS 4, ROCKIES 2. TORONTO SCORERS: INGE HAMMARSTROM (2), JIM MCKENNY, DAVE (TIGER) WILLIAMS. COLORADO SCORERS: GARY CROTEAU, DAVE HUDSON. This game was notable for its inflated shot totals. Colorado out-gunned the Maple Leafs 53-51 and the clubs combined for 46 shots in the third period alone (25-21 for the Rockies). Wayne Thomas turned in a supernatural performance in the Maple Leaf goal, making 51 saves. Michel Plasse was almost as good for Colorado. Thomas had lost his starting job to rookie Mike Palmateer earlier in the season, but Palmateer was sidelined with an eye injury. "When Wayne was struggling early in the season, he didn't show the life he's shown in the past week," praised Leaf coach Red Kelly. "When he's moving and challenging everybody, he's just one fine goalie — among the best in the league." Jim McKenny and Inge Hammarstrom scored third-period goals to break a 2-2 tie. McKenny's goal was controversial, as the Rockies complained the puck did not fully cross the goal-line. Hammarstrom's clincher was his seventh goal in seven games. A brief stick fight ensued when the game ended between Scott Garland of the Leafs and Steve Durbano of Colorado. Durbano sliced open Garland's nose. Garland then tried to spear Durbano in the face, but only grazed his cheek. This is how the final shots on goal totals appeared:

	1	2	3	T
Colorado....	11	17	25	53
Toronto......	15	15	21	51

CLEVELAND BARONS
[FRANCHISE DATE: July 14, 1976 / FINAL SEASON: 1977-78]

RICHFIELD COLISEUM, Mon. Nov. 1, 1976
MAPLE LEAFS 6, BARONS 3. TORONTO SCORERS: DARRYL SITTLER (2), LANNY McDONALD (2), GEORGE FERGUSON, BOB NEELY. CLEVELAND SCORERS: AL MacADAM (2), GREG SMITH. Moving east from Oakland didn't do much for the Barons' attendance figures, as evidenced by an embarrassingly small gethering to watch the Maple Leafs for the first time. Only 3,488 fans showed up in the 18,544-seat

Richfield Coliseum and the Leafs kept them quiet for most of the evening. Rookie goalie Mike Palmateer won for the third consecutive game since being called up to replace the struggling Wayne Thomas. Palmateer had previous victories in Detroit and Minnesota. The Leafs did big damage against Cleveland in the final minutes of the first period. With the Barons trailing 2-1, Lanny McDonald scored at 18:28 and Darryl Sittler at 18:54 to give the Leafs a comfortable advantage. Sittler scored again 17 seconds into the middle period and it was all over. Cleveland fought back to make it 5-3 in the third, but Palmateer then made a dazzling stop on veteran Jim Pappin of the Barons. He had also charged 35 feet out of his net in the second to thwart Wayne Merrick on a break. Tiger Williams of the Leafs was given a gross-misconduct penalty for pulling the hair of Cleveland's Fred Ahern during a second-period fight.

MAPLE LEAF GARDENS, Sun. Nov. 28, 1976
MAPLE LEAFS 5, BARONS 1. TORONTO SCORERS: BORJE SALMING, STAN WEIR, IAN TURNBULL, INGE HAMMARSTRON, JACK VALIQUETTE. CLEVELAND SCORER: DAVE GARDNER. The Maple Leafs eased to victory in Cleveland's first visit to the Gardens, capping off a busy sports day in Toronto. Earlier in the afternoon, Ottawa had beaten Saskatchewan in the 1976 Grey Cup Game at Exhibition Stadium on a last-minute touchdown pass from Tom Clements to Tony Gabriel. It took the Leafs far less time to thwart the Barons. Borje Salming got things rolling only 16 seconds after the opening faceoff, beating Gilles Meloche to put Leafs ahead 1-0. Stan Weir scored the eventual winner at 12:51 of the first. The Maple Leafs won for the second consecutive night at home, having defeated Boston 4-2 on Saturday. Leafs had won only three of their first nine home games prior to the weekend sweep. The Barons, on the other hand, were in a tailspin. "In four games we've scored four goals so it's clear what our problem is," said Cleveland coach Jack (Tex) Evans. Former Marlie great Dave Gardner scored the Barons' only goal, on the powerplay, at 4:36 of the second period. He later left the game with a knee injury.

———————————————————————

The second-largest expansion in the history of the NHL took place for the 1979-80 season. After seven years as a rival league (1972 - 1979), the World Hockey Association folded, and its four strongest franchises merged with the NHL — three of them representing Canadian cities.

HARTFORD WHALERS
[FRANCHISE DATE: June 22, 1979]

MAPLE LEAF GARDENS, Wed. Oct. 31, 1979
WHALERS 4, MAPLE LEAFS 2. TORONTO SCORERS: WALT
McKECHNIE, PAUL GARDNER. HARTFORD SCORERS: RAY
ALLISON, DAVE KEON, BLAINE STOUGHTON, GORDIE HOWE.
This night will always be remembered for the triumphant return of
hockey legends Gordie Howe and Dave Keon to Maple Leaf Gardens.
Both men had played in the WHA, but were now back in the NHL after
a lengthy absence. Howe, 51, hadn't played against the Maple Leafs since
retiring from the Detroit Red Wings in 1971, while Keon, 39, had bolted
the Leafs to join the Minnesota Fighting Saints in 1975. That Keon and
Howe both scored goals in Hartford's victory over the Maple Leafs made
the evening even more magical. Keon was still the Leafs' all-time scoring
leader and he received a long standing ovation when he appeared with
his Whaler teammates to start the game. The fans stood and cheered
again after his goal at 8:43 of the second period. Leaf goalie Mike
Palmateer came out of his net to cut down the angle on a shot by Blaine
Stoughton (another former Leaf) and Keon converted the rebound
before Palmateer could recover. It put Hartford in front to stay, 2-1. "The
reception was very nice," Keon said later. "I guess I expected some sort
of recognition, but nothing like that." Howe scored his goal at 8:57 of the
third period. While his son, Mark, cruised to the Leaf net as a decoy,
Gordie let fly with a 30-foot wrist-shot that beat a partially screened
Palmateer to the top right-hand corner. Again, the crowd stood and
cheered. "Toronto fans have always been my favourites," Howe said. "It
was great to see how they received Davey (Keon)." Walt McKechnie had
opened the scoring for Toronto at 3:56 of the first period. But, the Leafs
didn't score again until 10:29 of the third, and the Whalers had the game
well in hand. Keon was chosen the game's number-one star. Hartford
wore bright green road uniforms, with blue and white trim.

SPRINGFIELD CIVIC CENTER, Fri. Nov. 2, 1979
WHALERS 5, MAPLE LEAFS 3. TORONTO SCORERS: DARRYL
SITTLER (2), DAN MALONEY. HARTFORD SCORERS: GORDIE HOWE
(2), MARK HOWE, MIKE ROGERS, AL HANGSLEBEN. Two nights
after their victory in Toronto, the Whalers and Gordie Howe beat the
Maple Leafs once again. The roof of the Hartford Civic Center had caved
in under a heavy snowfall in January, 1978, so the Whalers played their

early NHL home games in Springfield, Mass. A sellout crowd of 7,621 saw Howe, the 51-year-old grandfather of two, score a pair of goals. He put Hartford ahead 2-0 midway through the first period, then gave the Whalers a 5-1 lead early in the third. "Winning these two games over the Leafs is a big boost for us," Howe said. "It's funny, but I have five goals on only a very few shots. I hope that scoring touch continues." Dave Keon also found his way onto the scoresheet once again, sending Al Hangsleben in alone for the Whalers' fourth goal. Struggling Leaf defenceman Ian Turnbull did not dress for the game, and he left the arena in a huff. "I don't really know why this happened because I haven't been told," Turnbull said. "But, it's their hockey club so they can do whatever they want." Darryl Sittler scored twice for the Leafs in a losing cause.

WINNIPEG JETS
[FRANCHISE DATE: June 22, 1979]

WINNIPEG ARENA, Sat. Nov. 10, 1979
MAPLE LEAFS 8, JETS 4. TORONTO SCORERS: DARRYL SITTLER (2), LAURIE BOSCHMAN (2), BORJE SALMING, ROCKY SAGANIUK, LANNY McDONALD, DAN MALONEY. WINNIPEG SCORERS: WILLY LINDSTROM, RON WILSON, GORD McTAVISH, PETER MARSH. The loud and ugly feud between Maple Leaf captain Darryl Sittler and recycled general manager Punch Imlach began two nights before this victory in Winnipeg. While the Leafs were in St. Louis, Imlach told reporters he thought Sittler had lost a step. Sittler said he would not apologize for the way he was playing, and the war was on. But the veteran center came through with a pair of goals in the Leafs' first-ever game against Winnipeg. He was part of a five-goal Maple Leaf explosion in a 4:49 span during the latter half of the second period. It converted a 4-2 deficit to a 7-4 advantage heading into the third. Rockey Saganiuk scored a controversial goal to cut Winnipeg's lead to 3-2 at 8:04 of the second period. And it rattled veteran goalie Gary Smith, who felt Saganiuk batted the puck in with a high stick. Smith caved in at that point, allowed the five Leaf goals, and was replaced by former Leaf Pierre Hamel for the third period. Bobby Hull played for the Jets and set up Peter Marsh's second-period goal. Hull would play 18 games in a Winnipeg uniform before finishing his pro hockey career later that season with Hartford. It was moments after this game that the famed

Mississauga, Ont. train derailment and explosion took place, forcing the largest peace-time evacuation in Canadian history. More than 250,000 residents of the town west of Toronto left their homes for two days as authorities feared an outbreak of illness from toxic fumes.

MAPLE LEAF GARDENS, Sat. Dec. 29, 1979
MAPLE LEAFS 6, JETS 1. TORONTO SCORERS: ROCKY SAGANIUK (2), WALT McKECHNIE, IAN TURNBULL, BOB STEPHENSON, DAVE (TIGER) WILLIAMS. WINNIPEG SCORER: BILL RILEY. The seven-week-long Sittler/Imlach feud came to a head before this game when Sittler cut the captain's "C" off his uniform. It was a reaction to Imlach's trade the previous day of prolific winger Lanny McDonald (Sittler's best friend) to Colorado. In a move heavily designed at weakening Sittler's influence on the club, Imlach dealt McDonald and defenceman Joel Quennville to the Rockies for forwards Wilf Paiement and Pat Hickey. It followed, by four days, the trade of another Sittler ally, Pat Boutette, to Hartford for unheralded winger Bob Stephenson. Sittler felt he could no longer perform the required duties of a captain, and his removal of the "C" before the game infuriated Imlach. "Unbelievable... he had all day to do it," growled Punch. "It just shows." The trades seemed not to hurt the Leafs in Winnipeg's first visit to the Gardens. Hickey and Stephenson both played; Stephenson scoring once and setting up another. "They both played well and I feel they'll get better," said coach Floyd Smith. "I know what kind of wheels Stephenson has because I saw him last year in the WHA when I was coaching Cincinnati and he was with Birmingham. I know what he can do." Leafs broke open a close game by scoring four unanswered goals in the third period. Paiement did not arrive in time to suit up.

EDMONTON OILERS
[FRANCHISE DATE: June 22, 1979]

NORTHLANDS COLISEUM, Sun. Nov. 11, 1979
MAPLE LEAFS 6, OILERS 3. TORONTO SCORERS: RON ELLIS (2), ROCKY SAGANIUK, JOHN ANDERSON, DAVE (TIGER) WILLIAMS, JERRY BUTLER. EDMONTON SCORERS: STAN WEIR, DAN NEWMAN, BRETT CALLIGHEN. After beating the Jets in Winnipeg, the Leafs moved west to play the Oilers for the first time and the Sittler

controversy sparked them to another lop-sided victory. Veteran Ron Ellis led the way with a pair of goals and the 34-year-old winger, who had been a part of both Punch Imlach eras, left no doubt as to whose side he was on. "I'd like to make it clear — and I know every player on the team would say the same — that we were playing for No. 27 this weekend," offered the normally soft-spoken Ellis. "Imlach can say what he wants, but it shows the character there is on this team." Added Lanny McDonald: "We all wanted to win these games for the captain. The two games this weekend were like playoff games for us because we had such intensity." Leafs jumped all over the Oilers and led 4-0 by the 10:57 mark of the opening period, at which time Edmonton coach Glen Sather replaced starting goalie Eddie Mio with veteran Dave Dryden. Eighteen-year-old Wayne Gretzky recorded his first of many career points against the Maple Leafs, setting up Brett Callighen's second-period goal.

MAPLE LEAF GARDENS, Wed. Nov. 21, 1979
MAPLE LEAFS 4, OILERS 4. TORONTO SCORERS: JOHN ANDERSON, WALT McKECHNIE, JERRY BUTLER, ROCKY SAGANIUK. EDMONTON SCORERS: WAYNE GRETZKY (2), BRETT CALLIGHEN, BLAIR MacDONALD. Wayne Gretzky flashed the brilliance that would make him hockey's greatest star of the 1980s when he scored twice and set up the other two Edmonton goals in his first-ever NHL game at the Gardens. It was the final leg of a seven-game eastern road swing that had taken the Oilers through Detroit, Boston, Washington, Philadelphia, Hartford and Buffalo, before arriving in Toronto. Gretzky netted the tying goal with a marvelous individual effort on the powerplay at 13:39 of the third period. "I felt I played a better game in Philadelphia, but it was a big one here, playing before both my grandmothers," Gretzky said after his great performance. The Oilers had only three victories in their previous 20 games. Rocky Saganiuk had given the Maple Leafs a 4-3 lead at 5:58 of the final period, taking a pass from Laurie Boschman and lifting the puck over a fallen Dave Dryden. Lanny McDonald was benched by Leaf coach Floyd Smith in the third period. "I don't know what it is with us," said Maple Leaf center Walt McKechnie. "It's as though our minds and legs aren't working together." To ensure that wouldn't continue, coach Smith pulled an Imlach-type move by ordering two workouts the following day — one at 9:30 a.m. and the other at 1:30 in the afternoon.

QUEBEC NORDIQUES
[FRANCHISE DATE: June 22, 1979]

THE COLISEE, Sun. Nov. 18, 1979
NORDIQUES 4, MAPLE LEAFS 2. TORONTO SCORERS: DARRYL SITTLER, DAN MALONEY. QUEBEC SCORERS: MICHEL GOULET (2), BOB FITCHNER, GARY LARIVIERE. Quebec goalie Michel Dion, who had played for Leaf coach Floyd Smith the previous year with Cincinnati of the WHA, turned in a sensational performance in the first-ever meeting between the Leafs and Nordiques. "I was psyched to play the Leafs, a team I had watched so many times as a kid," said Dion, a native of Granby, Que. The Maple Leafs came out strong and pressed hard for an early goal, but Dion made big saves on Darryl Sittler and John Anderson. Center Bob Fitchner put Quebec on the board at 6:31 with Ron Ellis in the penalty box, and Michel Goulet then clicked on a 4-on-1 break just more than a minute later. Sittler and Dan Maloney scored the Leaf goals, nine seconds apart, late in the second period. But, the Nordiques were already ahead 4-0. "We didn't know exactly what to expect playing in a new place with different fans," said veteran Leaf defenceman Dave Burrows. "The fans certainly gave their team a boost. We seemed to pick up when we started taking the body. But, it was too late by then. Maybe we should have started sooner."

MAPLE LEAF GARDENS, Sat. Jan. 5, 1980
NORDIQUES 7, MAPLE LEAFS 3. TORONTO SCORERS: WILF PAIEMENT, DARRYL SITTLER, JOHN ANDERSON. QUEBEC SCORERS: ROBBIE FTOREK (2), SERGE BERNIER, MARC TARDIF, REAL CLOUTIER, MICHEL GOULET, REG THOMAS. Quebec pounded the Maple Leafs in its first NHL visit to the Gardens, spoiling a milestone occasion for Darryl Sittler. The former Leaf captain scored his 300th career goal at 8:38 of the third period, but the Nords had an insurmountable 5-1 lead by that point. Sittler broke a 10-game scoring slump, becoming the 34th player in NHL history to reach 300 goals. He also moved into second place on the Maple Leafs' all-time points list with 714 (Dave Keon was still on top at the time with 858). Sittler wasn't in much of a mood to celebrate afterwards. "I was more concerned about going 10 games without a goal than getting number 300," he said. "Hopefully, I can start scoring again." Sittler scored the milestone goal on his one-time teammate, Ron Low. The third and fourth Quebec goals, scored 3:47

apart in the second period, occurred with the Nords holding a two-man advantage. Robbie Ftorek beat Leaf goalie Paul Harrison with a slapshot, then Marc Tardif converted Dale Hoganson's pass for the eventual winner. Leaf coach Floyd Smith was fuming after the game. "I've got nothing to say — write it as you saw it," he barked at reporters. With the loss, Leafs dropped into the Adams Division cellar, a point behind the expansion Nordiques.

After eight years in Atlanta, the Flames moved to Calgary for the 1980-81 season, becoming the NHL's seventh Canadian franchise.

CALGARY FLAMES
[FRANCHISE DATE: June 24, 1980]

STAMPEDE CORRAL, Thu. Oct. 23, 1980
MAPLE LEAFS 5, FLAMES 4. TORONTO SCORERS: ROCKY SAGANIUK (2), JOHN ANDERSON, LAURIE BOSCHMAN, RICK VAIVE. CALGARY SCORERS: BRAD SMITH, BOB MacMILLAN, ERIC VAIL, WILLIE PLETT. With the promise of a brand new arena (to be called the Olympic Saddledome), the Flames began their NHL tenure at the 6,492-seat Corral, on the Calgary Stampede grounds. And the Maple Leafs hog-tied them in their first visit to Cowtown. John Anderson, Laurie Boschman and Rocky Saganiuk scored first-period goals to give Toronto a 3-0 lead, but it was Saganiuk's second of the night — at 11:53 of the middle frame — that proved to be the winner. An overflow (standing-room) crowd of 7,243 watched the first-ever home-ice loss for the Calgary franchise. The victory improved the Maple Leafs' early season record to 5-1-1: the club's best start since 1944-45. Rick Vaive scored the key goal of the game at 6:58 of the second period. He converted Bill Derlago's pass only 25 seconds after Calgary's Bob MacMillan had cut Toronto's lead to 3-2. Future Maple Leaf Brad Smith ("Motor City Smitty" himself) scored the Flames' first goal. Eric Vail and Willie Plett beat Jiri Crha in the third period to make it close and Calgary almost tied the game in a scramble around the Leaf net with five seconds to go. "They kept fighting back and that's the sign of a good club," said Leaf coach Joe Crozier.

MAPLE LEAF GARDENS, Sat. Mar. 7, 1981
FLAMES 6, MAPLE LEAFS 4. TORONTO SCORERS: DARRYL SITTLER, WILF PAIEMENT, BRUCE BOUDREAU, RON SEDLBAUER. CALGARY SCORERS: KENT NILSSON (2), DON LEVER, GUY CHOUINARD, PHIL RUSSELL, BOB MacMILLAN. Goalie Pat Riggin, a native of Kincardine, Ont., stole the show in Calgary's first NHL visit to the Gardens. He made 44 saves as the Flames sent the Maple Leafs to their fourth consecutive defeat. Toronto outshot Calgary 17-8 in the second period and 21-15 in the third, but Riggin made a variety of dazzling saves. And he was pumped up for the game. "Are you kidding? I've had this weekend marked on the calendar ever since the start of the season," he said. "There was no way I was going to lose tonight." Riggin improved a personal hot streak to 9-1-1 in 11 starts. But he was not happy that the Flames had to catch a charter flight to Hartford after the game. "Of all the nights to be in such a damned rush," he said. "I've got like 40 people here to see me." Kent Nilsson scored twice for Calgary, mollifying Flames' general manager Cliff Fletcher, who told reporters in the second-period intermission he wanted Nilsson to shoot more. Asked how Nilsson had 37 goals, Fletcher replied, "Because he has 38 shots on net." Darryl Sittler scored his 35th goal of the season, reaching that total for the eighth consecutive year. Calgary led 3-0 after two periods.

The Colorado Rockies franchise, which had started in 1974-75 as the Kansas City Scouts, packed its bags once again for the 1982-83 season. After six years in Denver, the Rockies moved to East Rutherford, N.J.

NEW JERSEY DEVILS
[FRANCHISE DATE: June 30, 1982]

MAPLE LEAF GARDENS, Sat. Oct. 9, 1982
MAPLE LEAFS 5, DEVILS 5. TORONTO SCORERS: JOHN ANDERSON, JIM BENNING, BILL DERLAGO, WALT PODDUBNY, BORJE SALMING. NEW JERSEY SCORERS: CAROL VADNAIS, GLEN MERKOSKY, MERLIN MALINOWSKI, BOB LORIMER, HECTOR MARINI. The Maple Leafs botched up their 1982-83 season opener by blowing a 5-1 lead against New Jersey and had to settle for a tie in the Devils' first visit to Toronto. Hector Marini capped the New Jersey

comeback on the powerplay at 11:38 of the third period, with Maple Leaf Rocky Saganiuk in the penalty box. Maple Leaf owner Harold Ballard dropped the ceremonial first puck between captains Rick Vaive of Toronto and Don Lever of New Jersey. And the Gardens unvailed its new $1.48 million sportstimer (the current-day version) that night. Leafs led 4-1 after the first period and Borje Salming made it 5-1 early in the second. Then, in a play that seemed like it wouldn't have much bearing on the outcome, Devils' goalie Glenn (Chico) Resch stopped Maple Leaf Terry Martin on a penalty shot. "We were down 5-1 so there wasn't much pressure on me," Resch said. "I faked a lunge with my stick, he shot quick and the puck hit my pad." Glen Merkosky began the New Jersey comeback at 10:45 of the middle period. Leaf coach Mike Nykoluk was disappointed in the outcome. "We let them off the hook when we stopped skating and doing the things we did so well in the first 30 minutes," he lamented. "The players know they let down."

BRENDAN BYRNE ARENA, Wed. Dec. 1, 1982
DEVILS 7, MAPLE LEAFS 3. TORONTO SCORERS: RICK VAIVE, JIM BENNING, GREG TERRION. NEW JERSEY SCORERS: HECTOR MARINI (2), JEFF LARMER (2), RICK MEAGHER, GARRY HOWATT, MIKE ANTONOVICH. The Maple Leafs somehow got blown out in their first visit to the Meadowlands by a New Jersey team that had just one victory in its previous 20 games. A three-goal outburst by the Devils in a 1:50 span late in the second period broke open a 2-2 tie and sent the Maple Leafs to their sixth consecutive defeat. Jeff Larmer, Rick Meagher and Garry Howatt beat Mike Palmateer in that scoring flurry to give New Jersey a comfortable 5-2 cushion. Larmer's goal was the key, as it came only 14 seconds after Jim Benning had tied the game for the Maple Leafs. Toronto's road record dropped to 0-9-2 on the season, and 0-20-3 overall since its previous victory away from home, at Chicago, Jan. 31, 1982. "Yeah, it's the low point of the season," said Leaf coach Mike Nykoluk. "We just don't seem to have enough guys who want to stay (with the team). We've got to get guys who will stick their noses in there and play with some heart." With the loss, the Leafs' record on the season dropped to 4-13-5 for 13 points, one ahead of last-place Detroit in the Norris Division (and overall NHL standings).

The National Hockey League remained status quo with the same 21 teams for nine consecutive seasons (1982-83 to 1990-91). Then came the latest wave of expansion, and one more franchise relocation. Between 1991 and 1993, the NHL added five new clubs: two in California, two in Florida, and one in the nation's capital of Canada.

SAN JOSE SHARKS
[FRANCHISE DATE: May 9, 1990]

MAPLE LEAF GARDENS, Mon. Nov. 4, 1991
MAPLE LEAFS 4, SHARKS 1. TORONTO SCORERS: WENDEL CLARK (2), PETER ZEZEL, MIKE BULLARD. SAN JOSE SCORER: DAVID BRUCE. This game looked kind of dicey for the Maple Leafs. The expansion Sharks, riding a 12-game losing streak, held a 1-0 lead after two periods in their first visit to Toronto, but the Leafs prevailed with a strong final frame. A powerplay goal by David Bruce of San Jose at 7:49 of the second period held up until the 39-second mark of the third, when Peter Zezel finally got the Leafs on the board. Wendel Clark then put Toronto ahead at 6:49, snapping Gary Leeman's pass behind Jeff Hackett. Mike Bullard and Clark added late goals to pad the score in the Leafs' favour. "We realized that if they got a second goal, we'd be in deep trouble," said Leaf coach Tom Watt. "Wendel took charge. He's a leader — a guy who shows the way and sets the pattern for what needs to be done." In only his second game back from a 10-game absence with a knee injury, Clark typically shrugged off his performance. "I didn't do anything more than the other guys," he stated incorrectly. "The whole team, not just me, took charge in the third period." Leafs had just a 3-10-1 record going into the game.

COW PALACE, Fri. Nov. 22, 1991
MAPLE LEAFS 3, SHARKS 1. TORONTO SCORERS: DAVE ELLETT, CRAIG BERUBE, MIKE FOLIGNO. SAN JOSE SCORER: JEFF ODGERS. With the San Jose Arena under construction, the Sharks played their first two NHL seasons at the Cow Palace in Daly City, Calif., a suburb of San Francisco. Better known as the arena that hosted The Beatles' first U.S. concert, the Cow Palace had been home to the San Francisco Seals of the Western Hockey League in the 1960s. And, the NHL's Oakland Seals had played several home games there in the 1968-69 season. A sellout throng

of 10,888 saw the Maple Leafs' first visit to the Palace, and went home disappointed. Craig Berube and Mike Foligno combined to give Toronto the victory. Berube slammed Foligno's pass into the bottom left corner of the San Jose net at 17:39 of the second period, breaking a 1-1 tie. Foligno then took Berube's feed and beat Jeff Hackett with a low shot from the slot at 7:45 of the third. Mike Krushelnyski centered the line. "We're all big guys who like to muck out there," said Berube. "We just went in, banged around, and waited till we got a break." It was the Maple Leafs' first road victory in 12 starts that season. Played on the Friday night of Grey Cup Week, the game was overshadowed in Toronto by the Argonauts' presence in the 1991 CFL championship game. Two days later, at Winnipeg Stadium, the Argos and Raghib (Rocket) Ismail defeated the Calgary Stampeders for the title.

TAMPA BAY LIGHTNING
[FRANCHISE DATE: December 16, 1991]

MAPLE LEAF GARDENS, Thu. Oct. 15, 1992
MAPLE LEAFS 5, LIGHTNING 3. TORONTO SCORERS: DOUG GILMOUR, WENDEL CLARK, TODD GILL, MIKE KRUSHELNYSKI, NIKOLAI BORSCHEVSKY. TAMPA BAY SCORERS: PETER TAGLIANETTI, DANTON COLE, MIKAEL ANDERSSON. The Maple Leafs' first-ever game against opposition from the state of Florida coincided with the first victory for Pat Burns as Toronto coach. After two losses and a tie to start the 1992-93 season, the Leafs defeated Tampa Bay with a spirited, third-period comeback. Todd Gill, Mike Krushelnyski and Nikolai Borschevsky scored unanaswered goals to lift Toronto out of a 3-2 deficit. Having sat out the Leafs' first two games, Gill tied the score with a blast from just inside the blueline at 4:51. Lightning goalie Wendel Young complained that he was interefered with on the play, but referee Dan Marouelli disagreed. Mike Foligno's hard work behind the net led to the winner, at 6:57, as he passed in front to Krushelnyski. And Borschevsky clinched the victory on a breakaway at 11:36. Though announced as a sellout, only 12,672 fans showed up at the Gardens, and many of them booed the Leafs loudly during the first 40 minutes. "They had every right to," said Burns. "It was embarrassing out there for awhile." After the game, Toronto *Star* hockey columnist Bob McKenzie sought assault charges against Tampa Bay general manger Phil Esposito.

"He yelled at me to get out as I was interviewing Rob Ramage (in the Lightning dressing room)," said McKenzie. "I said, `I'm entitled to be in here.' At that point, he struck me and almost knocked me off my feet." The matter was eventually settled out of court.

EXPO HALL, Thu. Oct. 22, 1992
MAPLE LEAFS 5, LIGHTNING 2. TORONTO SCORERS: ROB PEARSON (2), NIKOLAI BORSCHEVSKY (2), WENDEL CLARK. TAMPA BAY SCORERS: BRIAN BRADLEY, ROB RAMAGE. With the Toronto Blue Jays hoping to clinch their first-ever World Series championship at SkyDome (against Atlanta), precious few sports fans in the Queen City cared or even realized that the Maple Leafs were making their inaugural trip to Florida. But, lo and behold, the Jays (and Jack Morris) lost Game 5 to the Braves, while the Maple Leafs beat the Lightning. Tampa Bay played its first NHL season at the Expo Hall on the Florida State Fairgrounds, and 9,344 showed up to see the Leafs. And Toronto won its first road game under coach Pat Burns. The turning point of the game occurred at 16:26 of the first period. With the Leafs leading, 2-1, ex-Leaf Brian Bradley of Tampa Bay was awarded a penalty shot. Leaf defenceman Bob Rouse had violated a rarely called rule about sweeping parts of a broken stick at an opponent in the defensive zone. Rookie goalie Felix Potvin did the splits and made the save. Rob Pearson scored twice for Toronto and later said, "I have to be a disturber to be effective. I have to be hit, myself. I want people to hit me from behind." Hmmmm.

OTTAWA SENATORS
[FRANCHISE DATE: December 16, 1991]

COPPS COLISEUM, Tue. Oct. 20, 1992
MAPLE LEAFS 5, SENATORS 3. TORONTO SCORERS: DIMITRI MIRONOV (2), MIKE KRUSHELNYSKI, WENDEL CLARK, DOUG GILMOUR. OTTAWA SCORERS: SYLVAIN TURGEON, NEIL BRADY, NORM MACIVER. With Game 4 of the 1992 World Series taking place at SkyDome, a small crowd of 7,186 showed up in Hamilton for the Maple Leafs' inaugural neutral-site game. And Leaf defenceman Dimitri Mironov scored his first two professional goals in the first NHL meeting between Toronto and Ottawa since 1933-34. A member of the Russian team that won the 1992 Olympic hockey tournament in Albertville,

Mironov had shown up at the Maple Leaf camp 10-15 pounds over-weight, and had watched the previous four games from the press box. Mironov blamed his weight problem on the excessive time it took getting his visa papers organized. "I was happy to score my first goal," he said. "It's too bad the Toronto fans didn't see it. With the game in Hamilton, there was no TV." The game also marked the first NHL win for Leaf goalie Felix Potvin. He made only 16 saves and at the final buzzer, Rob Pearson scooped up the puck and handed it to him. Wendel Clark's goal at 18:05 of the third period made it 4-2 Toronto and proved to be the winner. (The Maple Leafs and Ottawa played at the Gardens on Sat. Dec. 19, 1992. Leafs won 5-1).

OTTAWA CIVIC CENTER, Mon. Nov. 9, 1992
MAPLE LEAFS 3, SENATORS 1. TORONTO SCORERS: MIKE FOLIGNO (2), JOE SACCO. OTTAWA SCORER: SYLVAIN TURGEON. The Maple Leafs' first visit to Ottawa in 58 years cemented Felix Potvin's status as the club's number-one goaltender. Potvin made 36 saves in a terrific performance, lifting his record to 6-3-1 since taking over from an injured Grant Fuhr, Oct. 20. And after the game — with Fuhr ready to return — Leafs announced that Potvin would be staying with the team. Apart from Potvin, Toronto was very ordinary on this night, but coach Pat Burns expected a bit of a letdown after beating the Stanley Cup-champion Pittsburgh Penguins at the Gardens two nights earlier. "Hey, it's two points," he said. "After playing so well against Pittsburgh and coming in here against a team that hadn't won in 13 games, it was a dangerous situation." Ottawa's first-year record fell to 1-13-1 with the loss. Mike Foligno's second goal of the game, at 9:36 of the second period, gave Leafs a 2-0 lead and proved to be the winner. Foligno had been overlooked by Ottawa in the expansion draft and he spoke out after the game. "My goal this year is to make the other teams look bad at the end of the season and say, `Hey, we made a mistake by not taking him,'" Foligno crowed.

After 26 years in Bloomington, Minnesota (having joined the NHL in the six-team expansion of 1967), the North Stars re-located in Dallas for the 1993-94 NHL season, and dropped "North" from their nickname.

DALLAS STARS
[FRANCHISE DATE: March 10, 1993]

MAPLE LEAF GARDENS, Thu. Oct. 7, 1993
MAPLE LEAFS 6, STARS 3. TORONTO SCORERS: DAVE ANDREYCHUK (2), NIKOLAI BORSCHEVSKY, TODD GILL, ROB PEARSON, WENDEL CLARK. DALLAS SCORERS: MIKE MODANO (2), JAMES BLACK. The transplanted North Stars opened the 1993-94 NHL season at the Gardens and got trounced. Goals by Nikolai Borschevsky and Todd Gill 34 seconds apart in the third period broke a 2-2 tie and sent the Maple Leafs to victory. Borschevsky picked a small opening on the far side of Dallas goalie Andy Moog. Gill then smartly took the puck off the boards on his backhand, switched to his forehand, and beat Moog through the legs with a screened slapshot from inside the point. Gill was happy that so many of the veteran Maple Leaf players had returned from the previous year. "Our older guys have a lot of gas left," he said. "Everybody knows their job. We don't have to start re-building just yet." Roberto Alomar of the Blue Jays dropped the ceremonial first puck between captains Wendel Clark of the Leafs and Mark Tinordi of Dallas. The Jays had just returned home from Chicago with a 2-0 lead in the 1993 American League Championship Series.

REUNION ARENA, Mon. Nov. 1, 1993
MAPLE LEAFS 3, STARS 3. TORONTO SCORERS: DIMITRI MIRONOV, JOHN CULLEN, WENDEL CLARK. DALLAS SCORERS: ULF DAHLEN, MIKE MODANO, MIKE McPHEE. The Maple Leafs improved their early season record to 10-1-1 with a draw in their inaugural game in Texas. After an NHL-record 10-game win streak to start the season, the Leafs had lost their first game two nights earlier, in Montreal. Mike McPhee one-timed Neal Broten's pass behind Felix Potvin at 12:30 of the third period to produce the tie. Wendel Clark had two good chances to win it for the Maple Leafs in overtime. "I thought we responded well from our first loss," said coach Pat Burns. "It seemed like every game near the end of the streak was some kind of event — either our long winless streak in Chicago, or me going back to Montreal. Tonight was no event but we played well." Mike Modano's goal 33 seconds into the second period had given Dallas a 2-0 lead. But Dimitri Mironov and Clark tied it up before the period was out. Clark then put the Leafs ahead 3-2 at 5:54 of the third, taking a wonderful feed from Doug Gilmour to beat Andy Moog.

FLORIDA PANTHERS
[FRANCHISE DATE: June 14, 1993]

MIAMI ARENA, Thu. Oct. 21, 1993
MAPLE LEAFS 4, PANTHERS 3. TORONTO SCORERS: ROB PEARSON (2), DAVE ANDREYCHUK, KENT MANDERVILLE. FLORIDA SCORERS: TOM FITZGERALD, EVGENY DAVYDOV, ANDREI LOMAKIN. Rob Pearson banged in Wendel Clark's rebound at 2:17 of overtime, giving the Maple Leafs a victory in their first trip to south Florida. It also extended Toronto's unblemished record to 8-0-0, tying the NHL record for most victories to start a season. The 1934-35 Maple Leafs and the 1975-76 Buffalo Sabres had previously won their first eight games. The record-tying achievement was overshadowed in Toronto by Game 5 of the 1993 World Series, as the Blue Jays lost in Philadelphia to send the Series back to Toronto (where Joe Carter would win it two nights later). Rookie goalie Damien Rhodes made only his second NHL start for the Leafs and he robbed Dave Lowry of Florida with a fabulous glove save in the dying seconds of regulation. Andrei Lomakin had tied the score for the Panthers at 13:16 of the third period. "What's important for us is the big picture," said coach Pat Burns after the game. "Sure I'm happy we tied the record but it's not an issue for us at all. Nobody is talking about it." A crowd of 11,778 — about 3,000 short of capacity — watched the game in Miami.

MAPLE LEAF GARDENS, Wed. Nov. 3, 1993
MAPLE LEAFS 6, PANTHERS 3. TORONTO SCORERS: DAVE ANDREYCHUK (2), DAVE ELLETT, GLENN ANDERSON, WENDEL CLARK, KEN BAUMGARTNER. FLORIDA SCORERS: JESSE BELANGER, JAMIE LEACH, BRENT SEVERYN. The Maple Leafs improved to 11-1-1 on the season but lost winger Nikolai Borschevsky with a ruptured spleen. Borschevsky was crunched into the boards by Bill Lindsay of Florida midway through the first period. He left the ice and was thought to have a bruised rib. But when he returned in the second period, he suddenly became dizzy and was rushed by ambulance to Toronto Western Hospital. He later underwent surgery to remove his spleen. With Peter Zezel, Todd Gill and Rob Pearson already out of the Toronto line-up, an injury riddled season began to materialize. The Maple Leafs broke open a 1-1 tie with four unanswered goals in the

second period. Damien Rhodes played in net for the Leafs and looked bad on a meaningless goal with 1:22 left in the game. Anticipating that Brent Severyn of Florida would fire the puck into the corner, Rhodes cheated out of the goal. Instead, Severyn faked a shoot-in and blasted the puck into the vacant Toronto net before Rhodes could recover. The fans at the Gardens booed the rookie Leaf, which had Pat Burns fuming afterwards. "Rhodes saved our butt in the first period," the coach growled. "The players didn't appreciate the crowd's reaction at the end."

ANAHEIM MIGHTY DUCKS
[FRANCHISE DATE: June 15, 1993]

ARROWHEAD POND, Wed. Nov. 17, 1993
MAPLE LEAFS 4, MIGHTY DUCKS 3. TORONTO SCORERS: DAVE ANDREYCHUK (2), CHRIS GOVEDARIS, WENDEL CLARK. ANAHEIM SCORERS: TIM SWEENEY, ANATOLI SEMENOV, TERRY YAKE. In their first visit to Disneyland, the Maple Leafs built a 3-0 lead on Anaheim just more than 14 minutes into the game, but were life and death to hang on for the victory. Russian netminder Mikhail Shtalenkov started in goal for the Mighty Ducks but he gave up the three first-period goals on just five Maple Leaf shots. Guy Hebert replaced him for the second period. Anaheim fought back to tie the score at 3-3 by the 9:41 mark of the middle period. But Wendel Clark notched the eventual winner just more than four minutes later, beating Hebert with a bullet wrist-shot for his NHL-leading 18th goal of the season. "There are no more gimmees in the NHL anymore — forget it," said a relieved Pat Burns after the game. "You have to work hard every night." Damien Rhodes played goal for the Leafs and improved to 4-0-0 on the season. A crowd of 17,083 — the Mighty Ducks' first sellout since their season-opener against Detroit — watched the Maple Leaf victory.

MAPLE LEAF GARDENS, Wed. Dec. 15, 1993
MIGHTY DUCKS 1, MAPLE LEAFS 0. ANAHEIM SCORER: TIM SWEENEY. In the first of several neutral-zone-trap nightmares for the 1993-94 Maple Leafs, Anaheim pulled out a victory in its inaugural visit to the Gardens. Tim Sweeney scored a shorthanded goal at 6:15 of the third period and the Mighty Ducks held on for the win. Sweeney converted a perfect cross-ice feed from Terry Yake on a 2-on-1 break. With defencemen Todd Gill and Dave Ellett both injured, captain

Wendel Clark played the point on the Maple Leaf powerplay and was caught up ice on the goal. Guy Hebert was magnificent in net, stopping all 38 Maple Leaf shots for the Mighty Ducks' first-ever shutout. Leafs had numerous opportunities to score. Clark and Glenn Anderson both hit the goalpost dead on. And when referee Richard Trottier gave Anaheim's Bill Houlder a charging minor and 10-minute misconduct at 18:19 of the third period, the Leafs buzzed all around the Anaheim goal but failed to beat Hebert. The Toronto players were booed off the ice. "You've got to give them credit," said Leaf coach Pat Burns of the Ducks. "They force you to dump it in. There's no other way you can play against them."

RESULTS OF FIRST GAMES IN NEW (OR RENOVATED) ARENAS

MADISON SQUARE GARDEN (New York):
Feb. 28, 1968. New York 3, Toronto 1.

MONTREAL FORUM:
Nov. 14, 1968. Toronto 5, Montreal 3.

JOE LOUIS ARENA (Detroit):
Feb. 10, 1980. Toronto 4, Detroit 1.

HARTFORD CIVIC CENTER:
Apr. 1, 1980. Toronto 5, Hartford 4.

OLYMPIC SADDLEDOME (Calgary):
Nov. 5, 1983. Calgary 5, Toronto 3.

THE THUNDERDOME (St. Petersburg):
Oct. 23, 1993. Toronto 2, Tampa Bay 0.

SAN JOSE ARENA:
Nov. 9, 1993. Toronto 2, San Jose 2.

DATES OF FIRST GAMES IN 1994-95 NEW ARENAS

KEIL CENTER (St. Louis):
Sat. Oct. 22, 1994.

UNITED CENTER (Chicago):
Thu. Nov. 10, 1994.

TORONTO MAPLE LEAF
GENERAL MANAGERS
1964-65 to 1993-94
(*) PART OF SEASON

IMLACH, George (Punch)	1964-65 - 1968-69
	1979-80 - 1981-82
GREGORY, Jim	1969-70 - 1978-79
McNAMARA, Gerry	1981-82 - 1987-88
STELLICK, Gord	1988-89
BROPHY, John	1988-89*
DUFF, Dick	1988-89*
SMITH, Floyd	1989-90 - 1990-91
FLETCHER, Cliff	1991-92 - present

TORONTO MAPLE LEAF
HEAD COACHES
1964-65 to 1993-94

IMLACH, George (Punch)	1964-65 - 1968-69
	1979-80 - 1980-81
McLELLAN, John	1969-70 - 1972-73
CLANCY, Frank (King)	1966-67*- 1971-72*
KELLY, Leonard (Red)	1973-74 - 1976-77
NEILSON, Roger	1977-78 - 1978-79
SMITH, Floyd	1979-80*
DUFF, Dick	1979-80*
CROZIER, Joe	1980-81*
NYKOLUK, Mike	1980-81 - 1983-84
MALONEY, Dan	1984-85 - 1985-86
BROPHY, John	1986-87 - 1988-89*
ARMSTRONG, George	1988-89*
CARPENTER, Doug	1989-90 - 1990-91*
WATT, Tom	1990-91 - 1991-92
BURNS, Pat	1992-93 - present

TORONTO MAPLE LEAF
CAPTAINS
1964-65 to 1993-94

ARMSTRONG, George	1964-65 - 1968-69
KEON, Dave	1969-70 - 1974-75
SITTLER, Darryl	1975-76 - 1979-80
	1980-81
VAIVE, Rick	1981-82 - 1985-86*
RAMAGE, Rob	1989-90 - 1990-91
CLARK, Wendel	1991-92 - 1993-94
GILMOUR, Doug	1994-95 - present

LEADING SCORERS
1964-65 - 1993-94

YEAR	PLAYER	GP	G	A	PTS
1964-65	Frank Mahovlich	59	23	28	51
1965-66	Frank Mahovlich	68	32	24	56
1966-67	Dave Keon	66	19	33	51
1967-68	Mike Walton	73	30	29	59
1968-69	Norm Ullman	75	35	42	77
1969-70	Dave Keon	72	32	30	62
1970-71	Norm Ullman	73	34	51	85
1971-72	Norm Ullman	77	23	50	73
1972-73	Darryl Sittler	78	29	48	77
1973-74	Darryl Sittler	78	38	46	84
1974-75	Darryl Sittler	72	36	44	80
1975-76	Darryl Sittler	79	41	59	100
1976-77	Lanny McDonald	80	46	44	90
1977-78	Darryl Sittler	80	45	72	117
1978-79	Darryl Sittler	70	36	51	87
1979-80	Darryl Sittler	73	40	57	97
1980-81	Wilf Paiement	77	40	57	97
1981-82	Rick Vaive	77	54	35	89
1982-83	John Anderson	80	31	49	80
1983-84	Rick Vaive	76	52	41	93
1984-85	Rick Vaive	72	35	33	68

1985-86	Miroslav Frycer	73	32	43	75
1986-87	Russ Courtnall	79	29	44	73
1987-88	Ed Olczyk	80	42	33	75
1988-89	Ed Olczyk	80	38	52	90
1989-90	Gary Leeman	80	51	44	95
1990-91	Vincent Damphousse	79	26	47	73
1991-92	Doug Gilmour*	78	26	61	87
1992-93	Doug Gilmour	83	32	95	127
1993-94	Doug Gilmour	83	27	84	111

(*)- Acquired from Calgary Jan. 2, 1992

PENALTY MINUTE LEADERS
1964-65 to 1993-94

YEAR	PLAYER	GAMES	MINUTES
1964-65	Carl Brewer	70	177*
1965-66	Kent Douglas	64	97
1966-67	Jim Pappin	64	89
1967-68	Tim Horton	69	82
1968-69	Jim Dorey	61	200
1969-70	Rick Ley	48	102
1970-71	Jim Dorey	74	198
1971-72	Rick Ley	67	124
1972-73	Mike Pelyk	72	118
1973-74	Brian Glennie	65	100
1974-75	Dave Williams	42	187
1975-76	Dave Williams	78	299
1976-77	Dave Williams	77	338*
1977-78	Dave Williams	78	351
1978-79	Dave Williams	77	298*
1979-80	Rick Vaive#	69	188
1980-81	Rick Vaive	75	229
1981-82	Bob McGill	68	263
1982-83	Jim Korn	80	236
1983-84	Jim Korn	65	257
1984-85	Bob McGill	72	250
1985-86	Wendel Clark	66	227

1986-87	Wendel Clark	80	271
1987-88	Al Secord	74	221
1988-89	John Kordic	46	185
	Brian Curran	47	185
1989-90	Brian Curran	72	301
1990-91	Luke Richardson	78	238
1991-92	K. Baumgartner@	55	225
1992-93	Rob Pearson	78	211
1993-94	Rob Pearson	67	189

(*)- NHL Leader
(#)- Acquired from Vancouver Feb. 18, 1980
(@)- Acquired from New York Islanders Mar. 10, 1992

MAPLE LEAF PENALTY SHOTS
1964-65 to 1993-94

NOVEMBER 23, 1966: [Maple Leaf Gardens] Frank Mahovlich successful against Glenn Hall of Chicago. Final score: Toronto 6, Chicago 3.

FEBRUARY 8, 1967: [Maple Leaf Gardens] Pete Stemkowski unsuccessful against Roger Crozier of Detroit. Final score: Detroit 5, Toronto 2.

NOVEMBER 7, 1967: [Boston Garden] Bob Pulford unsuccessful against Gerry Cheevers of Bruins. Final score: Toronto 2, Boston 2.

MARCH 9, 1968: [Maple Leaf Gardens] Mike Walton successful against Roger Crozier of Detroit. Final score: Toronto 7, Detroit 5.

MARCH 10, 1968: [Chicago Stadium] Mike Walton unsuccessful against Jack Norris of Blackhawks. Final score: Chicago 4, Toronto 0.

JANUARY 22, 1970: [Los Angeles Forum] Norm Ullman unsuccessful against Wayne Rutledge of Kings. Final score: Toronto 3, Los Angeles 2.

OCTOBER 20, 1973: [Maple Leaf Gardens] Paul Henderson unsuccessful against Gilles Villemure of New York Rangers. Final score: Toronto 3, New York 2.

NOVEMBER 20, 1974: [Maple Leaf Gardens] Dave Keon successful against Gary Inness of Pittsburgh. Final score: Pittsburgh 8, Toronto 5.

MARCH 12, 1977: [Maple Leaf Gardens] Lanny McDonald unsuccessful against Jim Rutherford of Detroit. Final score: Toronto 6, Detroit 0.

OCTOBER 28, 1978: [Maple Leaf Gardens] Lanny McDonald successful against Gilles Gilbert of Boston. Final score: Boston 5, Toronto 3.

JANUARY 3, 1979: [Maple Leaf Gardens] Dan Maloney unsuccessful against Dan Bouchard of Atlanta. Final score: Atlanta 4, Toronto 1.

OCTOBER 9, 1982: [Maple Leaf Gardens] Terry Martin unsuccessful against Glenn Resch of New Jersey. Final score: Toronto 5, New Jersey 5.

OCTOBER 15, 1983: [Maple Leaf Gardens] Greg Terrion successful against Tony Esposito of Chicago. Final score: Toronto 10, Chicago 8.

JANUARY 14, 1984: [Maple Leaf Gardens] Greg Terrion successful against Murray Bannerman of Chicago. Final score: Toronto 2, Chicago 2.

JANUARY 1, 1986: [Maple Leaf Gardens] Dan Daoust unsuccessful against Patrick Roy of Montreal. Final score: Toronto 3, Montreal 2.

DECEMBER 4, 1986: [Los Angeles Forum] Rick Vaive successful against Darren Eliot of Kings. Final score: Los Angeles 4, Toronto 3.

MARCH 10, 1990: [Maple Leaf Gardens] Tom Kurvers unsuccessful against Bill Ranford of Edmonton. Final score: Toronto 3, Edmonton 2.

NOVEMBER 4, 1990: [Maple Leaf Gardens] Gary Leeman unsuccessful against Pete Peeters of Philadelphia. Final score: Philadelphia 7, Toronto 1.

NOVEMBER 24, 1993: [Olympic Saddledome] Wendel Clark successful against Trevor Kidd of Calgary. Final score: Calgary 5, Toronto 3.

MARCH 4, 1994: [Joe Louis Arena] Peter Zezel unsuccessful against Chris Osgood of Detroit. Final score: Toronto 6, Detroit 5 (OT).

MAJOR TRANSACTIONS
1964 to 1994

MAY 20, 1965: Maple Leafs acquire left-winger Larry Jeffrey, center Ed Joyal, right-winger Lowell MacDonald plus defencemen Marcel Pronovost and Aut Erickson from Detroit for right-winger Andy Bathgate, center Billy Harris and left-winger Gary Jarrett.

ANALYSIS: Bathgate and Pronovost were the key figures and the trade worked out fairly well for both teams. Bathgate scored an NHL-leading six playoff goals as Detroit advanced to the 1966 Stanley Cup Final, losing to Montreal. Pronovost provided the Maple Leaf defence with veteran savvy for the final five years of his career and was a key member of 1967 Stanley Cup champions. But, Toronto lost big in the end. Joyal and MacDonald went to Los Angeles in the 1967 expansion draft and wound up developing nicely. Joyal scored 33 goals in 1968-69 and was the second-best centerman (behind Red Berenson of St. Louis) in the new West Division. MacDonald later went to Pittsburgh and had seasons of 43, 34 and 30 goals.

MARCH 3, 1968: Maple Leafs acquire center Norm Ullman, left-winger Paul Henderson and right-winger Floyd Smith from Detroit for left-winger Frank Mahovlich, centers Pete Stemkowski and Garry Unger, plus the playing rights to retired defenceman Carl Brewer.

ANALYSIS: One of the most unpopular trades in the history of Toronto sports actually worked out not badly for the Maple Leafs. Ullman had seasons of 87, 85 and 77 points in a Leaf uniform, while Henderson averaged 25 goals per year between 1968-69 and 1973-74. Mahovlich had his best NHL season in '68-69, scoring 49 goals on a line with Gordie Howe and Alex Delvecchio. He was later traded to Montreal for Mickey Redmond, who twice topped 50 goals for the Red Wings. Detroit wasted Stemkowski, trading him to the Rangers in 1970 for unheralded defenceman Larry Brown. And the Wings really blew it with Unger, dealing him to St. Louis in 1971 for Red Berenson. Unger had eight consecutive seasons of 30 or more goals for the Blues.

MAY 23, 1968: Maple Leafs acquire veteran defenceman Pierre Pilote from Chicago for right-winger Jim Pappin.

ANALYSIS: The absolute worst trade of Punch Imlach's first tenure with the Leafs. After many distinguished years as captain of the Blackhawks, and having won the Norris Trophy three consecutive times in the early 1960s, Pilote had nothing left when he came to Toronto. He played one mediocre season for the Leafs and wisely retired. Pappin averaged 31 goals in seven years with the Blackhawks (scored 41 in 1972-73), playing on the club's top forward line with Pit Martin and Dennis Hull. Twice during his tenure in Chicago, the 'Hawks advanced to the Stanley Cup Final, losing on both occasions to Montreal.

FEBRUARY 1, 1971: Maple Leafs acquire goalie Bernie Parent and Philadelphia's 2nd-round choice in the 1971 amateur draft (Rick Kehoe) for goalie Bruce Gamble, center Mike Walton and Toronto's 1st-round choice in the 1971 draft (Pierre Plante).
ANALYSIS: A great trade initially was wasted when Harold Ballard allowed the best goalie in the world to defect to the newly formed WHA. Parent later came back to the NHL and depending on whom you ask, Ballard either didn't want him, or Parent's wife desired not to return to Canada. In any event, the Leafs traded him back to the Flyers for Doug Favell and Bob Neely. Philadelphia won two Stanley Cups and Parent earned the Conn Smythe Trophy both years. Leafs also erred with Kehoe, drafting him and then trading him to Pittsburgh in 1974 for Blaine Stoughton. Kehoe scored 55 goals for the Penguins in 1980-81. Stoughton had a big overtime goal for Toronto in the 1975 playoffs then jumped to the WHA, where he developed into a scoring star. Leafs could have had him back in 1979, but lost him to Hartford in the expansion draft. Stoughton went on to seasons of 56, 43, 52 and 45 goals with the Whalers.

MARCH 3, 1973: Maple Leafs acquire Boston's 1st-round choice in the 1973 amateur draft (Ian Turnbull) and future considerations (Ed Johnston) for goalie Jacques Plante and Toronto's 1st-round choice in the 1973 draft (Doug Gibson).
ANALYSIS: An excellent deal for the Maple Leafs as Jim Gregory landed a gem in Turnbull, who teamed with Borje Salming to provide the Leafs with an exceptionlly talented defence pairing in the 1970s. The Bruins felt Plante would help them win a third Stanley Cup in 1973, but Boston fell to the Rangers in five games in the opening round of the playoffs.

MARCH 13, 1978: Maple Leafs acquire left-winger Dan Maloney and Detroit's 2nd-round choice in the 1980 amateur draft (Craig Muni) for left-winger Errol Thompson, Toronto's 1st and 2nd-round choices in the 1978 draft (Brent Peterson and Al Jensen), and the Leafs' 1st-round choice in 1980 (Mike Blaisdell).

ANALYSIS: Leaf coach Roger Neilson wanted Dan Maloney so badly, he somehow talked general manager Jim Gregory into mortgaging the farm. But, Detroit screwed up with its draft picks and never prospered from the trade. Brent Peterson and Al Jensen were busts at the NHL level. The Red Wings could have had Al Secord, Steve Payne or Tony McKegney, any of whom would have made this trade look really bad on the Leafs. As it was, Toronto came out slightly ahead in the trade of veterans. Maloney's aggressiveness paid off when the Maple Leafs upset the New York Islanders in the 1978 quarterfinals. He hit the 20-goal mark only once in his four years with the club, and eventually became its head coach. Thompson, who teamed so well with Darryl Sittler and Lanny McDonald before breaking his wrist in 1976, scored 34 goals for Detroit in 1979-80, then finished his career in Pittsburgh.

JUNE 14, 1978: Maple Leafs acquire defenceman Dave Burrows from Pittsburgh for defenceman Randy Carlyle and center George Ferguson.
ANALYSIS: This looked like an exceptional deal for Toronto as Burrows had been one of the steadiest defencemen in the NHL for half a decade. But he got hurt early in his first season with the Maple Leafs and was never the same. Carlyle went on to a distinguished career with Pittsburgh and Winnipeg, earning the Norris Trophy as the NHL's top defenceman in 1980-81 after an 83-point season for the Penguins. A big edge for Pittsburgh in this one.

DECEMBER 29, 1979: Maple Leafs acquire right-winger Wilf Paiement and left-winger Pat Hickey from Colorado for right-winger Lanny McDonald and defenceman Joel Quennville.
ANALYSIS: Punch Imlach made this trade solely in spite of Leaf captain Darryl Sittler, with whom he was feuding, and it destroyed the franchise for more than a decade. A consumate professional, and extremely popular in Toronto, McDonald was at the peak of his brilliant career and Imlach made the deal chiefly to diminish Sittler's clout in the dressing room. It was a farcical move by a man with ulterior motives and it robbed some very loyal hockey fans of a franchise cornerstone. Almost as absurd was Colorado's trading of McDonald in 1981. Lanny eventually helped Calgary win a Stanley Cup and had a 66-goal season for the Flames in 1982-83. He is currently a member of the Hockey Hall of Fame. Paiement had a 40-goal season for the Leafs in 1980-81 but very few players could have adequately filled McDonald's shoes.

FEBRUARY 18, 1980: Maple Leafs acquire center Bill Derlago and right-winger Rick Vaive from Vancouver for left-winger Dave (Tiger) Williams and right-winger Jerry Butler.

ANALYSIS: It was probably an accident, but Imlach's frenzied purge of 1979-80 yielded one gem. Another of Sittler's allies, Williams had to be moved and Imlach was somehow able to milk Canucks' GM Jake Milford of his two brightest, young players. The pugnacious Tiger helped Vancouver make it to the 1982 Stanley Cup Final and became a staple on the Canadian west coast. But Vaive scored more than 50 goals in three consecutive seasons for Toronto while Derlago contributed seasons of 40, 35 and 34 goals. The only triumph in Imlach's pitiful second tenure as GM of the Leafs.

JANUARY 20, 1982: Maple Leafs acquire center Rich Costello, Philadelphia's 2nd-round choice in the 1982 amateur draft (Peter Ihnacak) and future considerations (Ken Strong) for center Darryl Sittler.

ANALYSIS: It took more than two years for the Maple Leafs to unload the disgruntled Sittler and they practically gave him away. Peter Ihnacak turned into a fairly reliable centerman throughout much of the 1980s, but the Leafs would have been better off acquiring *Lou* Costello than his namesake from the Flyers. Sittler had seasons of 43 and 27 goals for Philadelphia and finished his outstanding career in Detroit.

SEPTEMBER 4, 1987: Maple Leafs acquire center Ed Olczyk and left-winger Al Secord from Chicago for defenceman Bob McGill, left-winger Steve Thomas and right-winger Rick Vaive.

ANALYSIS: The Maple Leafs ultimately lost this mega-deal because Thomas turned into the best player in the trade. Otherwise, they got several productive seasons out of Olczyk and wound up trading him to Winnipeg for Dave Ellett: a key member of the early Pat Burns era. But Thomas, who was later dealt to the Islanders, became a prolific goalscorer and is still going strong. He notched a career-high 42 goals in 1993-94 to go with previous seasons of 40 and 37 and would have looked awfully good on the offensively shallow Leaf teams of the past two years.

JANUARY 16, 1991: Maple Leafs acquire center Peter Zezel and defenceman Bob Rouse from Washington for defenceman Al Iafrate.

ANALYSIS: Call this one a draw. While the Leafs have lacked a legitimate wheelhorse on the blueline since trading Iafrate, they prospered with the defensive steadiness of Rouse, and Zezel's penalty killing and faceoff expertise. They were both favourably suited for the disciplined approach of Pat Burns, wheras the more-talented but unpredictable Iafrate may have given the Leaf coach an ulcer. However, the unstable Maple Leaf powerplay of the past two seasons would almost certainly have been more productive with a "quarterback" like Iafrate.

SEPTEMBER 19, 1991: Maple Leafs acquire goalie Grant Fuhr, right-winger Glenn Anderson and left-winger Craig Berube from Edmonton for left-winger Vincent Damphousse, center Scott Thornton, defenceman Luke Richardson and goalie Peter Ing.
ANALYSIS: This trade must be judged by the spin-off deals that arose from it because only two of the seven principals (Richardson and Thornton) remain in place. And, if you subscribe to the "best player" theory, the Leafs have to come out on top, as this transaction ultimately netted them Dave Andreychuk. As well, Berube — while not the key figure — was part of the trade with Calgary that brought Doug Gilmour to Toronto. Add that to the obvious fact the Leafs are a much-better team than Edmonton, and Toronto gains a clear edge.

JANUARY 2, 1992: Maple Leafs acquire center Doug Gilmour, left-winger Kent Manderville, defencemen Jamie Macoun and Rick Nattress, and goalie Rick Wamsley from Calgary for right-winger Gary Leeman, left-winger Craig Berube, defencemen Michel Petit and Alexander Godyniuk, and goalie Jeff Reese.
ANALYSIS: All you have to say is two words: Doug Gilmour. The biggest trade in terms of numbers in NHL history may very well be the best deal the Maple Leafs have ever made. Gilmour was arguably the finest all-around forward in the NHL during his first two seasons in Toronto. This move hastened the anticipated development of the club by at least three years. Without it, the Leafs may not have been able to attract Pat Burns as head coach. The Flames have since rebounded, but the shock from this dreadful swap led them to plummet out of post-season contention in 1992-93.

FEBRUARY 2, 1993: Maple Leafs acquire left-winger Dave Andreychuk, goalie Darren Puppa and Buffalo's 1st-round choice in the 1993 amateur draft (Kenny Jonsson) for goalie Grant Fuhr and a conditional draft choice.
ANALYSIS: The rapid development of Felix Potvin enabled this trade to be a steal for the Maple Leafs. Andreychuk immediately fit hand-in-

glove with Gilmour and the big winger finished one, and embarked on a second 50-goal season in Toronto. The deal could become even more of a gem if Kenny Jonsson develops the way so many hockey people figure he will. Stay tuned.

MARCH 21, 1994: Maple Leafs acquire right-winger Mike Gartner from the New York Rangers for right-winger Glenn Anderson, defenceman Scott Malone and Toronto's 4th-round choice in the 1994 amateur draft (Alexander Korobolin).
ANALYSIS: Neither Gartner nor Anderson contributed significantly to their team's playoff fortunes in the spring of '94, although Gartner's overtime goal in Game 6 against San Jose kept the Leafs alive to win Game 7, and advance to the Western Conference final. Anderson was hardly a popular figure in New York but he has yet another Stanley Cup ring to show for the deal... his sixth. Gartner will likely stick around longer in Toronto than Anderson will in New York.

JUNE 28, 1994: Maple Leafs acquire center Mats Sundin, defenceman Garth Butcher and left-winger Todd Warriner from Quebec for left-winger Wendel Clark, defenceman Sylvain Lefebvre and right-winger Landon Wilson. The teams also exchange 1994 1st-round draft picks.
ANALYSIS: If you isolate the principal characters (Clark for Sundin) — and you subscribe to the "best-player" theory — Toronto gains an edge as the 23-year-old Sundin is the most talented skater in this deal. But Quebec is likely to fare better elsewhere. Lefebvre is one of the most reliable stay-at-home defencemen in the NHL, while Wilson is rated as a better prospect than Warriner. Sundin, however, should be playing pro hockey long after Clark is retired, and he solves the Maple Leafs' pursuit of a centerman to ultimately inherit the lead role from Doug Gilmour. In that regard, Leafs are a clear winner.

THEY WORE THE BLUE AND WHITE

In the 30 NHL seasons from 1964-65 to 1993-94, a total of **358** players wore the uniform of the Toronto Maple Leafs. How many do *you* know, or recall? An alphabetical listing follows.

[**SOURCE**: Toronto Maple Leafs 1993-94 Yearbook]

(*) MORE THAN ONE TENURE WITH THE MAPLE LEAFS

PLAYER	POS.	YEAR(S)	SWEATER NUMBER(S)
ACOMB, Doug	C	1969-70	22
ADAM, Russ	C	1982-83	16
ALEXANDER, Claire	D	1974-75 - 1976-77	20
ALLISON, Mike	LW	1986-87 - 1987-88	8
ANDERSON, Glenn	RW	1991-92 - 1993-94	10, 9
ANDERSON, John	RW	1977-78 - 1984-85	10, 28
ANDREYCHUK, Dave	LW	1992-93 - present	14
ARBOUR, Al	D	1965-66	3
ARMSTRONG, Tim	C	1988-89	8
ASHBY, Don	C	1975-76 - 1978-79	9, 20
AUBIN, Normand	C	1981-82 - 1982-83	24, 35
AUGUSTA, Patrick	RW	1993-94	24
BAILEY, Reid	D	1982-83	4
BATHGATE, Andy	RW	1964-65	9
BAUMGARTNER, Ken	D/LW	1991-92 - present	8, 22
BAUN, Bob	D	1964-65 - 1972-73*	21
BELANGER, Alain	RW	1977-78	17
BENNING, Jim	D	1981-82 - 1986-87	3, 15
BEREHOWSKY, Drake	D	1990-91 - present	29, 24, 55
BERG, Bill	LW	1992-93 - present	10
BERNHARDT, Tim	G	1984-85 - 1989-90	1
BERUBE, Craig	LW	1991-92	16
BESTER, Allan	G	1983-84 - 1990-91	31, 30
BIALOWIS, Frank	LW	1993-94	36

BLAISDELL, Mike	RW	1987-88 - 1988-89	22
BOIMISTRUCK, Fred	D	1981-82 - 1982-83	11
BOISVERT, Serge	RW	1982-83	12
BORSCHEVSKY, Nikolai	RW	1992-93 - present	16
BOSCHMAN, Laurie	C	1979-80 - 1981-82	12
BOUDREAU, Bruce	C	1976-77 - 1982-83	12, 19, 35
BOUTETTE, Pat	RW	1975-76 - 1979-80	15
BOWER, John	G	1964-65 - 1969-70	1
BOYER, Wally	C	1965-66	15
BRADLEY, Brian	C	1990-91 - 1991-92	44
BRENNEMAN, John	LW	1966-67	24
BREWER, Carl	D	1964-65 & 1979-80	2, 28
BRINDLEY, Doug	C	1970-71	17
BRITZ, Greg	RW	1983-84 - 1984-85	16, 32
BROSSART, Willy	D	1973-74 - 1974-75	25
BROTEN, Aaron	LW	1990-91	21
BRUBAKER, Jeff	LW	1984-85 - 1985-86	23
BULLARD, Mike	C/LW	1991-92	22
BURROWS, Dave	D	1978-79 - 1980-81	26
BUTLER, Jerry	RW	1977-78 - 1979-80	17
BYERS, Mike	RW	1967-68 - 1968-69	24
CAPUANO, Jack	D	1989-90	26
CARLETON, Wayne	LW	1965-66 - 1969-70	25
CARLYLE, Randy	D	1976-77 - 1977-78	23, 28
CARRIERE, Larry	D	1979-80	3
CIMETTA, Rob	LW	1990-91 - 1991-92	34, 14
CLANCY, Terry	D	1968-69 - 1972-73	7, 21
CLARK, Wendel	LW	1985-86 - 1993-94	17
CONACHER, Brian	LW	1965-66 - 1967-68	17, 22
COSTELLO, Rich	C	1983-84 & 1985-86	8, 16
COURTNALL, Russ	C	1983-84 - 1988-89	9, 16, 26
CRHA, Jiri	G	1979-80 - 1980-81	31
CULLEN, John	C	1992-93 - 1993-94	19
CURRAN, Brian	D	1987-88 - 1990-91	28
DALLMAN, Marty	C	1987-88	35, 15
DAMPHOUSSE, Vincent	LW	1986-87 - 1990-91	10
DAOUST, Dan	C	1982-83 - 1989-90	24
DAVIS, Kim	C	1980-81	
DEBLOIS, Lucien	RW	1990-91 - 1991-92	27

DEGRAY, Dale	D	1987-88	3
DERLAGO, Bill	C	1979-80 - 1985-86	19
DOMI, Tie	RW	1989-90	40
DOREY, Jim	D	1968-69 - 1971-72	8
DOUGLAS, Kent	D	1962-63 - 1966-67	19
DOWIE, Bruce	G	1983-84	1
DUNDAS, Rocky	LW	1989-90	34
DUNN, Dave	D	1974-75 - 1975-76	4
DUPERE, Denis	LW	1970-71 - 1973-74	17
DUPONT, Jerome	D	1986-87	2
DURIS, Vitezslav	D	1980-81 - 1982-83	23, 24
EASTWOOD, Mike	C	1991-92 - present	21, 32
ECCLESTONE, Tim	LW	1973-74 - 1974-75	16
EDWARDS, Don	G	1985-86	30
EDWARDS, Marv	G	1969-70	31
ELLETT, Dave	D	1990-91 - present	4
ELLIS, Ron	RW	1964-65 - 1980-81*	11,8,6
ERICKSON, Aut	D	1967-68	24
ESAU, Len	D	1991-92	36
EVANS, Chris	D	1969-70	
EVANS, Daryl	LW	1986-87	3
EVANS, Paul	C	1976-77 - 1977-78	17, 28,29
FARRISH, Dave	D	1979-80 - 1983-84	23, 28
FAUSS, Ted	D	1986-87 - 1987-88	2
FAVELL, Doug	G	1973-74 - 1975-76	33
FENTON, Paul	LW	1990-91	16
FERGUS, Tom	C	1985-86 - 1991-92	19
FERGUSON, George	C	1972-73 - 1977-78	10
FLETT, Bill	RW	1974-75	19
FOLIGNO, Mike	RW	1990-91 - 1993-94	15, 17
FORTIER, Dave	D	1972-73	22
FRANCESCHETTI, Lou	RW	1989-90 - 1990-91	15
FRYCER, Miroslav	RW	1981-82 - 1987-88	14
FUHR, Grant	G	1991-92 - 1992-93	31
GAGNE, Paul	LW	1988-89 - 1989-90	18, 41
GAMBLE, Bruce	G	1965-66 - 1970-71	1, 30
GAMBLE, Dick	LW	1965-66 - 1966-67	

GARDNER, Paul	C	1978-79 - 1979-80	18
GARLAND, Scott	C	1975-76 - 1976-77	25
GARTNER, Mike	RW	1993-94 - present	11
GAVIN, Stewart	LW	1980-81 - 1984-85	9, 17
GIBSON, John	D	1981-82	23
GILL, Todd	D	1984-85 - present	11,3,23
GILMOUR, Doug	C	1991-92 - present	93
GINGRAS, Gaston	D	1982-83 - 1984-85	11
GLENNIE, Brian	D	1969-70 - 1977-78	24
GODDEN, Ernie	C	1981-82	18
GODYNYUK, Alexander	D	1990-91 - 1991-92	93
GOVADERIS, Chris	LW	1993-94 - present	8
GRAHAM, Pat	LW	1983-84	23
GREIG, Mark	RW	1993-94 - present	11
GRISDALE, John	D	1972-73 - 1974-75	3
HALKIDIS, Bob	D	1991-92	33
HAMEL, Pierre	G	1974-75 - 1978-79	31,32,1
HAMMARSTROM, Inge	LW	1973-74 - 1977-78	11
HAMMOND, Ken	D	1988-89	29
HANNAN, Dave	C	1989-90 - 1991-92	9
HARLOCK, David	D	1993-94 - present	28
HARRIS, Bill	C	1964-65	15
HARRIS, Bill	RW	1981-82 - 1983-84	16
HARRIS, Duke	RW	1967-68	17
HARRISON, Jim	C	1969-70 - 1971-72	7, 12
HARRISON, Paul	G	1978-79 - 1979-80	30
HAWKINS, Todd	RW	1991-92	8
HENDERSON, Paul	LW	1967-68 - 1973-74	19
HICKEY, Pat	LW	1979-80 - 1981-82	15, 16
HIGGINS, Paul	RW	1981-82 - 1982-83	17
HILLMAN, Larry	D	1964-65 - 1967-68	2
HINSE, Andre	LW	1967-68	23
HODGSON, Dan	C	1985-86	16
HOPKINS, Larry	LW	1977-78	
HORTON, Tim	D	1964-65 - 1969-70	7
HOTHAM, Greg	D	1979-80 - 1981-82	4
HUBICK, Greg	LW	1975-76	19
HUTCHISON, Dave	D	1978-79 - 1983-84	22, 23

IAFRATE, Al	D	1985-86 - 1990-91	33
IHNACAK, Miroslav	LW	1985-86 - 1986-87	27
IHNACAK, Peter	C	1982-83 - 1989-90	18, 15
IMLACH, Brent	LW	1965-66 - 1966-67	9, 24
ING, Peter	G	1989-90 - 1990-91	31,1
JACKSON, Jeff	LW	1984-85 - 1986-87	12, 25
JAMES, Val	LW	1986-87	28
JARRY, Pierre	LW	1971-72 - 1973-74	8
JARVIS, Wes	C	1984-85 - 1987-88	12, 34,16
JEFFREY, Larry	LW	1965-66 - 1966-67	15, 12
JOHANSEN, Trevor	D	1977-78 - 1981-82*	2, 4
JOHNSON, Danny	C	1969-70	22
JOHNSON, Terry	D	1986-87	20
JOHNSTON, Ed	G	1973-74	1
JOHNSTON, Greg	RW	1990-91 - 1991-92	16
JONES, Jim	C	1977-78 - 1979-80	16
JOYAL, Ed	C	1965-66	24
KASZYCKI, Mike	C	1979-80 - 1982-83	14, 16
KEHOE, Rick	RW	1971-72 - 1973-74	16, 17
KELLY, Red	C	1964-65 - 1966-67	4
KENNEDY, Forbes	C	1968-69	22
KEON, Dave	C	1964-65 - 1974-75	14
KIRTON, Mark	C	1979-80 - 1980-81	20
KITCHEN, Bill	D	1984-85	26
KORDIC, John	RW	1988-89 - 1990-91	27
KORN, Jim	D/LW	1981-82 - 1984-85	20
KOTSOPOULOS, Chris	D	1985-86 - 1989-90	26
KURTENBACH, Orland	C	1965-66	25
KURVERS, Tom	D	1989-90 - 1990-91	25
KRUSHELNYSKI, Mike	C	1990-91 - 1993-94	26
KUDASHOV, Alexi	C	1993-94 - present	20
LACROIX, Eric	LW	1993-94 - present	37
LAFOREST, Mark	G	1989-90	1
LANDON, Larry	RW	1984-85	11
LANZ, Rick	D	1986-87 - 1988-89	4
LAROCQUE, Michel	G	1980-81 - 1982-83	1
LAUGHLIN, Craig	RW	1988-89	14, 18

LAWLESS, Paul	RW	1988-89 - 1989-90	20
LAROSE, Guy	RW	1991-92 - 1993-94	11
LAXDAL, Derek	RW	1986-87 - 1989-90	28, 35
LEEMAN, Gary	RW	1982-83 - 1991-92	4, 11
LEFEBVRE, Sylvain	D	1992-93 - 1993-94	2
LEY, Rick	D	1968-69 - 1971-72	26, 2
LIDDINGTON, Bob	LW	1970-71	26
LOISELLE, Claude	C	1990-91 - 1991-92	15
LOW, Ron	G	1972-73	30
LUCE, Don	C	1981-82	20
LUNDRIGAN, Joe	D	1972-73	2
MacKASEY, Blair	D	1976-77	16
MacMILLAN, Bill	RW	1970-71 - 1971-72	12, 23
MACOUN, Jamie	D	1991-92 - present	34
MAGGS, Darryl	D	1979-80	24
MAGNAN, Marc	LW	1982-83	35
MAGUIRE, Kevin	RW	1986-87 - 1991-92*	28, 18
MAHOVLICH, Frank	LW	1964-65 - 1967-68	27
MALONEY, Dan	LW	1977-78 - 1981-82	9
MANDERVILLE, Kent	LW	1991-92 - present	18
MANNO, Bob	D	1981-82	3, 18
MARCETTA, Milan	C	1966-67 (playoffs)	25
MARCHINKO, Brian	C	1970-71 - 1971-72	22
MAROIS, Daniel	RW	1988-89 - 1991-92	32
MARSH, Brad	D	1988-89 - 1990-91	3
MARSH, Gary	LW	1968-69	18
MARSHALL, Don	LW	1971-72	22
MARSHALL, Paul	LW	1980-81 - 1981-82	28
MARTIN, Matt	D	1993-94 - present	33
MARTIN, Terry	LW	1979-80 - 1983-84	25
MARTIN, Tom	RW	1967-68	
MAXWELL, Brad	D	1985-86	4
McADAM, Gary	LW	1985-86	12
McCLELLAND, Kevin	RW	1991-92	20
McCOURT, Dale	C	1983-84	12
McCREARY, Bill	RW	1980-81	28
McCUTCHEON, Darwin	D	1981-82	2
McDONALD, Lanny	RW	1973-74 - 1979-80	7
McGILL, Bob	D	1981-82 - 1992-93*	4, 15, 8

McINTYRE, John	C	1989-90 - 1990-91	44
McINTYRE, Larry	D	1969-70 - 1972-73*	25
McKECHNIE, Walt	C	1978-79 - 1979-80	11
McKENNA, Sean	RW	1987-88 - 1989-90	8
McKENNEY, Don	C	1964-65	17
McKENNY, Jim	D/RW	1965-66 - 1977-78	25, 18
McLACHLAN, Murray	G	1970-71	1
McLLWAIN, Dave	C	1991-92 - 1992-93	7
McNAMARA, Gerry	G	1969-70	1
McRAE, Basil	LW	1983-84 - 1984-85	26
McRAE, Chris	LW	1987-88 - 1988-89	32, 29
McRAE, Gord	G	1972-73 - 1977-78*	1, 31
McRAE, Ken	C	1992-93 - present	36, 40
MEEHAN, Gerry	C	1968-69	26, 27
MELROSE, Barry	D	1980-81 - 1982-83	26
MICKEY, Larry	RW	1968-69	12
MILLAR, Mike	RW	1990-91	36
MIRONOV, Dimitri	D	1992-93 - present	15
MOFFAT, Lyle	LW	1972-73 - 1974-75*	26
MONAHAN, Garry	LW	1970-71 - 1978-79*	20, 14
MOORE, Dickie	RW	1964-65	16
MULHERN, Richard	D	1979-80	8
MUNI, Craig	D	1981-82 - 1985-86	32, 33
MURRAY, Ken	D	1969-70 - 1970-71	3,7
MURRAY, Randy	D	1969-70	3
NATTRESS, Rick	D	1991-92	2
NEELY, Bob	D/LW	1973-74 - 1977-78	3
NELSON, Gord	D	1969-70	27
NIGRO, Frank	C	1982-83 - 1983-84	32
NYLUND, Gary	D	1982-83 - 1985-86	2
O'FLAHERTY, Gerry	LW	1971-72	
OLCZYK, Ed	C	1987-88 - 1990-91	16
OLIVER, Murray	C	1967-68 - 1969-70	11
OSBORNE, Mark	LW	1986-87 - 1993-94	12, 21
OSBURN, Randy	LW	1972-73	16
PAIEMENT, Wilf	RW	1979-80 - 1981-82	99
PALMATEER, Mike	G	1976-77 - 1983-84*	29

PAPPIN, Jim	RW	1964-65 - 1967-68	17, 18
PARENT, Bernie	G	1970-71 - 1971-72	30
PARENT, Bob	G	1981-82 - 1982-83	33
PARISE, Jean-Paul	LW	1967-68	19
PEARSON, Rob	RW	1991-92 - 1993-94	12
PEARSON, Scott	LW	1988-89 - 1990-91	18, 22
PELYK, Mike	D	1967-68 - 1977-78*	21,4
PERLINI, Fred	C	1981-82 - 1983-84*	8,28,29
PERREAULT, Yanic	C	1993-94	44
PETIT, Michel	D	1990-91 - 1991-92	22, 24
PICARD, Robert	D	1980-81	4
PILOTE, Pierre	D	1968-69	2
PLANTE, Cam	D	1984-85	11
PLANTE, Jacques	G	1970-71 - 1972-73	1
PODDUBNY, Walt	LW	1982-83 - 1985-86	12,8
POTVIN, Felix	G	1991-92 - present	29
PRATT, Tracy	D	1976-77	4
PRONOVOST, Marcel	D	1965-66 - 1969-70	3
PUPPA, Darren	G	1992-93	1
QUENNVILLE, Joel	D	1977-78 - 1978-79	3
QUINN, Pat	D	1968-69 - 1969-70	23
RAMAGE, Rob	D	1989-90 - 1990-91	8
REESE, Jeff	G	1987-88 - 1991-92	35,1
REID, Dave	LW	1988-89 - 1990-91	18
REYNOLDS, Bobby	LW	1989-90 - 1990-91	20
RHODES, Damien	G	1990-91 - present	31,1
RIBBLE, Pat	D	1979-80	3
RICHARDSON, Luke	D	1987-88 - 1990-91	2
RIDLEY, Curt	G	1979-80 - 1980-81	33,1
ROBERT, Rene	RW	1970-71 - 1981-82*	26, 14
ROOT, Bill	D	1984-85 - 1990-91*	25
ROUSE, Bob	D	1990-91 - 1993-94	28,3
RUPP, Duane	D	1964-65 - 1967-68	17,3,4
RUTHERFORD, Jim	G	1980-81	1
SABOURIN, Gary	RW	1974-75	15
SACCO, David	D	1993-94 - present	7
SACCO, Joe	LW	1990-91 - 1992-93	20, 24

SAGANIUK, Rocky	RW	1978-79 - 1982-83	8,7
ST. CROIX, Rick	G	1982-83 - 1984-85	1
SALMING, Borje	D	1973-74 - 1988-89	21
SAWCHUK, Terry	G	1964-65 - 1966-67	24, 30
SCHUTT, Rod	LW	1985-86	25
SECORD, Al	LW	1987-88 - 1988-89	20
SEDLBAUER, Ron	LW	1980-81	18
SEILING, Rod	D	1974-75 - 1975-76	16
SELBY, Brit	LW	1964-65 - 1970-71*	8,11,15
SELWOOD, Brad	D	1970-71 - 1971-72	3
SEMENKO, Dave	LW	1987-88	27
SEROWIK, Jeff	D	1990-91 - 1992-93	34
SHACK, Eddie	RW	1964-65 - 1974-75*	23
SHAND, David	D	1980-81 - 1982-83	3,4
SHANNON, Darryl	D	1988-89 - 1992-93	34, 29, 28
SHEDDEN, Doug	RW	1988-89 - 1990-91	27, 12
SITTLER, Darryl	C	1970-71 - 1981-82	27
SLY, Darryl	D	1965-66 - 1967-68	21
SMEDSMO, Dale	LW	1972-73	23
SMITH, Al	G	1965-66 - 1968-69	30,1
SMITH, Floyd	RW	1967-68 - 1969-70	17
SMITH, Gary	G	1965-66 - 1966-67	30,1
SMITH, Brad	RW	1985-86 - 1986-87	29
SNELL, Chris	D	1993-94 - present	38
SPENCER, Brian	LW	1969-70 - 1971-72	22, 15
STAMLER, Lorne	LW	1978-79	12
STANLEY, Allan	D	1964-65 - 1967-68	26
STASTNY, Marion	RW	1985-86	10
STEMKOWSKI, Peter	C	1964-65 - 1967-68	25, 12
STEPHENSON, Bob	RW	1979-80	15
STEVENS, Mike	LW	1989-90	26
STEWART, Bill	D	1983-84 - 1984-85	17
STEWART, Ron	RW	1964-65	12
STOTHERS, Mike	D	1987-88	25
STOUGHTON, Blaine	LW	1974-75 - 1975-76	17
STRONG, Ken	LW	1982-83 - 1984-85	23
SUTHERLAND, Bill	C	1968-69	15
SYKES, Bob	LW	1974-75	
TERRION, Greg	C	1982-83 - 1987-88	7

THIBAUDEAU, Gilles	C	1989-90 - 1990-91	7
THOMAS, Steve	LW	1984-85 - 1986-87	32, 12
THOMAS, Wayne	G	1975-76 - 1976-77	33, 30
THOMPSON, Errol	LW	1970-71 - 1977-78	12
THORNTON, Scott	C	1990-91	24
TOMLINSON, Dave	C	1991-92 - 1992-93	37, 14
TREMBLAY, Vincent	G	1979-80 - 1982-83	30,1
TROTTIER, Guy	RW	1970-71 - 1971-72	11
TURNBULL, Ian	D	1973-74 - 1981-82	2
ULLMAN, Norm	C	1967-68 - 1974-75	9
UNGER, Garry	C	1967-68	15
VAIVE, Rick	RW	1979-80 - 1986-87	20, 22
VALIQUETTE, Jack	C	1974-75 - 1977-78	8
VEITCH, Darren	D	1988-89 - 1990-91	26, 25
VERSTRAETE, Leigh	RW	1982-83 - 1987-88	28, 34
WALKER, Kurt	LW	1975-76 - 1977-78	26
WALTON, Mike	C	1965-66 - 1970-71	15, 16
WAMSLEY, Rick	G	1991-92 - 1992-93	30
WARD, Ron	C	1969-70	25
WARNER, Bob	D	1975-76 - 1976-77	16
WEIR, Stan	C	1975-76 - 1977-78	14
WESLEY, Blake	D	1985-86	28
WILLARD, Rod	LW	1982-83	28
WILLIAMS, Dave	LW	1974-75 - 1979-80	22
WILSON, Dunc	G	1973-74 - 1974-75	1
WILSON, Ron	RW	1977-78 - 1979-80	14, 11
WREGGET, Ken	G	1983-84 - 1988-89	31
YAREMCHUK, Gary	C	1981-82 - 1984-85	8
YAREMCHUK, Ken	C	1986-87 - 1988-89	34, 13,16
ZANUSSI, Ron	RW	1980-81 - 1981-82	39
ZEZEL, Peter	C	1990-91 - 1993-94	25